Remarkable Providences

Remarkable Providences

Readings on Early American History

REVISED EDITION

John Demos

BOSTON
Northeastern University Press

Northeastern University Press

Library of Congress Cataloging-in-Publication Data

Remarkable providences : readings on early American history /
[compiled by] John Demos. — Rev. ed.
p.   cm.
Rev. ed. of: Remarkable providences, 1600–1760. c1792.
ISBN 1–55553–097–4 — ISBN 1–55553–098–2
1. United States—Civilization—To 1783—Sources. I. Demos,
John I. Remarkable providences, 1600–1760.
E162.R46   1991
973.2—dc20   90–24536

Designed by David Ford

Composed in Weiss by European American Graphics, Gainesville,
Florida. Printed and bound by Maple Press, York, Pennsylvania.
The paper is Maple Antique, an acid-free sheet.

MANUFACTURED IN THE UNITED STATES OF AMERICA
97   96   95   5   4   3   2

Contents

Contents

Contents

Contents

Contents

Contents

Contents

Contents

Preface to the Revised Edition

The original edition of this book was published nearly twenty years ago, just as historical studies were entering a period of transition. The "old history," with its emphasis on political subjects, was passing into at least partial eclipse. And a "new history," broadly focused on social experience, was beginning to take shape. But the prospects for the future seemed quite uncertain. This was not, in fact, the first time that such a configuration had appeared in the scholarly firmament. And the previous times had yielded limited results overall. Change would, at best, proceed slowly and unevenly—and, at worst, might shrivel to the status of a fad. Acceptance would have to be won step by laborious step: first, presumably, among research historians, then in the broader confraternity of history teachers, and only thereafter (if at all) among a history-conscious "wider public."

The appearance, in such circumstances, of *Remarkable Providences* amounted to a pinpoint of new light—comparable, one might say, to a meteor so small and low in the sky as to be nearly invisible to the naked eye. It was—so its author believed—the first comprehensive "documents book" fully animated by the new history; at least he could think of no others in its field of coverage, early America. But events would prove its arrival to be definitely premature. Designed for use in the classroom, it did not fit courses that then dominated college and high school history curricula. Designed, too, for general readers of history, it lacked the informational context which that constituency requires. It did not go entirely without response; occasional and encouraging words came from other practitioners of the new history, but most of these touched scholarly, not pedagogic, concerns. In one surprising instance a fellow scholar was prompted to write a book of his own organized (in large part) around the documents in this collection. Encouraging—flattering even—but not in the anticipated ways. Within a few years the collection was out of print and hard to find.

The new edition of *Remarkable Providences* faces, one can reasonably hope, a very different prospect. Certainly, the horizons of history have changed between 1972 and 1991. The new history has progressed beyond the expectations even of its most enthusiastic early proponents. It now controls a vast amount of active, ongoing research, as manifest in published books and journals and at scholarly conferences and meetings. It has infiltrated a great many classrooms (and textbooks), at the college level and below. Its wider appeal is evident in book club adoptions and (at least occasionally) in impressive individual sales figures. The old history, while still strong and sometimes sparkling, must now share the skies.

Curiously, though, the "documents book"—as a publishing mini-genre—has been little affected by these changes. Most recent examples are still directed to *public* life; many offer compilations of the famous charters and official enactments that define the political shape of nations. Conversely, only a few touch the private and informal experiences that are otherwise so prominent on the agendas of historians. A need remains and indeed grows stronger with the passage of time.

The underlying structure of the original edition has been retained here. The documents are assembled, as before, in a series of concentric "rings," radiating out from the historical subject—that is, the individual person. (The only exception to this organizing principle is a special group of materials, presented first and treating the unique circumstances of settlement.)

However, the documents themselves have been sifted through a careful process of reconsideration and re-editing. Some have been dropped altogether; others, entirely new, have been added. The additions are designed both to reduce prior imbalance and to reflect recent trends in scholarship at large. For example, the original edition shows an unmistakable New England bias—unmistakable, and unavoidable (so it then seemed) because of the uneven preservation of evidence across the centuries. That bias has been reduced, if not eliminated, by the inclusion of new documents here. Moreover, the recent growth of interest and knowledge in black history underlies a new unit devoted entirely to that topic. And similarly, remarkable developments in the study of material culture are reflected at numerous points in the revised collection, chiefly by way of pictorial images. The result overall should be a fuller, deeper, and more representative sampling of the extant record—and of the life that lies behind that record.

It is, of course, the life that matters most of all. And these documents

Preface

have been chosen, in every case, for the way they reflect lived experience among average people in our colonial past. There is no real substitute for such primary evidence—no other way to capture the feel of events from day to day, year to year, generation to generation. Richard Frethorne, begging his parents for help in escaping the rigors of life in early Virginia; Mary Rowlandson, struggling to make sense of her "Indian captivity"; Sarah Lippit, dying triumphantly "with a smile on her lips"; Jonathan Ashley, methodically calculating his annual household expenses; Devereux Jarratt, remembering his youthful fear of "gentlefolk"; the three Neal children of Boston, dead at an early age and then linked together on a single gravestone (which survives today); and dozens of others remembered here in vivid detail: their stories *are* history, nothing less.

Watertown, Massachusetts   JOHN DEMOS
July 1990

Introduction

Few people alive in 1970 would, presumably, feel mystified by the notion of a distinctively American culture. The definition of this culture—its structure and inner substance—may well be a matter for vigorous debate, but its fundamental *reality* seems impossible to doubt.

By the same token, virtually no one alive in 1670 could have made any sense of such a concept. It is not just that the people of that time had no term precisely comparable to our "culture," no way to designate the underlying framework of values, customs, and institutions shared by the members of a particular society. Nor is it evident that in 1670 "America" conveyed only a very broad and generalized geographical meaning, and no political meaning at all. It is, more simply, that the settlers and those they had left behind in the mother country identified unquestioningly with one another. The Atlantic Ocean was for them a barrier of immense size and consequence, but it was (or seemed to be) only a spatial barrier. Ideas and traditions, like goods and people, moved readily across it in ships and emerged on the other side apparently unchanged. Until well along in the eighteenth century most residents of the British colonies in America continued to think of themselves as transplanted English people, as carriers of *the* culture to a distant land. Theirs was indeed a "New World," but it was new in a territorial sense alone.

We, of course, looking back from centuries later in time, may reach a different conclusion. But we should nonetheless be careful to recognize *their own* view of the matter, if only because it serves to highlight some of the problems inherent in this form of imaginative enterprise. We are proposing to study the beginning of American culture—and it is always difficult to unravel beginnings. In the process we must deal with people far removed from us in time—and people who were not aware of developing a distinctive way of life.

Students of American culture in later periods can amass a wealth of immediately pertinent materials, for Americans since the Revolution have been continually preoccupied with their own uniqueness. Indeed, these materials seem almost endless—hopeful definitions of national purpose, proud claims of special achievement, not to mention the painful thrusts received from a variety of foreign and domestic critics. For contemporaries and for scholars alike, all debate has proceeded from the assumption that America was, and remains, different. But the colonists, those "first Americans" as they have sometimes been called, produced very little such self-analysis. To be sure, they sustained their own form of introspectiveness, their own effort to define themselves in personal and political terms; but the framework of idea and feeling within which they faced these tasks was obviously derivative. The Puritan piety of the New England settlers, and the studied gentility of the Chesapeake planters—to take two of the most conspicuous attempts at self-definition—were rooted deeply in Old World traditions.

Lacking, then, any direct assistance from the people who made and lived the culture of early America, our inquiry must proceed largely by indirect methods—by deduction, by inference, by a kind of reading between the lines. But where are the data, and what is the interpretive strategy, best suited to such an undertaking? Many alternatives suggest themselves, no single one of which supplies an entirely satisfactory group of answers. But the preferences applied here, the preferences that determine the arrangement of all the documents presented in the succeeding pages, can and should be directly stated.

It is, I suggest, a network of *relationships* that especially reveals a culture of any type. The word "relationships" should be understood in its ordinary sense and will cover in this instance a wide range of interactions between units of varying size and character. The basic referent, however, will always be the individual person—an entirely hypothetical type of the "average" colonist. One person's experiences, assumptions, values *are* the culture, no more and no less; and the vital relationships that reveal this culture are also one person's. The word "vital" introduces another note of ambiguity, and every scholar may choose to construe it in a unique way. But certain simple categories seem obvious and unexceptionable.

We all have, for example, a family, a group of kinfolk among whom we spend much of our time and with whom we share some of our most profound and personal experiences. Similarly, we have a community of persons to which we feel we belong, a village, a neighborhood, a setting of human shapes and faces that are known in the course of immediate, everyday routine. At the same time, we all have some sense of strangers—people who are distinctly outside the community, who may or may not be enemies but are in any case *different*.

Introduction

But these categories need not be limited to units composed of persons. We all interact in countless ways with our natural environment: with the land, with the seasons, with all manner of animal and plant life. We have, moreover, still another set of attachments to a world beyond nature, a world of gods and devils, of chance and destiny, which may be no less real for being unseen. Finally, we have a relationship to our own lives; each personality is itself a network of inner relationships. We imply as much whenever we speak of someone as being "integrated," and the degree and character of such integration help to determine all forms of personal activity.

This way of approaching our task may be pictured as a design in which the individual colonist is the midpoint in a set of concentric circles, each one larger than the last. The smallest of the circles, the one nearest to the center, stands for the family; the others represent, successively, the community, the Indians, the natural setting, and the supernatural. Furthermore, if we examine the midpoint more closely we discover that it, too, is a circle, enclosing its own dense cluster of inner lines and shapes. The spatial distance from the point to the surrounding circles corresponds roughly to the personal distance from the individual colonist to the other units of analysis. The model must allow for interchange among the different circles: the family, for example, both supports and is nourished by the community; and relations with Indians are affected by religious doctrines. Yet in some deeper sense all lines of connection lead back to, and through, the midpoint—the individual person.

The rationale for the arrangement of this volume will now be obvious. Each circle of relationship is represented by one distinct group of readings. In addition, a separate section has been placed at the beginning to demonstrate the problems attendant on the earliest phase of settlement. These problems were special, in both kind and degree; no later generation of colonists had to face quite the same set of circumstances.

A few words are needed about the character of the documents themselves. They are intended, of course, to span a range of sorts and conditions, to represent the variety of materials available to the student of early American social history. However, they do have one general trait in common. They are all in some sense personal documents that reveal the impact of the culture at the level of individual experience. By the same token, institutional sources—formal decrees and statutes, official pronouncements by leaders of the community—have been left more or less to one side.

These choices express an underlying intent to approach the subject in essentially human terms. But in some measure this intent has been a limiting factor, for personal documents have survived on a rather arbitrary and irregular basis. Some aspects of human life are largely irrecoverable from centuries later in time: the more intimate dimensions of marriage, for instance, and important but largely unrecorded aspects of household and community routine. Moreover, in other matters the evidence seems to come preponderantly from one area of the colonies alone—and may on that count be at least a little suspect. (New England, for example, seems considerably overrepresented.) One must be candid about these difficulties in order to avoid later misunderstanding. Each document has been chosen because it demonstrates a specific form of human experience, but whether it is entirely typical remains an open question.

Questions of representative coverage are all the more troublesome since our subject is so broadly extended in time and space. We are asked to survey one hundred and fifty years of the American past, spread across tens of thousands of square miles. Every schoolchild knows that the setting of life varied considerably, as between South Carolina, Pennsylvania, and Massachusetts, and that the original settler can hardly be equated with the provincial gentleman or lady of a century later. All of this seems obvious and needs no elaboration here.

But how, then, can we manage to talk of *the* American culture, a single set of themes common to all or most of colonial experience? There is at least one way to reduce the element of variability, specifically the element of temporal variability, if only we will follow the historian's blind instinct to begin at the beginning. We can try to reconstruct the situation at the moment of settlement, at the time when people from England and northern Europe first came ashore with the aim of planting colonies. In this way we may find certain constants, certain basic trends and conditions that were present everywhere—whether in Virginia in 1607, Plymouth in 1620, New Amsterdam in 1626, Massachusetts Bay in 1630, and even Carolina in 1665.

Some of these conditions belonged wholly to the environment. There was, most simply, the awesome fact of the wilderness, the presence virtually everywhere along the Atlantic coast of a forest that seemed dark, dense, and profoundly mysterious. Most settlers had never seen anything like it, coming as they did either from towns or from well-developed areas of the rural countryside. They called the wilderness "howling"—the word quickly became a cliché, but it conveys nonetheless their sense of strangeness, of danger, as they began their "foundation work." What

Introduction

howled, and why? And what was needed to still the noise? These questions echoed in the hearts and minds of the settlers throughout the earliest years.

There were, quite literally, animals that howled. The average Englishman or woman of this period had no experience with wildlife of any sort. Domestic animals they knew—cows, sheep, pigs, goats, chickens perhaps, but was any settler prepared for the first encounter with a wolf? Or an alligator? Or a rattlesnake? At the outset all colonists regarded the animals of the wilderness as antagonists. Men traded information on ways to hunt them down and offered bounties to encourage their destruction. And yet, too, as time passed, a different, more pragmatic view took hold. Animals, especially dead ones, could be put to use—their flesh as food, their hides as clothing, and some of their other parts as medicinal antidotes and remedies. Indeed, the fur-bearing animals were from the beginning a most valuable stock-in-trade. For all these reasons the initial attitudes of fear rapidly gave way, and by the eighteenth century newer tendencies were evident as well. Some men began to hunt merely for sport; others developed an early form of scientific curiosity about their environment, a desire to describe and classify all the distinctive varieties of wildlife in the land.

There were other creatures, of human size and shape, that "howled" in the wilderness too. Of course, the colonists knew about the Indians even before they arrived, and Indians had figured directly in the plans they laid for the future. The missionary impulse, the trading impulse: these are familiar subjects in the history of settlement. They enclose a large and important area of cultural interchange—white and red people sitting down to deal with one another as comparable specimens of humankind. Considered on its face, all of this seems remarkably straightforward, controlled, matter-of-fact. Indeed, one could argue that the settlers were far more clear-headed in their dealings with the Indians than were Americans of any later period. All through the colonies people of the two races lived interspersed with one another on a basis of noninterference and often of genuine amity. Most colonists, especially in the rural areas, must have seen and known Indians as a matter of regular routine.

And yet there was another side. Unintended misunderstanding, calculated deceit, personal violence, and war: this, too, was part of the story from the beginning. Moreover, there was—there *had to be*—a set of psychological correlates to these bitter strands of interracial history, and occasionally they broke through into consciousness. Here, for example, was the emotional foundation of the famous captivity narratives. These tales of horror made the Indian seem virtually indistinguishable from the other creatures of the howling wilderness—brutal and arbitrary in personal conduct, constantly on the move, the exact antithesis of orderly, civilized modes of life. Behaving like a beast, the Indian deserved to be treated like a beast; or so, in moments of fear, the colonists would bitterly declare. In sum, they maintained opposite sets or clusters of attitudes: reasonableness and cooperation versus loathing and terror. If there is anything surprising here, it is the way the two sides were held apart. By what seems in retrospect a psychological sleight-of-hand, most colonists developed a form of split consciousness about the Indians. Perhaps, indeed, they felt impelled to do so: how to convert and trade with these strange and unpredictable people, if fear got in the way? And how to fight them effectively, if reason blunted the force of hatred?

So the wilderness vibrated with life of many sorts, and yet in another sense it was empty—entirely devoid of "civilized" forms and patterns. No aspect of the environment was more profoundly disturbing. The English of this era, like most people of any era, assumed a continuity of human tradition, an inherited matrix of community life, that would set boundaries to their experience. But the New World was literally boundless. Instinctively, blindly almost, the settlers would seek to fill the empty space with ways and traditions remembered from their homeland. Piece by piece, they would stitch together the threads of the culture that they still carried in their minds and would create a life that any one of their compatriots might recognize. Yet here and there, and all around them, the emptiness remained—a challenge for many future generations of people on the frontier.

The response to these environmental circumstances was at the deepest level a matter of personal adjustment. And in fixing our inquiry on the moment of settlement, we must take some measure of the settlers themselves. We must try to characterize them in terms, however broadly defined, that help us to understand their initial encounter with the American wilderness.

(1) They were, most obviously, nearly all white, and predominantly English. (The exceptions—the first of the blacks shipped from Africa; the Swedes, Finns, and Dutch scattered along the middle part of the coastline—can barely be noticed in what follows.)

(2) The majority were male and belonged to the age group between twenty and forty. (In this regard there was considerable variance among different settlements. In Virginia, for example, the earliest migrants were

Introduction

mostly young, unmarried adults, whereas in New England there was a strong tendency toward settlement by families from the very start.)

(3) They were drawn largely from the middle ranks of English society, from those categories usually designated by the terms "yeomen" and "husbandmen." Some were "gentlemen" and "ladies" (proprietors of landed estates or sons and daughters of proprietors, clergymen, military officers, merchants), but very few could lay claim to the status of nobility. Similarly, few among them came from the meanest groups in the English population—the "laborers" and "hirelings" with little or no property of their own, and the mass of "wandering persons," apparently unemployable, whose presence throughout the English countryside was so widely deplored.

(4) They belonged to a society still distinctly preindustrial. The bulk of the settlers came from villages and hamlets where agriculture remained the foundation of all human enterprise. Some were craftsmen—joiners, coopers, tanners, and the like—but these people, too, were accustomed to working the land.

(5) Their moral values and assumptions were rooted firmly in the Christian tradition. A personal and omnipotent God, an equally personal but menacing Devil, an array of supernatural forces on both sides, and a conviction of inherent human sinfulness: these were the decisive elements in their world-view. Of course, there was bitter dispute over many particular points of doctrine and worship, but everyone, whether Anglican or Puritan or Catholic, shared a certain core of religious commitment. English people of all sorts also shared a variety of beliefs that we might call "magical" and "superstitious"—venerable folk traditions bearing on the land and the weather, health and sickness, the foretelling of the future, the remembering of the past.

(6) As individual personalities, the settlers defy any effort at precise classification. But certain broad trends and tendencies can at least be suggested. Presumably, migration was itself a selective process that served to pull out unusually ambitious and resourceful elements from the larger English population. In one way or another (though not always consciously), they sought to better the basic circumstances of their lives, and in order to do so they were obliged to take risks and to accept the unknown as a regular part of experience. By so much they were set apart from the men and women they had left behind. Yet they could not entirely give up a more conservative orientation; and they also maintained a deep strain of passivity, of resistance to change, which marks them as heirs

of an age-old peasant culture. They were, in short, traditional people on the way to becoming modern.

Thus the setting, thus the people—it remains now to bring these various environmental and human forces together. And in so doing we shall concentrate on two broad themes that seem to have run through many of the settlers' earliest experiences. They can be briefly specified by the words "dependency" and "order." Indeed, we shall find that these two themes also provide a useful perspective on the later history of the colonies. Growth and change would shade them in different ways for successive generations, but there were obvious continuities as well. Each one reflected vital currents in the whole stream of life in the New World. The question of dependency touched many aspects of the relationship between the colonies and their mother country, and pointed in the end toward the American Revolution. The problem of order encompassed the effort of the colonists to find pattern and meaning in their affairs—both as groups of people bound to respect social imperatives, and as individuals wrestling in their own way with existential issues as old as humanity itself.

Whatever their character in specific cases, whatever resources they brought with them, all of the original settlers would be severely tested by their first encounter with the New World. The element of sheer physical hardship was nearly too much for them in the early years. Already weakened by weeks of confinement on shipboard, they came ashore quite unaccustomed to the local food supply and unprepared for the rigors of the North American climate. Often they added to their predicament by a poor choice of initial location. (Both Jamestown in Virginia and Charlestown in Massachusetts Bay were low and marshy sites, natural breeding grounds for disease-carrying insects.) For reasons of security they were obliged to live at very close quarters with one another. And there was the additional factor, almost inevitable given the huge distance from England and the small ships of the time, of woefully inadequate provisioning. So it was that each of the earliest settlements endured a period of disease and privation, a "starving time."

The record of these settlements is regrettably meager, but it does reveal in unmistakable terms a sense of perilous isolation from home, family, and reliable routine. Many people must have thought of recrossing the ocean, and quite a few actually did so. For all those who stayed, the need to maintain some thread of connectedness with England was overpowering. Life would be impossible, they felt, without money, goods, additional immigrants, approval, care, concern, love, prayers, arriving in a regular flow from the mother country. (The metaphor itself is illuminating.) Indeed *supplies*—in every sense of the term—became their overriding problem.

But this problem was compounded by all the difficulties of creating a viable form of community where none had existed before. A framework of orderly human relations seemed vitally necessary in a wilderness setting, yet it had to be established without the familiar supports of inherited custom and tradition. Authority became something visibly contrived—either by merchants and administrators overseas, or be lesser people on the scene—and so it was often precarious. At Jamestown, at Plymouth, at New Amsterdam, and even in Massachusetts Bay, the first years were characterized by chronic political and social flux. The threat of breakdown seemed very grave, and occasionally (as at Jamestown under the administration of President Wingfield) it was realized. The intense anxieties that circulated among the bulk of the settlers only made matters worse. There was an atmosphere of dog-eat-dog competitiveness, a pervasive sense that one person's gain would necessarily be another's loss. The first "plantations" in the New World seem, in retrospect, an apt model for Hobbes's "state of nature," where life was "nasty, brutish, and short."

Various strategies were tried as ways of coping with this situation. The famous Mayflower Compact of the Plymouth pilgrims provides an interesting case in point. William Bradford declared that it was "occasioned partly by the discontented and mutinous speeches that some of the strangers amongst them had let fall from them in the ship: that when they came ashore they would use their own liberty, for none had the power to command them." Ostensibly a democratic instrument, the Compact was designed expressly for a "better ordering" of the settlement. The key phrase was the one that bound the signers to give "all due submission and obedience" to the leadership. The early history of Massachusetts Bay shows an effort to achieve the same end, though by different means. For two years a small coterie of "magistrates" led by John Winthrop managed to use the charter of the parent company in order to concentrate all effective authority in their own hands. At Jamestown, moreover, the chaotic administration of Wingfield and his fellow "councillors" was followed in 1609 by a radical reorganization that left the colony under the rule of a single official endowed with almost dictatorial powers. The tenure of governors Thomas Gates and Thomas Dale has been remembered ever since as an extreme instance of repression in government—and as a prelude to the far milder regime begun by still another political reorganization in 1616. Here, as elsewhere in the New World, life seemed at first to oscillate unevenly between opposite poles of lawlessness and authoritarianism.

The seventeenth-century settlements along the North American coastline matured at varying speeds and in markedly different directions. But for most of them the extreme hardships of the early years were overcome with surprising rapidity. Virginia, Plymouth, and Maryland achieved a measure of permanence within a decade of their founding; in Massachusetts the process was even shorter, in New Amsterdam somewhat longer. The factors that served to hasten or retard development in each case included the rate of immigration, the extent and quality of available land, and relations with local Indians. For colonies begun later in the century (Pennsylvania and New Jersey, for example) there was the additional factor of proximity to the older settlements—which would serve as a valuable source of both goods and people.

In fact, after 1650 the general problem of supplies was rarely so critical as it had been earlier. Most of the settlements achieved a solid food base and a degree of protection against Indians that freed them from extreme reliance on the mother country. There was, of course, land in great abundance, and virtually every able-bodied man could assure himself of a regular subsistence. In some areas a start was made in commercial enterprise—witness the rapid development of tobacco cultivation in the tidewater area of Virginia, and the export of fish and timber from certain parts of New England. Moreover, there was remarkably little epidemic disease after the initial years, until well into the eighteenth century. Perhaps the most significant measure of overall progress was the highly favorable demographic regime that developed all through the colonies within a generation or so after settlement. From the evidence currently available it appears that the New World surpassed the Old on virtually every important index of life and health. Infant mortality, the mortality of women in childbirth, and the all-inclusive death rate were substantially reduced, while the birth rate and life expectancy rose correspondingly. The average man of twenty-one in seventeenth-century New England could expect to live another forty-five years: but in the mother country the comparable figure was nearer thirty.

Having rapidly outgrown the weakness of their beginnings, the colonies managed in time to achieve a startling degree of internal self-determination. In New England the process was a calculated one: Puritan dissenters were anxious to pursue their particular religious and social goals without interference from overseas. In the colonies farther south this was less a matter of conscious concern, but events moved steadily in a similar direction. The continuing problem of reliable communication across the Atlantic, plus the inevitable self-preoccupation of the English during the critical years of their own civil war and "inter-regnum," created conditions highly favorable to the development of colonial autonomy. This situation was to some extent reversed after the restoration of 1660, for the Stuart kings and their chief councilors were determined to impose a more orderly pattern of control on their far-flung empire. But the colonies, for their part, refused to fall obediently into line. The Navigation Acts, the establishment of the Board of Trade, the recall and revision of certain of the colonial charters, mark a thirty-year struggle to define the limits of imperial authority, in which the Crown was only partially successful. The accession of William and Mary in the Glorious Revolution of 1689 served, in effect, to scale down this struggle, and to fix the relationship between colonies and mother country at roughly the point to which it had then evolved.

But if the colonies became largely self-determining in a material and political sense, there were other forms of subordination that would long endure. For England loomed very large indeed in the minds and hearts of colonists of every generation. Within the settler group, according to one report, some "were, even to their eightieth year, still pleasing themselves with hopes of their returning to England." And among their American-born descendants there was an abiding curiosity to see the great land of which they heard so much. In fact, colonists continued until after the middle of the eighteenth century to speak of England as "home."

Travel to England was always a high priority for those with sufficient wealth and leisure. Merchants with business in London, political men bent on office or patronage, clergymen seeking contact with fellow worshipers, crossed and recrossed the ocean in substantial numbers. Vast quantities of personal correspondence testify to a similar orientation. Letters to England invariably begged for bits of social and political gossip and often carried detailed requests for scientific information or for new books and journals. There is a deferential, almost fawning tone in some of this material that projects with special clarity the dependency still inherent in the colonial relationship. For men and women in Boston or Philadelphia or tidewater Virginia, the Atlantic remained an indispensable lifeline to all that was most fine, most "civilized" in human experience.

Colonists everywhere, especially among the more privileged classes, looked to the mother country for their standards of good conduct, good manners, fashion, and indeed for a larger idea of whatever it was that constituted the good life. The planters of Virginia, for example, frequently pictured themselves as country gentlemen set down in the New World; and a visitor to the region in 1724 noted that their "habits of life, customs, computations, etc. . . . are much the same as about London, which they esteem their home." Many of the special artifacts and symbols of this genteel style were derived directly from England. Items such as perfumes, lacework, hats, fancy clothes, spices, precious stones, and billiard tables were frequently advertised in colonial newspapers as being "English-made" or "just arrived from England." Wig makers, tailors, and upholsterers working in the colonies found it advisable to announce some first-hand experience with the methods of their trade as practiced in England. A furniture dealer would declare that his goods were all "of the newest fashion, London-make." And a tutor "lately arrived" in a colonial city and looking for pupils would make it known that he had spent many years at the "education of Youth" in London. For that matter, the educational interchange between the colonies and England was quite extensive at all levels. Hundreds of merchants and planters sent their sons to schools in England, such as Eton, Harrow, and Winchester. In many cases young colonials went on from there to Oxford or Cambridge or Edinburgh, or to the Inns of Court in London. A considerable proportion of the staff at colonial colleges were graduates of one of the great British universities.

In all these ways the colonists remained beholden to England. The supplies they sought were, of course, scarcely comparable to those required in the earliest years of settlement. There is quite a difference between one man who begs for meat and tools and clothes as practical, day-to-day necessities and another who wants books for his library and perfume for his lady. It is the difference between the instinct of survival and the desire for a certain self-legitimization. Yet in a psychological sense, and from the single standpoint of dependency, the two are not so far apart. Both men have needs, both must look to England for the fulfillment of these needs, and there is in each case an undertone of real urgency. To put it somewhat crudely, there was a quality of special pleading in much of the *mail* that crossed the ocean from west to east during the colonial period.

Two aspects of this situation need a special note of emphasis. Colonial culture was profoundly derivative. The settlers and their descendants would eventually create a new society, but they remained all the while extremely attentive to the values and traditions of their English parent. Even as they faced away from the coast and moved on to the West,

Introduction

they would often look back over their shoulder, across the ocean toward the land they still called home. Furthermore, these tendencies diminished very little with the passage of time, and in some respects they may well have grown stronger. Recent scholarship of eighteenth-century America has uncovered evidence of increasing "anglicization"—in law, in social structure, in popular mores and custom. These findings suggest some interesting questions for further research. It is, for example, usually supposed that the Revolution occurred at the end of a long sequence of development in which the colonies grew progressively different from England. But perhaps a reverse hypothesis should be considered. Perhaps it was necessary for the colonies to become more *like* England before they could feel the need, and find the resources, to throw off their filial ties forever.

The problem of order, like that of dependency, was modified but never overcome in the later stages of colonial history. In fact, there are many aspects of colonial life that can be fruitfully examined as part of a dialectic between the opposing forces of tradition, security, and permanence on the one side and ambitiousness, fluidity, and change on the other. The first settlers were surprisingly successful in giving shape and meaning to their lives, but their achievement would barely outlive them. In this regard each succeeding generation would confront roughly the same predicament, for the creation of order was an ongoing process continuously renewed.

The story of the New England Puritans is the classic case in point. Nowhere else in the first half of the seventeenth century did life seem so powerfully controlled, so carefully patterned to a model of social perfection. Yet very soon the New England way began to fray around the edges, and well before 1700 the entire fabric was disintegrating. This was the "declension" that Puritan preachers decried from the pulpit in their celebrated "jeremiads." The later seventeenth century was, in fact, a time of upheaval in many parts of British America. In Virginia there was Bacon's Rebellion of 1676; in New York, Leisler's Rebellion of 1689; and similar disturbances occurred, though on a smaller scale, in Maryland and the Carolinas as well. Interpreted till recently as democratic uprisings in which average people sought to throw off the oppression of their social superiors, these events actually involved intense struggles among elite groups for control of the centers of power in their respective communities. As such, they testify to the presence of deep undercurrents of instability and social disorganization.

Instability was, in a sense, built into the ecological foundations of life in the New World. The land itself conspired against familiar structures of order. All of the early colonists expected that settlement would be compact, that houses and farms and places of business would be grouped together in tight little clusters. So it was in those parts of England from which they had come, and presumably the same imperatives would apply with added force amid the many difficulties of a wilderness environment. Yet almost everywhere events proved otherwise. The lure of new lands worked inexorably to wedge apart the fledgling communities in which people tried to recreate a secure network of human relationships.

This result was realized first in the region around Chesapeake Bay—and especially in Virginia. Confined for a decade to a few fortified settlements along the eastern shore, the colony began after 1620 to spread out dramatically. Several factors helped to speed the process. There was, first, a decision by the parent company in London to divide lands among the individual settlers and to offer "headrights" (fifty acres per person) to new arrivals. There was also the massacre sustained at the hands of local Indians in 1622—followed immediately by a devastating counterattack, which removed the danger from that quarter for more than a generation. If these were the necessary conditions of dispersion, the incentive lay in the soil itself. The profit to be made from the sale of tobacco was quickly evident to all Virginians (and Marylanders as well), and before midcentury the entire region had gone over to the cultivation of this one staple crop. Tobacco was hard on the land, however, so people tried continually to extend their holdings. They were encouraged in this by the shape of the countryside. The Chesapeake shoreline was unusually complex, with numerous little bays, inlets, streams, and rivers offering ready access to ocean-going ships. As a result the settlers could establish, on an individual basis, direct relationships with the important markets across the sea. There was little stimulus here to the development of towns—on the contrary, there was every inducement for people to scatter far and wide. An aerial view of the Chesapeake region in the 1640s or 1650s would have disclosed a situation radically at variance with traditional norms of settlement: hundreds of rather large farms, each with its own separate household, strung out irregularly along the various navigable waterways. Communities, in the familiar, *spatial* sense of that term, were simply not in evidence.

Farther north, in New England, the pressure to maintain cohesion was much greater. Leaders among the dominant Puritan group insisted that a tight pattern of settlement was vitally linked to the goals of their migration. Their departure from England had been, in part, a protest against ominous trends of social disintegration. They believed, for example, that England was overpopulated, was growing "weary of her inhabitants, so as man, which is the most precious of all creatures, is here more vile and base than the earth they tread upon." There was also the factor of human selfishness. Everywhere in "this sinful land" they observed a rising spirit of individualism, of personal greed. The result, as Robert Cushman put it, was that "each man is fain to pluck his means . . . out of his neighbor's throat." John Winthrop voiced the same protest in a series of rhetorical questions: "What means then the bleating of so many oppressed with wrong, that drink wormwood for righteousness? Why do many sheep that seek shelter at the judgment seats return without their fleeces? Why meet we so many wandering ghosts in shape of men, so many spectacles of misery in all our streets, our houses full of victuals and our entries of hunger-starved Christians, our shops full of rich wares and under our stalls lie our own flesh in nakedness?"

In contrast to all this, the Puritans aimed to recreate in America a spirit of harmony and brotherliness, an organic connection among men. Thus they proposed to live in a centralized community, to watch over one another, to worship in a common church, and to submit to a common government. Here was the meaning of Winthrop's famous model of a "city upon a hill"—*one* city, in which "we must be knit together . . . as one man . . . [and] . . . must delight in each other, make others' conditions our own, rejoice together, mourn together, labor and suffer together, always having before our eyes our commission and community in the work."

Yet almost from the beginning the Puritan city began to pull apart. Winthrop's design of a single, tightly bound community was immediately frustrated by various local exigencies; and within a year the settler group had dispersed to several different locations around Massachusetts Bay. The same centrifugal tendency was apparent in Plymouth Colony as well. The original plantation on Plymouth Bay divided in 1627 so as to permit the founding of a new town (at Duxbury); this was merely the prototype for a chain of similar fissions in the succeeding decades. The authorities of the colony watched this process with mounting alarm but felt powerless to reverse its direction. William Bradford expressed the official mood of resigned regret when he compared the original settlement to "an ancient mother grown old and forsaken of her children, though not in their affections yet in regard of their bodily presence and personal helpfulness; her

Introduction

ancient members being most of them worn away by death, and these of later time being like children translated into other families, and she like a widow left only to trust in God."

Even within the separate townships of New England there was a process of increasing fragmentation. Every settlement began in one designated center, with the meetinghouse and "home-lots" laid out in close and carefully arranged proximity. But after a time certain inhabitants would break away to form an additional village (or two, or three) in another corner of the town land. And often at least a few men contrived to live on farms that were effectively isolated from neighborhoods of any sort.

These trends, established so quickly and dramatically in the region around Chesapeake Bay and more gradually in New England, became in fact characteristic of all the colonies by the eighteenth century. The self-sufficient tobacco farm of Virginia foreshadowed the development of the rice and cotton plantations of Carolina and Georgia. The remarkable growth of Pennsylvania after 1680 depended heavily on the new city at Philadelphia, but the country to the west and north became a mazework of separate homesteads. Nearly everywhere the interior, the "back-country," provided the most striking of all the examples of human dispersion. To be sure, villages and hamlets were usually present, as centers of religious worship, legal process, and economic exchange; but most inhabitants regarded them in a utilitarian light—and not as a focus for personal and collective loyalties.

These ecological circumstances—above all, the sheer immensity of the land, as set against a relatively small and scattered population—trace one aspect of the problem of order in colonial America. But the same problem must be examined in more immediately political terms. For, as previously noted, the effort to transfer a stable framework of social and administrative organization from the Old World to the New was beset with difficulties from the very start; and it would in part remain so throughout the entire span of colonial history.

Always and everywhere, authority was the central consideration. In the minds of premodern Englishmen, on both sides of the Atlantic, authority was an assumed presence in all manner of human relationships. Validated by ancient tradition and reabsorbed by each succeeding generation, it was also tangibly embodied in crown and scepter, in cathedral and manor house, in wearing apparel, physical posture, and tonal inflection. Most important, authority was unitary in inner substance, and pyramidal in outward shape. Social position, material wealth, pedigree, and political influence were naturally joined in the same individuals and institutions.

Introduction

A rich man would expect to command office and prestige, and a high official must, by the same token, be visibly well-to-do. The theme of hierarchy informed the common wisdom of the day. Society was a graduated scale of ranks and statuses, "appointed . . . in a most excellent and perfect order." Power emanated from discrete source points and flowed ineluctably downward; obedience and submission simply reversed these lines of force. Top, middle, and bottom—and each of the intermediate conditions—were bound in a series of indissoluble linkages. The essential paradigm was captured in the following passage from a contemporary *Book of Homilies*: "Every degree of people, in their vocations, calling and office, hath appointed to them their duty and order. Some are in high degree, some in low; some kings and princes, some inferiors and subjects; priests and laymen, masters and servants, fathers and children, husbands and wives, rich and poor; and everyone have need of other."

This was, of course, an ideal, a goal, a touchstone of value and performance. It was nowhere perfectly realized, but it seemed—in the Old World—a reasonable standard to hold up against the actual course of human affairs. In the American colonies, however, the distance between the model and social realities widened significantly.

Consider, for example, the question of power—its origins, and its distribution in a variety of institutional agencies. The critical issue here was the relationship between local organs of government and the presumably superior resources of provincial authorities (governors, councils, assemblies, and the like). In fact, this relationship offered surprising advantages to the lesser units. By the middle of the seventeenth century the town meetings of New England and the county courts in the southern colonies had won for themselves a range of powers without precedent in the local administration of the mother country. Indeed, the whole inner balance of the pyramidal edifice seemed increasingly in jeopardy. The towns and counties were expected to support the system by sending representatives to the provincial assemblies and by carrying out the various decisions received from any branch of "higher" authority. In fact, full compliance could not be obtained on either count. Sometimes legislation by the assembly, and orders from the governor and his council, were simply ignored at the local level. Occasionally local communities neglected to send representatives to the assembly in the first place. Moreover, in some instances there was a plainly anomalous situation in which the lesser units came first in point of time—and themselves created the authority by which they would later be governed. This was true, for example, in the founding of both Rhode Island and Connecticut. In the eighteenth century there was difficulty in extending provincial authority over certain frontier communities. Scotch-Irish in Pennsylvania and Moravians in North Carolina (among others) wished to remain self-sufficient in both political and cultural affairs, and were reluctant to yield their autonomy to the central agencies of colonial administration.

The same problems can be presented more vividly from the standpoint of social structure, and of the individuals most critically placed in that structure. Ruling groups found their position inherently delicate, for wealth, power, and prestige did not always cohere in the expected ways. Certain men who came to America from humble backgrounds gained here the opportunity for rapid self-advancement. Their special qualities of energy and resourcefulness, combined perhaps with an element of sheer luck, enabled them to amass lands and other property, to build substantial houses, to affect at least some of the familiar accoutrements of gentility. Yet their prospects for obtaining commensurate political influence were none too certain. There were bound to be competing claims, both from men whose careers had traced a similar course and from others with preferred connections in England. Indeed, it is to this competition that modern historians have ascribed the special animus that infused some of the major social upheavals of the period. A statement by Nathaniel Bacon (leader of the Virginia rebellion that took his name) makes the point clearly enough. "We appeal to the country itself," he wrote in a famous manifesto, "what and of what nature their oppressions have been or by what cabal and mystery the designs of many of those whom we call great men have been translated and carried on. But let us trace these men in authority and favor to whose hand the dispensation of the country's wealth has been committed; let us observe the sudden rise of their estates [compared] with the quality in which they first entered this country or the reputation they have held here amongst wise and discerning men. And let us see whether their extractions and education have not been vile, and by what pretense and virtue they could so soon [enter] into employments of so great trust and consequence."

The whole connection with the mother country worked to skew lines of authority in awkward ways. Clearly, important decisions affecting the empire were made in London; every colonist who sought economic or political advantage was attentive to developments there. Personal contacts in the court bureaucracy were especially important and were cultivated with great care. Offices, contracts, land grants, and financial credits were among the rewards of effective maneuvering in this quarter. Yet English connections, even official ones, were not by themselves a guarantee of high rank in the colonies. Customs collectors, treasury agents, naval officers, and other appointed representatives of the prerogative would learn the limits of their authority quickly enough. Here were men with undeniable political clout—but often without much wealth or personal stature. Their recurrent difficulties in dealing with provincial merchants and planters owed much to this fact.

Above all, the disorderly tendencies in colonial life seemed a function of social mobility. Whatever the actual rates of mobility (and they have not yet been adequately studied), people *believed* they were high; and this belief became an important reality in its own right. Two short illustrations may be useful. One is an excerpt from the journal of John Winthrop, describing a "passage" between an inhabitant of Rowley, Massachusetts, and his servant: "The master, being forced to sell a pair of his oxen to pay his wages, told his servant he could keep him no longer, not knowing how to pay him the next year. The servant answered him [that] he would serve him for more of his cattle. 'But how shall I do,' saith the master, 'when all my cattle are gone?' The servant replied, 'you shall then serve me, and so you may have your cattle again.'" The humor of this episode was based in part on its peculiarity—its implicit affront to the norms of traditional society.

Of course, traditional society was not without the means to respond, and it is worth examining in this connection the notorious "sumptuary laws" of Massachusetts Bay. The background for this legislation was an alleged trend toward "excess in apparel." According to then current assumptions, clothing should visibly reflect (and thereby reinforce) the prevalent scale of status distinctions. In a well-ordered society humble people would dress in a humble way, while the rich and well-born wore finery. In Massachusetts, however, "men or women of mean condition, educations, or callings" were increasingly prone to "take upon them the garb of gentlemen, by the wearing of gold or silver lace, or buttons, or points at their knees, to walk in great boots; or women of the same rank to wear silk or tiffany hoods or scarves." The General Court of the colony, declaring its "utter detestation and dislike" of the trend, forbade such costume among all citizens whose personal assets totaled less than £200. The Court did make some exceptions, by declaring that "this law shall not extend to the restraint of any magistrate or other public officer of this jurisdiction, their wives and children, who are left to their discretion in wearing of apparel, or any settled military officer . . . or any other whose education and employments have been above the ordinary degree, or whose estates have been considerable, though now decayed." Taken as a whole, the legislation may be seen as a frontal attack on the problem of mobility. And the category of exceptions implies recognition of the special circumstances that prevailed in the New World. Magistrates and military officers would not invariably possess assets of £200, and others of excellent background might find their estates "decayed." Mobility operated in both directions, up *and* down; in either case it disturbed the equilibrium of society.

It is important, finally, to assess these trends at the level of ongoing human experience—to explore issues of personal style and behavior, in light of the whole complex interplay between individual colonists and their social and ecological environment. The famous question posed by J. Hector St. John de Crevecoeur in the revolutionary era is timelessly pertinent: "What then is the American, this new man?" Of course, there was no "American"—so identified and named—during the colonial period; but perhaps a "new man" was evolving all the same.

This possibility was occasionally considered at the time. When the Reverend John Clayton commented in reference to his Virginia hosts, "'tis strange in how many things besides they are remiss, which one would think Englishmen should not be guilty of," he was in a way anticipating Crevecoeur. There grew in some quarters a perception that the colonists were abandoning received conventions and were breaking out of a long-established mold that would otherwise have shaped their inner lives. It was hard to describe the process in so many words, and it is still hard to do so. But there were certain surface manifestations that anyone could see. For example, there was mobility, in both the geographical and the social meaning of the term. A man who chose to separate from his town (and family) of origin and to resettle himself in a more remote and perhaps isolated situation was taking a step of great psychological significance. The same can be said of another man who substantially increased his estate and began to wear silk doublets with silver buttons. They would, almost certainly, avoid seeing the implications of their behavior; they might well contrive to justify this behavior by reference to traditional values. Yet they were, all the same, gradually, ineluctably withdrawing from such values. And by just that much they were opening wider the door to something undeniably new—and even modern.

The balance between the traditional and the modern was always present in the colonists, but it was inherently unstable. The specific permutations and combinations of personality were as numerous and varied as the settlers themselves; but overall, and over time, the balance would shift decisively in favor of the more dynamic elements. The New World presented such an extraordinary range of opportunities for people ready to take advantage of them, that an active, even manipulative, style became increasingly the norm. People who had transformed a wilderness—clearing fields, building roads and houses, subduing animals and Indians—would take for granted an ability to shape the world to the pattern of their own wishes. Here, indeed, was a clear foreshadowing of the "go-ahead" spirit that became a hallmark of the new nation in the nineteenth century.

In some respects these changes were liberating. People experienced a palpable stretching of their talents, and their sense of themselves sharpened correspondingly. Personal identities gained at the expense of collective ones, and gradually through the eighteenth century the ground was laid for new values, new ideologies, a new ethos. People of the period could not see the trend for what it was, but they helped to create the individualism so loudly proclaimed by later generations of Americans. Yet there was also a cost. A more independent person was also more isolated and in some ways more vulnerable. Currents of fear, doubt, perplexity roiled the inner world of character and occasionally bubbled up to the surface. In a society increasingly fluid, individuals might feel a certain loss of bearings.

These circumstances may help to make intelligible one of the most striking traits of colonial Americans—their extreme sensitivity to the opinions and attitudes of others. The evidence of their own writings, especially their personal writings, is overwhelming here: one sees again and again their propensity to search for cues to behavior outside rather than within the self. Has one achieved an important goal, gained a new position or mark of honor?—one will describe in detail the admiration of friends and neighbors. Has one been disappointed in a quest of some type?—one will present the view of supposedly neutral parties that one should by all rights have succeeded. Has one been criticized or slighted by other members of the community?—one will immediately call them to account. Does such criticism have some reasonable foundation in fact?—one will jump to one's own defense and will probably try to shift the blame elsewhere. Is one uncertain as to one's particular worth and character?—one will ponder how others have defined one.

There is in all this a concern for reputation, an instinct of face-saving, a deep dread of appearing deficient in any way, which reached right to the center of personality. Colonial Americans—considered once again as a type—were not weak; they could act effectively when the occasion required. But often they were reluctant to claim the motives of action as their own. They preferred to picture themselves as responding to external influences, especially when their conduct might be open to reproach. They were, in short, not fully self-determining, and they were unable or unwilling to cultivate that existential awareness that modern people prize so highly. Their world was characterized less by stark confrontation with self and more by intense, face-to-face contacts with a variety of significant others.

It is necessary to emphasize the obvious fact that the colonists cannot be uniformly fitted to this set of specifications. For reasons too intimate to fathom from a distance of three centuries, some individual men and women varied widely from the predominant norms. Often such people became leaders in their communities; Benjamin Franklin might be a good case in point. But the evidence on average men and women strongly implies the characterological patterns already delineated.

There is the further question of the *roots* of these patterns. Surely they must be connected with the past, with still older trends and styles that prevailed among the first groups of settlers and their English progenitors. All across Europe in this period, as in preindustrial cultures elsewhere, the life of little communities was strung along a dense network of interpersonal contacts, and people were necessarily attentive to the disposition of neighbors. Moreover, the Puritan movement appears to have increased such pressures. Shame—the fear of being found out in sin by one's peers and ultimately by God—was fixed right at the core of Puritan character.

But the New World environment also played in here, fixing these trends in a distinctively American form. The point can be clarified somewhat by reference to the typology of character proposed by the sociologist David Riesman some years ago. Riesman elaborated three major variants of social character: "tradition-directed," "inner-directed," "other-directed." The first describes a person whose fundamental commitments are governed by values received from some vital cultural tradition. By contrast, inner-directed persons base their conduct on principles established within their own separate personalities, while the other-directed are guided by reactions they perceive in their peers. Riesman argues that western civilization has passed through each of these different orientations, moving from the traditional values of preindustrial society, to inner direction in the nineteenth century, to other direction today. His categories are useful, but the historical sequence he advances seems misleading. For colonial Americans were, by and large, notably other-directed—and appear to have become more so as time went along. Puritans had self-consciously rearranged their ties with the past, and non-Puritans found old ways and expectations simply irrelevant. It was, in fact, the sense of separation from the past that especially promoted the other-directed style. As the force of tradition wavered, people cast anxiously about for alternative guides to conduct. And in most cases they looked to others, to "public opinion," as we might say.

This tendency worked to counteract the disintegrative forces otherwise prevalent in colonial society. It was a kind of monitor within the individual against overly rapid change or deviance, an ally of those groups and structures that still represented order. Group pressure remained powerful precisely because people were so anxious about it. One finds in the records countless episodes in which the community tried to exploit such anxiety in order to prod recalcitrants back into line. These maneuvers did not always succeed, but even for people who resisted there was a painful inner cost. Of course, the great majority conformed (more or less), and for them the pressure of the group implied both danger and assurance. Amidst the many uncertainties of life it was sometimes a comfort to know that one's peers were watching.

But most of all, God was watching. No action, no motive, not even the most private and frivolous thoughts escaped His notice. His influence was everywhere, and the entire course of human history was shaped to His purposes. No matter how random the appearance of events, there was ultimate assurance that everything conformed to God's plan. Of course, this attitude was shared in all sectors of western culture during the preindustrial era. But for the men and women who settled the New World, it was intensified by the special circumstances in which they found themselves. "Providences" of one sort or another abounded—seemed, in fact, almost characteristic of the American environment.

And behind all this there was the twisted thread of experience itself. Whether for the first waves of settlers, their course radically deflected by the very fact of migration, or for their children and grandchildren, still set apart from traditional society, life was truly "remarkable." History had singled them out—to what end they could never be sure. Inevitably, as time passed, this sense of the extraordinary character of American experience became somewhat attenuated. And yet it continued to work beneath the surface of colonial life until the time of the Revolution—and beyond. It was there in the blustering self-consciousness of the new nation, in the determined moralism of the nineteenth-century reformers, in the relentless push against the frontier. It has survived into our own time as the rationale for trips to the moon and wars on the opposite side of the world. America "the great experiment," "the beacon of freedom," "the land of opportunity," "the last, best hope of the world"—truly a land of "remarkable providences."

Or so our history has invited us to believe.

Part One
Settlement

1
A Rationale for Migration

The motives of the people who founded "plantations" in the New World are extremely difficult to recover, from three centuries later in time. They were in any case as numerous, as varied, and as complex as the individual settlers themselves. But public discussion of such matters revolved persistently around certain particular issues. This discussion, and these issues, reveal much about the migrants—and about the culture from which they came. Migration was a grave undertaking that obliged people to rethink the assumptions that governed their lives. The condition of the society they left behind, the nature of the land to which they would go, the right relation of each person to family, neighbors, people of other countries and races, and God—these were questions that arose again and again.

"R.C.," author of the following document, cannot be positively identified. Very likely, however, he was Robert Cushman of Plymouth. A passenger on the *Mayflower* in 1620, Cushman returned to England a year later to act as business agent and promoter for the new settlement. His treatise on the "lawfulness" of migration was published in London in 1622 as part of a volume entitled *Mourt's Relation or a Journal of the Plantation of Plymouth*.

The official seal of the Massachusetts Bay Company, in use throughout the period 1629–84, makes its own point about the reasons for settlement.

Reasons and Considerations Touching the Lawfulness of Removing out of England into the Parts of America

(London, 1622)

Robert Cushman

Forasmuch as many exceptions are daily made against the going into, and inhabiting of, foreign desert places to the hindrance of plantations abroad and the increase of distractions at home: it is not amiss that some which have been ear witnesses of the exceptions made, and are either agents or abettors of such removals and plantations, do seek to give content to the world, in all things that possibly they can.

And although the most of the opposites are such as either dream of raising their fortunes here, to that than which there is nothing more unlike, or such as affecting their home-born country so vehemently as that they had rather with all their friends beg, yea, starve in it than undergo a little difficulty in seeking abroad; yet are there some who, out of doubt in tenderness of conscience and fear to offend God by running before they be called, are straitened and do straiten others from going to foreign plantations.

For whose cause especially, I have been drawn, out of my good affection to them, to publish some reasons that might give them content and satisfaction, and also stay and stop the wilful and witty caviller: and herein I trust I shall not be blamed of any godly wise, though through my slender judgment I should miss the mark and not strike the nail on the head, considering it is the first attempt that hath been made (that I know of) to defend those enterprises. Reason would [suggest], therefore, that if any man of deeper reach and better judgment see further or otherwise, that he rather instruct me than deride me.

And, being studious for brevity, we must first consider that—whereas God of old did call and summon our fathers by predictions, dreams, visions, and certain illuminations to go from their countries, places, and habitations to reside and dwell here or there, and to wander up and down from city to city, and land to land, according to His will and pleasure—now there is no such calling to be expected for any matter whatsoever, neither must any so much as imagine that there will now be any such thing. God did once train up His people, but now He doth not,

R.C., "Reasons and Considerations touching the lawfulness of removing out of England and into the parts of America," *Collections of the Massachusetts Historical Society*, Second Series, IX (Boston, 1832), pp. 64–73.

but speaks in another manner; and so we must apply ourselves to God's present dealing, and to His wonted dealing. And as the miracle of giving manna ceased when the fruits of the land became plenty, so, God having such a plentiful storehouse of directions in His holy word, there must not now any extraordinary revelations be expected. But now the ordinary examples and precepts of the Scriptures, reasonably and rightly understood and applied, must be the voice and word that must call us and direct us in every action.

Neither is there any land or possession now like unto the possession which the Jews had in Canaan, being legally holy and appropriated unto a holy people, the seed of Abraham, in which they dwelt securely and had their days prolonged—it being by an immediate voice said that He (the Lord) gave it [to] them as a land of rest after their weary travels, and a type of eternal rest in heaven. But now there is no land of that sanctimony, no land so appropriated, none typical [of it]—much less any that can be said to be given of God to any nation as was Canaan, which they and their seed must dwell in till God sendeth upon them sword or captivity. But now we are all in all places strangers and pilgrims, travelers and sojourners, most properly, having no dwelling but in this earthen tabernacle. Our dwelling is but a wandering, and our abiding but as a fleeting, and in a word our home is nowhere but in the heavens—in that house not made with hands, whose maker and builder is God, and to which all ascend that love the coming of our Lord Jesus.

Though then there may be reasons to persuade a man to live in this or that land, yet there cannot be the same reasons which the Jews had. But now, as natural, civil and religious bands tie men, so they must be bound; and as good reasons for things terrene and heavenly appear, so they must be led. And so here falleth in our question; how a man that is here born and bred, and hath lived some years, may remove himself into another country.

I answer: a man must not respect only to live and do good to himself, but he should see where he can live to do most good to others; for, as one saith, "He whose living is but for himself, it is time he were dead." Some men there are who of necessity must here live, as being tied to duties either to church, commonwealth, household, kindred, etc. But others [there are], and that many, who do no good in none of those, nor can do none, as being not able or not in favor, or as wanting opportunity, and [who] live as outcasts, nobodies, eye sores, eating but for themselves, teaching but themselves, and doing good to none, either in soul or body, and so pass over days, years, and months, yea, so live and so die. Now

5

such should lift up their eyes and see whether there be not some other place and country to which they may go to do good and have use towards others [by means] of that knowledge, wisdom, humanity, reason, strength, skill, faculty, etc. which God hath given for the service of others and His own glory.

But [I wish] not to pass the bounds of modesty so far as to name any, though I confess I know many, who sit here still with their talent in a napkin, having notable endowments both of body and mind, and [who] might do great good if they were in some places [but] which here do none, nor can do none, and yet through fleshly fear, niceness, straitness of heart, etc. sit still and look on, and will not hazard a dram of health nor a day of pleasure nor an hour of rest to further the knowledge and salvation of the sons of Adam in that new world, where a drop of the knowledge of Christ is most precious, which is here not set by. Now what shall we say to such a profession of Christ, to which is joined no more denial of a man's self? But some will say, what right have I to go live in the heathens' country?

Letting pass the ancient discoveries, contracts, and agreements which our Englishmen have long since made in those parts, together with the acknowledgment of the histories and chronicles of other nations who profess [that] the land of America from the Cape de Florida unto the Bay Canado (which is, south and north, three hundred leagues and upwards; and east and west, further than yet hath been discovered) is proper to the king of England, yet letting that pass—lest I be thought to meddle further than it concerns me or further than I have discerning—I will mention such things as are within my reach, knowledge, sight, and practice, since I have travailed in these affairs.

And first, seeing we daily pray for the conversion of the heathens, we must consider whether there be not some ordinary means and course for us to take to convert them, or whether prayer for them be only referred to God's extraordinary work from heaven. Now it seemeth unto me that we ought also to endeavor and use the means to convert them; or they [ought to] come to us. To us they cannot come, [for] our land is full; to them we may go, [since] their land is empty.

This then is a sufficient reason to prove our going thither to live lawful: their land is spacious and void, and they are few and do but run over the grass, as do also the foxes and wild beasts. They are not industrious, neither have [they] art, science, skill or faculty to use either the land or the commodities of it; but all spoils, rots, and is marred for want of manuring, gathering, ordering, etc. As the ancient patriachs therefore removed from straiter places into more roomy [ones], where the land lay idle and wasted and none used it, though there dwelt inhabitants by them (as in Gen. 13: 6, 11, 12, and 34: 21, and 41: 20), so is it lawful now to take a land which none useth and make use of it.

And as it is common land or unused and undressed country, so we have it by common consent, composition, and agreement, which agreement is double: First, the imperial governor, Massasoit, whose circuits in likelihood are larger than England and Scotland, hath acknowledged the king, majesty of England, to be his master and commander, and that once in my hearing, yea, and in writing under his hand to Captain Standish —both he and many other kings which are under him, [such] as Pamet, Nauset, Cummaquid, Narrowbiggonset, Namaschet, etc., with diverse others that dwell about the bays of Patuxet and Massachusetts. Neither hath this been accomplished by threats and blows or [by] shaking of sword and sound of trumpet; for as our faculty that way is small and our strength less, so our warring with them is after another manner, namely, by friendly usage, love, peace, honest and just carriages, good counsel, etc.—that so we and they may not only live in peace in that land, and they yield subjection to an earthly prince, but [also] that as voluntaries they may be persuaded at length to embrace the prince of peace, Christ Jesus, and rest in peace with Him forever.

Secondly, this composition is also more particular and applicatory, as touching ourselves there inhabiting; [for] the emperor [of the Indians] by a joint consent hath promised and appointed us to live at peace where [ever] we will in all his dominions, taking what place we will and as much land as we will, and bringing as many people as we will, and that for these two causes. First, because we are the servants of James, King of England, whose the land (as he confesseth) is; second, because he hath found us just, honest, kind, and peaceable, and so loves our company. Yea, and that in these things there is no dissimulation on his part, nor fear of breach (except our security engender in them some unthought of treachery, or our incivilities provoke them to anger) is most plain in other relations, which show that the things they did were more out of love than out of fear.

It being then, first, a vast and empty chaos, secondly, acknowledged the right of our sovereign king, [and] thirdly, by a peaceable composition in part possessed of diverse of his loving subjects, I see not who can doubt or call in question the lawfulness of inhabiting or dwelling there. But [it is clear] that it may be as lawful for such as are not tied upon some special occasion here to live there as well as here; yea, and as the enterprise is weighty and difficult, so the honor and fame of our dread sovereign, but chiefly to display the efficacy of power of the gospel both in zealous preaching, [and in] professing, and [in] wise walking under it, before the faces of these poor blind infidels.

As for such as object the tediousness of the voyage thither, the danger of pirates' robbery [and] of the savages' treachery, etc., these are but lions in the way; and it were well for such men if they were in heaven. For who can show them a place in this world where iniquity shall not compass them at the heels, and where they shall have a day without grief, or a lease of life for a moment; and who can tell but God what dangers may lie at our doors, even in our native country, or what plots may be abroad, or when God will cause our sun to go down at noondays and in the midst of our peace and security lay upon us some lasting scourge for our so-long neglect and contempt of His most glorious gospel.

But we have here great peace, plenty of the gospel, and many sweet delights and variety of comforts.

True indeed, and far be it from us to deny and diminish the least of these mercies; but have we rendered unto God thankful obedience for His long peace, whilst other peoples have been at wars? Have we not rather murmured, repined, and fallen at ears amongst ourselves, whilst our peace hath lasted with foreign power? Was there ever more suits in law, more envy, contempt, and reproach than nowadays? Abraham and Lot departed asunder when there fell a breach betwixt them, which was occasioned by the straitness of the land. And surely I am persuaded that, howsoever the frailties of men are principal in all contentions, yet the straitness of the place is such as each man is fain to pluck his means (as it were) out of his neighbor's throat; [and] there is such pressing and oppressing in towns and country, about farms, trade, traffic, etc. so as a man can hardly anywhere set up a trade but he shall pull down two of his neighbors.

The towns abound with young tradesmen, and the hospitals are full of the ancient; the country is replenished with new farmers, and the alms-houses are filled with old laborers; many there are who get their living with bearing burdens, but more are fain to burden the land with their whole bodies; multitudes get their means of life by prating, and so do numbers more by begging. Neither come these straits upon men always through intemperance, ill husbandry, indiscretion, etc., as some think; but even the most wise, sober, and discreet men go often to the wall, when they have done their best; wherein, as God's providence sway-eth all, so it is easy to see that the straitness of the place, having in it so many strait hearts, cannot but produce such effects more and more —so as every indifferent-minded man should be ready to say with father Abraham, "Take thou the right hand, and I will take the left", let us not thus oppress, straiten, and afflict one another, but seeing there is a spacious land, the way to which is through the sea, we will end this difference in a day.

[Consider] that I speak nothing about the bitter contention that hath been about religion, by writing, disputing, and inveighing earnestly one against another—the heat of which zeal, if it were turned against the rude barbarism of the heathens, it might do more good in a day than it hath done here in many years. Neither [do I speak] of the little love to the gospel and [the] profit which is made by the preachers in most places, which might easily drive the zealous to the heathens—who, no doubt, if they had but a drop of that knowledge which here flieth about the streets, would be filled with exceeding great joy and gladness, as that they would even pluck the kingdom of heaven by violence and take it as it were by force.

The greatest let that is yet behind is the sweet fellowship of friends and the satiety of bodily delights.

But can there be two nearer friends almost than Abraham and Lot or than Paul and Barnabas? And yet, upon as little occasions as we have here, they departed asunder, two of them being patriarchs of the church of old, the others the apostles of the church which is new. And their covenants were such as it seemeth might bind as much as any covenant between men at this day, and yet to avoid greater inconveniences they departed asunder.

Neither must men take so much thought for the flesh as not to be pleased except they can pamper their bodies with variety of dainties. Nature is content with little, and health is much endangered by mixtures upon the stomach; the delights of the palate do often inflame the vital parts, as the tongue setteth afire the whole body. Secondly, varieties here are not common to all, but many good men are glad to snap at a crust. The rent-taker lives on sweet morsels, but the rent-payer eats a dry crust often with watery eyes. And it is nothing to say what some one of a hundred hath, but [rather] what the bulk, body, and commonalty hath, which I warrant you is short enough.

And they also, which now live so sweetly, hardly will [see] their children attain to that privilege; but some circumventor or other will outstrip

9

them and make them sit in the dust, to which men are brought in one age but cannot get out of it again in seven generations.

To conclude, without all partiality: the present consumption which groweth upon us here, whilst the land groaneth under so many close-fisted and unmerciful men, being compared with the easiness, plainness, and plentifulness in living in those remote places, may quickly persuade any man to a liking of this course, and to practice a removal—which being done by honest, godly and industrious men, they shall there be right heartily welcome. (But [as] for others [of] dissolute and profane life, their rooms are better than their companies; for if here, where the gospel hath been so long and plentifully taught, they are yet frequent in such vices as the heathen would shame to speak of, what will they be when there is less restraint in word and deed?) My only suit to all men is that whether they live there or here they would learn to use this world as they used it not, keeping faith and a good conscience both with God and men, [so] that when the day of account shall come they may come forth as good and fruitful servants, and freely be received, and enter into the joy of their master.

Seal of the Massachusetts Bay Company, 1629

Archives of the Commonwealth of Massachusetts, Boston, Mass. Used with permission.

2

Passengers to the New World

The vast majority of the settlers were average men and women of their time. Many of them left no mark in the historical record, save for stray notations in documents like the passenger lists made out when ships embarked for the New World. But these lists contain valuable information. They show clearly that migrants were not distributed randomly through the entire range of the English population. They also reveal some of the demographic reasons for the diversity of social patterns that developed among different colonies. Consider, for example, the contrasts evident in the following two groups of migrants—the one bound for Virginia, the other for New England—in the year 1635.

Two Lists of Emigrants, Bound for New England and Virginia

(1635)

Ultimo July, 1635

These underwritten names are to be transported to Virginia, embarked in the *Merchant's Hope*, Hugh Weston, Master, per examination by the minister of Gravesend touching their conformity to the Church discipline of England, and have taken the oaths of allegiance and supremacy:

Edward Towers	26	Allin King	19
Henry Woodman	22	Rowland Sadler	19
Richard Seems	26	Jo. Phillips	28
Vyncent Whatter	17	Daniel Endick	16
James Whithedd	14	Jo. Chalk	25

New England Historical and Genealogical Register, XV (1861), p. 142; XXV (1871), pp. 13–15.

Jonas Watts	21		Jo. Vynall	20
Peter Loe	22		Edward Smith	20
Geo. Brocker	17		Jo. Rowlidge	19
Henry Eeles	26		Wm. Westlie	40
Jo. Dennis	22		Jo. Smith	18
Tho. Swayne	23		Jo. Saunders	22
Charles Rinsden	27		Tho. Bartcherd	16
Jo. Exston	17		Tho. Dodderidge	19
Wm. Luck	14		Richard Williams	18
Jo. Thomas	19		Jo. Ballance	19
Jo. Archer	21		Wm. Baldin	21
Richard Williams	25		Wm. Pen	26
Francis Hutton	20		Jo. Gerie	24
Savill Gascoyne	29		Henry Baylie	18
Rich. Bulfell	29		Rich. Anderson	50
Rich. Jones	26		Robert Kelum	51
Tho. Wynes	30		Richard Fanshaw	22
Humphrey Williams	22		Tho. Bradford	40
Edward Roberts	20		Wm. Spencer	16
Martin Atkinson	32		Marmaduke Ella	22
Edward Atkinson	28			
Wm. Edwards	30		*Women*	
Nathan Braddock	31		Ann Swayne	22
Jeffrey Gurrish	23		Eliz. Cote	22
Henry Carrell	16		Ann Rice	23
Tho. Ryle	24		Kat. Wilson	23
Gamaliel White	24		Maudlin Lloyd	24
Richard Marks	19		Mabell Busher	14
Tho. Clever	16		Annis Hopkins	24
Jo. Kitchin	16		Ann Mason	24
Edmond Edwards	20		Bridget Crompe	18
Lewes Miles	19		Mary Hawkes	19
Jo. Kennedy	20		Ellin Hawkes	18
Sam Jackson	24			

Primo die Augusti, 1635

These underwritten names are to be transported to Virginia, embarked in the *Elizabeth de Lo*, Christopher Browne, Master, examined by the minister of Gravesend touching their conformity to the order and discipline of the Church of England; the men have taken the oaths of allegiance and supremacy:

Jo. Benford	20	Wm. Thurrowgood	13
Lodowick Fletcher	20	Samuel Mathew	14
Jo. Bagbie	17	Tho. Frith	17
Robt. Salter	14	Jo. Austin	24
Edward White	18	Paul Fearne	24
Stephen Pierce	30	Thomas Royston	25
Rich. Beanford	18	Jo. Tayler	18
Rich. Chapman	18		
Andrew Parkins	18	*Women*	
Jo. Baker	16	Katherine Jones	28
Jo. Walker	16	Eliz. Sankster	24
Jo. Vaughan	17	Ellin Shore	20
Yeoman Gibson	16	Alice Pindon	19
Tho. Leed	16	Sara Everedge	22
Geo Trevas	18	Margaret Smith	28
Wm. Shelborn	20	Elizab. Hodman	20
Samuel Growce	38	Moules Naxton	19
Wm. Glasbrooke	21	Marie Burback	17
Edward Dicks	30	Eliz. Rudston	40
Jo. Bennett	18	Eliz. Rudston	5
Michael Saundby	25		

Bound for New England

Weymouth, the 20th of March, 1635
1. Joseph Hull, of Somerset, a minister, aged 40 years
2. Agnes Hull, his wife, aged 25 years
3. Joan Hull, his daughter, aged 15 years
4. Joseph Hull, his son, aged 13 years
5. Tristram, his son, aged 11 years
6. Elizabeth Hull, his daughter, aged 7 years
7. Temperance, his daughter, aged 9 years
8. Grissell Hull, his daughter, aged 5 years
9. Dorothy Hull, his daughter, aged 3 years
10. Judith French, his servant, aged 20 years
11. John Wood, his servant, aged 20 years
12. Robert Dabyn, his servant, aged 28 years

13. Musachiell Bernard, of Batcombe, clothier in the county of Somer-
    set, 24 years
14. Mary Bernard, his wife, aged 28 years
15. John Bernard, his son, aged 3 years
16. Nathaniel, his son, aged 1 year
17. Rich. Persons, salter and his servant, 30 years
18. Francis Baber, chandler, aged 36 years
19. Jesope, joyner, aged 22 years
20. Walter Jesop, weaver, aged 21 years
21. Timothy Tabor, in Somerset of Batcombe, tailor, aged 35 years
22. Jane Tabor, his wife, aged 35 years
23. Jane Tabor, his daughter, aged 10 years
24. Anne Tabor, his daughter, aged 8 years
25. Sarah Tabor, his daughter, aged 5 years
26. William Fever, his servant, aged 20 years
27. John Whitmarke, aged 39 years
28. Alice Whitmarke, his wife, aged 35 years
29. James Whitmarke, his son, aged 11 years
30. Jane, his daughter, aged 7 years
31. Onseph Whitmarke, his son, aged 5 years
32. Rich. Whitmarke, his son, aged 2 years
33. William Read, of Batcombe, taylor in Somerset, aged 28 years
34. [name not entered]
35. Susan Read, his wife, aged 29 years
36. Hannah Read, his daughter, aged 3 years
37. Susan Read, his daughter, aged 1 year
38. Rich. Adams, his servant, 29 years
39. Mary, his wife, aged 26 years
40. Mary Cheame, his daughter, aged 1 year
41. Zachary Bickewell, aged 45 years
42. Agnes Bickewell, his wife, aged 27 years
43. John Bickewell, his son, aged 11 years
44. John Kitchin, his servant, 23 years
46. George Allin, aged 24 years
47. Katherine Allin, his wife, aged 30 years
48. George Allin, his son, aged 16 years
49. William Allin, his son, aged 8 years
50. Matthew Allin, his son, aged 6 years
51. Edward Poole, his servant, aged 26 years
52. Henry Kingman, aged 40 years

53. Joan, his wife, being aged 39
54. Edward Kingman, his son, aged 16 years
55. Joanne, his daughter, aged 11 years
56. Anne, his daughter, aged 9 years
57. Thomas Kingman, his son, aged 7 years
58. John Kingman, his son, aged 2 years
59. John Ford, his servant, aged 30 years
60. William King, aged 40 years
61. Dorothy, his wife, aged 34 years
62. Mary King, his daughter, aged 12 years
63. Katheryn, his daughter, aged 10 years
64. William King, his son, aged 8 years
65. Hannah King, his daughter, aged 6 years
66. Thomas Holbrooke, of Broadway, aged 34 years
67. Jane Holbrooke, his wife, aged 34 years
68. John Holbrooke, his son, aged 11 years
69. Thomas Holbrooke, his son, aged 10 years
70. Anne Holbrooke, his daughter, aged 5 years
71. Elizabeth, his daughter, aged 1 year
72. Thomas Dible, husbandman, aged 22 years
73. Francis Dible, sawyer, aged 24 years
74. Robert Lovell, husbandman, aged 40 years
75. Elizabeth Lovell, his wife, aged 35 years
76. Zacheus Lovell, his son, 15 years
77. Anne Lovell, his daughter, aged 16 years
78. John Lovell, his son, aged 8 years
79. Ellyn, his daughter, aged 1 year
80. James, his son, aged 1 year
81. Joseph Chickin, his servant, 16 years
82. Alice Kinham, aged 22 years
83. Angell Hollard, aged 21 years
84. Katheryn, his wife, 22 years
85. George Land, his servant, 22 years
86. Sarah Land, his kinswoman, 18 years
87. Richard Jones, of Dinder
88. Robert Martin, of Batcombe, husbandman, 44
89. Humphrey Shepard, husbandman, 32
90. John Upham, husbandman, 35
91. Joan Martin, 44
92. Elizabeth Upham, 32

93. John Upham, Junior, 7
94. Sarah Upham, 26
95. William Grane, 12
96. Nathaniel Upham, 5
97. Elizabeth Upham, 3
98. Dorset Richard Wade, of Simstyly, cooper, aged 60
99. Elizabeth Wade, his wife, 6[?]
100. Dinah, his daughter, 22
101. Henry Lush, his servant, aged 17
102. Andrew Hallett, his servant, 28
103. John Hoble, husbandman, 13
104. Robert Huste, husbandman, 40
105. John Woodcooke, 2[?]
106. Rich. Porter, husbandman, 3[?]

         JOHN PORTER, Deputy Clerk to Edward Thoroughgood.

3

What to Bring: A Checklist

The Reverend Francis Higginson was among the first group of settlers in Massachusetts Bay. He arrived in 1629 and made his home at Salem. He subsequently became minister to the congregation of that town. Higginson was also the author of one of the earliest books on the settlement of this region. His little volume entitled *New England's Plantation* was published in London in 1630. It contained, among other things, a wealth of practical advice for future migrants. The "catalogue" of "needful things," printed below, is interesting both for what is included and for what is left out. On the whole it appears to be a sensible list. One wonders, though, how much use a settler would have for a sword and suit of armor?

A Catalogue of Such Needful Things as Every Planter Doth or Ought to Provide to Go to New England

(1630)

Francis Higginson

Victuals for a whole year for a man, and so after the rate for more.
8 bushels of meal,
2 bushels of peas,
2 bushels of oatmeal,
1 gallon of aqua-vita,
1 gallon of oil,
2 gallons of vinegar,
1 firkin of butter.

Apparel.
1 Monmouth cap,
3 falling bands,
3 shirts,
1 waistcoat,
1 suit of canvas,
1 suit of frieze,
1 suit of cloth,
3 pair of stockings,

Francis Higginson, "New England's Plantation" (London, 1630), in Alexander Young, ed., *Chronicles of the First Planters of the Colony of Massachusetts Bay* (Boston, 1846), pp. 266–267.

Chapter 3

4 pair of shoes
2 pair of sheets
7 ells of canvas, to make a bed
    and bolster,
1 pair of blankets,
1 coarse rug.

Arms
1 armor, complete
1 long piece,
1 sword,
1 belt,
1 bandoleer,
20 pound of powder,
60 pound of lead,
1 pistol and goose shot.

Tools
1 broad hoe,
1 narrow hoe,
1 broad axe,
1 felling axe,
1 steel handsaw,
1 whipsaw,
1 hammer,
1 spade,
2 augers,
4 chisels,

2 piercers, stocked,
1 gimlet,
1 hatchet,
2 frowers,
1 handbill,
1 grindstone,
1 pickaxe,
nails, of all sorts.

Household Implements
1 iron pot,
1 kettle,
1 frying pan,
1 gridiron,
2 skillets,
1 spit,
wooden platters,
dishes,
spoons,
trenchers.

Spices
Sugar,
Pepper,
Cloves,
Mace,
Cinnamon,
Nutmegs, Fruit.

Also, there are diverse other things necessary to be taken over to this plantation, [such] as books, nets, hooks and lines, cheese, bacon, kine, goats, etc.

4

Advice to Planters in
New Netherland

The Dutch colony of New Netherland was founded in 1626 and lasted until being taken over by the English in 1664. (It was then, of course, renamed New York.) The directors of the Dutch West India Company managed the province and sought in a variety of ways to encourage its development. Perhaps their most imaginative device was the "patroonship"—a broad tract of land, and an equally broad measure of authority, granted to any company member who would undertake to colonize fifty families at his own expense. Many of these grants never materialized as functioning settlements, but New Netherland seemed to retain a more "feudal" character than most of its neighbors.

In 1650 Cornelius Van Tienhoven, secretary of the province, wrote a report on its present and future prospects. Presented here in an early and somewhat stilted translation from the Dutch, this document reveals some of the fundamental assumptions from which all colonization proceeded.

Chapter 4   Advice to Planters in New Netherland

Information Relative to Taking up Land in New Netherland, in the Form of Colonies or Private Boweries

(1650)

Cornelius Van Tienhoven
(Secretary of the Province)

If any man be disposed to begin, either by himself or others, colonies, boweries, or plantations in New Netherland, lying in the latitude of one and forty degrees and a half, he shall first have to inform himself fully of the situation of the lands lying on rivers, havens, and bays, in order thus to select the most suitable and particularly the most convenient grounds. It is therefore to be borne in mind that the lands in New Netherland are not all level and flat and adapted to raising of grain, inasmuch as they are, with the exception of some few flats, generally covered with timber [and] in diverse places also with large and small stones.

In order, then, first to describe those lands which are actually the most convenient and best adapted for early occupancy—where and how [they are] located—I shall enumerate the following places, and commend the remainder to the consideration of proprietors of this country.

I begin, then, at the most easterly corner of Long Island, being a point situated on the main ocean [and] enclosing within, [to the] westward, a large inland sea adorned with diverse fair havens and bays fit for all sorts of craft. This point is entirely covered with trees, without any flats, and is somewhat hilly and stony; [it is] very convenient for cod fishing, which is most successfully followed by the natives during the season. This point is also well adapted to secure the trade of the Indians in wampum (the mine of New Netherland), since in and about the above-mentioned sea and the islands therein situated lie the cockles whereof wampum is made—from which great profit could be realized by those who would plant a colony or hamlet on the aforesaid hook for the cultivation of the land, for raising all sorts of cattle, for fishing, and the wampum trade. It would be necessary, in such [a] case, to settle on the aforesaid land some persons thoroughly conversant with agriculture and others with the fishery.

Oyster Bay [is] so called from the great abundance of fine and delicate oysters which are found there. This bay is about a short mile across

Cornelius Van Tienhoven, "Information Relative to Taking Up Land in New Netherland," in E. B. O'Callaghan, ed., *The Documentary History of the State of New York*, IV (Albany, N.Y., 1851), pp. 27–35.

(or in width, at the mouth), deep and navigable, without either rocks or sands. [It] runs westward in proportion and divides itself into two rivers, which are broad and clear; on which said rivers lie fine maize lands, formerly cultivated by the Indians, some of which they still work. (They could be had for a trifle.) This land is situated on such a beautiful bay and rivers that it could at little cost be converted into good farms fit for the plow; there are here, also, some fine hay valleys.

Martin Gerritsen's Bay, or *Martinnehouck*, is much deeper and wider than Oyster Bay and runs westward in; [it] divides into three rivers, two of which are navigable. The smallest stream runs up in front of the Indian village called Martinnehouck, where they have their plantations. This tribe is not strong and consists of about 30 families. In and about this bay there were formerly great numbers of Indian plantations, which now lie waste and vacant. This land is mostly level and of good quality, well adapted for grain and [the] rearing of all sorts of cattle. On the rivers are numerous valleys of sweet and salt meadows; all sorts of river fish are also caught there.

Schout's Bay, on the East River, [is] also very open and navigable, with one river running into it; on said river are also fine maize lands, level and not stony, with right beautiful valleys. Beyond said river is a very convenient hook of land, somewhat large, encircled by a large valley and river, where all descriptions of cattle can be reared and fed—such convenience being a great accommodation for the settlers, who otherwise must search for their cattle frequently several days in the bush.

The country on the East River between Greenwich and the island Manhattan is for the most part covered with trees, but yet [is] flat and suitable land, with numerous streams and valleys—right good soil for grain—together with fresh hay and meadow lands.

Wiequaeskeck, on the North River five miles above New Amsterdam, is very good and suitable land for agriculture; [there is] very extensive maize land, on which the Indians have planted. Proceeding from the shore and inland 'tis flat and mostly level, well watered by small streams and running springs. This land lies between the Sintinck and Armonck streams, situated between the East and North rivers.

In the bay of the North River, about two miles from Sandy Hook, lies an inlet or small bay; on the south shore of said bay, called *Neyswesinck*, there are also right good maize lands which have not been cultivated by the natives for a long time. This district is well adapted for raising and feeding all sorts of cattle, and is esteemed by many not ill-adapted for fisheries. A good trade in furs could also be carried on there; and 'tis likewise accessible to all large vessels coming from sea, which are often obliged to lie or anchor behind Sandy Hook, either in consequence of contrary winds or for want of a pilot.

The district inhabited by a nation called Raritangs is situated on a fresh-water river that flows through the center of the lowland which the Indians cultivated. This vacant territory lies between two high mountains, far distant the one from the other. This is the handsomest and pleasantest country that man can behold, [and] it furnished the Indians with abundance of maize, beans, pumpkins, and other fruits. This district was abandoned by the natives for two reasons; the first and principal [one] is, that finding themselves unable to resist the Southern Indians they migrated further inland; the second [is] because this country was flooded every spring like Rensalaer's colony—[the floods] frequently spoiling and destroying their supplies of maize which were stored in holes underground. Through this valley pass large numbers of all sorts of tribes, on their way north or east; this land is therefore not only adapted for raising grain and rearing all descriptions of cattle, but also [is] very convenient for trade with the Indians.

On both sides of the South Bay and South River also lie some handsome lands, not only suitable but very convenient for agriculture and trade.

I have already stated where the first colonists should, in my opinion, settle—regard being had to the convenience of those lands in the possession of which, other nations being anticipated, they would not be able to extend their pretended limits further, and great peace and security would [thereby] be afforded to the inhabitants. I shall here further state the time when those emigrating hence to and arriving in New Netherland will take up land, and how each shall afterwards earn a living and settle in the most economical manner according to the fashion of the country.

Boors and others who are obliged to work at first in colonies ought to sail from this country in the fore or latter part of winter, in order to arrive with God's help in New Netherland early in the spring, [such] as in March or at [the] latest in April, so as to be able to plant during that summer garden vegetables, maize, and beans, and moreover [to] employ the whole summer in clearing land and building cottages as I shall hereafter describe.

All, then, who arrive in New Netherland must immediately set about preparing the soil, so as to be able, if possible, to plant some winter grain, and to proceed the next winter to cut and clear the timber. The trees are usually felled from the stump, cut up and burnt in the field, except such as are suitable for building—for palisades, posts, and rails, which must be prepared during winter so as to be set up in the spring on the new-made land which is intended to be sown, in order that the cattle may not in any way injure the crops. In most lands is found a certain root, called red wortel, which must, before plowing, be extirpated with a hoe expressly made for that purpose. This being done in the winter, some plow right around the stumps, should time or circumstances not allow these to be removed; others plant tobacco, maize, and beans at first. The soil even thus becomes very mellow, and they sow winter grain the next fall. From tobacco can be realized some of the expenses incurred in clearing the land. The maize and beans help to support both men and cattle. The farmer, having thus begun, must endeavor every year to clear as much new land as he possibly can and sow it with such seed as he considers most suitable.

It is not necessary that the husbandman should take up much stock in the beginning, since clearing land and other necessary labor do not permit him to save much hay and to build barns for stabling. One pair of draft horses or a yoke of oxen only is necessary to ride the planks for buildings, or palisades, or rails from the land to the place where they are to be set. The farmer can get all sorts of cattle in the course of the second summer when he will have more leisure to cut and bring home hay [and] also to build barns and houses for men and cattle.

Of the Building of Houses at First

Before beginning to build it will above all things be necessary to select a well located spot, either on some river or bay, suitable for the settlement of a village or hamlet. This is, previously, [to be] properly surveyed and divided into lots, with good streets according to the situation of the place. This hamlet can be fenced all around with high palisades or long boards and closed with gates, which is advantageous in case of attack by the natives who heretofore used to exhibit their insolence in new plantations. Outside the village or hamlet other land must be laid out, which can in general be fenced and prepared at the most trifling expense.

Those in New Netherland and especially in New England, who have no means to build farm houses at first according to their wishes, dig a square pit in the ground, cellar fashion, six or seven feet deep [and] as long and as broad as they think proper. [They] case the earth inside with wood all around the wall, and line the wood with the bark of trees or something else, to prevent the caving in of the earth. [They] floor this cellar with plank and wainscot it overhead for a ceiling, raise a roof of spars, [and] clear up and cover the spars with bark or green sods —so that they can live dry and warm in these houses with their entire families for two, three, and four years, it being understood that partitions are run through those cellars which are adapted to the size of the family. The wealthy and principal men in New England, in the beginning of the colonies, commenced their first dwelling houses in this fashion for two reasons: firstly, in order not to waste time building and not to want food [for] the next season; [and] secondly, in order not to discourage poorer laboring people whom they brought over in numbers from [the] fatherland. In the course of three or four years, when the country became adapted to agriculture, they built themselves handsome houses, spending on them several thousands.

After the houses are built in the above described manner or otherwise, according to each person's means and fancy, gardens are made and planted in season with all sorts of pot herbs—principally parsnips, carrots, and cabbage—which bring great plenty into the husbandman's dwelling. The maize can serve as bread for men and food for cattle.

The hogs, after having picked up their food for some months in the woods, are crammed with corn in the fall. When fat they are killed and furnish a very hard and clean pork—a good article for the husbandman, who gradually and in time begins to purchase horses and cows with the produce of his grain and the increase of his hogs, and, instead of a cellar as aforesaid, builds good farm houses and barns.

Of the Necessary Cattle

The cattle necessary in a colony or private bowery in New Netherland are: good mares and sound stallions; yoke oxen for the plow (inasmuchas in new lands, full of roots, oxen go forward steadily under the plow, and horses stand still, or with a start break the harness in pieces); milch cows of kindly disposition, and good bulls; sheep, sows, etc. Fowls are well adapted to boweries.

These cattle are abundant in New Netherland and especially in New England and [are] to be had at a reasonable price, except sheep which the English do not sell and [which] are rare in New Netherland.

Prices of Cattle

In New Netherland:

A young mare with her second or third foal costs	fl. 150 to 160	=	$60
A four- to five-year-old stallion about	130	=	52
A milch cow with her second or third calf	100	=	40
A year-old sow	20 to 24	=	8 to 10
A sheep, being a ewe	20 to 24		

In New England:

A good mare sells for	fl. 100 to 120
A stallion	100
A milch cow	60 to 70
A yearling cow	12 to 14
Sheep are not sold here.	

It is to be observed that in a colony each farmer has to be provided by his landlord with at least one yoke of oxen (or with two mares in their stead), two cows, one or two sows for [the] purpose of increase, and the use of the farm and the support of his family. If the above cattle multiply in [the] course of time with God's blessing, the boweries can be fully stocked with [the] necessary cattle and new boweries set off with the remainder—as is the practice in Rensalaer's Colony and other places, as so on *de novo*, so as to lay out no money for stock. All farming implements necessary for the land must be also procured, except [a] wagon and [a] plow which can be made there. And as it is found by experience in New Netherland that farmers can with difficulty obtain from the soil enough to provide themselves with necessary victuals and support, those who propose planting colonies must supply their farmers and families with necessary food for at least two or three years. If not altogether, it must be done at least in part.

Necessary Supplies for the Farmer

If no wheat or rye can be had for bread, maize can be always had in seasons from the Indians at a reasonable price. The skepel costs ordinarily 10 to 15 stivers when bought from the Indians.

Meat	Vinegar
Pork	Pease, and
Butter or Oil instead	Beans

Salad oil and vinegar are not easy to be had in that country, except at an excessively high price from the Dutch traders.

All this being arranged, it must be noted what description of people are best adapted for agriculture in New Netherland and [are likely] to perform the most service and [to] return the most profit in the beginning.

First, a person is necessary to superintend the working men; he ought to be acquainted with farming.

Industrious country people [are also necessary], conversant with the working and cultivation of land, and possessing a knowledge of cattle.

It would not be unprofitable to add to these some Highland boors, from the Veluwe, Gulick, Cleef, and Berg.

Northerners are a people adapted to cutting down trees and clearing land, inasmuch as they are very laborious and accustomed to work in the woods. Northerners can do almost anything—some can build much, others a little, and [they can] construct small craft which they call yawls. [It is also necessary to have] carpenters who can lay brick; smiths conversant with heavy work, [adept at] curing cattle and provided with suitable medicines; one or more surgeons, according to the number of the people, with a chest well supplied with all sorts of drugs; one or more coopers; a clergyman, comforter of the sick, or precentor who could also act as schoolmaster; a wheelwright.

All other tradesmen would [be required] in time; the above mentioned mechanics are the most necessary at first. In order to promote population through such and other means the people must be provided with freedoms and privileges, so as to induce them to quit their fatherland and emigrate with their families beyond the sea to this far distant New Netherland. And as poor people have no means to defray the cost of passage and other expenses, it were desirable that wealthy individuals would expend some capital to people this country or at their own expense remove themselves, like the English of New England, with funds and a large body of working men, and provide those without means with land, dwelling, cattle, tools, and necessary support—and [continue] that until they could derive the necessary maintenance from the soil and the increase of cattle, after which time they would be able to pay yearly a reasonable quitrent to their lords and masters from the effects in their possession.

By the population and cultivation of the aforesaid lands those who shall have disbursed funds for the removal of the laboring classes, the purchase of cattle, and all other expenses, would, in [the] process of some years, after God had blessed the tillage and the increase of the cattle, derive a considerable revenue in grain, meat, pork, butter, and tobacco, which form at first the earliest returns. In time [their estates] can be improved by industry, such as the making [of] pot and pearl ashes, clapboards, knees for ship building, staves, all sorts of pine and oak plank, masts for large ships, square timber, and ash and hickory planks (in which a staple trade could be established). The English of New England put this in practice, as is to be seen, after the land had been first brought to proper condition. They sell their provisions at the Caribbean Islands, staves at Madeira and the Canaries, masts and fish in Spain and Portugal, and bring in return all sorts of commodities; [and] so much of which returns as they do not consume are again distributed by them throughout all the islands known and inhabited in the northern part of America. So that through the variety of the returns, which of necessity were received, a profitable trade is already established in New England—which can also be right well set on foot by the Netherlanders if the population of the country were promoted.

The Following Is the Mode Pursued by the West India Company in the First Planting of Boweries.

The Company, at their own cost and in their own ships, conveyed several boors to New Netherland, and gave these the following terms:

The farmer, being conveyed with his family over [the] sea to New Netherland, was granted by the Company for the term of six years a bowery, which was partly cleared, and a good part of which was fit for the plow. The Company furnished the farmer a house, barn, [and] farming implements and tools, together with four horses, four cows, sheep and pigs in proportion (the usufruct and enjoyment of which the husbandman should have during the six years, and on the expiration thereof [should] return the number of cattle he received). The entire increase remained with the farmer. The farmer was bound to pay yearly one hundred guilders ($40) and eighty pounds of butter [in] rent for the cleared land and bowery. The country people who obtained the above-mentioned conditions all prospered during their residence on the Company's lands. Afterwards the cattle belonging to the Company in New Netherland were distributed for some years among those who had no means to purchase stock.

The risk of the cattle dying is shared in common; and after the expiration of the contract the Company receives, if the cattle live, the number the husbandman first received; and the increase which is over [this number] is divided half and half, by which means many people have obtained stock, and even to this day the Company have still considerable cattle among the colonists, who make use on the above conditions of the horses in cultivating the farm. The cows serve for the increase of the stock and for the support of their families.

The foregoing is what is necessary to be communicated at present, respecting the establishment of one or more colonies and relative to supplies. What regards the government and preservation of such colonies, and what persons ought to be in authority there, and who these ought to be, I leave to the wise and prudent consideration of your noble High Mightinesses. Meanwhile I pray [to] the Creator of Heaven and Earth to endow your High Mightinesses with the spirit of grace and wisdom, so that all your High Mightinesses' deliberations may tend to the advantage of the country and its inhabitants.

5

Blueprint for a
New England Community

The leaders of the "planting" at Massachusetts Bay assumed that their colony would be confined to a small geographical area. Such a pattern would be necessary, they believed, both for effective defense against the Indians and for the preservation of godly ways and purposes. But events did not confirm their expectations. Within two years the original company was scattered through a dozen small villages around the bay, and by the end of a decade Massachusetts had established some new settlements much farther to the west. One of these was Springfield, founded in 1636 by a group of migrants from the town of Roxbury. William Pynchon, a wealthy and much-respected "gentleman," was the leader of the group. Springfield grew rapidly in the 1640s and 1650s, and Pynchon became the most important man in the entire western part of Massachusetts—a magistrate, and a highly successful entrepreneur in the fur trade.

When Pynchon and his fellow "adventurers" first reached Springfield, they framed "Articles of Agreement" to specify their plans. These articles illustrate a model of settlement that obtained, with minor variations, in towns all over New England.

Articles of Agreement, Springfield, Massachusetts

(1636)

May the 14th, 1636

We whose names are underwritten, being by God's providence engaged together to make a plantation at and over against Agawam upon Connecti-

Articles of Agreement, among the first settlers of Springfield, in *New England Historical and Genealogical Register*, XIII (1859), pp. 295–297.

30

cut, do mutually agree to certain articles and orders to be observed and kept by us and by our successors, except we and every [one] of us for ourselves and in our own persons shall think meet upon better reasons to alter our present resolutions.

1ly. We intend by God's grace, as soon as we can, with all convenient speed, to procure some Godly and faithful minister with whom we purpose to join in church covenant to walk in all the ways of Christ.

2ly. We intend that our town shall be composed of forty families, or, if we think meet after[ward] to alter our purpose, yet not to exceed the number of fifty families, rich and poor.

3ly. That every inhabitant shall have a convenient proportion for a house lot, as we shall see meet for everyone's quality and estate.

4ly. That everyone that hath a house lot shall have a proportion of the cow pasture to the north of End Brook lying northward from the town; and also that everyone shall have a share of the Hassokey Marsh over against his lot, if it be to be had, and everyone to have his proportionable share of all the woodland.

5ly. That everyone shall have a share of the meadow or planting ground over against them, as nigh as may be on Agawam side.

6ly. That the long meadow called Masacksick, lying in the way to Dorchester, shall be distributed to every man as we shall think meet, except we shall find other conveniency for some for their milch cattle and other cattle also.

7ly. That the meadow and pasture called Nayas, toward Patuckett on the side of Agawam lying about four miles above in the river, shall be distributed [erasure of six lines] as above said in the former order—and this was altered with consent before the hands were set to it.

8ly. That all rates that shall arise upon the town shall be laid upon lands according to everyone's proportion, acre for acre of house lots and acre for acre of meadow, both alike on this side and both alike on the other side, and for farms that shall lie further off a less proportion as we shall after agree; except we shall see meet to remit one half of the rate from land to other estate.

9ly. That whereas Mr. William Pynchon, Jeheu Burr, and Henry Smith have constantly continued to prosecute this plantation when others fell off for fear of the difficulties, and [have] continued to prosecute the same at great charges and at great personal adventure: therefore it is mutually agreed that forty acres of meadow lying on the south of End Brook under a hillside shall belong to the said parties free from all charges forever

—that is to say, twenty acres to Mr. William Pynchon and his heirs and assigns for ever, and ten acres to Jeheu Burr, and ten acres to Henry Smith, and to their heirs and assigns for ever—which said 40 acres is not disposed to them as any allotments of town lands, but they are to have their accommodations in all other places notwithstanding.

10ˡʸ. That whereas a house was built at a common charge which cost 6£, and also the Indians demand a great sum to buy their right in the said lands, and also [considering] two great shallops which was requisite for the first planting: the value of these engagements is to be borne by inhabitants at their first entrance, as they shall be rated by us, till the said disbursements shall be satisfied. Or else in case the said house and boats be not so satisfied for, then so much meadow [is] to be set out about the said house as may countervail the said extraordinary charge.

11ˡʸ. It is agreed that no man except Mr. William Pynchon shall have above ten acres for his house lot.

12ˡʸ. [Cancelled] It is also agreed that if any man sell any timber out of his lot in any common ground [and] if he let it lie above three months before he work it out, it shall be lawful for any other man to take it that hath present use of it.

13ˡʸ. Whereas there are two cow pastures, the one lying toward Dorchester and the other northward from End Brook, it is agreed that both these pastures shall not be fed at once, but that the town shall be ordered by us in the disposing of [them] for times and seasons, till it be lotted out and fenced in severally.

May 16th, 1636

14. It is agreed that after this day we shall observe this rule about [the] dividing of planting ground and meadow: in all planting ground to regard chiefly persons who are most apt to use such ground; and in all meadow and pasture to regard chiefly cattle and estate, because estate is like to be improved in cattle, and such ground is aptest for their use. And yet we agree that no person that is master of a lot, though he have no cattle, shall have less than three acres of mowing ground; and none that have cows, steers, or year-olds shall have under two acres apiece; and [for] all horses not less than four acres. And this order in dividing meadow by cattle [is] to take place [on] the last of March next; so that all cattle that then appear, and all estate that shall then truly appear

at 20£ a cow, shall have this proportion in the meadows on Agawam side, and in the long meadow [called] Masacksick, and in the other long meadow called Nayas, and in the pasture at the north end of the town called End Brook.

15. It is ordered that for the disposing of the Hassokey Marsh and the granting of home lots these five men undernamed (or their deputies) are appointed to have full power—namely, Mr. Pynchon, Mr. Mitchell, Jeheu Burr, William Blake, Henry Smith. It is ordered that William Blake shall have sixteen poles in breadth for his home lot, and all the marsh in breadth abutting at the end of it to the next high land, and three acres more in some other place.

Next [to] the lot of William Blake [to the] northward lies the lot of Thomas Woodford, being twelve poles broad, and all the marsh before it to the upland.

Next [to] the lot of Thomas Woodford lies the lot of Thomas Ufford, being fourteen rods broad, and all the marsh before it to the upland.

Next [to] the lot of Thomas Ufford lies the lot of Henry Smith, being twenty rods in breadth, and all the marsh before it; and [it is] to run up in the upland on the other side to make up his upland lot [of] ten acres.

Next [to] the lot of Henry Smith lies the lot of Jeheu Burr, being 20 rods in breadth, and all the marsh in breadth abutting at the end of it, and as much upland ground on the other side as shall make up his lot [of] ten acres.

Next [to] the lot of Jeheu Burr lies the lot of Mr. William Pynchon, being thirty rods in breadth, and all the marsh at the east end of it, and an addition at the further end of as much marsh as makes the whole twenty-four acres, and as much upland adjoining as makes the former house lot thirty acres—in all together fifty-four acres.

Next [to] the lot of Mr. Pynchon lies the lot of John Cable, fourteen rods in breadth, and four acres and a half in marsh at the fore end of his home lot.

The lots of Mr. Matthew Mitchell, Samuel Butterfield, Edmond Wood, [and] Jonas Wood are ordered to lie adjoining to Mill Brook—the whole being to the number of twenty-five acres—to begin, three of them, on the great river, and the fourth on the other side of the small river.

It is ordered that for all highways that shall be thought necessary by the five men above named, they shall have liberty and power to lay them out where they shall see meet, though it be at the ends of men's lots, giving them allowance for so much ground.

We testify to the order abovesaid, being all of us first adventurers and undertakers for the said plantation.

William Pynchon   Edmond Wood
Matthew Mitchell   the mark T
Henry Smith   of Thomas Ufford
the mark L   John Cable
   of Jeheu Burr
William Blake

6

The Trials of a Leader

The development of the colony begun at Jamestown, Virginia, in 1607 was for some years extremely troubled and uncertain. The settlers failed to create a stable pattern of relations with the local Indian tribes or to assess accurately the natural resources of the country. There was, in addition, a fundamental problem of establishing effective internal discipline.

At first the colony was governed by a council of leading gentlemen, one of whom was designated as president. Edward Wingfield played an important, if unhappy, role in the administration of this early period; his *Discourse of Virginia* was written in defense of his own "presidentship." The chaotic situation that Wingfield describes seemed to require a drastic remedy; and, in fact, two years later the administration of Virginia was reorganized so as to rest supreme power in the hands of a single "governor." In the great wilderness of the New World there were, it seemed, few alternatives to anarchy and authoritarianism.

A Discourse of Virginia

(1608)

Edward Maria Wingfield

Here Followeth What Happened in James Town, in Virginia, after Captain Newport's Departure for England.

Captain Newport, having always his eyes and ears open to the proceedings of the Colony, three or four days before his departure asked the President how he thought himself settled in the government—whose answer was that no disturbance could endanger him or the Colony but it must be

Edward Maria Wingfield, "A Discourse of Virginia," in *Transactions and Collections of the American Antiquarian Society*, IV (Boston, 1860), pp. 77–98.

wrought either by Captain Gosnold or Mr. Archer. For the one was strong with friends and followers, and could if he would; and the other was troubled with an ambitious spirit, and would if he could. The Captain gave them both knowledge of this, the President's opinion, and moved them with many entreaties to be mindful of their duties to His Majesty and the Colony.

June, 1607, the 22nd: Captain Newport returned for England, for whose good passage and safe return we made many prayers to our Almighty God.

June the 25th, an Indian came to us from the great Powhatan with the word of peace—that he desired greatly our friendship, that the werowances [chiefs] Pasyaheigh and Tapahanah should be our friends, that we should sow and reap in peace or else he would make wars upon them with us. This message fell out true; for both those werowances have ever since remained in peace and trade with us. We rewarded the messenger with many trifles which were great wonders to him. This Powhatan dwelleth 10 miles from us, upon the River Pamunkey which lies north from us. The Powhatan in the former journal mentioned (a dweller by Capt. Newport's faults) is a werowance and under this great Powhatan, which before we knew not.

July—the 3rd of July, seven or eight Indians presented the President a deer from Pamaonke, a werowance desiring our friendship. They inquired after our shipping, which the President said was gone to Croutoon. They fear much our ships; and therefore he would not have them think it far from us. Their werowance had a hatchet sent him. They were well contented with trifles. A little after this came a deer to the President from the Great Powhatan. He and his messengers were pleased with the like trifles. The President likewise bought, diverse times, deer of the Indians [and] beavers and other flesh, which he always caused to be equally divided among the Colony.

About this time diverse of our men fell sick. We missed above forty before September did see us, amongst whom was the worthy and religious gentleman Capt. Bartholomew Gosnold, upon whose life stood a great part of the good success and fortune of our government and Colony. In his sickness time the President did easily foretell his own deposing from his command—so much differed the President and the other councillors in managing the government of the Colony.

July—the 7th of July, Tapahanah, a werowance [and a] dweller on Salisbury side, hailed us with the word of peace. The President, with a shallop well manned, went to him. He found him sitting on the ground crosslegged, as is their custom, with one attending on him which did often say, "This is the werowance Tapahanah"; which he did likewise confirm with stroking his breast. He was well enough known, for the President had seen him diverse times before. His countenance was nothing cheerful, for we had not seen him since he was in the field against us; but the President would take no knowledge thereof, and used him kindly, giving him a red waistcoat which he did desire. Tapahanah did inquire after our shipping. He received [the same] answer as before. He said his old store was spent, that his new [one] was not a full growth by a foot, [and] that as soon as any was ripe he would bring it; which promise he truly performed.

The ——— of ——— Mr. Kendall was put off from being [a member] of the Council and committed to prison, for [the reason] that it did manifestly appear he did practice to sow discord between the President and Council. Sickness had not now left us six able men in our town. God's only mercy did now watch and ward for us; but the President hid this our weakness carefully from the savages, never suffering them in all this time to come into our town.

September—the 6th of September, Pasyaheigh sent us a boy that was run from us. This was the first assurance of his peace with us; besides, we found them no cannibals. The boy observed the men and women to spend the most part of the night in singing or howling, and that every morning the women carried all the little children to the river side; but what they did there he did not know. The rest of the werowances do likewise send our men renegades to us home again, using them well during their being with them; so as now, they being well rewarded at home at their return, they take little joy to travel abroad without passports.

The Council demanded some larger allowance for themselves, and for some sick [persons], their favorites—which the President would not yield unto without their warrants. This matter was before propounded by Capt. Martin, but so nakedly as that he neither knew the quantity of the store to be but for 13 weeks and a half, under the captain-merchant's hand. He prayed them further to consider the long time before we expected Capt. Newport's return, the uncertainty of his return (if God did not favor his voyage), the long time before our harvest would be ripe, and the doubtful peace that we had with the Indians (which they would keep no longer than opportunity served to do us mischief).

It was then therefore ordered that every meal of fish or flesh should excuse the allowance for porridge, both against the sick and [against the] whole. The Council, therefore, sitting again upon this proposition [and being] instructed in the former reasons and order, did not think fit to break the former order by enlarging their allowance, as will appear by the most voices ready to be showed under their hands. Now was the common store of oil, vinegar, sack, and aquavita all spent, saving two gallons of each. The sack [was] reserved for the Communion Table, [and] the rest for such extremities as might fall upon us, which the President had only made known to Capt. Gosnold, of which course he liked well. The vessels were, therefore, bunged up. When Mr. Gosnold was dead, the President did acquaint the rest of the Council with the said remnant; but, Lord, how they then longed for [a chance] to sup up that little remnant! For they had now emptied all their own bottles, and all others that they could smell out.

A little while after this the Council did again fall upon the President for some better allowance for themselves and [for] some few [of] the sick, their privates. The President protested he would not be partial; but, if one had anything of him, every man should have his portion according to their places. Nevertheless [he said] that, upon [being shown] their warrants, he would deliver what [it] pleased them to demand. If the President had at that time enlarged the proportion according to their request, without doubt in [a] very short time he had starved the whole company. He would not join with them, therefore, in such ignorant murder without their own warrant.

The President, well seeing to what end their impatience would grow, desired them earnestly and oftentimes to bestow the Presidentship among themselves, [and said] that he would obey, [as] a private man, as well as they could command. But they refused to discharge him of the place, saying they might not do it; for [they said] that he did His Majesty good service in it. In this meantime the Indians did daily relieve us with corn and flesh, [so] that in three weeks the President had reared up 20 men able to work; for, as his store increased, he mended the common pot, [and] he had laid up, besides, provision for three weeks' wheat beforehand.

By this time the Council had fully plotted to depose Wingfield, their then President, and had drawn certain articles in writing amongst themselves, and took their oaths upon the Evangelists to observe them—the effect whereof was, first: to depose the then President; to make Mr. Ratcliffe the next President; not to depose the one the other; not to take the deposed President into [the] Council again; not to take Mr. Archer into the Council, or any other, without the consent of every one of them. To these [articles] they had subscribed, as out of their own mouths at several times it was easily gathered. Thus had they forsaken His Majesty's government, [as] set [for] us down in the instructions, and made it a triumvirate. It seemeth [that] Mr. Archer was nothing acquainted with these articles. Though all the rest crept out of his notes and commentaries that were preferred against the President, yet it pleased God to cast him into the same disgrace and pit that he prepared for another, as will appear hereafter.

September—the 10th of September, Mr. Ratcliffe, Mr. Smith, and Mr. Martin came to the President's tent, with a warrant subscribed under their hands, to depose the President, saying they thought him very unworthy to be either President or [a member] of the Council; and therefore [they] discharged him of both [positions]. He answered them that they had eased him of a great deal of care and trouble [and] that, long since, he had diverse times proffered them the place at an easier rate. And [he said] further, that the President ought to be removed (as appeareth in His Majesty's instructions for our government) by the greater number of 13 voices, [the] Concillors, [and] that they were but three; and therefore [he] wished them to proceed advisedly. But they told him [that] if they did him wrong they must answer [for] it. Then said the deposed President, "I am at your pleasure. Dispose of me as you will, without further garboils."

I will now write what followeth in my own name, and give the new President his title. I shall be the briefer, being thus discharged. I was committed to a sergeant, and sent to the pinnace; but I was answered with, "If they did me wrong, they must answer [for] it."

The 11th of September, I was sent for to come before the President and Council upon their court day. They had now made Mr. Archer [the] recorder of Virginia. The President made a speech to the Colony [for the reason] that he thought it fit to acquaint them why I was deposed. (I am now forced to stuff my paper with frivolous trifles, [in order] that our grave and worthy Council may the better strike those veins where the corrupt blood lieth, and that they may see in what manner of government the hope of the Colony now travaileth.) First, Master President said that I had denied him a penny-whistle, a chicken, a spoonful of beer, and [had] served him with foul corn; and with that [he] pulled some grain out of a bag, showing it to the company. Then started up Mr. Smith and said that I had told him plainly how he lied; and that I [had] said [that] though we were equal here, yet, if he were in England, he would think scorn his name should [he] be my companion. Mr. Martin followed with, "He reporteth that I do slack the service in the Colony,

39

and do nothing but tend my pot, spit, and oven; but he hath starved
my son and denied him a spoonful of beer. I have friends in England
[who] shall be revenged on him, if ever he come in London."

I asked Mr. President if I should answer these complaints and whether
he had aught else to charge me withal. With that he pulled out a paper
book, loaded full with articles against me, and gave them [to] Mr. Archer
to read. I told Mr. President and Council that, by the instructions for
our government, our proceeding ought to be verbal, and [that] I was
there ready to answer; but they said they would proceed in that order.
I desired a copy of the articles and time given me to answer them likewise
by writing; but that would not be granted. I bade them then please themselves. Mr. Archer then read some of the articles—when, on the sudden,
Mr. President said, "Stay, stay! We know not whether he will abide [by]
our judgment, or whether he will appeal to the King." [He continued],
saying to me, "How say you: will you appeal to the King, or no?" I
apprehended presently that God's mercy had opened [for] me a way,
through their ignorance, to escape their malice; for I never knew how
I might demand an appeal. Besides, I had secret knowledge how they
had forejudged me to pay five-fold for anything that came to my hands,
whereof I could not discharge myself by writing; and [I knew] that I
should lie in prison until I had paid it.

The Captain Merchant had delivered me our merchandise, without
any note of the particulars, under my hand; for [he] himself had received
them in gross. I likewise, as occasion moved me, spent them in trade
or by gift amongst the Indians. So likewise did Capt. Newport take [out]
of them, when he went up to discover the King's river, what[ever] he
thought good, without any note of his hand mentioning the certainty.
And [he] disposed of them as was fit for him. Of these, likewise, I could
make no account; only I was well assured I had never bestowed the value
of three penny-whistles to my own use nor to the private use of any
other; for I never carried any favorite over with me, or entertained any
there. I was all [to] one and one to all. Upon these considerations I
answered Mr. President and the Council that His Majesty's hands were
full of mercy and that I did appeal to His Majesty's mercy. Then they
committed me [as a] prisoner again to the master of the pinnace, with
these words, "Look to him well; he is now the King's prisoner."

Then Mr. Archer pulled out of his bosom another paper book full
of articles against me, desiring that he might read them in the name
of the Colony. I said [that] I stood there, ready to answer any man's
complaint whom I had wronged; but no one man spoke one word against

me. Then was he willed to read his book, whereof I complained; but I was still answered, "If they do me wrong, they must answer [for] it." I have forgotten the most of the articles, [for] they were so slight (yet he glorieth much in his penwork). I know well the last—and a speech that he then made savored well of a mutiny—for he desired that by no means I might lie prisoner in the town, lest both he and others of the Colony should not give such obedience to their command as they ought to do; which goodly speech of his they easily swallowed.

But it was usual and natural to this honest gentleman, Mr. Archer, to be always hatching of some mutiny in my time. He might have appeared an author of three several mutinies. And he (as Mr. Pearsy sent me word) had bought some witnesses' hands against me to diverse articles, with Indian cakes (which was no great matter to do after my deposal, and considering their hunger), persuasions, and threats. At another time he feared not to say, openly and in the presence of one of the Council, that, if they had not deposed me when they did, he had gotten twenty others to himself which should have deposed me. But this speech of his was likewise easily digested. Mr. Crofts feared not to say that, if others would join with him, he would pull me out of my seat and out of my skin too. Others would say (whose names I spare) that, unless I would amend their allowance, they would be their own carvers. For these mutinous speeches I rebuked them openly, and proceeded no further against them, considering therein of men's lives in the King's service there. One of the Council was very earnest with me to take a guard about me. I answered him [that] I would [have] no guard but God's love and my own innocence. In all these disorders was Mr. Archer a ringleader.

When Mr. President and Mr. Archer had made an end of their articles above mentioned, I was again sent prisoner to the pinnace; and Mr. Kendall, taken from thence, had his liberty, but might not carry arms. All this while the savages brought to the town such corn and flesh as they could spare. Pasyaheigh, by Tapahanah's mediation, was taken into friendship with us. The Councillors, Mr. Smith especially, traded up and down the river with the Indians for corn; which relieved the Colony well.

As I understand by a report, I am much charged with starving the Colony. I did always give every man his allowance faithfully, both of corn, oil, aquavita, etc., as was by the Council proportioned; neither was it bettered after my time, until, towards the end of March, a biscuit was allowed to every working man for his breakfast, by means of the provision brought us by Capt. Newport, as will appear hereafter. It is further said [that] I did much banquet and riot. I never had but one squirrel roasted, whereof I gave part to Mr. Ratcliffe, then sick—yet was that squirrel given [to] me. I did never heat a flesh-pot but when the common pot was so used likewise. Yet how often Mr. President's and the Councillor's spits have night and day been endangered to break their backs—so laden with swans, geese, ducks, etc.! How many times their flesh-pots have swelled, many hungry eyes did behold to their great longing. And what great thieves and thieving there hath been in the common store since my time—I doubt not but it is already made known to his Majesty's Council for Virginia.

The 17th day of September I was sent for to [come to] the Court to answer a complaint exhibited against me by Jehu Robinson; for [he charged] when I was President I did say [that] he with others had consented to run away with the shallop to Newfoundland. At another time I must answer Mr. Smith for [the charge] that I had said he did conceal an intended mutiny. I told Mr. Recorder [that] those words would bear no actions—that one of the causes was done without the limits mentioned in the patent granted to us. And therefore [I] prayed Mr. President that I might not be thus lugged with these disgraces and troubles; but he did wear no other eyes or ears than grew on Mr. Archer's head. The jury gave the one of them 100 pounds and the other 200 pounds damages for slander. Then Mr. Recorder did very learnedly comfort me, [saying] that if I had wrong I might bring my writ of error in London; whereat I smiled.

I, seeing their law so speedy and cheap, desired justice for a copper kettle which Mr. Croft did detain from me. He said I had given it [to] him. I did bid him bring his proof for that. He confessed he had no proof. Then Mr. President did ask me if I would be sworn [that] I did not give it him. I said I knew no cause why to swear for mine own [property]. He asked Mr. Croft if he would make oath [that] I did give it him; which oath he took, and won my kettle from me, that was in that place and time worth half his weight in gold. Yet I did understand afterwards that he would have given John Capper the one half of the kettle to have taken the oath for him; but he would [have] no copper on that price. I told Mr. President I had not known the like law, and prayed they would be more sparing of law until we had more wit or wealth. [I said] that laws were good spies in a populous, peaceable, and plentiful country, where they did make the good men better and stayed the bad from being worse; yet we were so poor as they did but rob us of time that might be better employed in service in the Colony.

The ——— day of ——— the President did beat James Read, the smith.

The smith struck him [back] again. For this he was condemned to be hanged; but before he was turned off the ladder he desired to speak with the President in private—to whom he accused Mr. Kendall of a mutiny, and so escaped himself. What indictment Mr. Recorder framed against the smith I know not; but I know it is familiar for the President, Councillors, and other officers, to beat men at their pleasure. One lieth sick till death, another walketh lame, the third crieth out of all his bones; which miseries they do take upon their consciences to come to them by this their alms of beating. Were this whipping, lawing, beating, and hanging in Virginia known in England, I fear it would drive many well-affected minds from this honorable action of Virginia.

This smith, coming aboard the pinnace with some others about some business two or three days before his arraignment, brought me commendations from Mr. Pearsy, Mr. Waller, Mr. Kendall, and some others, saying they would be glad to see me on shore. I answered him [that] they were honest gentlemen and had carried themselves very obediently to their governors. I prayed God that they did not think of any ill thing unworthy [of] themselves. I added further that upon Sunday if the weather were fair I would be at the sermon. Lastly, I said that I was so sickly, starved, [and] lame, and did lie so cold and wet in the pinnace, as I would be dragged thither before I would go thither any more. Sunday proved not fair; I went not to the sermon.

The ———— day of ———— Mr. Kendall was executed, being shot to death for a mutiny. In the arrest of his judgement he alleged to Mr. President that his name was Sicklemore, not Ratcliffe, and so [he] had no authority to pronounce judgement. Then Mr. Martin pronounced judgement.

Somewhat before this time the President and Council had sent for the keys of my coffers, supposing that I had some writings concerning the Colony. I requested that the Clerk of the Council might see what they took out of my coffers; but they would not suffer him or any other. Under color hereof they took my books of accounts and all my notes that concerned the expenses of the Colony, and [the] instructions under the Captain Merchant's hand of the store of provisions, diverse other books, and trifles of my own proper goods, which I could never recover. Thus was I made good prize on all sides.

The ———— day of ———— the President commanded me to come on shore, which I refused [to do], as not rightfully deposed. And [I] desired that I might speak to him and the Council in the presence of ten of the best sort of the gentlemen. With much entreaty some of them were

sent for. Then I told them [that] I was determined to go into England
to acquaint our Council there with our weakness. I said further [that]
their laws and government were such as I had no joy to live under them
any longer, [and] that I did much mislike their triumvirate, having forsaken
His Majesty's instructions for our government; and therefore [I] prayed
there might be more made of the Council. I said further [that] I desired
not to go into England, if either Mr. President or Mr. Archer would
go, but was willing to take my fortune with the Colony; and [I] did
also proffer to furnish them with £100 towards the fetching home [of]
the Colony, if the action was given over. They did like of none of my
proffers, but made diverse shot at me in the pinnace. I, seeing their resolutions, went ashore to them—where, after I had stayed a while in conference, they sent me to the pinnace again.

December—the 10th of December Mr. Smith went up the river of
the Chickahominy to trade for corn. He was desirous to see the head
of that river; and, when it was not possible with the shallop, he hired
a canoe and an Indian to carry him up further. The river—the higher
[he went]—grew worse and worse. Then he went on shore with his guide
and left Robinson and Emmery, two of our men, in the canoe—which
were presently slain by the Indians, Pamunkey's men. And he himself
[was] taken prisoner, and by the means of his guide his life was saved.
And Pamunkey, having him prisoner, carried him to his neighbors' werowances to see if any of them knew him for one of those which had
been, some two or three years before us, in a river amongst them [to
the] northward and [had] taken away some Indians from them by force.
At last he brought him to the great Powhatan (of whom before we had
no knowledge), who sent him home to our town the 8th of January.

During Mr. Smith's absence the President did swear [in] Mr. Archer
[as] one of the Council, contrary to his oath taken in the articles agreed
upon between themselves (before spoken of), and contrary to the King's
instructions, and without Mr. Martin's consent; whereas there were no
more but the President and Mr. Martin then of the Council.

Mr. Archer, being settled in his authority, sought how to call Mr.
Smith's life in question, and had indicted him upon a chapter in Leviticus
for the death of his two men. He had had his trial the same day of
his return and, I believe, his hanging the same or the next day—so speedy
is our law there. But it pleased God to send Captain Newport unto us
the same evening, to our unspeakable comfort; whose arrival saved Mr.
Smith's life and mine, because he took me out of the pinnace and gave
me leave to lie in the town. Also by his coming was prevented a parlia-

ment, which the new Councillor, Mr. Recorder, intended there to summon. Thus error begot error.

Captain Newport, having landed, lodged, and refreshed his men, employed some of them about a fair storehouse, others about a stove, and his mariners about a church—all which works they finished cheerfully and in short time.

January—the 7th of January our town was almost quite burnt with all our apparel and provision; but Captain Newport healed our wants, to our great comforts, out of the great plenty sent us by the provident and loving care of our worthy and most worthy Council.

This vigilant Captain, slacking no opportunity that might advance the prosperity of the Colony, having settled the company upon the former works, took Mr. Smith and Mr. Scrivener (another Councillor of Virginia, upon whose discretion liveth a great hope of the action) [and] went to discover the River Pamunkey on the further side whereof dwelleth the Great Powhatan, and to trade with him for corn. This river lieth north from us, and runneth east and west. I have nothing but by relation of that matter, and therefore dare not make any discourse thereof, lest I might wrong the great desert which Captain Newport's love to the action hath deserved—especially himself being present, and best able to give satisfaction thereof. I will hasten, therefore, to his return.

March—the 9th of March he returned to Jamestown with his pinnace well laden with corn, wheat, beans, and peas to our great comfort and his worthy commendations.

By this time the Council and Captain, having attentively looked into the carriage both of the Councillors and other officers, removed some officers out of the store, and [especially] Captain Archer, a Councillor whose insolency did look upon that little himself with great-sighted spectacles, derogating from others' merits by spewing out his venomous libels and infamous chronicles upon them, as doth appear in his own handwriting; for which, and other worse tricks, he had not escaped the halter, but that Captain Newport interposed his advice to the contrary.

Captain Newport, having now dispatched all his business and set the clock in a true course (if so the Council will keep it), prepared himself for England upon the 10th of April, and arrived at Blackwall on Sunday, the 21st of May, 1608.

7

Two Letters Home

It is very difficult for us to imagine fully the predicament of the first colonists in America. There is no equivalent in our twentieth-century world to the sense of strangeness, the material hardship, and the isolation that was the everyday experience of the settlers at Jamestown or Plymouth or Boston. But luckily a few personal documents have survived from these earliest and most difficult years, and they are highly evocative. They help us to realize both the utter dependency of the settlers on support from the mother country and the extreme tenuousness of such support.

Richard Frethorne and ——— Pond belonged to the faceless legions of ordinary people who have "made" history. All we know of them is contained in the letters printed below.

Richard Frethorne, to His Parents

(Virginia, 1623)

Loving and kind father and mother:

My most humble duty remembered to you, hoping in God of your good health, as I myself am at the making hereof. This is to let you understand that I your child am in a most heavy case by reason of the nature of the country, [which] is such that it causeth much sickness, [such] as the scurvy and the bloody flux and diverse other diseases, which maketh the body very poor and weak. And when we are sick there is nothing to comfort us; for since I came out of the ship I never ate anything but peas, and loblollie (that is, water gruel). As for deer or venison I

Richard Frethorne, Letter to his father and mother, March 20, April 2 and 3, 1623, in Susan M. Kingsbury, ed., *The Records of the Virginia Company of London*, IV (Washington, D.C., 1935), pp. 58–62. I am grateful to the Keeper of Public Records in the Public Record Office, London, for permission to reprint this document. The manuscript is held in the Public Record Office.

never saw any since I came into this land. There is indeed some fowl, but we are not allowed to go and get it, but must work hard both early and late for a mess of water gruel and a mouthful of bread and beef. A mouthful of bread for a penny loaf must serve for four men which is most pitiful. [You would be grieved] if you did know as much as I [do], when people cry out day and night—Oh! that they were in England without their limbs—and would not care to lose any limb to be in England again, yea, though they beg from door to door. For we live in fear of the enemy every hour, yet we have had a combat with them on the Sunday before Shrovetide, and we took two alive and made slaves of them. But it was by policy, for we are in great danger; for our plantation is very weak by reason of the death and sickness of our company. For we came but twenty for the merchants, and they are half dead just; and we look every hour when two more should go. Yet there came some four other men yet to live with us, of which there is but one alive; and our Lieutenant is dead, and [also] his father and his brother. And there was some five or six of the last year's twenty, of which there is but three left, so that we are fain to get other men to plant with us; and yet we are but 32 to fight against 3000 if they should come. And the nighest help that we have is ten miles of us, and when the rogues overcame this place [the] last [time] they slew 80 persons. How then shall we do, for we lie even in their teeth? They may easily take us, but [for the fact] that God is merciful and can save with few as well as with many, as he showed to Gilead. And like Gilead's soldiers, if they lapped water, we drink water which is but weak.

And I have nothing to comfort me, nor there is nothing to be gotten here but sickness and death, except [in the event] that one had money to lay out in some things for profit. But I have nothing at all—no, not a shirt to my back but two rags (2), nor no clothes but one poor suit, nor but one pair of shoes, but one pair of stockings, but one cap, [and] but two bands. My cloak is stolen by one of my own fellows, and to his dying hour [he] would not tell me what he did with it; but some of my fellows saw him have butter and beef out of a ship, which my cloak, I doubt [not], paid for. So that I have not a penny, nor a penny worth, to help me to either spice or sugar or strong waters, without the which one cannot live here. For as strong beer in England doth fatten and strengthen them, so water here doth wash and weaken these here [and] only keeps [their] life and soul together. But I am not half [of] a quarter so strong as I was in England, and all is for want of victuals; for I do protest unto you that I have eaten more in [one] day at home

47

than I have allowed me here for a week. You have given more than my day's allowance to a beggar at the door; and if Mr. Jackson had not relieved me, I should be in a poor case. But he like a father and she like a loving mother doth still help me.

For when we go up to Jamestown (that is 10 miles of us) there lie all the ships that come to land, and there they must deliver their goods. And when we went up to town [we would go], as it may be, on Monday at noon, and come there by night, [and] then load the next day by noon, and go home in the afternoon, and unload, and then away again in the night, and [we would] be up about midnight. Then if it rained or blowed never so hard, we must lie in the boat on the water and have nothing but a little bread. For when we go into the boat we [would] have a loaf allowed to two men, and it is all [we would get] if we stayed there two days, which is hard; and [we] must lie all that while in the boat. But that Goodman Jackson pitied me and made me a cabin to lie in always when I [would] come up, and he would give me some poor jacks [to take] home with me, which comforted me more than peas or water gruel. Oh, they be very godly folks, and love me very well, and will do anything for me. And he much marvelled that you would send me a servant to the Company; he saith I had been better knocked on the head. And indeed so I find it now, to my great grief and misery; and [I] saith that if you love me you will redeem me suddenly, for which I do entreat and beg. And if you cannot get the merchants to redeem me for some little money, then for God's sake get a gathering or entreat some good folks to lay out some little sum of money in meal and cheese and butter and beef. Any eating meat will yield great profit. Oil and vinegar is very good; but, father, there is great loss in leaking. But for God's sake send beef and cheese and butter, or the more of one sort and none of another. But if you send cheese, it must be very old cheese; and at the cheesemonger's you may buy very good cheese for twopence farthing or halfpenny, that will be liked very well. But if you send cheese, you must have a care how you pack it in barrels; and you must put cooper's chips between every cheese, or else the heat of the hold will rot them. And look whatsoever you send me—be it never so much—look, what[ever] I make of it, I will deal truly with you. I will send it over and beg the profit to redeem me; and if I die before it come, I have entreated Goodman Jackson to send you the worth of it, who hath promised he will. If you send, you must direct your letters to Goodman Jackson, at Jamestown, a gunsmith. (You must set down his freight, because there be more of his name there.) Good father, do not forget me, but have mercy and pity my miserable case. I know if you did but see me, you would weep to see me; for I have but one suit. (But [though] it is a strange one, it is very well guarded.) Wherefore, for God's sake, pity me. I pray you to remember my love to all my friends and kindred. I hope all my brothers and sisters are in good health, and as for my part I have set down my resolution that certainly will be; that is, that the answer of this letter will be life or death to me. Therefore, good father, send as soon as you can; and if you send me any thing let this be the mark.

ROT   Richard Frethorne,
                                                 Martin's Hundred

The names of them that be dead of the company [that] came over with us to serve under our Lieutenants:

John Flower	George Goulding
John Thomas	Jos. Johnson
Thos. Howes	our lieutenant, his
John Butcher	father and brother
John Sanderford	Thos. Giblin
Rich. Smith	George Banum
John Olive	a little Dutchman
Thos. Peirsman	one woman
William Cerrell	one maid
	one child

All these died out of my master's house, since I came; and we came in but at Christmas, and this is the 20th day of March. And the sailors say that there is two-thirds of the 150 dead already. And thus I end, praying to God to send me good success that I may be redeemed out of Egypt. So *vale in Christo*.

Loving father, I pray you to use this man very exceeding kindly, for he hath done much for me, both on my journey and since. I entreat you not to forget me, but by any means redeem me; for this day we hear that there is 26 of [the] Englishmen slain by the Indians. And they have taken a pinnace of Mr. Pountis, and have gotten pieces, armor, [and] swords, all things fit for war; so that they may now steal upon us and we cannot know them from [the] English till it is too late—[till the time] that they be upon us—and then there is no mercy. Therefore if you love or respect me as your child, release me from this bondage and save my life. Now you may save me, or let me be slain with infidels. Ask this man—he knoweth that all is true and just that I say here. If you do redeem me, the Company must send for me to my Mr. Harrod; for so is this Master's name. April, the second day,

Your loving son,
Richard Frethorne

Moreover, on the third day of April we heard that after these rogues had gotten the pinnace and had taken all furnitures [such] as pieces, swords, armor, coats of mail, powder, shot and all the things that they had to trade withal, they killed the Captain and cut off his head. And rowing with the tail of the boat foremost, they set up a pole and put the Captain's head upon it, and so rowed home. Then the Devil set them on again, so that they furnished about 200 canoes with above 1000 Indians, and came, and thought to have taken the ship; but she was too quick for them—which thing was very much talked of, for they always feared a ship. But now the rogues grow very bold and can use pieces, some of them, as well or better than an Englishman; for an Indian did shoot with Mr. Charles, my master's kinsman, at a mark of white paper, and he hit it at the first, but Mr. Charles could not hit it. But see the envy of these slaves, for when they could not take the ship, then our men saw them threaten Accomack, that is the next plantation. And now there is no way but starving; for the Governor told us and Sir George that except the *Seaflower* [should] come in or that we can fall foul of these rogues and get some corn from them, above half the land will surely be starved. For they had no crop last year by reason of these rogues, so that we have no corn but as ships do relieve us, nor we shall hardly have any crop this year; and we are as like to perish first as any plantation. For we have but two hogsheads of meal left to serve us this two months, if the *Seaflower* do stay so long before she come in; and that meal is but three weeks bread for us, at a loaf for four [men] about the bigness of a penny loaf in England—that is but a halfpennyloaf a day for a man. Is it not strange to me, think you? But what will it be when we shall go a month or two and never see a bit of bread, as my master doth say we must do? And he said he is not able to keep us all. Then we shall be turned up to the land and eat barks of trees or molds of the ground; therefore with weeping tears I beg of you to help me. Oh, that you did see my daily and hourly sighs, groans, and tears, and [the] thumps that I afford mine own breast, and [the way I] rue and curse the time of my birth, with holy Job. I thought no head had been able to hold so much water as hath and doth daily flow from mine eyes.

But this is certain: I never felt the want of father and mother till now; but now, dear friends, full well I know and rue it, although it were too late before I knew it.

I pray you talk with this honest man. He will tell you more than now in my haste I can set down.

Your loving son,

Virginia, 3rd April, 1623   Richard Frethorne

——— Pond, to His Parents

(Massachusetts, 1630)

To my loving father William Pond, at Etherston in Suffolk, give this.
Most loving and kind Father and Mother:

My humble duty [be] remembered unto you, trusting in God you are in good health. And, I pray, remember my love unto my brother Joseph, and thank him for his kindness that I found at his hand at London, which was not the value of a farthing. I know, loving father, and do confess that I was an undutiful child unto you when I lived with you and by you, for the which I am much sorrowful and grieved for it, trusting in God that He will guide me that I will never offend you so anymore; and I trust in God you will forgive me for it.

[The reason for] my writing this unto you is to let you understand what a country this New England is, where we live. Here are but few Indians; a great part of them died this winter; it was thought it was [because] of the plague. They are a crafty people, and they will cozen and cheat, and they are a subtle people. And whereas we did expect great store of beaver, here is little or none to be had; and their Sackemore John wastes it, and many of us truck with them, and it layeth us many times in eight shillings a pound. They are proper men and clean-jointed men, and many of them go naked with a skin about their loins, but now some of them get Englishmen's apparel. And the country is very rocky and hilly, and [there is] some champion ground, and the soil is very flete. And here is some good ground and marsh ground, but here is no

——— Pond, Letter to William Pond, in *Proceedings of the Massachusetts Historical Society*, Second Series, VII (Boston, 1892–1894), pp. 471–473.

Michaelmas. Spring cattle thrive well here, but they give small store of milk. The best cattle for profit is swine, and a good swine is here at five pounds' price; a goose is worth two pounds, a good one got. Here is timber [in] good store, and acorns [in] good store; and here is good store of fish, if we had boats to go for [it] and lines to serve fishing. Here are good stores of wild fowl, but they are hard to come by. It is harder to get a shot than it is in old England. And people here are subject to disease, for here have died of the scurvy and of the burning fever nigh two hundred and odd. Besides, as many lyeth lame; and all Sudbury men are dead but three, and [some] women and some children; and provisions are here at a wonderful rate. Wheat meal is 14 shillings a bushel, and peas 10 shillings, and malt 10 shillings, and Einder seed wheat is 15 shillings, and their other wheat is 10 shillings. Butter [is] 12 pence a pound, and cheese is 8 pence a pound, and all kind of spices [are] very dear and [there are] almost none to be got.

If this ship had not come when it did, we had been put to a wonderful strait, but thanks be to God for sending of it in. I received from the ship a hogshead of meal, and the Governor telleth me of a hundred-weight of cheese, the which I have received part of it. I humbly thank you for it. I did expect two cows, the which I had none; nor I do not earnestly desire that you should send me any, because the country is not so [suitable] as we did expect it. Therefore, loving father, I would entreat you that you would send me a firkin of butter and a hogshead of malt unground, for we drink nothing but water; and a coarse cloth of four pounds price, so it [will] be thick. [As] for the freight, if you of your love will send them I will pay the freight. For here is nothing to be got without we had commodities to go up to the East parts amongst the Indians to truck; for here where we live, here is no beaver. Here is no cloth to be had to make no apparel; and shoes are at five shillings a pair for me; and that cloth that is worth two shillings [and] eight pence a yard is worth here five shillings. So I pray, father, send me four or five yards of cloth to make us some apparel. And, loving father, though I be far distant from you, yet I pray you remember me as your child. And we do not know how long we may subsist, for we cannot live here without provisions from old England. Therefore, I pray, do not put away your shop stuff, for I think that in the end, if I live, it must be my living. For we do not know how long this plantation will stand, for some of the magnates that did uphold it have turned off their men and have given it over. Besides, God hath taken away the chiefest stud in the land, Mr.

Johnson, and the lady Arabella, his wife, which was the chiefest man of estate in the land and one that would have done most good.

Here came over 25 passengers, and there came back again four score and odd persons; and as many more would have come if they had wherewithal to bring them home. For here are many that came over last year, which was worth two hundred pounds before they came out of old England, that between this [time] and Michaelmas will hardly be worth 30 pounds. So here we may live if we have supplies every year from old England; otherwise we cannot subsist. I may, as I will, work hard, set an acre of Einder wheat; and if we do not set it with fish (and that will cost 20 shillings), if we set it without fish, they shall have but a poor crop. So, father, I pray, consider of my case; for here will be but a very poor being—no being—without, loving father, your help with provisions from old England. I had thought to have come home in this ship, for my provisions were almost all spent; but [you should know] that I humbly thank you for your great love and kindness in sending me some provisions, or else I should and might have been half famished. But now I will—if it please God that I have my health—I will plant what corn I can; and if provisions be not cheaper between this [time] and Michaelmas, and [assuming] that I do not hear from you what I was best [advised] to do, I purpose to come home at Michaelmas.

My wife remembers her humble duty unto you and to my mother; and my love to my brother Joseph and to Sarah Myler. Thus I leave you to the protection of the Almighty God.

From Watertown in New England, the 15 of March, 1630.

[no signature]

We were wonderful sick, as we came at sea, with the small pox. No man thought that I and my little child would have lived. My boy is lame and my girl too, and there died in the ship that I came in 14 persons.

8

The Early Days Remembered

The difficulties of the settlement era were long, sometimes lovingly, re-membered; they became in time the stuff of legend. The following letter shows the form and tone of such remembrance at a still early date. The writer, the Reverend Samuel Smith (then of Hadley, Massachusetts), had participated as a boy in the founding of Wethersfield on the "great" (that is, Connecticut) River. He was here responding to a direct inquiry from his son Ichabod (then residing in Suffield, Connecticut).

The Reverend Samuel Smith to Ichabod Smith

(1699)

Hadley, Massachusetts Colony
Jan. the first 1698/99

My dear and dutiful son:

I was at so tender an age at the death of my beloved father that I am possessed of but little of the information for which you seek. My reverend father was an ordained minister of the Gospel, educated at Cam-bridge in England, and came to the land by reason of the great persecution by which the infamous Archbishop Laud and the Black Tom Tyrant (as Mr. Russell was always wont to call the Earl of Strafford) did cause the reign of His Majesty Charles the First to lose favor in the sight of the people of England. My father and mother came over in 1636/37, first to Watertown, which is near Boston, and after a year or two to Wethers-field on the great river, where he became the first settled pastor. Concern-ing of the early days, I can remember but little save hardship. My parents had brought both menservants and maidservants from England, but the maids tarried not but till they got married, which was shortly for there

Rev. Samuel Smith, Letter to Ichabod Smith, January 1, 1699, quoted in Helen Evertson Smith, *Colonial Days and Ways* (Hartford, Conn., 1900), pp. 49–51. The original of this letter does not survive.

was a great scarcity of women in the colonies. The men did abide better. One of them had married one of my mother's maids, and they did come with us to Wethersfield, to our great comfort for some years, until they had many little ones of their own. I do well remember the face and figure of my honored father. He was 5 foot, 10 inches tall, and spare of build, though not lean. He was as active as the redskinned men and sinewy. His delight was in sports of strength, and with his own hands he did help to rear both our own house and the first meetinghouse of Wethersfield, wherein he preached years too few. He was well-featured and fresh-favored with fair skin and long curling hair (as near all of us have had), with a merry eye and sweet smiling mouth, though he could frown sternly enough when need was.

The first meetinghouse was solidly made to withstand the wicked onslaughts of the redskins. Its foundations was laid in the fear of the Lord, but its walls was truly laid in the fear of the Indians, for many and great was the terrors of them. I do mind me [i.e., remember] that all the ablebodied men did work thereat, and the old and feeble did watch in turns to espy if any savages was in hiding near[by], and every man kept his musket nigh to his hand. I do not myself remember any of the attacks made by large bodies of Indians whilst we did remain in Wethersfield, but did oftimes hear of them. Several families which did live back a ways from the river was either murdered or captivated in my boyhood, and we all did live in constant fear of the like. My father ever declared [that] there would not be so much to fear if the redskins was treated with such mixture of justice and authority as they could understand, but if he was living now he must see that we can do naught but *fight* them and that right heavily.

After the redskins the great terror of our lives at Wethersfield, and for many years after we had moved to Hadley to live, was the wolves. Catamounts were bad enough, and so was the bears, but it was the wolves that was the worst. The noise of their howlings was enough to curdle the blood of the stoutest, and I have never seen the man that did not shiver at the sound of a pack of them. What with the way we hated them and the good money that was offered for their heads, we do not hear them now so much, but when I do I feel again the young hatred rising in my blood; and it is not a sin, because God made them to be hated. My mother and sister did each of them kill more than one of the gray howlers, and once my oldest sister shot a bear that came too near the house. He was a good fat one, and kept us all in meat for a good while. I guess one of her daughters has got the skin.

As most of the Wethersfield settlers did come on foot through the wilderness and brought with them such things only as they did need at the first, the other things was sent round from Boston in vessels to come up the river to us. Some of the ships did come safe to Wethersfield, but many was lost in a great storm. Amongst them was one which held all our best things. A good many years later, long after my father had died of the great fever and my mother had married Mr. Russell and moved to Hadley, it was found that some of our things had been saved and kept in the fort which is by the river mouth, and they was brought to us. Most of them was spoiled with seawater and mold, especially the books and the plate. Of this there was no great store, only the tankard, which I have, and some spoons, divided among my sisters, which was all so black [that] it was long before any could come to its own color again.

[Editor's note: The earliest surviving copy of this letter breaks off just here; undoubtedly, the original contained more.]

Part Two
Life History

9

An Ipswich Tailor

A culture has, of course, no existence apart from the experience of the persons who belong to it. For the student of culture there is much to be learned from the careful investigation of individual lives. Every person struggles to find in his or her personal history some underlying pattern, some inner thread of connectedness that provides a basis for sorting out discrete events and situations. Sometimes the struggle has a negative outcome: one finds only *dis*connectedness and *non*pattern in the course of a life. But this, too, is worth analyzing.

The study of autobiographical documents thus obtains a dual significance. There is, first, the evident interest of the events themselves, all the particular interactions with other people and settings. And there is also the meaning the writer finds in the whole sequence—one's sense of having "lived" or "been lived by" one's own life. The latter type of concern is often especially prominent in the case of an older person. Consciously or unconsciously, one asks oneself which experiences have been most profound, most valuable, most disappointing. And in answering such questions, one is very much the child of one's culture.

We must recognize some special problems in working with life histories. Three lives from all of early America hardly provide a representative sample, especially when two of them are set in the same geographical area and all three are men. Still, there is no reason to regard John Dane or John Barnard or Devereux Jarratt as *un*typical in any important ways. They seem, on the whole, to have been men of average talents, and they were subject to most of the dominant influences on people of their time. The same statement could not be made about *The Autobiography of Benjamin Franklin*—to cite an alternative case.

John Dane was born in England, the son of a tailor, in about the year 1612. He was himself trained as a tailor, and during his early manhood he worked at his trade in a variety of different locations. He crossed the ocean a little before 1640. He settled first at Roxbury in

Massachusetts Bay and then moved to Ipswich, where he lived until his death in 1684. His short autobiography was written near the end of his life, apparently in order to instruct and inspire his descendants in Christian conduct.

A Declaration of Remarkable Providences
in the Course of My Life

(1670s?)

John Dane

And [I speak] first of a family providence. In my infancy—and yet I very well remember it—my father removed his habitation from Berkhampstead to Stortford. There he bought a house, and brought his family thither; and he went back again to finish matters with him [whom] he had sold his [house] to, and my mother and her children were at Stortford. Not being among any acquaintances, and my father staying longer than she thought he would (or himself either), my mother met with some wants and was troubled and wept. I doubt not but she laid open her wants to God, for she was a serious woman. And my sister How—she was but a little girl—she went into the yard and sat down in the sun under the window; and laying her hand on the ground to rise up, there lay a shilling under her hand. She brought it in. I, being a little boy, asked her where she found it. She showed me. I went and scrabbled with my fingers in the place and found another. It being in the nick of time in her wants, she took great notice of it, and I doubt not but [she] made good improvement thereof, with great acknowledgement of God's mercy at that time.

I shall mention one more [providence] concerning my mother. When she lived in Stortford, one night in her sleep she fell into a dream, and [upon] waking she was much taken with it. She told my father, and could not keep it out of her mind. And it was that such a minister (I have forgot his name) should preach [on] such a week and such a day at Elsenham, on such a text. The thoughts of it did so take with her that she inquired; and, as she dreamed, so it was—the same man, the same day, the same text. She and my brother How heard him. I, then being so

John Dane, "A Declaration of Remarkable Providences in the Course of My Life," *New England Historical and Genealogical Register,* VIII (1854), pp. 149–156.

young, cannot remember every thing; but I doubt not but that she made good improvement of that sermon.

Concerning myself: when I was but a little boy, being educated under godly parents, my conscience was very apt to tell me of evils that I should not do. Being now about eight years old, I was given much to play and to run out without my father's consent and against his command. [Once up]on a time, I having gone out for most part of the day, when my father saw me come home he took me and basted me. I then kept home and followed my business two or three days. My father and mother commended me and told me that God would bless me if I obeyed my parents, and what the contrary would issue in. I then thought in my heart—oh, that my father would beat me more when I did amiss! I feared, if he did not, I should not be good.

Not long after I, being alone on the shopboard, [was] ripping open a pair of britches of a gentleman who had a hole in his pocket and [had] sewed [it] up again, through which hole he had had lost or dropped into his knees of his linings a piece of gold—which, when I saw [it], I thought I might have it, for I thought nobody knew of it nor could know of it. I took the gold and hid it, and sat upon the shopboard to work; but, thinking of it, I thought—it is none of mine. I fetched it again, but upon more pondering I went and hid it again. When I had done so I could not be quiet in my mind, but fetched it again, and thought [that] though nobody could know of it, yet God, He knew of it. So I gave it to my father, who gave it to the gentleman. I can't but take notice of God's goodness in then giving me restraining grace to preserve [me] from such a temptation, though then I slightly passed over many such providences.

I did think myself in a good condition. I was convinced that I should pray and dared do no other, and read and hear sermons and dared do no other; yet I was given to pastime and to dancing, and that I thought lawful. Now [once] upon a time, when I was grown [to] eighteen years of age or thereabouts, I went to a dancing school to learn to dance. My father, hearing of it, when I came home told me [that] if I went again he would baste me. I told him [that] if he did he should never baste me again. With that my father took a stick and basted me. I took it patiently and said nothing for a day or [two], but one morning betimes I rose and took two shirts on my back and the best suit I had and [put] a Bible in my pocket and set the doors open and went to my father's chamber door and said "good-bye father, good-bye mother." "Why, whither are you going?" "To seek my fortune," I answered. Then said my mother, "go where you will, God, He will find you out." This word, the point of it, stuck in my breast; and afterwards God struck it home to its head.

Although I thought my father was too strict—I thought Solomon said, "be not holy over much," and David was a man after God's own heart, and he was a dancer—but yet I went [on] my journey, and was [away] from him half a year before he heard where I was. I first settled in Berk-hampstead, and there wrought on a shopboard that had been improved that way. On a night when most folks was abed, a maid came into the shopboard and sat with me, and we jested together; but at the last she carried it so, and put herself in such a posture, as that I made as if I had some special occasion abroad and went out; for I feared [that] if I had not [gone] I should have committed folly with her. But I often thought that it was the prayers of my parents that prevailed with God to keep me. I then gave myself much to dancing and staying out and heating myself and lying in haymows, the people being abed where I abode, [with the result] that I lost my color and never recovered it again.

I then went and wrought at Hertford, and went to an inn for my lodging. The next day I went and got work in the town. It was near the time of the Assizes at Hertford, and my master had many sergeants' coats to make; and I sat up three nights to work, and then I went to my inn to lodge. The door was locked, and I knocked hard. I heard one of the maids say, "there is one at the door." I heard one say, "'tis no matter, it is none but the tailor." So they opened the door, and the hostess sat in a chair by the fire in her naked shift, holding her breasts open. She said to me, a chair being by her [and] she holding out her hand, "come, let us drink a pot," and several times reiterated her words. I said I was so sleepy that I could not stay with her now, but I would drink a cup with her in the morning; and so I hastened away to my chamber. Here I took no notice of the goodness of God in restraining me, but rather ascribed it to myself, although I had as wretched a nature as I have been since more sensible on than before.

Awhile after, there was a cockpit built to fight cocks in, and many knights and lords met there; and there followed to the town many brave lasses. And [once] upon a day, as I remember, there came one from Stort-ford that I was wonderful glad to see, that I might inquire of my friends there. I invited him to this inn to drink; and there was one of these brave lasses there which dined at the table I dined at, and it is likely that I might [have offered] drink to her and she to me; but this I know, that I never touched her. The night after, I came to go to bed and asked for a light. My hostess said, "we are busy, you may go up without [one, for] the moon shines." And so I did. And when I came in the chamber I went to my bedside and pulled off all my clothes and went in, and there was this fine lass in the bed. I slipped on my clothes again and went down and asked my hostess why she would serve me so. "Oh," said she, "there's nobody would hurt you." I told her [that] if I hired a room I would have it to myself, and showed myself much angry. So she gave me a light into another chamber, and there I lay; but in the morning I went to that chamber I used to lie in, for I had left a little bundle of things on the bed's tester. I came to the door and gave the door a shove, and this fine mistress reached out her hand out of the bed and opened the door. So I went in. "I doubt, miss, I am troublesome to you." "No," said she, "you are welcome to me." I told her [that] I had left a small trifle on the tester of the bed, and I took it and went my way. For all this and many other [restraints] of the like [sort], I thank God I never yet knew any but those two wives that God gave me. But when I consider my wretched heart and what I might with shame and blushing speak that way, I cannot but say—oh, wonderful, unspeakable, and unsearchable mercies of a God that taketh care of us when we take no care of ourselves.

I now being at Hertford, Mr. Goodwin preached there, and he preached concerning prayer. But on Sabbath day, not being in that trim that I would have been in (I had a great band that came over my shoulders that was not clean, and [lacked] some other things that I would have had), I would not go to meeting but walked in the fields close by a meadow side. There was, whether fly, wasp, or hornet I cannot tell; but it struck my finger, and water and blood came out of it and pained me much. I went up to a house and showed it [to the people there], but they knew not what a sting I had at my heart. Now I thought of my mother's words, that God would find me out. I hastened home to the chamber I lay in, at my master's house; and when I came there I took my Bible and looked over some instructions my father had written, and I wept sorely. The pain and swelling increased and swelled up to my shoulder. I prayed earnestly to God that He would pardon my sin and heal my arm. I went to a surgeon and asked him what it was. He said it was "the take". I asked him what he meant. He said it was taken by the providence of God. This knocked home on my heart what my mother said, "God will find you out." Now I made great promises that if God would hear me this time I would reform.

It pleased God in a short time to ease me, and I did reform and stood in awe of God's judgments, though I had a lingering mind after my former pastime. I then wrought with Mr. Tead, that lives at Charlestown, He was a young man then. He and I were going to a dancing on a night and it began to thunder, and I told him I doubted we were not in our way; and he and I went back again. But about a month or six weeks after, I had a mind to visit a friend, of a Sabbath day, four miles out of Hertford; but I took a good while pondering whether I might [do so] or no. I knew Mr. Goodwin was a good man, and that the other was naught; but, to quiet my mind, I thought that Christ said concerning the Pharisees—they sat in Moses' chair, hear them. I thought he might preach [some] good matter. And thus I blinded my eyes and went. And when I came there, they were gone to meeting; and I flattered myself, [thinking] it may be I shall meet them coming home. And so I went into a wood; and there I cried bitterly, and now concluded that God, God had found me out. I was now utterly forlorn in my spirit, and knew not what to do, thinking that God now had utterly forsaken me and that He would hear me no more. And when I had cried so long that I could cry no longer, I rose up in a forlorn condition and went home to Hertford. I then, in a restless condition, knew not what to do. I was thinking what to do to throw off this trouble; and at this time, awhile after, there was one Master Scofield, who was a minister and my god-father, that had a son that was bound to Saint Christopher's, and he was at me to go with him. I readily agreed. And when the time was come that we should go, there came news that Saint Christopher's was taken by the Spaniards.

Then was I at a sore loss, and considered what I should do. I drew up this conclusion, that I would go and work journey-work through all the counties in England, and so walk as a pilgrim up and down on the earth. But at last I had some thoughts to go first home to my father's house; but I thought he would not entertain me. But I went; and when I came home my father and mother entertained [me] very lovingly, and all the neighbors. Yet my mind was still troubled, though I had some secret thoughts that God might still do me good. Mr. Harris— preaching at Stortford on that text, "Am I my brother's keeper?"—declared that we ought to be one another's keepers. Upon which I spake to one that I was acquainted with, [saying] that if he saw me either do or say that that was not meet, that he would tell me of it. At that time when I heard any[one] read a chapter that there was any of the promises in, my tears would run down my cheeks. I saw a young man coming in the street, and I feared that he would call me out. I left the shopboard and went into a backhouse, and prayed to God to keep me that I might not be overcome.

After a while that I had abode with my father, Mr. Norton, coming to my father's, wished him to put me [out] to Mr. Barenton's. That was a very religious family, [as much so] as ever I came in. And I went thither and was butler; there I kept company with the choicest Christians. I went to hear Mr. Farecloth, three or four miles [away]—I have forgot[ten] the town's name. The words of Mr. Farecloth's text were these: "Ye that were aliens and strangers from the commonwealth of Israel hath He reconciled to Himself." In this sermon he did so set forth the love of Christ [and] His readiness and willingness to entertain poor sinners, that I believe there were very few dry eyes in the meeting house, nor without doors (for many could not come in). It was great encouragement to me.

Soon after this I married, and went and dwelt at a place called Woodrow, in Hatfield. Soon after I had the palsy taking me, which did much weaken my brain and spoil my memory. And just it was with God that it should be so, for I cannot but acknowledge of what God had then bestowed on me. I went to a physician, and he told me that it was too late to do me any good. I was so [sick] as that I could scarce go to bed or from bed without help. And my mother having been servant to the Lady Denny, [and] she speaking of it to the Lady, she told her of a medicine that had cured an old woman of three score years old. My mother, diligently attending to the method of the business, came to me and applied the same to me, and it cured me; though I have the marks of it on my face to this day. Then I lived on Woodrow Green, on Hatfield forest. No sooner one trouble was at an end, but another ensued. There was one Muschen [who] lived under the same roof that I lived in, only he lived at one end and I at the other. There were farmers' and yeomen's sons [who] met there; and I was among them, thinking no harm. But they were contriving to have a merry meeting at that Muschen's house and invited me to be one of them. And being among them, they would contrive their business with me, and told me that they would have four bushels of barley out of a barn (the owner of which, one of these was his son); and this Muschen was to turn it into malt, and brew it, and drink it there. I dared not cross them, [for] they were such blustering lads; but I was in a sad tune and knew not what to do. But I went to my brother How's father and advised with him. He was a very honest man; and he told me [that] I should by no means be among them when they did act that business, but [that I should] make some journey some

way or other, and he would do the business for me. So I did. And he
acquainted the woman of the house, a prudent woman. And at the time
appointed they went to the barn. The woman, having had foreknowledge
of it, stood after supper at her hall window listening, the barn not being
far distant from the house; and she heard a noise at the barn, and sent
suddenly to the barn, and took them with four bushels of barley, carried
out of the barn in a sack. The thing being discovered, the men were
in a bad toss, but they suspected me; and the yeoman's son came flattering
to me, to know if I did not tell of it; and [he] said it is well that it
was found out, but needs he would know if I did not tell some of the
family. I told him I had not spoken with any of the family since we
were together. Many words passed, but nothing did appear but suspicion.
But one of the company (as afterwards I was informed, and I myself suspected him and escaped his hands) came with a sword to my shop to
kill me.

This was no sooner over but [there] comes a new trouble. I then went
to live in the chief place in Hatfield town, and took an apprentice and
kept a journeyman. And the tailors were so disgusted at it that they
made [complaints] earnestly to the old Lady Barenton, Sir Francis Barenton's widow, and to Mr. Sir Thomas Barenton, to get me out of the
town; for, said they, he takes up all our work, and we know not how
to live. This was so eagerly prosecuted as that Mr. Robert Barenton told
me that he would give me his ears, if he did not send me out of town.
And after [being] three times sent for before Sir Thomas Barenton by
warrant, and pleaded against (and [they] could not prevail), they summoned me to the quarter sessions; but God of His goodness stood by
me, and afterwards I found great friendship from those that were my
professed adversaries.

When these storms were a little over, there was a great coming to
New England; and I thought that the temptations there were too great
for me. I then bent myself to come to New England, thinking that I
should be more free here than there from temptations; but I find here
a devil to tempt, and a corrupt heart to deceive. But to return to the
way and manner of my coming; when I was much bent to come I went
to Stortford to my father to tell him. My brother How was there then.
My father and mother showed themselves unwilling. I sat close by a table
where there lay a Bible. I hastily took up the Bible, and told my father
[that] if, where I opened the Bible, there I met with anything either to
encourage or discourage, that should settle me. I opening of it, not knowing no more than the child in the womb, the first [line] I cast my eyes

on was: "Come out from among them, touch no unclean thing, and I will be your god and you shall be my people." My father and mother never more opposed me, but furthered me in the thing, and hastened after me as soon as they could.

My first coming was to Roxbury. There I took a piece of ground to plant of a friend. And I went to plant; and having kept long in the ship, [and] the weather being hot, I spent myself and was very weary and thirsty. I came by a spring in Roxbury street, and went to it, and drank, and drank again many times; and I never drank wine in my life that more refreshed me, nor was [anything] more pleasant to me in my life, as then I absolutely thought. But Mr. Norton being at Ipswich, I had a mind to live under him. And one time I came to Ipswich alone when there was no path but what the Indians had made; sometimes I was in it, sometimes out of it, but God directed my way. By the way I met in one place with forty or fifty Indians, all of a row. The foremost of them had a long staff that he held on his forehead like a unicorn's horn. Many of them were powwows; and as I passed by them I said, "what cheer." They all, with a loud voice, laughing, cried out, "what cheer, what cheer," [so] that they made the woods ring with noise. After I parted with them about a mile, I met with two Indians, one of them a very lusty sannup. I had a packet under my arm, and he took hold of it and peeked into it. I snatched it away, with an angry countenance, and he made no more of it. So I came to Ipswich, and agreed with Goodman Metcalf's vessel to bring me from Boston, where I had brought my goods. I brought a year's provision with me, but I soon parted with it. My meal I parted with for Indian [corn] the next year. I thought if one had it, another should not want. There came a neighbor to me and said he had no corn. He made great complaints. I told him I had one bushel and I had no more, but he should have half of it. And he had; and after[ward] I heard of certain [people] that at the same time he had a bushel in his house. It troubled me to see his dealings and the dealings of other men.

Many troubles I passed through, and I found in my heart that I could not serve God as I should. What they were, were too tedious to mention. But [once] upon a time, walking, with my gun on my shoulder charged, in the mile brook path beyond Deacon Goodhewe's, I had several thoughts [which] came flocking into my mind that I had better make away [with] myself than to live longer. I walked discoursing with such thoughts [for] the best part of an hour, as I judged it. At length I thought [that] I ought of two evils to choose the least, and that it was a greater evil to live and to sin against God than to kill myself—with many other

satanical thoughts. I cocked my gun, and set it on the ground, and put
the muzzle under my throat, and took up my foot to let it off. And
then there came many things into my head; one [was] that I should not
do evil that good might come of it. And at that time I no more scrupled
to kill myself than to go home to my own house. Though this place
is now a road, then it was a place that was not much walked in. I was
then much lost in my spirit; and, as I remember, the next day Mr. Rogers
preached, expressing himself that those were blessed that feared God and
hoped in His mercy. Then I thought that blessedness might belong to
me, and it much supported my spirit.

[Once] upon a time we were in some present want in the family, and
my wife told me she had nothing for the children. She desired me to
take my gun and see if I could get nothing. And I did go; and I had
one pig then that was highly esteemed on, and that followed me a great
way into the marshes. I thought the providence of God seemed to tell
me that I should not go out today. So I returned back again with my
pig; and when I came within less than forty rods of my house a company
of great gray geese came over me and I shot and brought down a gallant
goose in the very nick of time.

In [sixteen] sixty-one, my house was burnt, as nearly as I can remember; and it was a most violent fire. At that time I could not but take
notice of several providences concurring with [it]. I do not know that
I did murmur at it, but was silent—looking up to God to sanctify it
to me. It pleased God to stir up the hearts of my loving friends to help
me to the carrying on of another. I had been ill before, and [was] not
well fitting to go abroad, and could not endure wet on my feet. When
the carts went into the woods I went with them, and many times in
the swamps [I] broke in up to the knees, in cold water, in the winter.
And it pleased God [that] I grew better than before, which I looked
on as a special hand of God. A second providence was this; that, though
my provisions were all burnt, I had a stock of fine swine; and the corn
that was burnt—when the flowers fell down and the fire [was] out—
these swine fell to eating the burnt corn, and fattened to admiration,
and that in a small time; so that I had good pork for the workmen to
carry on the work.

Thus God hath all along preserved and kept me all my days. Although
I have many times lost His special presence, yet He hath returned to
me in mercy again. Once in England at Mr. Barenton's house in Christmas
time, the company in the hall was showing tricks in the night, and Mrs.
Barenton came and stood by. I being there, I took notice that my mistress

changed her countenance, and the tears ran down her cheeks and she turned away. I presently thought that her thoughts were better improved than mine. It put me upon a serious meditation of the joys of heaven and the vanities of this world. It took such an impression of my heart as that, though it was a time of jollity, I could scarce hear music nor see wantonness, [and] that I was [not] able [at such times] to show my face without shedding of tears.

The like impression had my thoughts brought to me upon a question in our private meetings, upon a question of that text—God's love constrains us to love Him that has loved us first. Beating my thoughts on God's infinite love took such an impression of my heart as that I thought I could do anything for God or suffer anything for God. Oh, loving relations, have a care of quenching such notions of God's spirit, lest you bring sorrow and affliction onto your heads and hearts, as many others have done to their great grief and sorrow; and I can speak it, to the grief of my soul, by woeful experience.

10

A Marblehead Clergyman

The beginning of John Barnard's life overlaps with the end of John Dane's by three years, but they knew very different worlds. Dane remembered Massachusetts when it was merely a collection of villages joined by rude "paths," and he remembered, too, vivid personal encounters with Indians who lived nearby. The only mention of Indians in Barnard's *Autobiography* is a reference to a book about "Maucompus, the giant Indian" by a certain "worthy divine of this country." History was already at work transforming these native Americans into objects of academic concern.

Barnard's world—though still "provincial," still very much beholden to the mother country—was a world of education, genteel manners, some economic complexity, and a considerable degree of material comfort. Barnard accepted all this as given; and he also accepted a wide range of opportunities to travel—to test himself in other geographical and social settings. His account of the various experiences to which these travels exposed him affords an engaging picture of a young New Englander of the early eighteenth century, as seen from several different vantage points.

For reasons of space we cannot here follow Barnard's life beyond its thirty-fifth year, but that is a reasonable stopping place. It was then that Barnard finally managed to settle himself in a long-term ministerial position, and in marriage. The later parts of the *Autobiography* are chiefly reflections on his mature life as a clergyman; they reveal much less about personal change and development.

Barnard was evidently a man of very sturdy physical constitution, and he continued as pastor at Marblehead almost to the time of his death in 1770. The *Autobiography* was written when he was eighty-four years old, in response to the "earnest desire" of several younger clerical colleagues. It does not seem to have been intended for publication.

Chapter 10   A Marblehead Clergyman

Autobiography of the Reverend John Barnard: Excerpts

(1767)

John Barnard

I, John Barnard, was born at Boston, 6th Nov., 1681. [I was] descended from reputable parents, viz. John and Esther Barnard, remarkable for their piety and benevolence, who devoted me to the service of God in the work of the ministry, from my very conception and birth, and accordingly took special care to instruct me themselves in the principles of the Christian religion, and kept me close at school to furnish my young mind with the knowledge of letters. By the time I had a little passed my sixth year I had left my reading school, in the latter part of which my mistress made me a sort of usher, appointing me to teach some children that were older than myself, as well as smaller ones; and in which time I had read my Bible through thrice. My parents thought me to be weakly, because of my thin habit and pale countenance, and therefore sent me into the country, where I spent my seventh summer, and by the change of air and diet and exercise I grew more fleshy and hardy; and [in order] that I might not lose my reading [I] was put to a school-mistress, and returned home in the fall.

In the spring of my eighth year I was sent to the grammar school, under the tuition of the aged, venerable, and justly famous Mr. Ezekiel Cheever. But after a few weeks, an odd accident drove me from the school. There was an older lad [who] entered the school the same week with me; we strove who should outdo; and he beat me by the help of a brother in the upper class, who stood behind master with the accidence open for him to read out of; by which means he could recite his [illegible] three and four times in a forenoon, and the same in the afternoon; but I who had no such help, and was obliged to commit all to memory, could not keep pace with him; so that he would be always one lesson before me. My ambition could not bear to be outdone, and in such a fraudulent manner, and therefore I left the school. About this time [there] arrived a dissenting minister from England, who opened a private school for reading, writing, and Latin. My good father put me under his tuition, with whom I spent a year and a half. The gentleman, receiving but little encouragement, threw up his school, and returned me to my father, and again I was sent to my aged Mr. Cheever, who placed me in the lowest

John Barnard, "Autobiography of the Rev. John Barnard," *Collections of the Massachusetts Historical Society*, Third Series, V (Boston, 1836), pp. 178–189, 196–219.

class; but finding I soon read through my [illegible], in a few weeks he advanced me to the [illegible], and the next year made me the head of it.

In the time of my absence from Mr. Cheever, it pleased God to take to Himself my dear mother, who was not only a very virtuous but [also] a very intelligent woman. She was exceedingly fond of my learning, and taught me to pray. My good father also instructed me, and made a little closet for me to retire to for my morning and evening devotion. But, alas! how childish and hypocritical were all my pretensions to piety, there being little or no serious thoughts of God and religion in me.

Just as I had completed my eighth year, my father saw cause to take a second wife, a virtuous woman, an excellent wife, and an extraordinarily good mother-in-law, in whom God graciously very much made up my loss; who, though she could not be supposed to have the love of me which she had of her own children by my father, yet was she constant in her dutiful regard to and care of me and a younger brother. I remember to have heard persons of figure, who knew her, say to me when I was grown up a young man, that they never knew but two good mothers-in-law, and mine was one of them. My honored father died in December, 1732, having just completed his 78th year; my good mother-in-law out-lived him twenty-six years, and died January the last day, in 1758, being in her 94th year.

Though my master advanced me, as above, yet I was a very naughty boy, much given to play, insomuch that he at length openly declared, "You, Barnard, I know you can do well enough if you will; but you are so full of play that you hinder your classmates from getting their lessons; and therefore, if any of them cannot perform their duty, I shall correct you for it." One unlucky day one of my classmates did not look into his book, and therefore could not say his lesson, though I called upon him once and again to mind his book; upon which our master beat me. I told master the reason why he could not say his lesson was, his declaring he would beat me if any of the class were wanting in their duty; since which this boy would not look into his book, though I called upon him to mind his book, as the class could witness. The boy was pleased with my being corrected, and persisted in his neglect, for which I was still corrected, and that for several days. I thought, in justice, I ought to correct the boy, and compel him to a better temper; and therefore, after school was done, I went up to him, and told him I had been beaten several times for his neglect; and since master would not correct him I would, and I should do so as often as I was corrected for him; and then [I] drubbed him heartily. The boy never came to school any more, and so that unhappy affair ended.

Though I was often beaten for my play and my little roguish tricks, yet I don't remember that I was ever beaten for my book more than once or twice. One of these was upon this occasion. Master put our class upon turning Aesop's Fables into Latin verse. Some dull fellows made a shift to perform this to acceptance; but I was so much duller at this exercise that I could make nothing of it; for which master corrected me, and this he did two or three days going. I had honestly tried my possibles [i.e. my hardest] to perform the task; but having no poetical fancy nor then a capacity opened of expressing the same idea by a variation of phrases though I was perfectly acquainted with prosody, I found I could do nothing; and therefore [I] plainly told my master, that I had diligently labored all I could to perform what he required, and perceiving I had no genius for it, I thought it was in vain to strive against nature any longer; and he never more required it of me. Nor had I anything of a poetical genius till after I had been at college some time, when upon reading some of Mr. Cowley's work, I was highly pleased, and a new scene opened before me.

I remember once, in making a piece of Latin, my master found fault with the syntax of one word, which was not so used by me heedlessly, but designedly, and therefore I told him there was a plain grammar rule for it. He angrily replied, there was no such rule. I took the grammar and showed the rule to him. Then he smilingly said, "Thou art a brave boy; I had forgot it." And no wonder; for he was then above eighty years old.

While I was a schoolboy, I experienced many signal deliverances from imminent danger, on the land, and in the waters. I mention two signal deliverances: The one [occurred] in the year 1692, in my eleventh year, [when] I fell from a scaffold at the eaves of the old North Meeting House, eighteen feet high, between two pieces of timber that lay on the ground, without touching them. I lay upon the ground until somebody ran to my father's house, about two hundred feet off, and acquainted him with my fall; who came and took me up, without any apparent signs of life in me, and carried me home; where, by the blessing of God upon the means used, in some hours I recovered breath and sensation, and had no bone broken nor dislocated, though I complained of inward ails; but through the divine mercy soon got well.

The other is a more remarkable instance of the goodness of God to me. In June, 1693, in my twelfth year, Sir Francis Wheeler, with his fleet, which had in vain made an attempt upon Martinique, came to Boston, and brought with him a violent and malignant distemper called the scarlet fever, by which he lost many hundreds of his men. The distemper soon spread in Boston, of which many persons died—and that within two or three days of their being taken ill. It pleased God I was seized with it, and through the rampancy of the fever and a violent pain at my heart, which rendered every breath I drew to be as though a sword had pierced me, I was so bad that life was despaired of. On the third night (I think) it seemed to me that a certain woman, wife of a doctor, who used to supply my father's family with plasters upon occasion, came and brought me some small dark-colored pills, and directed me to put one in my mouth and hold it there till it grew mellow, then squeeze it flat betwixt my thumb and finger and apply it to my right nipple; it would soak in, and before I had used them all so, I should be well. I followed the prescription, and when I had used the third pill, my pain and fever left me, and I was well. My tender father, very early the next morning, came into my bedchamber to inquire how it was with me. I told him I was quite well, and intended to get up presently, and said the pills Mrs. (naming her) had given me last night had perfectly cured me. He said to me, "Child, I believe she was not here; I heard nothing of it." To confirm him I said, "Sir, I have the remaining four pills now in my hand," and put my hand out of bed to show them, but they dropped out of my hand into the bed. I then raised myself up to look for them, but could not find them. He said to me, "I am afraid, child, you are out of your senses." I said to him, "Sir, I am perfectly awake and in my senses, and find myself truly well." He left the room with the supposition that I was delirious, and I saw by his countenance that he was ready to give me over for lost. He then inquired of all the house whether that woman had been at the house the day or evening before. They all let him know that they had not seen her here. He betook himself to his closet, and in about an hour came to me again; [I] continued firm in the story I had told him. He talked to me of some other things, and found by my answers that I was thoroughly awake and, as he now thought, under the power of no distraction; [he] was better satisfied, and left me with a more placid countenance. By noon I got up, and was perfectly recovered from my sickness. I thought I would have given ever so much to know what the pills were, that others might receive the benefit of them. Finding that the abovesaid woman had not been at our house, and I was perfectly healed, I could not help thinking that a merciful God had sent an angel, as He did Isaiah to Hezekiah, to heal me; and to this very day I cannot but esteem it more than an ordinary dream or the wild ramblings of a heated imagination. It seemeth to me a sort of heavenly vision. And what less can you, sir, make of it? The kind offices of the ministering spirits are, doubtless, more than we are aware of. However, thus has God mercifully appeared for my help, when I was brought very low, and in this manner rescued me from the jaws of death. Forever blessed be His holy name! But to return.

From the grammar school I was admitted into the college, in Cambridge, in New England, in July, 1696, under the Presidentship of the very reverend and excellent Dr. Increase Mather, (who gave me for a thesis, *Habenti dabitur,*) and the tutorage of those two great men, Mr. John Leverett (afterwards President) and Mr. William Brattle (afterwards the worthy minister of Cambridge). Mr. Leverett became my special tutor for about a year and a half, to whom succeeded Mr. Jabez Fitch (afterwards the minister of Ipswich with Mr. John Rogers, who at the invitation of the church in Portsmouth, New Hampshire, removed to them). Upon my entering into college, I became chamber-mate, the first year, to a senior and a junior sophister, which might have been greatly to my advantage, had they been of a studious disposition and made any considerable progress in literature. But, alas! they were an idle pack, who knew but little and took no pains to increase their knowledge. When, therefore, according to my disposition, which was ambitious to excel, I applied myself close to books and began to look forward into the next year's exercises, this unhappy pair greatly discouraged me and beat me off from my studies, so that by their persuasions I foolishly threw by my books and soon became as idle as they were. Oh! how baneful it is to be linked with bad company! and what a vile heart had I to hearken to their wretched persuasions! I never, after this, recovered a good studious disposition while I was at college. Having a ready, quick memory, which rendered the common exercises of the college easy to me, and being an active youth, I was hurried almost continually into one diversion or another, and gave myself to no particular studies, and therefore made no great proficiency in any part of solid learning.

There were two accidents which happened while I was an undergraduate, that somewhat startled and awakened me. The one [occurred] in the winter of my freshmanship, when a number of us went a skating upon what is called Fresh Pond in Watertown. Two lovely young gentlemen, John Eyre, of our class, son of Justice Eyre of Boston, and Maxwell, [of] the class above me, a West Indian (which two only of all the company had asked leave of the Tutors to go out of town upon the diversion), being both good skaters, joined hand in hand, and flew away to the farther end of the pond, and as they were in like manner returning, they ran upon a small spot in the middle of the pond called the boiling hole (because rarely frozen over), which was open the day before but now had a skim of ice upon it about half an inch thick, and both of them broke the thin ice and plunged into the water. Maxwell rose not again, it being supposed he rose under the ice; Eyre rose in the hole they had broken [and] attempted to get upon the ice, but it gave way under him and plunged him [in] anew. I, who happened to be nearest to them, ran towards the hole, called to Eyre only to keep his head above water by bearing his arms upon the thin ice, and we would help him with boards, which the rest of the company ran to fetch from a new house building by the edge of the pond, not twenty rods off; but he kept on his striving to get up, till it so worried him he sunk and rose no more; and thus both were drowned. It threw me into grievous anguish of mind to think I was so near my dear friend, within two rods, and yet it was impossible for me to help him. I went to the utmost edge of the thick ice, and raised my foot to take another step, but saw I must fall in as they had done. The boards arrived to the place within five minutes of Eyre's last sinking. The sight was truly shocking to me, and I plainly saw how soon and suddenly the providence of God might, by one means or another, snatch me out of the world, and what need I had to be always ready; and [I] lifted up my heart in thankfulness to God, who had spared me, whose turn it might have been instead of theirs. Thought I, if God had taken me away instead of them, oh, what would have become of me! But since God had mercifully spared me, I would endeavor for the future to live devoted to His service. But, alas! how soon did such serious thoughts and purposes die away! Eyre was taken up that afternoon, but Maxwell could not be found until the next day.

The other instance happened the summer following, when a great number of the scholars went to bathe and cool themselves in the river, upon a very hot day. George Curwin, a freshman, who could not swim, went up to his waist near the foot of the bridge, ducking and trying to learn to swim. It being near high water, the tide came round the foot of the bridge with a strong current and, ere he was aware, carried him past his depth, and soon hurried him into the current of the arch, which threw him a great way into the river, where he was dabbling and drowning. One of the tallest and stoutest young men immediately swam off to his relief, [and] bid him get upon his back, and he would carry him ashore. He got upon the back of the young man, but unhappily, instead of taking him round the neck, he embraced both the arms of the young man so strongly that he could not extend them to swim; who became now as much in danger of drowning as Curwin. He tried to shake him off but could not, and both were now tumbling in the water. I happened to be upon a pier of the bridge, and called to the company now on shore (who cared not to go off to their help lest they should be alike entangled) to wade, the tallest up to his chin, and make a string to the shore, and I would try to save them. Upon which I immediately swam away to the helpless couple, kept myself from their laying hold on me, and continually pushed them forward till they were got within the reach of the outmost man and were recovered, seemingly at the last gasp; and thus, through divine goodness, they were both preserved. This filled me with thankfulness to God in sparing the young men and making me instrumental in their preservation, and awakened in me many serious thoughts and resolutions; but ah! soon did I sin them away. Mr. Curwin afterwards was fixed in the church at Salem, from whence he sprung, a co-pastor with the aged Rev. Mr. Nicholas Noyes; and after serving them about three years and a half [he] died Nov. 23, 1717, aged 35, an excellent young man, leaving the aged Mr. Noyes to bewail his death. I was called, and even compelled, to preach his funeral sermon, upon a public Thanksgiving —a printed copy whereof I herewith send you.

In the last year of my being at college it pleased God, in righteous judgment, so far to deliver me up to the corrupt workings of my own heart that I fell into a scandalous sin, in which some of my classmates were concerned. This roused me more seriously to bethink myself of the wickedness of my heart and life; and though I had kept up some little show of religion, yet now I saw what a terrible punishment it was to be left of God and exposed to His wrath and vengeance, and [I] set myself upon seeking an interest in the favor of God, through the blessed Mediator, and [I] resolved, through the grace of God assisting of me, to lead a sober, a righteous, and a godly life, and improve my time and talents in the service of my Maker and Redeemer; and [I] applied myself more closely to my studies. But I found I could not recover what I had lost by my negligence.

In July, 1700 I took my first degree, Dr. Increase Mather being President; after which I returned to my honored father's house, where I betook myself to close studying, and humbling myself before God with fasting and prayer, imploring the pardon of all my sins, through the mediation of Christ [and] begging the divine Spirit to sanctify me throughout, in spirit, soul, and body, and [to] fit me for and use me in the service of the sanctuary, and [to] direct and bless all my studies to that end. I joined to the North Church in Boston under the pastoral care of the two Mathers. Some time in November, 1702 I was visited with a fever and sore throat; but, through the mercy of God to a poor sinful creature, in a few days I recovered a good state of health; and from that time to this— November, 1766—I have never had any sickness that has confined me to my bed.

While I continued at my good father's I prosecuted my studies, and looked something into the mathematics, though I gained but little—our advantages therefore being no ways equal to what they have, who now have the great Sir Isaac Newton, and Dr. Halley, and some other mathematicians, for their guides. About this time I made a visit to the college, as I generally did once or twice a year, where I remember, the conversation turning upon the mathematics, one of the company who was a considerable proficient in them, observing my ignorance, said to me he would give me a question, which, if I answered in a month's close application, he should account me an apt scholar. He gave me the question. I, who was ashamed of the reproach cast upon me, set myself hard to work, and in a fortnight's time returned him a solution of the question, both by trigonometry and geometry, with a canon by which to resolve all questions of the like nature. When I showed it to him he was surprised, said it was right, and owned he knew no way of resolving it but by algebra, which I was an utter stranger to. I also gave myself to the study of the Biblical Hebrew, turned the Lord's Prayer, the creed, and part of the Assembly's Catechism into Hebrew (for which I had Dr. Cotton Mather for my corrector), and entered on the task of finding the radix of every Hebrew word in the Bible with [a] design to form a Hebrew Concordance; but when I had proceeded through a few chapters in Genesis, I found the work was done to my hand by one of the Buxtorfs. So I laid it by.

The pulpit being my great design, and divinity my chief study, I read all sorts of authors, and, as I read, compared their sentiments with the sacred writings, and formed my judgment of the doctrines of Christianity by that only and infallible standard of truth; which led me insensibly into what is called the Calvinistical scheme (though I never to this day have read Calvin's works, and cannot call him master)—which sentiments, by the most plausible arguments to the contrary that have fallen in my way (and I have read the most of them), I have never yet seen cause to depart from.

Through the importunity of my friends I preached my first sermon, from Proverbs viii, 17, to a society of young men, meeting on Lord's

day evening for the exercises of religion (to which I belonged), in the
August twelvemonth after I took my first degree; and some months after
[I] preached publicly at Gloucester. By August, 1702, I became almost
a constant preacher, both on week days and on the Lord's day, privately
and publicly, insomuch as that I have sometimes preached every day of
the week but Saturday, and both parts of the Sabbath, before and after
—and, as my fond friends who heard me said, to good acceptance. At
this time I preached for the Rev. Mr. John Danforth of Dorchester, who
was pleased to compliment me upon it in such strains of commendation
as would not be modest in me to mention. This constant preaching took
me off from all other studies. About two months before I took my second
degree the reverend and deservedly famous Mr. Samuel Willard, then
Vice-President, called upon me (though I lived in Boston), to give a
common-place in the college hall; which I did, the latter end of June,
from 2 Peter i, 20,21, endeavoring to prove the divine inspiration and
authority of the holy Scriptures. When I had concluded the President
was so good as to say openly in the hall, *"Bene fecisti, Barnarde, et gratias
ego tibi."* Under him I took my second degree in July, 1703.

Here suffer me to take occasion to show you the manner of my studying
my sermons, which I generally pursued when I had time for it, and which
upon some special occasions I made use of even in my advanced years.
Having in a proper manner fixed upon the subject I designed to preach
upon, I sought a text of scripture most naturally including it; then I read
such practical discourses as treated upon the subject; I read also such
polemical authors, on both sides of the question, as I had by me— sometimes having ten or a dozen folios and other books lying open around
me—and compared them one with another, and endeavored to make their
best thoughts my own. After having spent some time (perhaps two or
three days) in thus reading and meditating upon my subject, I then applied
myself to my Bible, the only standard of truth, and examined how far
my authors agreed or disagreed with it. Having settled my mind as to
the truth of the doctrine I had under consideration, I then set myself
to the closest meditation upon the most plain and natural method I could
think of for the handling of the subject. Sometimes, not always, I penned
the heads of the discourse. Then I took the first head and thought over
what appeared to me most proper to confirm and illustrate it, laying it
up in my mind; [and] so I went through the several heads; and when
I had thus gone over the whole in its several parts, then I went over
all in my meditation, generally walking in my study or in my father's
garden. When I thought myself ripe for it I sat down to writing, and

being a swift penman I could finish an hour and a quarter's discourse, with rapid speaking, in about four hours' time. This manner of studying sermons cost me, 'tis true, a great deal of time, perhaps a week or fortnight for a sermon and sometimes more; but I had this advantage by it, that there was a greater stock laid up in my memory for future use, and I found it easy to deliver my discourses *memoriter*; and by the full and clear view I had of my subject I could correct the phraseology in my delivery. I kept indeed my notes open and turned over the leaves as though I had read them, yet rarely casting my eye upon my notes, unless for the chapter and verse of a text which I quoted. When I was settled in the ministry I found this method too operose, yet when called to special public services, if I had time, I practiced it—only penning head by head as I meditated on them. Observing also that the aged Mr. Samuel Cheever, with whom I settled, very much failed in his memory (for he was wholly a *memoriter* preacher), I thought I might be reduced to his circumstances if I lived to old age, and therefore betook myself to reading my notes; and I find the advantage of it, since it hath pleased God to spare me to a great old age.

In June, 1704, the church at Yarmouth sent for me to assist their pastor, the Rev. Mr. John Cotton, who was taken off from public service by a paralytic disorder; and having spent two months with them I returned home. They fetched me again to them in July, 1705, where I preached to them [for] some time; but having galled my right hand by some hard labor I was not used to, it turned to an ulcerous sore, insomuch that [when] a probe [was] put in at the roots of my fore and middle finger [on] the inside of my hand, it would come out at the middle of the back of my hand; which made me fear the loss of the use of it. For which reason I determined to return to Boston to get my hand cured. Accordingly I took my passage on board a coaster the middle of September; and falling in with a number of shallops that were catching mackerel, I, who loved the sport, could not resist the temptation of hauling the line with my sore hand—by which means the salt water so rinsed and cleansed the ulcer that, when I showed it to the doctor at Boston and let him know what had happened by the way, he told me I had cured the sore, and with some innocent salves to the orifices it soon became well. Thus kindly did Divine Providence deal with me, when I thought my danger had been very great. I returned to Yarmouth again according to my promise, at their desire, in November. The February following, Mr. Cotton died, and then the church and people proceeded to invite me to a settlement among them. There was but one man who withheld his vote from me; and even the Quakers in the town, of which there were several, were approving of it. The reverend ministers also in the neighborhood seemed to be pleased with it. I wrote to my honored father about it, and he seemed to be backward in consenting to the motion, partly because of the distance of about 85 miles, and partly (what he saw into further than I did) that it would not be a comfortable settlement to me. So I put a stop to their proceedings and returned home the latter end of March following, 1705.

My constant preaching went on as usual. In October, 1705, the Rev. Mr. Colman first invited me into his pulpit; I preached from 2 Corinthians iv, 17. In the week-time after it, the good gentleman meeting me, carried me to dine with him; after dinner he took me into his study and told me with great tenderness the reason why he had not asked me to his pulpit long before—[which] was because some of the chief of his people had esteemed me but as a mimic and tool of the Mathers, whom they were displeased with, and desired he would not invite me to preach among them; but they had now been with him, and with tears confessed their unjust thoughts of me, and said they would never trust to idle reports [any] more, even for my sake, and desired him to improve me as often as he pleased. Mr. Colman then opened his heart to me, acquainted me with a very great part of his travels in England [and] his familiar converse with the famous Philomela, and showed me several of his poetical compositions; and from this time [he] became a kind father and intimate and fast friend to me, as long as he lived.

In the spring of 1707 I was appointed by Governor Dudley [as] one of the chaplains to the army which was sent to Port Royal (now Annapolis) to reduce that fort—and with it Acadia, or Nova Scotia—to obedience to the crown of England. . . .
[A small section has been omitted here, in which Barnard describes in detail the military arrangements for the Port Royal expedition and inserts some passages from a journal he kept during the voyage.]
We went to Port Royal, landed in an orchard, were ambushed and lost about fourteen men, drove the enemy before us, returned to the orchard, spent a few days there, and then embarked our men. But about 110 French[men], mostly privateers, with their captain at their head (who arrived in our absence), came and lay hid[den] in the thicket of the woods and underbrush, just without a log fence, where Capt. Talbot with forty men were placed as a guard to the orchard. And [they] observed [us] till our men were mostly embarked and the boats were ashore for the last freight and Capt. Talbot [was] called off from the guard; and then

they broke in upon the orchard, where were only some of the officers besides Talbot's guard and a few others with myself, and poured in their shot upon us, and killed [of those with] us seven men. I had a shot [that] brushed my wig, and was mercifully preserved. A few boat-loads of men going off immediately put back; and we soon drove them out of the orchard, killed a few of them, [and] desperately wounded the privateer captain; and after that we all embarked and returned for Boston as fast as we could. When we came home, the General found it to be sadly true, what I suggested to him at Port Royal. Not only was he reprimanded and slighted by the Government, but [also he was] despised and insulted as he walked the streets by the populace—the very children, at the sight of him, crying out "wooden swords!" Though he was in himself a valiant man, yet I think his capacity was below the post he sustained. Nor did I go without my share of obloquy, for a little piece of imprudence while I was absent; for which my pastors treated me cruelly, for reasons best known to themselves; by which my reputation sunk among some people. But the more thinking persons looked upon it as a vile treating of me and continued their respects to me, especially the excellent Mr. Colman; so that I was almost constantly employed in preaching.

1708. Capt. John Wentworth, of Piscataqua (afterwards Governor of it), meeting me in Boston, greatly urged me to go [as] his chaplain in a ship of 500 tons, [with] 20 guns and 40 men, to Barbados and London. I proposed it to my good father, who told me [that] if I were not settled in the ministry before this time twelvemonth he would consent to my taking a voyage. I continued my itinerant preaching; and in the winter of 1708, preaching at Watertown, I returned in the evening to sup at Cambridge with the Rev. Mr. Brattle. While we were at supper, the ringing of the college bell, with the tidings that the college was on fire, was brought to us. I immediately left the table, ran across the pastures to the college, [and] found the area filled with the scholars (President Leverett at the head of them) and a multitude of the town's people, staring upon Stoughton Hall; but [I] knew not where the fire was, [though] the smoke [was] pouring out at the eaves from one end of the hall to the other. I stepped to the President and told him I would see where the fire was, stripped off my coat and wig, tied a handkerchief about my head, ran up the stairs of the northerly entry, and discovered where the fire was. Then [I] ran to the President and said, "Sir, please to order a ladder at the window of such a chamber, and supply me with water, and I will go in and quench the fire." Accordingly I went into the chamber; it was on fire all round. I ran to the window to open it, but it was fastened so as I could not find how to open it; and I could stay no longer in the chamber than I could hold my breath—the smoke was so exceedingly thick [that] it would have suffocated me to have drawn a breath. But observing the bulk of the fire was at the bed (for while President and scholars were at prayers in Harvard Hall, a spark, as it seemed, had snapped from the hearth and set fire to the calico curtains), I ran and told the President to order somebody to cut up the floor over the bed and pour water [on it] till they had extinguished the fire there. He did so; and then we soon mastered the fire. The President was pleased to observe upon it [that] if I had not providentially been there the college [would] have been consumed.

The summer of 1709 arrived, and I [was] not settled, when, meeting Capt. Wentworth at Boston, he again urged me to take the same voyage with him [that] he last year proposed. I obtained my good father's consent, and we sailed from Nantasket Road [on] July 9, 1709, and arrived with an easy, comfortable passage, in one and twenty days, at Barbados. As we were running down the latitude, a seeker bore down upon us, fell into our wake, and chased us with all the sail he could make; but our ship (the *Lusitania*), being a prime sailer, kept her distance. Capt. Wentworth got his ship ready, kept his course steadily, and before noon we raised the island, and [we] came to anchor before Bridgetown in the afternoon. Thus kind Providence preserved us. There was no congregation of Dissenters in this place; but I constantly attended public worship at church. A small number of considerable and valuable gentlemen, knowing I was a preacher, entreated me to entertain them upon a Lord's day; but I told them [that] I should not be here above two Sabbaths more, and I thought it would not be prudence to give any disturbance to the Episcopal clergy for so little a time; and [so I] refused their offer. While I was here I had some acquaintance with several of the clergy. Mr. Beresford, the chief minister upon the island, kindly invited me to dine with him, and entertained me with great civility. He was a gentleman of considerable learning, sobriety, and virtue.

After about five weeks stay at Barbados we set sail, under the convoy of Commodore Logg in the *Weymouth* and Capt. Norborough in the *Lark*, men-of-war, with about sixty sail, some bound for North America but mostly for London. The day after we sailed [there] came on a violent storm, something of a hurricane; the strength of which lasted about eight hours, when we could not hear one another speak upon deck without turning our face to the ear of the man we spoke to, neither could we put a light into the poop lantern without a man crawling upon his belly, and a second holding him by the heels, and a third [holding] him in like manner, to secure him. The storm parted the fleet; some fell in with the *Weymouth*, others with the *Lark*; and though the violence abated, yet it continued a very heavy storm for twelve or fourteen days, by which several of the fleet were much damaged, especially in their rigging. Commodore Logg was very careful and assisted the disabled ships that were with him. After the storm was over we spied three sail to leeward. The Commodore, who had made Wentworth a chasing ship, being a prime sailer, and ordered him to wear a broad pendant, now made signal for a chase. Wentworth bore away, the man-of-war after him, at more than a mile astern. Our ship outsailed the man-of-war, sparing her all our topgallant and studding-sails. By four in the afternoon we overhauled the sternmost of the three, so as to fling a shot across her forefoot; she brought to. But the man-of-war left us to stand for the fleet, who kept their course, and had long been out of sight; and the men-of-war were now out of sight, when we spied a tall ship to windward bearing down towards us, whose signals, which she made, we understood not; therefore [we] concluded it was one of the French fleet sailing from Martinique, [at] the same time we did from Barbados. Capt. Wentworth called his officers and men aft and said to them, "you see, gentlemen, the fleet and man-of-war have left us; it will cost us darkness before we can take the prize under command. A tall ship, probably a French man-of-war, is coming towards us. I am shipped upon convoy; if we needlessly leave the convoy and any mischance should befall us, we must make good all damages. I called you together to ask your advice what you would have me to do, whether we had best run all hazards, or forego the prize and make the best of our way for the convoy." Though the men had an eager desire to [take] the prize (a ship of 250 tons, well loaded from Martinique), yet they honestly answered, "sir, since your freight is shipped under convoy, we think you cannot safely and justly lose the convoy." Away we then stood for the fleet, and Jack Frenchman rejoiced at their narrow escape. A few days before we reached the channel of England, the *Lark* and those of the fleet that parted from us in the storm joined us; and I think we had no one vessel missing. When we entered the chops of the channel in the night, we fell in with a fleet of tall ships, which by their actions we knew to be men-of-war, and concluded it to be De Guy's squadron, which we heard was out upon a cruise. Wentworth's ship being an excellent sailer, he slung his yard and got everything ready [so] that, if it should prove an enemy, he might make a running fight and possibly escape. But now were we surprised when in the first peep of day we saw an eighty-gun ship, within pistol shot, upon our starboard quarter. For the men-of-war had placed themselves, by the help of a spy-boat running among the fleet in the night, close alongside of each of our fleet [which] they took to be a ship of force. As the day came on Capt. Norborough in the *Lark* knew the ship that was alongside of him to be an Englishman, and immediately fired a salute, which dissipated our fears and filled us with joy. It proved to be my Lord Dursley's squadron, sent out to look for De Guy. They spared us three capital ships to guard us up the channel. Going up channel we descried three French privateers lying a-hull, one of 30 guns. Our men-of-war took one of them and recovered two prizes from them; the other escaped. We cast anchor the next day in the Downs; the day after [we] were piloted up the river to Gravesend, where I and some passengers took boat and arrived at Billinsgate, London, that evening, [in] the beginning of November, after a long passage. It was truly pleasant sailing up the river. Some days after our arrival Commodore Logg came to me on the 'Change, and in a very complaisant manner desired me, if there was occasion, to be witness of his care of the fleet.

I had letters [of introduction] to Dr. Calamy, Dr. Oldfield, Mr. Fleming, and Mr. Pomfret, ministers; and I took my opportunity to wait upon them, who received me with a great deal of goodness. [I also had letters] to Sir William Ashurst, Mr. Harrison, and Mr. Parkhurst—to whom I sent my letters. After some weeks spent in London I first preached for Mr. Fleming, and then at Mr. Reynolds', Mr. Ratcliff's Mr. Mauduit's, Dr. Calamy's, Dr. Oldfield's, Mr. Anderson's, Mr. Pomfret's, Mr. Masters'; and [I] prayed, upon a Fast-day, both at Mr. Reynolds' and Dr. Hunt's. Besides which, I was employed at a small congregation near Eltham, the chief of which were Sir Alexander Carr and Esquire Stoddard—the rest were a poor people. This was as my parish, to which I preached constantly —unless called to preach in the city, and then I sent another in my stead. When I preached one morning by candle-light at Dr. Calamy's, after the service was over I was conducted into the vestry, with three or four gentlemen, to eat a piece of bread and butter and drink a glass of sack. While I was there, [there] came to us an aged gentlewoman (hearing I was of New England) to inquire after her brother, Col. Shrimpton, whom I knew well; and she brought a young lady (properly so called) with her, who was very pleasant with me. She asked me if all the people of my country were white, as she saw I was; for being styled in the general West Indians, she thought we were all black, as she supposed the Indians to be. She asked me how long I had been in the kingdom. When I told her a few months, she said she was surprised to think how I could learn their language in so little a time. "Methinks," said she, "you speak as plain English as I do." I told her [that] all my country-people, being English, spoke the same language I did. With many such like questions she diverted me. What strangers were even the [people of the] city of London to New England, excepting a few merchants who traded with us! [I] being invited by Dr. Calamy to dine with him, there was present the pious and excellent lady of the famous Col. Gardiner, and a young daughter of hers, about 13 or 14 years old. I was very kindly and pleasantly entertained by the Dr. and that lady. The Dr., among other things, surprised me by saying to me, "Mr. Barnard, you don't think, I hope, to carry Philomela (Miss Singer) away from us?"—which occasioned a very agreeable conversation upon that lady and her writings. Before we broke up, Mrs. Gardiner very kindly invited me to go with her and her daughter in her coach down to Scotland, obligingly telling me my journey should cost me nothing. I had a strong inclination to have embraced her generous offer; but [I] was forced to tell her [that] the time of the ship I came in, returning to New England (with which I purposed to go) was so near at hand that I could not prudently run the risk of being absent when she sailed. But I most humbly thanked her for her obliging request and was heartily sorry I could not gratify my own inclination so far as to comply with it. I preached for Mr. Fleming, who was taken off from his public services by the palsy, especially in his tongue. After my first preaching to them they were fond of my continuing in their service, especially the chief of the congregation, insomuch that my friends and acquaintances in London began to congratulate me upon the prospect of my settling in as good a congregation as most in London; and indeed the people sought for no other help, until Dr. Sacheverel's mob gutted and burnt the bowels of Mr. Daniel Burgess' meeting-house; and then he wanting a place to preach in, and they [some]one to preach to them, they united and I was thrown out. [I] preaching for Mr. Anderson, a worthy Scotch minister, at St. James' (where was a great concourse of the Scotch nobility and gentry), he with several of his vestry-men expressed themselves highly pleased with my public performance and private conversation, and greatly urged me to stay and spend my days in the kingdom, saying, "We very much want men of your abilities and vigor," and [also saying] that he (Mr. Anderson) and some others he knew had a great respect for me [and] would use their best endeavors to procure as good a congregation for me as any in London. I told him [that] I could be content to spend a few years among them, but that I chose to return to New England and there improve the remainder of my life in the service of the Gospel. "Well," said he, "if you will not abide with us, we will take no further concern about you." I returned him thanks for his kind respects to me.

While I preached at Mr. Flemings's, a gentleman that was of his congregation, who had been captain of a troop under King William at the battle of the Boyne, was pleased to persuade me very much to stay in the kingdom, saying, "I expect an insurrection shortly in favor of the Pretender, and we very much want men of your principles, knowledge, and activity. I always keep two horses ready-saddled in my stable to mount at a minute's warning; and one of them, with a pair of jack-boots, shall be at your service, to mount as a chaplain with us." I smiled and thanked him.

Having some considerable acquaintance with Mr. Ratcliff, at Rotherhithe, for whom I preached several times, I cannot well refuse to take notice of that pious and ingenious gentleman's catechising and instructing [of] children, who came to him every Tuesday from all parts round about and from every sect; in which work he generally spent the day. His manner was to place the males and females by themselves from ten to sixteen years old, and class them according as they could say the catechism. Beginning with prayer, he then heard the girls and then the boys, till he had gone through the catechism with them; and then [he] dismissed the girls, giving them a reward of a farthing or half-penny as they performed, but still retained the upper class, to whom he proposed a question to be disputed by them. He asked each boy which side of the question he was for, whether yea or nay, then placed the yeas and the nays by themselves, then asked one of the yeas what he had to say in proof of his opinion, then asked one of the nays what he had to say, and so went to the yeas and nays, one after another alternately, till he had gone through the class—when, as moderator, he summed up the force of the reasoning on both sides and gave the true solution of the question. You would have admired and been pleased with the reasons the youth advanced for the part they held. I remember [that] the question disputed upon, when I was present, was "Which is best, virtue or riches?" They said many things on both sides, which I should have thought vastly exceeded the capacity of such youths. One prompt lad, in arguing for the preference of virtue, observed among other things that riches would not make a man good, but would tend to improve his wickedness. "There is," said he, "the Pope of Rome, who is the richest man in the world and yet the wickedest man alive." This came from a boy of about thirteen years old, of poor circumstances, and low education ([having none] but what he received here). When the instruction was over, Mr. Ratcliff gave each of these boys a penny to buy them bread for their dinner (which they had gone without for the sake of the catechism), being supplied with this stock from gentlemen of substance, as well as of his own.

I contracted a very considerable friendship with Esquire Stoddard, of the small congregation I preached to near Eltham, dined often at his house, was treated by him with great civility—and [likewise] by the gentlewoman, his housekeeper. She treated me once with a glass of currant wine of her own making. I was greatly pleased with it and begged a recipe of it. After consulting several ministers [as to] whether she could, with safety to her promise, divulge the secret to a foreigner, bound out of the kingdom, and [whether she] was no ways likely to hurt him from whom she had the recipe, she gave it to me; and when I returned home I soon spread it among my acquaintances.

It happened that Dr. Sacheverel's trial came on some months after I arrived in London, and I attend the trial in Westminster Hall one day, and had the pleasure of seeing the most brilliant assembly of lords, and ladies, and gentry; but, to my disappointment, the House of Lords adjourned presently after my coming in to consider a point of law; so that I heard none of the pleadings.

With some pleasant company, my own countrymen, I took a tour to Oxford, where, under the conduct of Mr. Caswell (professor of astronomy, an ingenious, most humble, and meek man), we were entertained with a view of the colleges, walks, gardens, theatre, libraries, and museum, and were diverted with the strange account [that] the keeper of the museum gave us of its rarities, especially those from New England, which we knew much better than he did. While we were at Oxford we set out in the rain to see Blenheim House, built by the nation in honor to the great Duke of Marlborough, fixed upon him and heirs forever. Though it was not finished, it appeared a magnificent and superb building, its gardens containing about sixty acres of land.

At another time (at the desire of Mr. Mico, a merchant, brother to our Mr. Mico of Boston, to accompany a Connecticut farmer who went to look after an estate he supposed he had right to there) I took a journey as far as Staffordshire, through St. Albans (where I viewed Duke Humphrey's sepulchre, or dined with Duke Humphrey, as 'tis called), Dunstable, Woburn, Northampton, Coventry, to Litchfield, where we put up. We had the company of an elder and a 25-year-old gentlewoman with us in the coach, who were at first very fearful and shy of us, as absolute strangers; but before we had traveled far they became very easy and pleasant, being thoroughly gratified with our modest and entertaining conversation. The young lady we parted with the next day at noon— [she] being received by a gentleman and lady in their coach, who waited for her at an appointed place. The elder lady still traveled with us to Litchfield. When we came to the inn, I was in a hurry for horses to carry us about seven miles farther, to Rudgley. The good old lady, seeing me about to move off, said to me, "Sir, I can't part with you yet; I must treat you with a glass of burnt claret. I was somewhat fearful of you at first, as strangers, as we are often treated somewhat rudely by such in traveling with them; but really, sir, I never traveled with more agreeable company, nor was better pleased than with your conversation and behavior." I thanked her for her great compliment. "No, sir," said she, "it is no compliment; and I have been thinking how to acknowledge your civility. Will a recipe of the best bacon in England be acceptable to you?" I answered her, "Yes, madam, with my most hearty thanks for it." She sat down and wrote me a recipe which, when I came home, I scattered abroad; and from thence came all the right good bacon made in New England.

Upon my journey it was my custom to send to the parson of the parish, after dinner, to come and take a glass of wine with a stranger, by which means I had the opportunity of seeing and sounding several clergymen, and found them generally very empty and warm Jacobites. I lodged at Rudgley near a fortnight, and the first Sabbath attended the church service of the place, one Mr. Taylor being curate; and, as my custom was, [I] waited upon the parson after the service was over, where I found four or five of the chief men of the parish. Mr. Taylor soon fell into a high encomium of Dr. Sacheverel (who had a day to two before passed through Litchfield with a numerous cavalcade, as in triumph), who he esteemed the great defender of the church, which he thought would have gone near to have been pulled down by the Whigs if it had not been for his famous (but really infamous) sermon. I made myself to appear to them as a stranger to, and very much unconcerned about, the controversy. However, I observed one thing to him, that I should have liked the Dr. better if in his speech upon his trial he had abode by his principles in his sermon—whereas it seemed to me that they did not well agree together. The parson said he could not think it possible for the Dr. not to be true and consistent with himself. I asked him if he had seen the sermon and speech. He replied [that] he had seen neither of them. I thought so from this wild talk about them; and though I had both of them in my pocket, yet [I] secreted them from

him. One of the gentlemen present said, "Sir, I believe you have had
a liberal education." I said to him, "Sir, I may not deny that I have had
the advantage of such an education as my country affords, but [I] am
sorry I have made no better improvement of it." Upon which the parson
abruptly took me by the hand and said, "Sir, let us take a turn into the
garden." We did so, and left the company. He sent for the bottle and
glass, and entertained me with idle chat about the flowers, etc.; so I
quickly withdrew and went to my lodgings. Being come there, I showed
the gentleman of the house (who was one of them at the parson's) Dr.
Sacheverel's sermon; he had scarce read a page before he broke forth
into violent exclamations against him, and thought he deserved to be
hanged for preaching and printing such stuff. (It is to be noted that I
traveled with a long wig, a sword by my side with mourning hilt, and
black clothes—the court being then in mourning for the Prince of Den-
mark, Queen Anne's husband—by which means I was taken for a small
courtier and treated as such by many country squires and knights I met
withal.) The Sabbath after, I attended at a parish church, about three
miles distant from my lodging, where I heard a venerable, grave, ancient
gentleman, who preached much in the strain of our Dr. I Mather, with
great plainness and fidelity, as one that aimed at making his hearers real
Christians—which was a rare thing to be heard in the Church. I waited
upon him after service, and found him and his aged wife two good, devout
Christians; we spent the remainder of the day very agreeably and profitably together. About sunset I was for taking my leave; the good old gentleman would in his great civility accompany me, as I thought he designed,
a few rods. But when we had gone over half a mile I said to him, "Sir,
I am ashamed to put you to so long a travel in your great age; I heartily
thank you for your respects shown to me and wish you a good night."
"No, sir," said he, "I cannot part with you yet. I'll accompany you a
little farther"; and he did so, notwithstanding all I could say, till we came
to my lodgings. We refreshed ourselves a little after our walk, and then
he arose to return home. I thought myself obliged to [show] the like
civility to him, and therefore accompanied him to his house, being favored
with a bright moon, and again bade him a good night; but the good
old gentleman would walk with me back again. When we arrived at a
brook, about half way, I stopped and said to him, "Sir, your goodness
to me is so great that I am ashamed I cannot make you suitable returns;
and though I have been entertained and pleased with your conversation
and company, beyond what I have met with in England, yet I am even

compelled, against my inclination, to say [that] I would not take a step farther unless he allowed me to take leave of him." He replied, "Sir, though I have been greatly gratified with your company, yet, since it must be so, I wish you a good night; and may the blessing of God be with you." So we parted, I think the good man's name was Ridgley, an excellent Christian, a man of good learning, an apostolical preacher of admirable meekness and humility and great civility. While I was at Rudgley I visited Uttoxeter, Wolverhampton, and Burton, from whence comes the best, stoutest, and finest ale in England; where, having occasion to converse with some lawyers upon the affairs which carried me there, I was taken by them for a considerable lawyer. At length I returned to London.

There were many kind and pleasing proposals made to me, besides that of Madame Gardiner's, which I neglected for the same reason I did hers: —my design to return in the ship I came in. Mr. William Whitingham (whom I knew in Boston) had a pleasant seat and living at Boston in Lincolnshire; and meeting me in London, [he] strongly invited me to go with him to his seat and spend some time there, telling me the journey should cost me nothing. Capt. Robert Robinson (formerly an apprentice to my good father, whose son, an admiral, has married my brother's only daughter), commander of Her Majesty's yacht, the *Carolina*, who then was about to carry over to Holland the great Duke of Marlborough, with other nobles and their retinue, earnestly invited me to go with him, assuring me my trip to Holland should cost me nothing. But, above all, the famous Mr. Rowe invited me to bear him company to Agford when he was going down to marry the incomparable Philomela, whom I longed to see, saying my journey should be no charge to me. All of which I thought myself obliged to refuse for the reason mentioned. Yet I was persuaded to stay longer in London, and I let the ship depart without me.

Attending at Dr. Brey's church to hear Bishop Burnet, I had the favor of the Bishop's blessing.

Praying upon a fast at Mr. Reynolds' and Mr. Hunt's, I was invited to sup with the ministers, which I did to my great satisfaction with their learned and devout conversation—when I took the opportunity of such a number of grave divines being together to read to them, with their leave, the history of Maucompus, the great Indian, sent over by me from a learned, worthy divine of this country as a specimen of a work he was about to offer to the world: But those great men, while they acknowledged the vast reading and ingenuity of the author, yet thought he was too credulous and easily imposed upon, and therefore concluded [that] this was no recommendation of the larger work from whence it was extracted.

When my Lord Wharton was about to go over to Ireland as Lord Lieutenant, he desired a gentleman of great learning and ready wit, with whom I was particularly acquainted, to look out [for] an agreeable chaplain for him. The gentleman immediately addressed himself to me, urging me to take the gown and embrace this opportunity of going [as] his chaplain; for he was the best-natured nobleman in the kingdom, of regular life, the greatest friend to the Dissenters, would treat me with all goodness, and I should be in a fair way for preferment. After a considerable debate upon the affair I said to the gentleman, "Sir, you know I was bred a Dissenter; and I could make many exceptions to the articles, the rubric, and the practices of the Church of England." Yet, to make short of it, [I said that] I had read all I could meet with on both sides of the controversy, and was settled in my own judgment, but was no bigot, as he knew; and if he could give me any clear proof, and tolerable satisfaction, that the great Head of the church had empowered any man or number of men, civil or ecclesiastical, upon earth, to give law to His church, to appoint the regimen, modes of worship, and what ceremonies he or they pleased, I would turn churchman tomorrow. But since the only Head of the church seemed to me to have reserved this power to Himself alone, and [to have] ordered His ministers to teach only what He had commanded, I thought myself obliged to refuse coming under the yoke of bondage to any merely human authority; and therefore I could not accept his kind offer. After weighing in his mind what I had said, he found himself at a loss for a satisfactory answer and said, "Then I find I must look out for another;" and this put an end to our conference about it.

In my conversation with some great merchants I perceived that there was something moved at Court that tended to the prejudice of New England; and they observed [that] we very much wanted an agent to appear on our behalf, and that Mr. Jeremiah Dummer, a courtier and one intimate with the excellent ministry then at the helm, was as proper a person as we could get, being our own countryman, of admirable capacity and diligent application. I immediately dispatched letters to the Governor, Speaker of the House, and some other persons of figure and influence, laid what I had heard before them, and recommended Mr. Dummer to them; upon which he was presently appointed their agent and diverted what was threatening to us. Two years after, in the latter end of Queen

Anne's reign, under her bad ministry, the court seemed to be fixed upon taking away the New England charter, when Mr. Agent Dummer appeared and wrote a pamphlet showing that the New England charter was not an act of grace from the throne but a contract between the king and our fathers, that we had fulfilled our part of the contract, and therefore it would be the highest injustice to deprive us of what we had bought at the expense of so much blood and treasure; which put a stop to the proceedings against us. That piece was reprinted in the time of the struggle about the stamp act; and I counted myself happy in being, in some small degree, instrumental in thus serving my native country.

Nothing could be more obsequious and cringing, even to meanness, than a great number of candidates for the ministry from Scotland and Ireland were to the standing ministry to put them into places. I have had several of them paying their court to me, sometimes two or three in a morning before I was out of bed, importuning me to open the way, to direct and recommend them to settlements in New England. But I let them know that I looked upon myself [as] a stranger to their education and manners, and therefore I could not honestly comply with their desires; and forasmuch as we had a college which furnished both the churches and the magistracy with able men, it would be highly injurious to my *alma mater* for me to endeavor to supply the churches from abroad, seeing we needed them not.

When I was about to return home, I was earnestly courted by several considerable merchants and some West India gentlemen of my acquaintance to go into trade, and they offered to send by me what goods I pleased. One of them went so far as to engage sending a thousand a year sterling from London and all the rum and molasses from his large plantation in Antigua, and obliged me to take the name of his overseer and his orders upon him. But I thanked them for their generous offer, and told them [that] I wholly devoted myself to the service of God in the work of the ministry, and [that], God assisting me, no worldly considerations should take me off from it.

At length I took passage in the *Buckingham Frigate*, a ship of about 250 tons—Ephraim Breed, commander—which sailed to Portsmouth to be under the convoy of Commodore Littleton, who was to take care of the fleet bound to the West Indies. The latter end of July I traveled in the stage flying coach, which reached Portsmouth in one day, where I stayed with three New England passengers [for] about a month waiting for the convoy. While I was here I was acquainted with several families of good fashion, which treated me with peculiar respect and goodness. Here I

preached to the dissenting church one part of a Lord's day to good accept-
ance. There happened to be an army under Lord Shannon, lying at
Cowes, bound to New England and thence to Canada. We four New
England passengers had a great inclination to see it. We ferried over to
Ryde on Saturday and traveled to Newport on the Isle of Wight, where
we visited Carisbrook castle, an ancient and decayed pile, intending on
Monday morning to go to Cowes. Lord's day evening as we discoursed of
our voyage to New England, our landlord overheard us and said to us,
"Gentlemen, I wish [that] you are not very disappointed; I heard the
signal guns for sailing fired very early this morning, and the wind was
fair, but small." It put us, as well it might, into a great surprise; but
it was too late in the night then to think of going to Ryde, seven miles
distant; we therefore went to bed, rose on Monday before the sun, [and]
set away for Ryde. There we found the fleet had come to sail the morning
before; but, in going round St. Helen's Point, the tide was too strong
for the wind and they were forced to come to anchor. What should we
do now? Our clothes and effects were all on board ship, the wind [was]
fair and strong, the fleet [was] under sail, and [there was] no boat to
carry us to them. Within a quarter of an hour the ferry-boat from Portsmouth landed at Ryde; but the wind was high and the sea foaming. I
begged of my companions not to lisp a word of our being bound out
with the fleet, and [to] content themselves to submit to my measures,
or we should never get on board our ship. They promised they would.
I then went up to the ferryman, as he landed, and said, "Ferry-man,
you have had a hard passage of it. I see your company are wet, and
I suppose you will not care to go off again presently." "No, master," said
he, "the wind and sea are turbulent; I must stay till it abates a little."
We then mixed ourselves with other company and talked of a passage
to Portsmouth. The ferryman soon learned [that] there were four of us
men, bound over to Portsmouth, as he thought; which was a great fare
with him. I called for bread and cheese and a mug of ale for our breakfast,
and sat down, seemingly very easy. Anon the ferryman came to us and
said, "Masters, if you are bound over, the wind seems to be somewhat
abated; I think we may go." I said to him, "Don't be in too great a hurry;
we shall be ready presently." He came a second time; we then rose and
followed him into the boat. After we had got a little way from shore
I said to my companions, "There is an honest, worthy gentleman, bound
off in that fleet; I should be very glad to take leave of him; perhaps
we may never see him again." "I should be glad to see him," said my

companions, one and all. I understood a small boat, and was determined
to take the helm myself if fair means would not prevail with him to carry
us to the ship; and I think, in such necessitous circumstances, I should
have done nothing but what was right. But I said, "Well, ferryman, what
shall I give you to take a run to that hindmost ship, [so] that we may
shake hands with an honest gentleman?" "O! master," said he, "the wind
is high and scant, the sea so rough, and the distance so great [that]
I cannot possibly go thither." "Come," said I, "I'll give you half a crown
for it." "Indeed I cannot," said he. "Well," said I, "I'll give you a crown"
—which I knew was as much as he ordinarily got in two or three days.
He paused and said, "Well, masters, to oblige you I will try what I can
do; but you must not detain me." We told him we would not hinder
him one quarter of an hour. So he steered for our ship, which lay by
for us, the fleet being mostly round the Point. As soon as we got on
board we gave him the crown, handed him a few biscuits and a bottle
of rum, and then told him we would detain him no longer. He broke
out, as [if] in great anguish, "What! am I catched?" We replied, "Yes,
and we are well escaped; so fare you well." Had he known our circumstances we should have come off well at the price of a guinea a man
—so biting are these sharpers.

We came to sail, soon got up with the fleet, and put in at Torbay.
I landed at Brixham, a poor small fish-town. The second day [we] came
to sail, and put in at Plymouth on Saturday, and on the next day set
sail upon our voyage (August 27). [We] took our departure from Scilly
[on] Aug. 31, 1710. On Sept. 5 [we] parted with the convoy, and the
fleet separated on their different courses for their several ports, and we
soon found ourselves a lone ship. Our ship was either ill built, or ill
loaded; [she] was so crank that she could not hold up her sides to a
smart gale. We were often necessitated to settle our mainyard to Portland,
and once to strike our topmasts; so that we had a very long passage.
[On] Sept. 7 we saw a tall ship standing after us, which we took for
a French man-of-war; but night coming on we altered our course and
lost her—a happy escape, through a kind Providence. Sept. 23: Very
hard north-west wind and a mountainous sea, which put us to difficulties.
Sept. 28: By bad steering, or a strong current, or both, we fell so much
southward of our course as to make the islands of Corvo and Flores.
Oct. 14: Hoisted out our boat, it being calm; tried the current, found
it set between three and four knots to the south, something westward;
and took two tortoises, about sixty weight apiece. Oct. 20: Fell in with

a large fleet, about four o'clock in the morning, saw their top and poop lights, which stood away north-east. We kept our course and lost them by daylight.

Oct. 28 and 29: Many fowls of different sorts came about us, and some lodged on our rigging. The water was of a light green color, and we concluded we were on the banks in lat. 43°11', long. 62°11'. We hoisted out our boat and sounded with 160 fathoms, but found no bottom. Oct. 30: sounded again but had no bottom. Nov. 6: about four o'clock P.M. we got sounding in about 35 fathoms, brought up hake's teeth and some shells. The captain, being confined with the gout, came not upon deck, but being told the depth and showed the bottom, he, with the two mates and a captain passenger, concluded we were in the South Channel, and it being a fair wind, the captain ordered such a course to be steered, saying, "We shall be abreast with the table land of Cape Cod by morning and [shall] have the whole day before us to run up the bay for Boston." Observing the talk of the several officers, I confess I was greatly concerned in mind lest we should be running among the shoals of Nantucket, but I said nothing to them, trusting in God and not [in] man to preserve us. Before we had stood our course three hours, a strong north-west wind clapped all the sails a-back in a moment. We lay by for three or four days, kept the lead going every watch, found little or no alteration in the depth of the water and not much in the bottom brought up. Nov 11th, in the morning watch, they brought up white sand, upon which they all agreed we were upon the back of Martha's Vineyard. I then asked them where they thought we were when we set our course upon our first getting soundings. They answered me [that] we were certainly running upon Nantucket shoals, and had we continued that course two hours longer we should unavoidably have perished among them. I then observed to them what abundant cause we had of thankfulness to a gracious God, who, in mercy to us, caused the wind so suddenly to blow in our teeth, and stop our way—though doubtless we (some of us) thought it against us. Let this great deliverance which a good God has given us never be forgotten by us.

The wind being favorable, we stood for the Vineyard, and in about two hours raised it, and got to anchor that day (it being Saturday) by one o'clock. Some of the passengers crossed [on] the ferry that afternoon and set out for Boston, another passenger and myself chose to stay the Sabbath over at the Vineyard. Tuesday morning we went over [on] the ferry and put away on horseback for Boston. We traveled but leisurely. As we drew towards Boston we understood Thursday was a day of public thanksgiving; we stopped at Braintree and attended the public service there; and I arrived at my good father's house after candle-lighting that evening, just before they were going to sit down to supper. And a joyful thanksgiving it was, both to my parents and myself—to my parents and brethren, who had been in great distress about me; for all the vessels that came out with us had arrived, the last of them above a week before us; though the passengers who set out from the Vineyard arrived at Boston Nov. 14, and informed my parents I was well at the Vineyard, and would be here in a day or two—and to myself, who, after a very tedious passage of eleven weeks, having escaped the dangers of the sea and the enemy and been signally preserved from perishing by shipwreck, was now arrived safe, after more than a year and four months' absence, to join with my good parents and brethren on such a special day in our thankful praises to God for His great goodness to us.

The Wednesday evening after I came home I preached at a private meeting of devout Christians, who monthly upheld such meetings at each other's houses alternately, from Isaiah xxxv., 10. "The ransomed of the Lord shall return, and come to Zion with songs and everlasting joy upon their heads." Which I considered as ultimately referring to the joy and triumph with which the redeemed of the Lord shall arrive at the heavenly world, from all the dangers and temptations they had met with in this; in which also I described my own particular case, yet decently couched, with thankfulness. There was a crowded house, of four rooms upon a floor, who hung upon my lips. Soon after, I preached the same sermon upon the Sabbath at Mr. Colman's meeting-house, with great satisfaction to the hearers.

A few days after my arrival I waited upon Governor Dudley at Roxbury, to pay my duty to him and deliver some books with letters I brought for him. He diligently inquired of me about the circumstances of the times in England. I gave him the best account I could; and among other things [I] told him the new ministry, St. John's and Harley and the others, were supposed by those who best understood affairs to be driving at the preparing [of] the way for the Pretender, and had persuaded Her Majesty he was her real brother, and she seemed to be willing to resign the crown to him. [I also reported] that the inferior clergy were nineteen in twenty in the Pretender's interest, and [that] it was expected it would not be long before the nation would be embroiled in a civil war upon the account. He replied to me, "Child, you should not divulge such things; you will endanger the bringing [of] yourself into mischief; you are too far from the Court to know the secrets of it." I said to him, "Sir, I do not make this common talk, but I thought it my duty to acquaint your Excellency with it." Soon after King George I came to the throne, in the year 1715, the kingdom was invaded and insurrections made in behalf of the Pretender. Meeting Governor Dudley after the tidings arrived to us of the insurrection, among other conversation I said to him, "Sir, your Excellency may remember some accounts I gave you of affairs at home, which you were pleased to check me for. What does your Excellency think of it now?" "Ah, child," said he, "we old men dream dreams, but you young men see visions."

The pulpits in Boston and round about the country were soon open to me, so that between the public and private preaching I had constant employment. And it gave me some diversion to hear (as I passed along the streets) people in their shops saying to one another, "How much better he preaches now than before he went to England"—though I often preached the sermons I had made before.

In the summer of 1711 there was a fair prospect, from the generality of the people being fond of it, that I should have settled at Reading. But a very worthy gentleman accidentally traveling through the town, they invited him to preach to them the next Sabbath. He did so; and a wise Providence so ordered it that when they came to a choice the vote turned out for him. In the latter end of 1711 it was concluded by my friends, from the affection the people had for me, that I should have been fixed at Jamaica, a parish in Roxbury. I confess it pleased me because it was within five miles of Boston. But happening to attend a lecture at Roxbury, Governor Dudley, who saw me come in, threw open his pew door to me. Some of the chief persons of Jamaica were present, and, observing the respect the Governor showed me, [they] concluded I should be a Governor's man, as they called it; and though they were particularly set for me before, yet from some disgust they had to the Governor [they] altered their minds and threw me off. [In] the latter end of 1712 the people of Newton had a great inclination to settle me among them; but one of the chiefs made a visit to ———— to consult him about it, [and] he only answered with a forbidding shrug, and so put an end to it. There were the prospects of my settling in several other places; but a good and wise Providence overruled it for the best.

In the year 1713 a number of the brethren of the North Church in Boston to which I belonged, fourteen in number, concluded, with the assistance of several of the first men of the church and congregation, to build a new meetinghouse with [a] design to settle me into it. I knew nothing of their designs for me till the house was raised, when at the dinner, to which I was invited, one of the chief of them said to me, "Sir, I hope within a little while to see you settled in this new house." When the house was near finished the aged Dr. I. Mather sent for the aforesaid fourteen members, one by one, closeted them, appeared against their settling a *manifesto* man (as he styled me because of the great friendship Mr. Colman showed to me), and extorted from as many as he could a promise that they would not vote for me. By the direction of the Mathers the said fourteen men got into a private room and combined into a church. Soon after they proceeded to the choice of a minister; five would not vote at all because they had been made to promise they would not vote for me. So a minister was chosen and afterwards settled by five persons out of fourteen, when the other nine were evidently for another person. The conduct of the Mathers was wondered at by all. Within a few days, I made a visit to Dr. C. M. as I generally visited him once a week or fortnight; and in all my visits to him before this he never said one word to me about the new house, nor I to him; but now he opened himself to me and said, "Mr. Barnard, do you think we could easily bear to have the best men in our house leave us, [such] as Capt. Charnock, Capt. Bant, Mr. Greenwood, Mr. Ruck, and it may be counsellor Hutchinson, and Mr. Troisel? No, sir, we cannot part with such men as these."— which was a plain telling me [that] the grand reason of their opposition to my settlement in the new house was the fear that those gentlemen would leave them to sit under my ministry in case I was fixed there (as I understood afterwards several of them designed). Soon after the choice of Mr. Webb I made a visit to Mr. R. in an evening, where I found counsellor Hutchinson and his brother, E. Hutchinson, discoursing of the management of the affairs of the new house. And presently counsellor H. applied himself to me, saying, "It is cruel hard treatment, when the house was built designedly for you, and most, if not all, the members of the church aimed at settling you with them, to have it so clandestinely and unjustly, contrary to their minds, wrested from you. But I will see who shall be settled in it." (It is to be noted that he had generously given the ground it stood upon, but had not yet given them a deed for it.) "I'll shut the doors of the house and see who will dare to open them without my leave." I said to him, "Sir, you will greatly endanger a controversy between you and your ministers if you should do so." He replied with some warmth, "Sir, I have already borne heavy things from them; but this is too much to bear calmly. If they will contend with me, my back is broad enough to bear it." I then said to him, "Sir, I humbly entreat you to consider what will be the natural effect of it.

It will disturb your mind, prejudice you against your ministers, endanger your losing the benefit of their ministry, and will render you a sufferer in your best interest. I therefore earnestly beseech you, sir, to engage in no controversy with them upon my account; but leave me to the care of Divine Providence, which does all things well and I trust will provide for me." I saw he was pleased with my answer to him; and [I] presently diverted the discourse another way. I never knew till this time that this honorable gentleman had any particular regards to me or was [in] any ways inclined to see me fixed in the new house. Within a few weeks he gave the society a deed for the ground; and they settled among them a much better man than myself. And I was truly thankful to God that he was pleased to make use of me as an instrument to quench the flame that was kindling, which doubtless would have burnt very fiercely had it not been stifled.

I preached in the new house, the second Sabbath of their meeting, on May 23, 1714, from Gen. xxviii, 17 [on] the dedication of the house to the worship and service of God, and the gate of heaven. Within a few years something happened in Mr. Webb's conduct, about settling a colleague with him, which gave occasion to the Mathers [for] repenting of their treatment of me—insomuch that Dr. C. M. said, "Johnny Barnard would not have treated them so."

After so many disappointments, and being now turned of my thirty-second year, I began to be discouraged and [to] think whether Providence designed me for the work of the ministry, [or] whether I was not called upon to lay aside my own inclination and betake myself to some other business. But I considered my parents' and my own solemn dedication to this service; and hearing from several parts of the country that many had been greatly profited by my preaching, and ministers informing me that this and the other person had given them an account that my preaching such or such a sermon was the means of their being first awakened and turning into the path of religion and virtue, I was encouraged to keep to my studies and go on in the work of the gospel, as I had opportunity, and to commit my case to God and wait His pleasure. I often thought [that] if my father's circumstances would have afforded it (which they could not), I would live all my days at Cambridge near the College and preach to any people who needed help, but never come under the awful charge of a church, but [rather] give myself wholly up to studying.

The aged and Rev. Mr. Samuel Cheever, pastor of the church in Marblehead, needing assistance, the church and town nominated Mr. Edward Holyoke (now President), Mr. Amos Cheever, and myself, to preach to them, upon probation for three months, alternately. The committee came to me in August, 1714, to acquaint me with their design and [to] desire my compliance with it. I went and preached to them [on] August 11 and took my turn with the others, until the church in January came to a choice, and the vote finally came out for me; and the town concurred in it, voting a salary. The committee brought me the votes, both of choice and maintenance, and desired my acceptance of them. I thanked them for their respects to me and their generous provision for my support; but knowing [that] there were two of the church and some chief men of the town who swayed many others, [who] were very fond of settling Mr. Holyoke with them, which would occasion a controversy among them, I deferred complying with their request and told them I would take some time to consider it. Some months after [this], they came to me again to receive my answer. I told them I had heard there was a considerable strife in the town for the settling of Mr. Holyoke, which was very discouraging to me; and [I] asked them if they thought the town was large enough to require another house. They answered me [that] they believed there were people enough to fill another house. I then asked them if they had anything against Mr. Holyoke's settling among them. They said, no—if the vote of the church had turned out for him, they should have been entirely satisfied. Then said I to them, "Why may not Mr. Holyoke's friends in Marblehead be allowed to build a house for him, as well as the church enjoy their inclination to settle me with them?" They said [that] if it could be done peaceably they had nothing against it; upon which I asked if any of Mr. Holyoke's Marblehead friends were in town. They informed me [that] such were come to treat with him. I then desired [that] they would seek them out and appoint a meeting with them, either at Mr. Holyoke's or at my father's, and I would wait upon them in the evening and try if we could compromise matters. Accordingly all met at Mr. Holyoke's father's. I told them what I had proposed; and after some discourse upon it among themselves I said to them, "Gentlemen, if you can amicably agree that Mr. Holyoke shall settle among his friends, I will accept the offer of the church to settle with them; otherwise I know not how to comply with your request. For I do not care to fix in a town under the disadvantage of strife and contention." Mr. Holyoke then said, "If Mr. Barnard will go to Marblehead, I will go also; else not." They presently fell into an agreement to build a new house for Mr. Holyoke, and my friends promised to use their influence with the town to consent to it; and so they parted good friends.

Upon the 9th of November, 1715, I removed, upon the people's desire, to Marblehead; the day before, Mr. Holyoke's people first opened their new house, in which several neighboring ministers kept a day of prayer for the divine direction and blessing upon their intended settlement. In January following Mr. Holyoke left his tutorship at the college and came to live in Marblehead, and [he] was ordained the next April. I carried on part of the labors of the Sabbath with my venerable father Cheever, till I was ordained [on] July 18, 1716. When we returned from the public to his house, the good man broke out, before all the ministers, "Now, Lord, lettest thou thy servant depart in peace." And having obtained help from God, I am continued to this day, ministering unto my people in much weakness, fear, and trembling, [and] preaching none other things than what the Law and the Prophets, Jesus Christ and his Apostles have made known—testifying, both to Jew and Gentile, repentance towards God and faith towards the Lord Jesus Christ.

The 18th of September, 1718, I married Miss Anna Woodbury from Ipswich, an only child whose parents were both dead, a young gentlewoman of comely personage and good fortune, but above all strictly virtuous and of admirable economy; who is yet living, though now crippled by paralytic or rheumatic disorders in her right leg. It has pleased God to deny children to us; and we are satisfied with the divine allotment, which is always wisest and best. . . .

11

A Virginia Minister

Devereux Jarratt was, like John Barnard, a clergyman. But there the
similarity ends. Jarratt was a Virginian, of extremely humble birth and
upbringing, and his ministry was Church of England, not Congregational. His autobiographical memoir, first set down in a series of letters
to a colleague and published toward the end of his life, is very nearly
unique among *non*-New England sources.

Jarratt's progress up the social scale was, if not unique, unusual for
his time. The steps and stages along the way were strikingly varied:
from parents to older brothers to local employers and patrons; from
farmhand to stable boy to carpenter's apprentice to schoolmaster and
(after many years) to minister.

But the memoir presents much more than its personal subject. Here,
indeed, is a cultural cross-section of eighteenth-century Virginia, with
"gentlefolk" and "plain" and several gradients in between. Jarratt shows
us, for example, the power of social deference, as experienced bottom-
side. And the importance of books and book learning (in a community
where any such was scarce). And the rudimentary state of organized
religion. And the amusements, the "sport," of country people.

As with the Barnard autobiography, we limit this selection to the
first half (or so) of life. In fact, Jarratt's later years spilled out of the
colonial era altogether—and thus lie beyond our present concerns.

The Life of the Reverend Devereux Jarratt,
Written by Himself: Excerpts

(1806 [1733])

. . . I was born in New Kent, a county in Virginia, about 25 miles below Richmond, on January 6th, 1732–3, O. S. [Old Style]. I was the youngest child of Robert Jarratt and Sarah his wife. My grandfather was an Englishman, born, I believe, in the city of London, in Devereux County, in Essex Street, which is so called from Robert Devereux, Earl of Essex. From this circumstance, perhaps, or from his being a soldier in the army of the Earl of Essex, he named his first son Robert, and his second son Devereux. He had only these two sons and one daughter, who was married to Walter Clopton of new Kent. But from whencesoever the name Devereux was derived, it is certain, as far as I have known or heard, [that] my uncle was the first who had that name in Virginia, or even in America, and it was confined to our family for 50 or 60 years. But after I became a minister of this parish (Bath) a number of people, out of respect to me, called one of their sons after my name.

My grandmother, as I was told, was a native of Ireland. Both she and my grandfather died before I was born, and I have had no account of them, except that they were poor people, but industrious, and rather rough in their manners. They acquired a pretty good tract of land, of near 1200 acres, but they had no slaves—probably they were prejudiced against that kind of property. The family of the Jarratts have been remarkably short-lived, and very few of the name are to be found now living.

My father was brought up to the trade of a carpenter, at which he wrought till the very day before he died. He was a mild, inoffensive man, and much respected among his neighbors. My mother was the daughter of Joseph Bradley, of Charles City, a county bordering on New Kent. None of my ancestors, on either side, were either rich or great, but had the character of honesty and industry, by which they lived in credit among their neighbors, free from real want, and above the frowns of the world. This was also the habit in which my parents were. They always had plenty of plain food and raiment, wholesome and good, suitable to their humble station, and the times in which they lived. Our food was altogether the produce of the farm or plantation, except a little sugar, which was rarely used; and our raiment was altogether my mother's

Devereux Jarratt, *The Life of the Reverend Devereux Jarratt, Written by Himself* (Baltimore, 1806), pp. 12–55.

manufacture, except our hats and shoes, the latter of which we never put on but in the winter season. We made no use of tea or coffee for breakfast or at any other time; nor did I know a single family that made any use of them. Meat, bread, and milk was the ordinary food of all my acquaintance. I suppose the richer sort might make use of those and other luxuries, but to such people I had no access. We were accustomed to look upon what were called *gentle folks* as being of a superior order. For my part, I was quite shy of them, and kept off at a humble distance. A periwig, in those days, was a distinguishing badge of gentle folk— and when I saw a man riding the road, near our house, with a wig on, it would so alarm my fears, and give me such a disagreeable feeling, that, I dare say, I would run off, as for my life. Such ideas of the difference between *gentle* and *simple* were, I believe, universal among all of my rank and age. . . .

My parents neither sought nor expected any titles, honors, or great things, either for themselves or [their] children. Their highest ambition was to teach their children to read, write, and understand the fundamental rules of arithmetic. I remember also they taught us short prayers, and made us very perfect in repeating the church catechism. They wished us all to be brought up in some honest calling, that we might earn our bread by the sweat of our brow, as they did. Two of their children died in infancy before I was born; and only four lived to years of maturity, three sons and a daughter. I was a great favorite, as being the youngest.

When I was between six and seven years of age I had the misfortune to lose my father, by a very sudden stroke. I remember, on the morning in which he died, I saw him go out of the house about his business as usual, and by nine o'clock I saw him expiring in his chamber. His sudden exit was attributed to his taking a dose of *tartar emetic* as he complained of being something unwell. The remembrance of this event has made me cautious of *tartar* all my days. I never knowingly took a grain of it; though I suspected that a physician once gave me some of it in disguise, but it almost put an end to me. It brought on the same symptoms of the cramps and cold sweat, which came on my father just before he expired—but I, being of a stronger constitution than he, survived the attack.

My father, dying so suddenly and unexpectedly, had made no will; the consequence was that my elder brother, Robert, heired all the landed estate. Of the perishable estate an equal division was made, and my part, as well as the rest, amounted to £25 current money of Virginia, which I was to receive at the age of twenty-one. . . .

Both my brothers were taught the trade of a carpenter and millwright, at which they wrought for the most part of their lives. They both died about the meridian of life. My sister is still living. But I shall say no more of my family—but proceed to those things which more particularly relate to myself.

At a very early period, as I have been told, I discovered a pregnancy of genius in some things not very common, and was frequently called *parson*; and some of my friends would sometimes say they thought I would be a parson. I can myself remember this, and can now recollect that the retentiveness of my memory was very extraordinary. Before I knew the letters of the alphabet I could repeat a whole chapter in the Bible, at a few times hearing it read, especially if the subject of it struck my fancy. The 16th chapter of *Judges*, and some other parts of the history of *Samson*, I soon learned to repeat; because I was so much taken with his strength, exploits, and vengeance on the Philistines for his two eyes. And the odiousness of Delilah's character, who so basely betrayed him into the hands of his enemies, made such an impression on my mind, as, I believe, contributed to that utter abhorrence, which I have had to that kind of vermin, all the days of my life.

I had indeed an aptitude in learning several things, but more especially those in which the memory was mostly concerned. I have never conversed with any person in my life whose memory seemed equal to mine. Nor did I ever know one who could repeat so many lines in an English or Latin poet as I could, in the same space of time. My voice was remarkably tuneable, and soft or sonorous as the case required on which it was exercised. So that as my memory enabled me to repeat the stanzas of the longest songs, I could sing them with an air and grace which excited attention and admiration. The number of songs I could repeat and sing when but a child might seem incredible to relate. The old song of *Chevy Chase*, which Mr. Addison has honored with a critic in the Spectator and considers as a work of merit and genius, I learned to repeat and sing by hearing it a few times only, though it contained near a hundred stanzas. The traces made on my brain by the chapters and songs I then learned to repeat have never been erased to the present moment. As what I have here said respecting my memory, etc. relate merely to gifts of nature, which I had no hand in acquiring, there can be no vanity in writing them down. But I cannot help regretting that I had no better subjects offered for a display of such talents than paltry songs, as most of those were which then took my attention.

At eight or nine years old I was sent to an English school in the neighborhood. And I continued to go to one teacher and another, as opportunity served (though not without great interruptions) till I was 12 or 13. In this time I learned to read in the Bible (though but indifferently) and to write a sorry scrawl, and acquired some knowledge of arithmetic. With this small fund I left school, and my mother dying about this time, no further care was bestowed on my education.

I now fell into the hands of my eldest brother. In his way he was exceeding kind to me. He allowed me in all the indulgences a depraved nature and an evil heart could desire. I mean, he was at no pains to correct my morals or restrain me from any of the vices of the times. I followed the way of my own heart, and walked in the sight of mine own eyes, not considering, as everyone ought, *that for all these things God would bring me into judgement.* While with my brother I was employed in three kinds of business: (1) in keeping and exercising race-horses for the turf; (2) in taking care of, and preparing gamecocks for a tach and main; (3) in ploughing, harrowing, and other plantation work. The first two were then agreeable enough—but the last, in which I was most constantly employed, was very irksome. Thus I continued till about 17 years of age, when I was allowed to quit the plough and to betake myself to the business of a carpenter with my second brother Joseph. But he was fractious, and often had recourse to hard words and severe blows. These I did not at all relish, but I continued to labor with him till the latter end of the year 1750, or 1751.

Before I proceed, I must take a little time to reflect on the danger of my situation at that period. During the five or six years I continued with my brothers I do not remember ever to have seen or heard anything of a religious nature, or that tended to turn my attention to the great concerns of eternity. I know not that I ever heard any serious conversation respecting God and Christ, Heaven and Hell. There was a church in the parish within three miles of me, and a great many people attended it every Sunday. But I went not once in a year. And if I had gone ever so often, I should not have been much the wiser, for the parish minister was but a poor preacher—very unapt to teach or even to gain the attention of an audience. Being very near-sighted, and preaching wholly by a written copy, he kept his eyes continually fixed on the paper, and so near, that what he said seemed rather addressed to the cushion than to the congregation. Except at a time when he might have a quarrel with anybody— then he would straighten up and speak lustily, that all might distinctly hear. I remember to have heard [that] he had once a quarrel with his clerk, and strove hard in vestry to turn the poor man out of his place, but failed in the attempt. The next Sunday he had prepared a scolding for him, and did vilify him stoutly right over his head. The clerk sat it out to the last, and as soon as the angry sermon ended he rose up, according to custom, to sing a psalm. He wished to return the parson like for like, but was not allowed, there, to say anything but [what] was contained within the lids of the Prayer-Book. However, to suit the discourse and pay the minister in kind, he gave out the 2nd psalm, and with an audible voice read the first stanza thus:

> With restless and ungoverned rage,
> Why do the heathen storm?
> Why in such rash attempts engage,
> As they can ne'er perform?

The parson saw what he was at, and ordered another psalm. This is no fiction. And [is] what is to be expected from such pastors.

In circumstances so unpromising it is not very wonderful that I remained ignorant of God and careless about religion. I only copied the example of my elders and superiors, and the example of such has great influence —especially a bad example. But so far were those who ought to have set me a good example, and restrained me from the company, the conversation, and the practice of the ungodly, from doings that by precept and example I was directly led into all these, and encouraged therein. Cards, racing, dancing, etc., which are still the favorite sport and diversion of the wicked and ungodly, were then much in vogue. In these I partook as far as my time and circumstances would permit, as well on Sundays as any other day. In these I vainly sought my felicity, but never found [it].

The blessed author of my being, who made me for himself, and ordained that I should seek happiness in him, was forgotten—though, blessed be his goodness, he did not even then leave me without a witness, and I was less free from inward than outward restraint. Conscience would check, and I had at times awful forebodings of a judgement to come. The thoughts of death were terrible, and every threatening dispensation gave great alarm. I was sensible [that] I was not so good as I ought to be, and wished at such seasons that I were good. But what real goodness was, or how to attain unto it, I knew not, and therefore came to no settled purpose of going in pursuit of it, but dismissed such uneasy sensations as soon as I could. I so totally neglected the means of religion that, during those years, I do not remember I ever retired for private prayer, or in reality prayed at all.

I was not contented with the small degree of learning I had acquired, and wished for more knowledge, especially in figures. My friends and acquaintances, I dare say, thought me a topping scholar—but I knew better. I had not gone far in arithmetic, and was very superficial in the rules I had been hurried through. To understand figures well we reckoned the height of learning. Philosophy, rhetoric, logic, etc. we never heard of. There were no books on such subjects among us. Arithmetic was all and all. To acquire this I borrowed a plain book in manuscript, and while the horse, with which I harrowed or ploughed, was grazing an hour or two at noon, I frequently spent the time in application to that book. And being now of an age for better discovering the nature of things, I made a greater progress in the real knowledge and use of figures in one month than I had done in years while at school. But I had no thought then of commencing [as] a teacher, yet, while at the plough or axe, I seemed out of my element. Neither of these, as time evinced, was the business for which I was designed, and to which providence gradually opened and prepared the way.

One of the most remote means, as I consider it, which led me to that station which I now fill was my being called from the axe to the quill. This took place in the nineteenth year of my age, when I was thinking of nothing less. I was so well skilled in the *division of crops*, the *rule of three*, and *practice* that, you may be sure, the fame of my learning sounded far. One Jacob Moon, living in Albemarle County about one hundred miles from New Kent, had also heard how learned I was. He, being a native of New Kent and perhaps prejudiced in favor of his old country folk, sent me word that he should be glad to employ me as a schoolmaster, and supposed I might get as many pupils in his neighborhood as would make it worth my while to set up a school. I readily embraced the proposal, and soon packed up my all, which consisted in things as made no great baggage, for I think I carried the whole on my back except one shirt. In this plight I took my departure from the place of my nativity. My whole dress and apparel consisted in a pair of coarse breeches, one or two oznaburg shirts, a pair of shoes and stockings, an old felt hat, a bearskin coat, which, by the by, was the first coat I ever had made for me since my childhood. And that I might appear something more than common in a strange place, and be counted somebody, I got me an old wig which, perhaps being cast off by the master, had become the property of his slave, and from the slave it was conveyed to me. But people were not obliged, you know, to ask how I came by it, and, I suppose, I was wise enough not to tell them. I had not, however, a farthing of money, and, I believe, I had never owned five shillings cash in all my life. I had neither horse nor saddle, but my brother lent me both, which I was to return in a month or two. On the second or third day after I set out I arrived at Moon's place of residence. Moon was then an overseer for Col. Richard Cocke of Surrey County. We soon entered on the business of raising a school. But I quickly discovered the number of pupils would be far short of what I had been made to expect. The prospect was gloomy and forbidding at that time, nor did it brighten much for some years, yet I have reason to adore the providence of God that brought me here.

I opened my little school, though the promised income, as might be foreseen, would scarce afford me clothing of the coarsest sort. However, I was content with a little, which I could call my own. I behaved so well in my new station that I gained the confidence of Moon so far that he trusted me with as much checks as made me two new shirts. This was something better than I had been used to before. I considered myself well off, as I never looked for or expected greater matters. But on my way to New Kent, where I was obliged to go to return my brother's horse and saddle at the time appointed, I had the sad misfortune to lose one of my new shirts, which I never recovered again. The place of which I was obliged to supply with one made of very rough oznaburg, as I would not extravagantly impose on the kindness and generosity of my landlord Moon, by asking credit for another check shirt. I was contented and cheerful from day to day.

With respect to religious advantages my situation was not at all mended, but rather worse. Moon's family, in which I lived, were just as ignorant of religion as I was, and as careless about it. And as Albemarle was then nearly a frontier county, the manners of the people were generally more rough and uncivilized than in the more interior parts of the country. In the interior counties there were churches and ministers to perform divine service every Sunday. But in Albemarle there was no minister of any persuasion, or any public worship, within many miles. The Sabbath day was usually spent in sporting, and whether this was right or wrong, I believe no one questioned.

Sometime in the course of that year Mr. Whitefield's eight sermons, preached in Glasgow, were left by someone at Moon's. This being the first sermon book I ever had seen, or perhaps heard of, I had the curiosity to look into it. I was but a poor reader and understood little of what I did read. And what I did understand in those sermons had no effect—

supposing I had no concern in the contents, as the author, I was told, was a New Light, and consequently what he said was nothing to Churchmen. I wish such ignorance had been peculiar to myself. But it is a reigning evil, of very extensive influence, and is very pernicious to mankind. It would be well if people would examine not who wrote, but whether what is said or written be agreeable to the word of God and the standard of truth.

My constitution had been always strong, and I had seldom known what sickness was. But, living now on the banks of James River and between two bold creeks (called Bremo) which ran into the river above and below the house, I was violently attacked with a quotidian ague, which in a little while changed to a tertian, and at last terminated in a quartan, which followed me eight or nine months. In the paroxisms I frequently wept at the thought of my being in a land of strangers at a great distance from the place of my nativity and my nearest relations. But of God, and my estrangement and distance from him, of the salvation of my soul and a future state, I had little or no concern. Such a degree of blindness and insensibility had fallen upon me.

When my year expired at Moon's, my ague still continuing, I thought it advisable to move my quarters and get a school at another place. I did so. Here again my expectation failed me, as my second school was less profitable than the first. The first brought me in £9, the second £7. I boarded altogether with Moon the first year, but now my quarters were more unsettled: I was to board among my employers, proportioning the time to the number of the children they sent. I first took up at the house of one Abraham Childers. Here I wished to pitch my tent for the whole year, as I found the manners of that family very much to the taste of my depraved mind. I always had a great turn for merriment, banter, buffoonery, and such like. The members of the family had the same turn; consequently we met the approbation of each other. As my ambition was always to excel in everything I had a mind to, so I strove to excel in these and every other species of levity and folly. And I did excel so much that, whether from envy or something else, I sometimes met with a check or kind of reproof, even from the members of that ungodly family. In the time of my residence here I met with considerable hardships which, together with the quartan ague which regularly continued its periodical attacks, were enough, one would think, to have cowed any spirits less audacious than mine. But all had no effect on me; I continued thoughtless of my Maker and the interests of my soul.

111

Having finished the quota of time I had to stay in this family, my quarters were to be moved. I did move, but with great reluctance. However, in the issue this movement proved a peculiar blessing to me.

I went now to board with a gentleman whose name was Cannon. He was a man of great possessions, in land, slaves, etc. As I had been always very shy of gentlefolk, and had never been accustomed to the company and conversation of the rich, you may imagine how awkwardly and with what confusion I entered his house. There was another very fearful circumstance, which added to my perplexity; for I had been told that the lady of the house was a New Light, and of sentiments so rigid and severe that all levities of every kind must be banished from her presence, and every species of ungodliness must expect a sharp reproof from her. I was put upon some serious reflections and considerations, how to demean myself in her presence so as to give no cause for reproof, and also induce the pious matron to think I was not destitute of religion. This put me upon a project entirely new to me—I mean, to act the hypocrite. I had no intention of being religious, but wished to appear so, in order to gain her good opinion. Oh, how thoughtless—how inconsiderate—how foolish is man! While restraining myself, that I might appear fair in the eyes of a worm like myself, I considered not that I was at all times exposed to the view of that Holy Being to whom I must render an account for all my words and actions.

It was on a Sunday P.M. when I first came to the house—an entire stranger both to the gentleman and his lady. Though they had sent their niece and daughter to me for about three months, yet I had no personal acquaintance with them, as the school had been made up without my presence. The interview, on my part, was the more awkward as I knew not how to introduce myself to strangers, and what style was proper for accosting persons of their dignity. However, I made bold to enter the door, and was viewed in some measure as a phenomenon. The gentleman took me (if I rightly remember) for the son of a very poor man in the neighborhood, but the lady, having some hint, I suppose, from the children, rectified the mistake, and cried out, *it is the school-master.*

I found her reading a religious book, and the gravity of her appearance gave me an unusual feeling, which perhaps might increase the disadvantage under which I appeared. I felt miserable, and said little, the whole evening. I was truly out of my element, and was glad, when the morning arose, to get off to my little school, that I might once more be [out] from under the eye of restraint.

The custom of this lady was, as I soon discovered, to read a sermon in *Flavel* every night—to which she wished me to attend. I had, indeed, little relish for such entertainment, yet, agreeable to my purpose of playing the hypocrite and gaining a favorable opinion, I affected a very close attention. And that I might excel in this art and more effectually answer my purpose, I would sometimes after a long discourse was finished (Flavel's sermons being all lengthy) ask her to read another—though probably I understood not the tenth part of what was read. Flavel's sermons are too experimental and evangelical for one so ignorant of divine things as I was to comprehend. When she was weary of reading, she would ask me to read in my turn. But so poor a hand did I make of the business that reader and hearer were rather abashed than edified. Yet I could not decently refuse. She soon desisted asking me to read, and took the whole task on herself. This custom continued for six or eight weeks, without any other effect on me but fatigue and drowsiness, which I supported with much fortitude and self-denial, rather than give the least reason for suspicion that I could be weary of good things. I should, no doubt, have eloped some evenings and passed the evening at my former stand, but as I was to carry the two little girls to school every day on horseback, one behind and the other before me, I was obliged to stand to my charge.

But it pleased God, on a certain night while she was reading as usual, to draw out my attention and fix it on the subject in a manner unknown to me before. The text of the sermon was, "Then opened he their under-standing;" from which words were pointed out what new discoveries would open to the eye of the mind by means of spiritual illumination etc. The subject was naturally as dark to me as any of the former, and yet I felt myself impressed with it, and saw my personal interest in the solemn truths—and truths I believed them to be. But at the same time I was conscious that I was a stranger to that spiritual illumination and its conse-quent discoveries, and of course was yet in a dark and dangerous state. I must have known before this that I was a sinner, and all things were not right with me, but nothing ever came home to my heart so as to make a lasting impression till now. The impression followed me to bed —arose with me in the morning—and haunted me from place to place, till I resolved to forsake my sins and try to save my soul. But my resolution was made in my own strength, for I had not yet learned how weak and frail we are by nature, and that all our suffering is of God.

It may be worthy of remark that my distress then did not arise from a painful sense of any particular sin or sins in general, but from a full persuasion that I was a stranger to God and true religion, and was not prepared for death and judgement. The alteration in my conduct effected by these impressions on my mind soon became visible to my benefactress, which was matter of great joy. And as she was the first I had ever known to be truly and experimentally acquainted with *vital religion*, and I was the first she had ever seen in her family who was desirous to be acquainted with the same, she was not willing I should go away till the year was ended to board anywhere else. Accordingly I spent the rest of the year there.

My religious concern continued during my abode here, but not at all times alike. I went altogether on a legal, self-sufficient plan; I asked mercy of God, but not for grace to help in time of need. The consequence was that the best resolutions I made were too weak to bear the shock of temptation, and I was too often carried into such extravagancies from the right, that all my hopes were slain, and I had all my religion to begin afresh. I strove against sin and folly, but got no ground, because I strove in my own strength. Sometimes I seemed to stand fast for a few days—and then be overtaken in a fault, which would throw me back again. I remember once, being in bad company, I acted so contrary to my resolutions that, on reflection, I ran and leaped, tore my hair and cried out, like one distracted. The power of sin and [my] natural inclination to indulge myself as formerly were so strong, and would make such violent struggles for gratification, that at times I was ready to give up the contest and all further efforts in religion. But this thought would immediately occure—*Damnation will be the consequence*. This I could not bear, and therefore still resolved to strive, rather than *burn in hell to all eternity*.

I had never heard the gospel preached in all my life, nor had I an opportunity of hearing it. All the external helps I had were my landlady and Flavel's sermons. These sermons were explicit enough in pointing out the lost and helpless state of man—the necessity of divine aid, and of a better righteousness than I could furnish—yet I could not readily comprehend this, nor easily correct that legal bias which is so natural to all men. I had no conception of being justified by the righteousness of Christ, or any other righteousness but my own. On these accounts my religion continued in a state of fluctuation for a great while. I had religion enough to make me frequently uneasy, but never to make me happy. Sinning and repenting, repenting and sinning, was the round in which I went for many months. Yet it was apparent that there was a change in my life for the better.

This was the state in which I was at the conclusion of that year— when necessity obliged me to change my place of abode. I mentioned above that my school here was small, and the income about £7, and

I found it would be still less should I continue another year. So I looked out for a school somewhere else. Moon wished to employ me again, and I went there, with the prospect of having a greater number of pupils than before. I now got a school of twelve or thirteen scholars, at twenty shillings per scholar, which was the usual price in those days. I again boarded with Moon all that year.

Remembering how blind, careless, and insensible Moon and the rest of the family were respecting religion when I lived there before, and seeing no alteration for the better, I was concerned for their souls and did what I could to make them sensible of the danger they were in. But they made light if it—turned all off with a laugh—imputing the whole to *New Light cant*, which they supposed I had catched from Mrs. Cannon, the lady of whom I have spoken. Moon and his wife, being Church people as they said, could listen to nothing but what came through that channel. But in truth, they knew no more of the principles of the Church of England than of any other, and this case is not peculiar to them but is very common in the world.

I was myself at that time but little acquainted with the principles of the church. Nor did I understand the meaning of many scriptures which I read, but I understood enough to know that except we repent we must perish—and except a man be born again, he cannot see the kingdom of God. These truths I insisted on in the family, and especially the necessity of being born again. This they did not deny. "We must all be born again," said they, "but that is to be after we are dead."

I wished to be better acquainted with the meaning of the scriptures. I wanted some instructor. I had not a single book in the world, nor was I able to buy any books, had I known of any for sale. But by some means I got hold of a little old book, in a smoky condition, which I found to be Russel's seven sermons. I borrowed the book, and read the sermons again and again. This book was of much service to me, and I remember I was deeply impressed with the account of Francis Spira, which is given in one of the sermons. But I still wanted help in understanding the scriptures. I had never heard of any expositor, nor did I know there was any such in the universe; yet I thought it necessary there should be a book of that sort. Mentioning, perhaps, my desire of an expositor to some person, I was told of a very large book belonging to a gentleman, about five or six miles distant across the river, which explained all the New Testament. I resolved to get the reading of that book, if possible. By my living so long with Mr. Cannon, and the resort of gentlemen to his house, I had worn off some of my clownish rusticity, and had become less shy of persons in the upper ranks of life. I therefore determined on a visit to the gentleman who owned the book, and in a short time went to his house. Here I found no less a treasure than that most excellent exposition *Burkett on the New Testament*. I asked the loan of it, which was readily granted. And, taking up the folio in my arms, I brought home the prize. I was wonderfully pleased with the book, not only for the light and instruction I gained by it, but also because I found the writer to have been a minister of the church—hoping this circumstance would gain the attention of the family to such parts as I should wish them to hear me read. But it was not so. As I had no candle, my custom was in an evening to sit down flat on the hearth, erect the volume on the end of a chest which stood near, and by the light of the fire read till near midnight. It pleased God mightily to improve my understanding by these means—and I soon became what was called a good reader, and my relish for books and reading greatly increased.

I acquired considerable views of the nature and plan of salvation through Jesus Christ, but I did not yet think I had attained a living faith in his blood. For some time I had withdrawn myself from the company of the wicked, had quitted dancing, racing, cards, etc., and in the course of the year had twice or thrice heard the gospel preached in a lively manner by a Presbyterian, which much affected me. By such helps I was kept pretty steady in my religious pursuits for eight or nine months of that year. But before the close I met with a dreadful rebuff. This circumstance I will simply relate.

My annual income, as already said, had been very small, yet by frugality I had saved enough to procure me a small pony and a saddle. I began also to get some credit in a store, and having [the] prospect of getting £13 at the end of that year, ventured to go in debt for a tolerable suit of clothes; my linen, on Sundays, was finer than formerly, and I began no doubt to be a little too vain and to think more highly of myself than I ought. Thus furnished, I determined on a visit to my friends in New Kent. My brothers, whom I dearly loved, still lived there—whom I had not seen for a long time—and I believe I was equally beloved by them.

I made the visit and was received with the utmost cordiality. My brothers and their wives, and all the black people on the plantation, seemed overjoyed at my coming. The pleasure of seeing each other was mutual, and our congratulations are not easily described. Nothing was thought too good for me which their houses afforded, and they wished to entertain me in the most agreeable manner. It was in the season of autumn, when the cellars in that quarter were generally stored with good sound cider.

These were set open with great liberality. But by the by this was no great temptation, as you know, I am not very fond of spiritous liquors. But they knew I had been very fond of company and merriment, and wished to entertain me with frolic and dance. This proposal I rejected, and told them my reason for so doing. This was a disappointment they did not expect, and they soon discovered there was a great alteration in me, and that my mind was turned to religion. This, I suppose, might put some damp on their spirits, though they allowed that all people ought to be better than they were—but they thought I had overshot the mark, and carried matters quite too far. "We all ought to be good," say they, "but sure[ly] there can be no harm in innocent mirth, such as dancing, drinking, and making merry, etc." I doubt not but I told them the views I had of such things, and also what I had discovered of my own guilt and danger, and what my determinations were. I talked to them, as well as I knew how, for their profit—but to no good effect. I visited other relations also, and discoursed with them on religious concerns. In a word I stood fast about five days. But through the influence of my brethren and their strategems to take me in, I was insensibly—and at unawares —drawn from my integrity in the course of one week.

Being one day on a visit to my uncle Clopton, I was to return to my brother's that evening. I did so. But in my absence he had contrived to gather a considerable company of people, of different sexes and ages, for the purpose of drinking cider and dancing, as liked them best. I was surprised, when I rode up, to see such numbers both within and without doors. Without, the tankard went briskly round, while the sound of music and dancing was heard within. I was strongly solicited to join the company within—but I held back for some time. But too soon I found the Apostle's words realized—*evil communications corrupt good manners*—for here was I drawn in once more to join those vanities and follies which I thought I had forever abandoned. At first I joined with reluctance—but I soon found myself shorn of all my strength, and, like Samson, was become weak *like another man.* And here I was tempted to fix my staff, and take up my rest. I thought it vain for me to attempt a religious life anymore (at least as yet) and therefore I might as well give a loose to my passions, and get what little happiness I could in sports and sensual gratifications. From this night I had no more to say about religion—my mouth was shut up on that subject.

For two or three months from that time I had but little relish for anything of a religious nature, though I was not without some severe twinges of conscience which I bore without much flinching. I endeavored to be as airy as I could, and as I possessed a great degree of vivacity and was extremely jocose, my company was very acceptable to the ungodly and courted by persons much my superior in family and fortune. This must have been very flattering to my vanity, and tickling to a depraved heart. It was a wonderful mercy indeed that I had not, like many others in like circumstances, been carried down the stream and abandoned religion forever. But, blessed be the Lord, it was not many months before *the snare was broken, and I was delivered.*

From the time I returned from my visit to New Kent I still boarded with Moon. But from some circumstances I determined to stay there no longer than till I should finish the year. This determination being made known, Mr. Cannon invited me to return to him to teach his little son, who by this time was old enough to be put to school. I gladly accepted the invitation, and again took up residence at his house, where I continued for some years at the rate of £15 per annum standing wages.

On my return to this family, I found my benefactress as much engaged in religion as before; and her conversation and example soon revived in me former desires and resolutions. About this time also a Presbyterian minister had obtained a settlement in the county of Cumberland, contiguous to Albermarle, and preached once in four weeks within four miles of my lodgings. This afforded me better helps for religious improvement than ever I had before. Nor did I neglect them. I constantly attended all the sermons, and frequently had the pleasure of the minister's company and conversation at our house, and also at other houses in the settlement. He was not, indeed, the best of men, nor was he a good preacher— yet I gained considerable advantages by him, as by his means I was brought to an acquaintance with a number of very excellent books written by men of the greatest eminence for learning and piety, such as Baxter, Watts, Dodderidge, Young, etc. These I read with pleasure and profit. The preaching of the gospel had also some good effects on several in the neighborhood, and increased the number of religious friends, which I consider as another advantage to me. With these I frequently conversed, to our mutual edification. And as I neglected none of the public ordinances of religion and means of grace, and my moral character was irreproachable, I was received and held as a Christian by all the professing people in the different counties where I was known. I believe, indeed, I had true religion then, as far as it went—but was subject to continual doubts, whether to draw the happy conclusion in my favor or not. At times I felt comfortable—but soon sunk in doubts and fears. The stake was of great value, and we can never make too sure of the prize—but a too hasty conclusion, or a decision not well founded, might be attended with fatal consequences. Such considerations prevent many pious souls from drawing a conclusion hastily for fear of a deception in so weighty a case.

While in this state of suspense I was assaulted with very uncommon trials; and a perplexing thought followed me, that my case was singular, and that no man in the world had such trials, oppositions, and enemies to contend with as I had. No book I read, no sermon I heard, seemed to touch my perplexing case, which might with some show of reason confirm me in the singularity of it, and cause me to fear there was no promise applicable to it. This state of trial, sorrow, trouble, and perplexity continued long and painful—perhaps for twelve months. But still I was naturally so vivacious, and had such command on my countenance, [that] hardly anyone suspected otherwise but that I was happy all this while. I never spake to any man respecting it, except the minister, and then but partially. He told me he had been in the same situation, which afforded me some relief for the present, but it lasted not long. The Lord relieved me at last—I well remember the time and place—when and where I was sitting, with a good book in my hand. In this I read a great many discouraging cases described by the author, with the promises adapted to such cases. I paid great attention to every case and promise—and, perhaps, [was] not without hope that God would be my friend. But not finding my case, I was still thinking it nameless and altogether singular, and consequently there could be no promise in the Bible suitable to it. At last I cast my eye on *Isaiah* 62:12: *Thou shalt be called, sought out, a city not forsaken*. These words appeared very applicable to a nameless case, and I was enabled to apply them as such to the great comfort of my soul. I saw and believed that though my case were nameless and hid from all the men upon earth, yet God knew it and would search me out for good, and not forsake me, or give me over into the hand of the enemy. I was blessed with faith to believe, not one promise only, but all the promises of the gospel with joy unspeakable and full of glory —I saw such a fullness in Christ, to save to the uttermost, that, had I ten thousand souls as wretched and guilty as mine was, I could venture all on his blood and righteousness without one doubt or fear. The comforts I then felt were beyond expression and [were] far superior to anything I had ever known before that memorable hour. . . .

Not that I suppose I never had true religion before this—I believe I had real religion, or I could not have gone through so many trials— but such a bright manifestation of the redeemer's all-sufficiency and willingness to save, and such a divine confidence to rely on him, I never had till that moment. It was a little heaven upon earth, so sweet, so ravishing, so delightful. I uttered not a word, but silently rejoiced in God my Savior.

For some time before this period I began to exercise my talents for the good of souls. I had acquired a considerable knowledge of Divinity and some gift in *extempore* preaching—and in reading with readiness and propriety I had much improved. I was thought to read any book well, but especially books of sermons and treatises on religious subjects. I acquired the gift of *extempore* prayer, by officiating as chaplain in Mr. Cannon's family, from the first time family prayer was set up in it, which was shortly after my becoming a member of it the second time.

The way in which I exercised my talents was by appointing meetings every Sunday when the minister was not to preach in the neighborhood. In these meetings I used to make prayer, sing Watts's hymns and psalms, and read some lively and practical discourse. Considerable congregations used to attend those meetings; solemn attention was paid—impressions were frequently made on the hearers, and I hope some good was done. I never pretended to preach, but only read a printed sermon, with the addition sometimes of a few words, either to point or explain a sentence. But at the same time I took care to interweave the additional words so naturally with the rest that the whole might appear to be read in the book. I had no conception of any man's presuming to preach the gospel before he had gone through an introductory course of necessary education —nor then, unless he were duly ordained to the ministerial office, by those who have authority to ordain. None thought of preaching without these qualifications and credentials. . . .

Having continued this exercise for some time, several of my friends wished me to turn my attention toward the ministry, suggesting I had talents suitable for such an office, and that I might be of more service by devoting myself entirely to the preaching of the gospel. But I looked upon the idea as fanciful, and paid little regard to suggestions of that sort. Not that I was averse to the office—but how it was possible I could be qualified, so as to be admitted to it, I had no conception. I was wholly among the Presbyterians—had received all my knowledge of religion from them, and was peculiarly attached to them and their church, and had no notion then of being a minister or member of any other. I had never examined the principles of the Church of England, and by what I knew of the lives and preaching of the clergy I had imbibed strong prejudices against that church. I knew also that the Presbyterians required the knowledge of Latin, Greek, etc. in all who took part with them in the ministry.

This obstacle appeared insuperable, as I was totally ignorant of these languages and without the means of acquiring the knowledge of them.

I had by the time taught school five or six years, and was under such a character as a teacher that, I suppose, I could have got business anywhere. Having stayed with Mr. Cannon as long as convenient, I went into Cumberland and set up a school at Mr. Thomas Tabb's, a gentleman who had lately joined the Presbyterians. I boarded in his house, performed the office of a chaplain in the family morning and evening, and still kept up the custom of meeting on Sundays, either at my school-house or other private houses. Here I was living when N. Davies, a gentleman of Cumberland, solicited and obtained a young man from the college of New Jersey to come to his house to instruct his son in the Latin, etc. This young man's name was Alexander Martin. . . . I was now more than ever pressed on by my friends to turn my attention to the ministry; and for this purpose they advised me to put myself under the tuition of Mr. Martin. I was still without money—for, of late, I had laid out what money I could spare in buying books, and a very good collection of Divinity, Poetry, etc. I had got. The want of money was the only obstacle in the way, but the hand of providence interposed and removed it. Mr. John Cannon, with whom I had lived, and Captain John Hunter, uncle to Mr. Martin, kindly offered me such assistance as should enable me to go through my studies. This they did unsolicited and *gratis*. Such a generous proposal I could not reject, and in a little while [I] entered Mr. Martin's school as his pupil—being then about twenty-five years and four months old, or thereabouts.

I had never seen the rudiments of the Latin tongue in all my life, nor had I learned a word in any grammar whatever. But such was the strength of my memory then that in eight days I could so perfectly repeat every part of the grammar that I began to construe, give the parts of speech, rules, etc. In seven months I began to read Suetonius, one of the most difficult Latin authors in prose. In a word I acquired such knowledge of the Latin and Greek in that year that my generous friends were released from their burden, as I was capable of improving myself and teaching others also.

In the following year Mr. Martin returned to the Jersies, and I took the school upon myself, and continued with Mr. N. Davis as tutor of his son for a year and a half. I was next employed by Mr. Thompson Swann to teach his children and some others, for which he agreed to give me forty pounds a year and my board at his house. I continued with him one year; at this place I once more, to my sorrow, experienced the baneful effects of trifling and ungodly company. Mr. Swann's house was a place of good resort. Scarce a week in the year passed without a company for cards, dancing, etc. The same was the case, more or less, with all the wealthy families in the neighborhood. It was therefore all but impossible for me to avoid being with such company in the situation I was, and sure enough it had a very undue effect on my mind. I thank God I never gave way then to any overt acts of sin—but I found the company had a very cooling influence on religion, and greatly abated my zeal and the fervors of devotion, rendered me vain and trifling in my life and conversation, and—I fear—would have carried me quite away, had I continued longer in that place. . . .

It was in the spring, 1762, when I quit my school, and began to prepare for an immediate entrance into Holy Orders. . . .

12

A Connecticut Farmer

Biography and (as in the preceding cases) autobiography reflect the shape of entire lives. But they cannot show the pace of events from season to season or day to day. For that, we must turn to personal diaries.

In fact, the still extant diaries from early America are few in number and biased in provenance; most come from the "elite" group (ministers, magistrates, leading merchants, and planters). The diary of Thomas Minor is, however, a rare and valuable exception. Minor lived almost his entire life in the town of Stonington, Connecticut. He was a land-owner, a farmer, a husband, a father, and something of a civic leader. All aspects are represented in the diary he kept over a period of more than thirty years.

His individual diary entries are admittedly brief—and extremely spar-ing as to detail. But they do add up. For example, they help us to trace the specific rhythms of life in a premodern, rural community: the bursts of activity around spring planting and autumn harvesting, and the relatively slack periods of winter and midsummer. They afford, too, recurrent glimpses of village-level sociability, of local governance, of household economy, and even of the mentality that framed all such expe-rience.

The selection presented here comprises one full year of diary entries, those for 1672. It follows the older, Julian calendar (in wide use until the mid-eighteenth century); thus March is "the first month," and Febru-ary the last.

The Diary of Thomas Minor, Stonington, Connecticut:
Excerpt
(1672)

An almanac for the year of our Lord 1672; from the Creation, 5621; and the first year after the leap year; and the 24th of the reign of our Lord King Charles the Second.

March is the first month, and hath 31 days. Friday [is] the first. Thursday the 7th, we made the country rate, and mended the cart bridge. Mr. Noyes was here, and Joseph, his wife, and children. Friday the 8th, my wife took physic [i.e., medicine]. Tuesday the 12th, goodman Dart was here. Wednesday the 13th, the meeting was at Moses Palmer's. Thursday the 14th, I showed John Lewis his lot. Friday the 15th, a meeting at Mr. Richardson's about the meeting house. The 18th day of this month, we ran the line from Weakapoug to Mystic. Friday [the] 22nd, I began to sow wheat. The 25th, I sowed wheat. Friday the 29th. Sabbath day the 31st, Mr. Noyes taught out of the 12th chapter of the [Book of] Revelations and the 9th verse.

The second month is April, and hath 30 days. Monday the 1st, we made the hedge at the water side. Tuesday the 2nd, I was at Mr. Stanton's about his Indian Jean. Wednesday the 3rd, the meeting was at our house. Monday the 8th. Tuesday the 9th, I was with Deacon Park. Captain Denison did bring hither five pounds of flax. The 10th day, Deacon Park and we were at Quaquataug. The 11th day, Mr. Noyes and Deacon Park and the company was here. I agreed with Mr. Noyes and Thomas Park. The 15th day, Monday, we met at Mr. Richardson's. Ralph Park came in. The 17th day, I was at New London. Monday the 22nd, we were at Mr. Richardson's. Wednesday, we met at Mr. Samuel Cheesborough's, being [the] 24th. Thursday [the] 25th, there was a training [at?] Misstucksuck. Tuesday the 30th, we chose deputies. Clement and Mannasah's wives were here the same day. Mannasah's bay mare came home again.

The third month is May, and hath 31 days. Wednesday [was] the first. Sabbath day the 5th, there was a sacrament at New London. Monday and Tuesday, I and my wife was at the farm. And Wednesday the 8th, we covered the cellar. And Wednesday the 15th the church at New London met. Nathaniel Cheeseborough was ill. The 16th day, the cattle was

Sidney H. Miner and George D. Stanton, Jr., eds., *The Diary of Thomas Minor, Stonington, Connecticut* (New London, Conn., 1899), pp. 108–115.

to go to the farm. Tuesday the 21st, the doctor let Nathaniel Cheeseborough's blood. Mr. Parker had the oats aboard, 40 bushels, to bring me
two barrels of molasses. Wednesday the 22nd, we made hedge upon the
wall. Wednesday the 29th, I and my three sons, Clement, Ephraim, and
Mannasah, was at Stratford. The 30th, a day of humiliation. Friday [the]
31st. 22 cattle at the farm [on] the 16th day of May. The first of June,
1672, coming from Stratford, I failed in taking a cup of cider too much,
to the grieving of my sons, Clement, Ephraim, and Mannasah.

The fourth month is June, and hath 30 days. Saturday [was] the first.
Tuesday the 4th, I came home. I had my horse shoed at Lam's. Saturday
the 8th, I was at [the] mill. Samuel fetched Munchapeg. The committee
met at New London [on] the 12th and 13th. I was at Poquanump [on]
the 15th. Saturday the 16th, the magistrates were here. The 17th, we
plowed in the plain. The 18th, we were at the farm. Mr. Noyes was
here. H. G. was married. Saturday the 22nd, cleaving pales. The 24th,
and midsummer day, I was at [the] mill, and at Mr. Richardson's, and
Joseph was here. The 26th and the 27th day, we fetched our mallaces
from Mr. Parker. We took up goods at Raymond's to the value of 11
02s 09p, and paid [for] a firkin of butter to Mr. Hill, one pound, 11
shillings. Saturday the 29th, I was at Rebecca's to greet Mr. Baldwin.
Sabbath day the 30th, Clement and Mary was here.

The fifth month is July, and hath 31 days. The first is Monday. The
2nd day, the committee met with squmacut people. The 3rd day, I and
my wife was at the farm. The 5th day, we were at Ephraim's house [with?]
the whole town. Monday the 8th, I was at New London. The 10th day,
my wife and I was with Mr. Stanton. The 12th day, I was at the farm.
The 14th day, the sacrament was. The 15th day, Monday, we put the
wheels to the cart that Clement made us. The 18th day, Friday, Hannah
Steerie was delivered. The 20th, we reaped our rye. The 22nd, we were
cutting off oats, and fetching in the summer wheat and peas. Monday
the 29th, we cut winter wheat. Wednesday [the] 31st, we made an end
of reaping.

The sixth month is August, and hath 31 days. Thursday [was] the
first. Saturday the third I had all the English corn with into [sic] house.
Clement and Mannasah went home. Monday the 5th, I fetched home
the meat. Abraham began to mow. My wife was at New London. There
was a court at Mr. Stanton's. The 7th day, Wednesday, Elizabeth Witter
was buried. We were at plowing of the plain. I and my wife was at Edmund
Fanning's. Thursday the 8th, I was a-threshing wheat. The 12th day was
the eclipse. We had our oxen to the farm. The 14th, my wife was at

Fanning's. We laid out 20 acres of land for the smith. The oxen came from the farm. Thursday the 15th, we made hay and fetched 2 loads of wood. Thursday the 20th, we were at Rebecca's house. Wednesday, we came to New London, to Mr. Bradstreet's. Thursday [the] 22nd, we came home. We had 2 pair of shoes. The butter weighed 73 [pounds?]. Thursday [the] 29th, we had 17 loads of hay home. Samuel plowed the first acre for wheat. I was lame. Saturday [the] 31st. The 29th [of] August I sowed wheat.

The seventh month is September, and hath 30 days. Sabbath day [was] the first. The 2nd day, I fetched the calves from the farm. The 6th day, I made an end of sowing wheat. The 5th day, I rode about Mr. Noyes, his rate. Sabbath day [the] 8th. Monday [the] 9th, we had the hay by the creek stacked. We were about Sam Colver and Martha Fish. [The] 10th, 11th, and 12th, we were upon the same account. We sent Samuel Colver to jail. We traced [?] the Indian corn, and made one barrel of cider. The 19th day is Thursday. I came from the court.

The 7th of October, 1672, Ann Mason was married.

Cary Latham's account for the year 1672, 24th October.

The 30th of October, 1672, Mr. Stanton said he had married Thomas Brand.

The eighth month is October, and hath 31 days. Tuesday [was] the first. The 2nd day, I was at Mr. Stanton's about Indian business. That night goodwife Burroughs died. The 3rd and 4th day, we mended the chimney. The 5th, I fetched shovels. I had a pair of horse shoes of John Denison, it being Saturday. The 8th day, I went to the court. The 19th day, I came home. The 31st, one day is appointed to be a day of Thanksgiving. The 29th and 30th days, I fetched pales. The 24th day, I reckoned with Cary. There was 3 [pounds?] due me. The 30th day, the carpenters fetched their tools with our canoe, and my wife was at New London.

The ninth month is November, and hath 30 days. Friday [was] the first. The 6th and 7th days, our sons killed their swine. Samuel was at Poquatuck. I was at the farm. The 8th day, the rams were brought from the island, it being Friday. The 9th day, Augustine was here with his boat and Steven Wilcox. My wife went in the boat to New London. Sam fetched home the canoe. The 10th day was the great tide. The 11th day, Monday, I fetched my wife from New London. The 14th day, I brought beans from the farm. The 15th day, Friday, I fetched 3 loads of wood. The 20th day, Samuel brought home the swine. [The] 21st, I was at New London. [The] 22nd, Friday, we fetched the cedar bolts. [The] 23rd, we drawed timber for the meeting house. Sabbath day [the]

24th, Mr. Noyes taught first, after he came from the Bay. Tuesday [the] 26th, Hannah was very ill in her face. Samuel went to Fleming's. Thursday the 28th day, we killed our swine. Francis Thorne was apprehended. Friday [the] 29th. Saturday the 30th day, my canoe was at Mr. Chester's vessel.

The tenth month is December, and hath 31 days. Sabbath day [was] the first. The 6th day, I was at New London. Sabbath day, the 8th, Monday the 9th, and the 10th, I was at New London. Lieutenant Samuel Mason sent two swine. Sabbath day the 15th [was] sacrament day. The 16th day, we brought Clement and William Minor to Tagwonk. The 17th day, Clement went home, and had a cow with him. The 18th day, I began to thresh wheat. The 28th day, I winnowed and had 17 bushels of winter wheat. The 26th day, we had a court at Mr. Stanton's. The 30th day, Monday, I was at [the] mill with 2 bushels of wheat and 2 of Indian corn. My wife went to New London. Tuesday the 31st. The 17th day, Lam had the steer.

The eleventh month is January, and hath 31 days. Wednesday [was] the first. And Wednesday the 8th, I made an end of threshing of winter wheat and rye. Thursday [the] 9th, Clement was here. Saturday the 11th, he went home. He had the two mares and the colt with him. Monday the 13th, we cleared the trees about the new meeting house. And Wednesday the 15th and the 16th days, we raised the meeting house. Tuesday [the] 21st, we winnowed oats, 38 bushels and a half. Robert Fleming mended the saddle. Wednesday [the] 22nd. Thursday [the] 23rd, we had a court at Samuel Cheeseborough's. The 24th was the great storm of rain. [The] 29th, Wednesday. Friday the 31st, I had four score bushels of oats and three.

The twelfth month is February, and hath 28 days. Saturday [was] the first. The 4th day, Tuesday, I was at New London. I had two pair of plain shoes of My. Royce. I owe him two shillings. Saturday the 8th, Samuel was at the farm. Thursday the 13th, we were at the new meeting house and appointed how many seats to make. Friday the 14th, we agreed with goodman Wheeler for 26 to make the seats, to cart and provide all about them but nails. Saturday the 15th, I fetched all the iron works from Lam. There was due to him 02 06s. 00d. And the steer paid for. Wednesday the 19th, I looked out and pitched upon a place for my fifty acres. Thursday the 20th, Clement and Martha was married by Mr. Witherell, Commissioner. Saturday [the] 22nd. And Friday the 28th.

Part Three
Family and Household

13

The Physical Setting

It is important in assessing the culture of the settlers to form some picture of the material basis of their lives. What were the familiar objects of their everyday experience? What items were necessary to insure their continued health and prosperity?

One way to answer such questions is to examine the estate inventories drawn up following the death of property owners. These were, of course, important legal documents—details of inheritance depended on them—and the executors in charge took great care to see that everything of value was included. John Smith, whose inventory is printed here, was a miller and very much an average citizen of Providence, Rhode Island. The executors listed his properties according to location ("chamber," "lower room," "mill")—a method that permits us to reconstruct the disposition of objects within the household.

William Fitzhugh of Stafford County, Virginia, was a planter of considerable local importance, and he maintained an ample, even elaborate household. We are fortunate to have a full description of his estate, in Fitzhugh's own hand. In 1686 he conceived a plan to resettle himself in England. He asked his brother-in-law, Dr. Ralph Smith, then residing in Bristol, to try to arrange a swap: Fitzhugh's Virginia plantation for an English town house or landed estate of equivalent value. In this connection he wrote out a detailed account of all his property. There is no record that such an exchange was ever worked out, and Fitzhugh certainly continued to live in Virginia for the rest of his life.

This unit concludes with a series of photographs of period furnishings, utensils, and tools.

An Inventory of the Estate of John Smith, Miller of This Town of Providence, Deceased

(1682)

Item		lb	s	d
It.	A small three year old steer	2	0	0
It.	A two year old heifer	1	0	0
It.	A three year old heifer	2	0	0
It.	A year old bull very small of growth	0	15	0
It.	A small two year old bull	1	1	0
It.	An old mare and a two year old horse	2	10	0
It.	A year old horse	0	15	0
It.	A mare and a two year old mare	2	8	0
It.	Sixteen swine great and small together	10	0	0
		22	9	0
It.	To corn in the mill	1	3	0
It.	To a hide in the mill	0	6	0
It.	To flax in the mill & dwelling house	0	10	0
It.	To corn in the crib	0	10	0
It.	To a barrel & half full of pork in the cellar	1	0	0
It.	To a barrel with some beef and venison in it in the cellar	0	6	0
It.	To three old casks in the cellar	0	3	0
It.	Two small tubs with a little salt in one of them in the cellar	0	2	0
It.	To an old cask with a little soap in it in the cellar	0	2	0
It.	To two tubs and tobacco in the cellar	0	5	6
		4	7	6
It.	To a felling axe, and three old ones and a piece of one	0	8	0
It.	To two broad hoes	0	4	0
It.	To an old shovel	0	0	6
It.	To an old scythe and piece of one with rings and nebs	0	2	0
It.	To sawn pine boards	1	10	0

"An Inventory of the Estate of John Smith," in *The Early Records of the Town of Providence, Rhode Island*, VI (Providence, R.I., 1894), pp. 72–75.

Item		lb	s	d
It.	To the cart, and plough, and all tackling thereunto belonging, with the horse tackling also	2	0	0
It.	To a pair of chisels and a gouge	0	2	0
It.	Three old augers and an old hand saw	0	3	0
		4	9	6
	Up in the chamber of the dwelling house			
It.	To Rye	0	6	0
It.	To two bedsteads with the beds and bedding to them belonging	2	0	0
It.	To two pieces of meat, and a little salt	0	6	0
		2	12	0
	In the lower room of the dwelling house			
It.	To one bedstead with the bed and bedding thereunto	3	0	0
It.	To a brass kettle	2	10	0
It.	To a small copper kettle	0	5	0
It.	To an old broken copper kettle	0	1	0
It.	To a chest with the Book of Martyrs in it	0	15	0
It.	To a small piece of homemade cloth	1	10	0
It.	To a pair of bottle rings & three wedges	0	2	3
It.	To a frying pan	0	3	0
It.	To two guns	1	1	0
It.	To a small box	0	1	0
It.	To a chamber pot	0	2	0
It.	To two small old pewter platters	0	2	0
It.	To two basins and three porringers	0	4	6
It.	To two quart glasses	0	0	9
It.	To three iron pots	0	12	0
It.	To a trammel, & fire shovel, & tongs	0	9	0
It.	Two spinning wheels, & old cards	0	7	0
It.	To an old Bible, some lost & some of it torn	0	0	9
It.	To four old chairs	0	1	6
It.	To several wooden dishes	0	2	0
It.	To a wooden bottle	0	1	0
It.	To some old trenchers	0	0	6
It.	To a pail, and a can	0	2	0
It.	To four old spoons	0	1	0

Item		lb	s	d
It.	To a spit, and a small grater	0	1	3
It.	To about two pounds of tallow candles	0	1	0
It.	To an old bridle	0	0	6
It.	To lumber of very little worth if any	0	1	6
		11	18	6
It.	The corn mill with the house over it, and all such other things as do thereunto belong or appertain	40	0	0
It.	The seventh part of the saw mill adjoining to the corn mill, with the old millstone that lyeth by	3	10	0
		43	10	0

Debts due

It.	By William Ingram of Swansey	0	15	0
As to what other debts due or owing yet not fully known: the sum total, errors excepted in casting, is		90	1	9

A true and fair appraisal of what was made [to] appear unto us to be the estate of John Smith (miller), deceased, taken by us upon the eighth day of April, one thousand six hundred and eighty two, as witness our hands,

John Whipple, Jr.
William Hopkins

Letter from William Fitzhugh, of Stafford County, Virginia, to Dr. Ralph Smith, of Bristol, England

(1686)

Doctor Ralph Smith,   April 22, 1686

In order to [facilitate] the exchange [which] you promised to make for me, and [which] I desired you to proceed therein—[that is] to say to exchange an estate of inheritance in land there of two or three hundred pounds a year, or in houses in any town of three or four hundred pounds a year—I shall be something particular in the relation of my concerns here, that is to go in return thereof. As, first, the plantation where I now live contains a thousand acres, at least 700 acres of it being rich thicket, the remainder good hearty plantable land, without any waste either by marshes or great swamps. The commodiousness, conveniency, and pleasantness your self well knows. Upon it there is three quarters well furnished, with all necessary houses, ground, and fencing, together with a choice crew of Negroes at each plantation, most of them [in] this country born, the remainder as likely as most in Virginia, there being twenty-nine in all, with stocks of cattle and hogs at each quarter. Upon the same land is my own dwelling house, furnished with all accommodations for a comfortable and genteel living, [such] as a very good dwelling house, with 13 rooms in it, four of the best of them hung, nine of them plentifully furnished with all things necessary and convenient; and all houses for use well furnished with brick chimneys; four good cellars, a dairy, dovecoat, stable, barn, henhouse, kitchen, and all other conveniences, and all in a manner new; a large orchard of about 2500 apple trees (most [of them] grafted), well fenced with a locust fence which is as durable as most brick walls; a garden a hundred foot square, well paled in; a yard wherein is most of the foresaid necessary houses, pallisaded in with locust puncheons, which is as good as if it were walled in and more lasting than any of our bricks; together with a good stock of cattle, hogs, horses, mares, sheep, etc. and [the] necessary servants belonging to it for the supply and support thereof. About a mile and half distant [there is] a good water gristmill, whose toll I find sufficient to find my own family with wheat and Indian corn for our necessities

Letter from William Fitzhugh to Dr. Ralph Smith, April 22, 1686, in Richard Beale Davis, ed., *William Fitzhugh and His Chesapeake World, 1676–1701* (Chapel Hill, N.C., 1963), pp. 175–176. I am grateful to the Virginia Historical Society, owner of the copyright to this book, for permission to reprint Fitzhugh's letter.

and occasions. Up the river in this country [I have] three tracts of land more; one of them contains 21996 acres, another 500 acres, and one other 1000 acres—all good, convenient, and commodious seats, and which in a few years will yield a considerable annual income. [There is also] a stock of tobacco with the crops and good debts lying out of about 250000 lb., besides sufficient [quantity] of almost all sorts of goods to supply the family's and the quarter's occasions for two, if not three, years. Thus I have given you some particulars [from] which I thus deduce [that] the yearly crops of corn and tobacco together with the surplus of meat more than will serve the family's use will amount annually to 60000 lb. tobacco which at 10 shillings per Ct. is £300 per annum; and the Negroes' increase, [they] being all young, and a considerable parcel of breeders, will keep that stock good for ever. The stock of tobacco, managed with an inland trade, will yearly yield 60000 lb. [of] tobacco without hazard or risk, which will be both clear, without charge of housekeeping or disbursements for servants' clothing. The orchard in a very few years will yield a large supply to plentiful housekeeping, or, if better husbanded, [will] yield at least 15000 lb. tobacco annual income. What I have not particularly mentioned, your own knowledge in my affairs is able to supply. If any are so desirous to deal for the estate without the stock of tobacco, I shall be ready and willing; but I will make no fractions of that, either all or none at all shall go. I have so fully discoursed [to] you in the affair that I shall add no further instructions, but leave it to your prudent and careful management. And [I] would advise that if any overtures of such a nature should happen, immediately give an account thereof to Mr. Nicholas Hayward, Notary Public near the Exchange [in] London, both of the person treating, and the place, situation, quantity, and quality of the estate, who will take speedy and effectual care, to give me a full and ready account thereof, which I hope you will for all opportunities do.

To Doctor Ralph Smith, in Bristol,

Sir, Your
William Fitzhugh

Furnishings (New England)

Joined great chair, Dedham, Massachusetts, dated 1652. Note the enclosed area, with seat serving as lid, at bottom. This provided storage space for books, chamber pots, or textiles, at the owner's discretion. Dedham Historical Society, Dedham, Mass. Used with permission.

Joint stool, Newbury, Massachusetts, late seventeenth century. Stools of this type were widely used throughout the colonies for seating. Henry Francis duPont Winterthur Museum, Winterthur, Del. Used with permission.

Board chest. Board chests, of this and related types, were the most common form of case furniture in colonial America. They could be used for almost any kind of storage, especially important in a precloset era. Mabel Brady Garvan Collection, Yale University Art Gallery. Used with permission.

Joined form, Massachusetts, second half of the seventeenth century. Forms or benches like this one (and cruder variants) provided seating alongside a table. Henry Francis duPont Winterthur Museum, Winterthur, Del. Used with permission.

Board and trestles, Massachusetts, early eighteenth century. This simple table, and others like it, could be disassembled and put away when not in use. Frederick Brown Fund and Helen and Alice Colburn Fund, Museum of Fine Arts, Boston. Used with permission.

Tools and Utensils (New England)

A collection of wooden tableware: spoons, plates, bowls, and cups, the most common categories of table utensils in colonial America. Wood was the material most often used in making them. Pilgrim Hall, Plymouth, Mass. Used with permission.

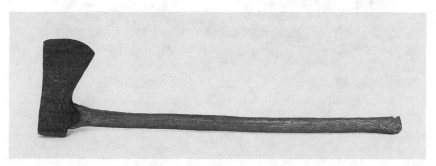

Felling axe, New England, ca. 1725. With tools like this one, colonists cleared their land of trees and hewed their wood into shape for use in domestic construction. Essex Institute, Salem, Mass. Used with permission.

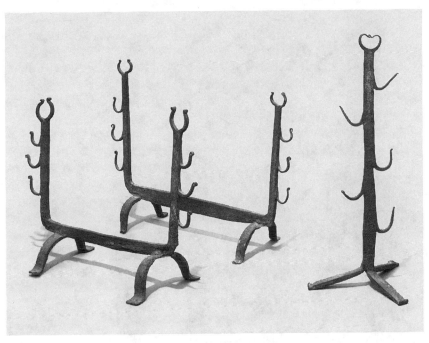

Firedogs and tree, New England, first half of the eighteenth century. Firedogs of this type were used along with rotated spits for roasting meat; the associated tree was a place to hang cooked meat, near the fire, until it was served. Samuel Putnam Avery Fund, Museum of Fine Arts, Boston. Used with permission.

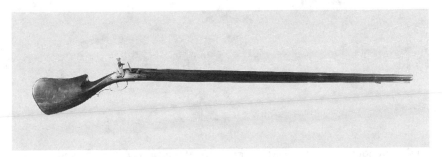

Doglock musket, Charlestown, Massachusetts, ca. 1665. Weapons of this general type were essential to the conquest of the New World environment and its human denizens. The example shown here is five and one-half feet long and heavy; the "doglock" was its firing mechanism. Historic Deerfield, Inc., Deerfield, Mass. Used with permission.

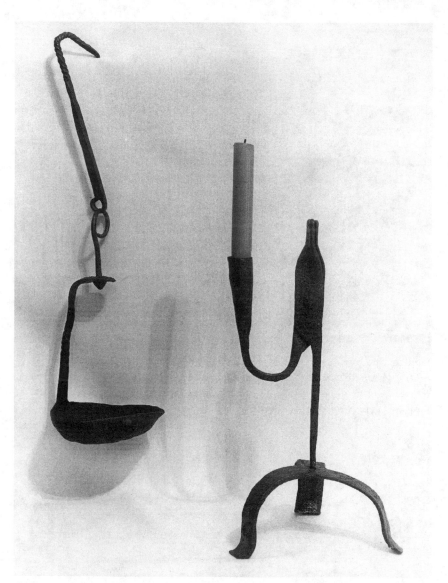

Rushlight holder and oil lamp, New England, eighteenth century. Together with candles, wrought iron lamps of these (and other) types cut the darkness of evening in colonial households. Personal collection of the author.

14

A Household Budget

What were the necessities for maintaining a household in colonial America? And what were their costs?

The answer, in one case, is provided by a family budget worked out by Jonathan Ashley of Deerfield, Massachusetts, in 1751. Ashley was the minister at Deerfield, and his "computation of . . . expenses" (presumably for an entire year) formed part of a plea to his congregation for a salary increase.

A minister would, to be sure, expect a higher standard of living than the average for his community. And all such budgets would vary from one instance to the next, depending on time and place, social class and personal predilection. Still, the Ashley budget cannot have been wholly atypical, at least in its basic categories (food, clothing, medical expenses, and the like). It shows us, as few other documents could, the practical underpinnings of life under fully premodern conditions.

Computation of the Expenses of a Family Consisting of a Man, a Woman, 4 Children, and a Maid
Jonathan Ashley

(Deerfield, Massachusetts, 1751)

Wheat, 40 bushels at 22/6	45	00	00
Beef, 500 lb. at 12d.	25	00	00
Pork, 17 score [?] & ½ at 18d	26	05	00
Mutton & veal	10	00	00
Fish	03	00	00
Indian corn, 12 bushels at 11/8	07	00	00
Malt, 11 bushels	11	00	00

Jonathan Ashley, "Computation of the Expenses of a family . . . ," ms. original at Pocumtuck Valley Memorial Association Library, Deerfield, Mass. Used with permission.

Cider, 12 barrels	18	00	00
Rum, wine, metheglin, etc.	20	00	00
Sugar, 100 lbs.	25	00	00
Tea, chocolate, & rice [?], etc.	12	00	00
Butter, 200 lb. at 3/6	35	00	00
Milk, 2 quarts per day	35	00	00
Apples	04	00	00
Turnips	02	00	00
Spices, raisins, etc.	06	00	00
Salt	04	00	00
Peas	01	00	00
Cheese, 60 lb. at 3s.	09	00	00
Tallow, 27 lb. at 3s.	04	01	00
Clothing for the family	125	00	00
Doctor's bill	20	00	00
Pocket expenses	10	00	00
Blacksmith's bill	05	00	00
Keeping a horse	15	00	00
Pipes & tobacco	04	00	00
Books	02	00	00
Paper, ink, & quills	02	00	00
Schooling girls	07	00	00
Maid's work	47	00	00
Man's help	10	00	00
House repair & wear of house- hold goods	25	00	00
	587	01	00

15

Dependents: Young People and Servants

In theory, the typical household of the colonial period was organized along strict hierarchical lines. The man was the "head"; the wife was his "helpmeet"; the children and servants were subordinates—enjoined to attitudes of obedience and submission. In practice there was considerable deviation from this model. The openness, the fluidity of New World society gradually eroded traditional forms of authority; persons who were officially dependent could sometimes find ways to strike out on their own.

The normative standards for childrearing are nicely summarized in a short statement written by the Reverend Cotton Mather of Boston near the start of the eighteenth century. Mather, in fact, describes practice as much as purpose here. His comments on discipline are especially striking: children, he suggests, must be shamed—not beaten—when they "do amiss." At the same time he urges praise and prayer as parallel means of "instruction." His overall posture is one of deep parental concern; more than many of his modern counterparts, Mather seems to have been an active, involved father.

The indenture of Gabriel Ginings exemplifies a common practice in colonial times—a practice that historians have not been able fully to understand. For reasons nowhere made explicit, the parents of young Ginings "bound him out" into a foster family for the remainder of his childhood. Although the document is silent on the subject of motive, it does declare the practical side of such arrangements—the promises made on both sides.

When George Willys, Jr., went from Hartford, Connecticut, to England in 1638, he left his father a written promise to return as soon as his business was done. Nothing could illustrate more vividly the norm of filial obligation that obtained throughout this culture. But it is also notable that the promise was not kept, for Willys never did come back to New England.

Only a relative few among the colonists had much formal education, and college was largely for those with ambitions to become clergymen. Admission to college was a solemn moment—and a fit occasion for the receipt of advice from one's elders. The letter from the Reverend Thomas Shepard of Cambridge, Massachusetts, to his son when the boy entered Harvard expounds a comprehensive view of the learning process.

Young women, of course, had no chance at college; they prepared for a different future, by another route. A handwritten offering of "advice to my daughters" by the Reverend Solomon Williams of Lebanon, Connecticut, expressed a widely prevalent standard.

Conflict between masters and servants was a chronic problem in every one of the colonies. Servants were charged with many forms of dereliction: running away without permission, theft, refusal to follow orders, and so forth. Masters, on the other hand, were accused of ignoring *their* obligations, too. The court case between Richard Preston and his servants, in Calvert County, Maryland, puts some of these difficulties in focus.

Some Special Points, Relating to the Education
of My Children

(1706)

Cotton Mather

I. I pour out continual prayers and cries to the God of all grace for them, that He will be a Father to my children and bestow His Christ and His grace upon them, and guide them with his councils, and bring them to His glory.

And in this action I mention them distinctly, every one by name, unto the Lord.

II. I begin betimes to entertain them with delightful stories, especially scriptural ones. And still conclude with some lesson of piety, bidding them to learn that lesson from the story.

"Some Special Points, Relating to the Education of My Children," in Worthington C. Ford, ed., *The Diary of Cotton Mather*, 2 vols. (Boston, 1911), I, pp. 534–537.

And thus, every day at the table, I have used myself to tell a story before I rise, and make the story useful to the olive plants about the table.

III. When the children at any time accidentally come in my way, it is my custom to let fall some sentence or other that may be monitory and profitable to them.

This matter proves to me a matter of some study and labor and contrivance. But who can tell what may be the effect of a continual dropping.

IV. I essay betimes to engage the children in exercises of piety, and especially secret prayer, for which I give them very plain and brief directions, and suggest unto them the petitions which I would have them to make before the Lord, and which I therefore explain to their apprehension and capacity. And I often call upon them: *Child, don't you forget every day to go alone, and pray as I have directed you!*

V. Betimes, I try to form in the children a temple of benignity. I put them upon doing of services and kindnesses for one another and for other children. I applaud them when I see them delight in it. I upbraid all aversion to it. I caution them exquisitely against all revenges of injuries. I instruct them to return good offices for evil ones. I show them how they will by this goodness become like to the good God and His glorious Christ. I let them discern that I am not satisfied except when they have a sweetness of temper shining in them.

VI. As soon as 'tis possible, I make the children learn to write. And when they can write, I employ them in writing out the most agreeable and profitable things that I can invent for them. In this way I propose to freight their minds with excellent things, and have a deep impression made upon their minds by such things.

VII. I mightily endeavor it that the children may betimes be acted by principles of reason and honor.

I first beget in them an high opinion of their father's love to them, and of his being best able to judge what shall be good for them.

Then I make them sensible [that] 'tis a folly for them to pretend unto any wit or will of their own; they must resign all to me, who will be sure to do what is best. My word must be their law.

I cause them to understand that it is a hurtful and a shameful thing to do amiss. I aggravate this on all occasions, and let them see how amiable they will render themselves by well doing.

The first chastisement which I inflict for an ordinary fault is to let the child see and hear me in an astonishment and hardly able to believe that the child could do so base a thing, but believing that they will never do it again.

I would never come to give a child a blow, except in case of obstinacy or some gross enormity.

To be chased for a while out of my presence I would make to be looked upon as the sorest punishment in the family.

I would by all possible insinuations gain this point upon them, that for them to learn all the brave things in the world is the bravest thing in the world. I am not fond of proposing play to them as a reward of any diligent application to learn what is good, lest they should think diversion to be a better and a nobler thing than diligence.

I would have them come to propound and expect at this rate: *I have done well, and now I will go to my father. He will teach me some curious thing for it.* I must have them count it a privilege to be taught, and I sometimes manage the matter so that my refusing to teach them something is their punishment.

The slavish way of education, carried on with raving and kicking and scourging (in schools as well as families) 'tis abominable, and a dreadful judgement of God upon the world.

VIII. Though I find it a marvelous advantage to have the children strongly biassed by principles of reason and honor (which, I find, children will feel sooner than is commonly thought for), yet I would neglect no endeavors to have higher principles infused into them.

I therefore betimes awe them with the eye of God upon them.

I show them how they must love Jesus Christ, and show it by doing what their parents require of them.

I often tell them of the good angels who love them and help them and guard them, and who take notice of them—and therefore must not be disobliged.

Heaven and Hell I set before them, as the consequences of their behavior here.

IX. When the children are capable of it, I take them alone, one by one, and after my charges unto them to fear God and serve Christ and shun sin, I pray with them in my study and make them the witnesses of the agonies with which I address the throne of grace on their behalf.

X. I find much benefit by a particular method, as of catechising the children, so of carrying the repetition of public sermons unto them.

The answers of the catechism I still explain with abundance of brief questions, which make them to take in the meaning of it, and I see that they do so.

And when the sermons are to be repeated, I choose to put every truth into a question, to be answered still with *yes*, or *no*. In this way I awaken their attention, as well as enlighten their understanding. And in this way I have an opportunity to ask, *Do you desire such or such a grace of God?* and the like. Yea, I have an opportunity to demand, and perhaps to obtain, their consent unto the glorious articles of the new covenant. The spirit of grace may fall upon them in this action, and they may be seized by Him and held as His temples through eternal ages.

Indenture of Gabriel Ginings

(Portsmouth, Rhode Island, 1663)

This indenture, made the first day of the month called August in the year one thousand, six hundred [and] sixty-three, between William Wodell of Portsmouth in Rhode Island in New England, husbandman, on the one part, and Thomas Ginings and his son Gabriel of the aforesaid town, on the other part, witnesseth that Thomas Ginings aforesaid, hath by these presents put his said son Gabriel as an apprentice unto the aforesaid William Wodell, for the full and just term and time of fourteen years and two months from the day of the date hereof to be completely ended, during which term of time the said Gabriel is faithfully and truly as an apprentice to serve the said William Wodell, his wife, heir, or whomsoever of his children he, the said Wodell, shall appoint the said Gabriel to serve. And he, the said Gabriel Ginings, is to be obedient unto all the just commands of the said Wodell, his wife, heirs, or whom as aforesaid he shall appoint him to serve. And in all things he the said Gabriel is duly and truly to behave himself as such an apprentice ought to do, during the said term and time. During all which term and time the aforesaid William Wodell, his wife, heirs, or whom[ever] he shall dispose of the said Gabriel unto as aforepromised, is faithfully and truly to provide the said Gabriel sufficient food and raiment suitable for such an apprentice, and at the end of the term when the said Gabriel hath served the full time aforesaid, then the said William Wodell, his wife,

Indenture of Gabriel Ginings, in *The Early Records of the Town of Portsmouth, Rhode Island* (Providence, R.I., 1901), pp. 412–413.

heirs, or whom[ever] aforesaid he shall appoint the said Gabriel to serve is to deliver unto the said Gabriel in the aforesaid town of Portsmouth two suits of apparel, one cow, and one mare foal weanable. And if the said Gabriel should be taken away by death within two years of the end of the aforesaid term, then the said William Wodell, his wife, heirs, or whom[ever] he shall as aforesaid appoint the said Gabriel to serve, is to deliver a cow or a mare foal to whomsoever the said Gabriel shall give it, or to be otherwise disposed of by those in power in such cases. And further, this may testify that this indenture was made with the free and voluntary consent of Ann Ginings, the wife of the said Thomas Ginings and mother of the said Gabriel, as also with the said Gabriel's free consent. And in testimony to the truth of this indenture the aforesaid parties have interchangeably set to their hands and seals in Portsmouth aforesaid [on] the day and year above written, which is the first day in August in the year aforesaid.

Signed Sealed and Delivered

in presence of   Thomas Ginings

John Roome   Gabriel Ginings

John Sanford   Ann Ginings

George Wyllys' Promise and Oath, to His Father

(Hartford, Connecticut, 1639)

Whereas by God's permission, I, George Wyllys, Jr., intend a voyage into England by the appointment of my father, George Wyllys, for the true and faithful performance of such trust as my said father shall commit to my charge and care, both concerning the sale of his lands in Warwickshire there and disposing of the money that shall be received for the same by me and my appointment, as also for the marrying of myself if my necessity require and fit opportunity be offered, wherefore for the better assurance to my said father of my reality for the accomplishment thereof [I] do both promise and swear:

By the name of the everlasting God, that I will do the best of my endeavors [in] every way for the sale of the aforesaid land by the first

George Wyllys' Promise and Oath, in *Collections of the Connecticut Historical Society*, XXI (Hartford, Conn., 1924), p. 6. I am grateful to the Connecticut Historical Society for permission to reprint this document.

opportunity, and lay out the said money that shall be paid for the same according to my father's directions. As far as my necessity require and providence offer an opportunity of marriage, I shall readily and really attend and take council and follow the same of those parties deputed for that purpose by my father. And as soon as I shall dispatch the sale of that land and other such business commended and committed to me by my father, I will (the Lord not letting or hindering) return again into New England to this place to my said father, to settle my abode and dwelling as my father shall advise, as near unto him as may be for his comfort by me. And all this to the best of my skill I promise and swear to perform without fraud, deceit, or reservation, so help me God through Jesus Christ.

Letter from the Reverend Thomas Shepard to His Son at His Admission into the College

(Massachusetts, 1672)

Dear Son,

I think meet (partly from the advice of your renowned grandfather to myself at my admission into the College, and partly from some other observations I have had respecting studies in that society) to leave the remembrances and advice following with you, in this great change of your life, rather in writing, then *viva voce* only; that so they may be the better considered and improved by you, and may abide upon your heart when I shall be (and that may be sooner than you are aware) taken from thee and speak no more: requiring you frequently to read over, and seriously to ponder, and digest, as also conscientiously to put in practice the same through the Lord's assistance.

I. Remember the end of your life, which is a coming back again to God and fellowship with God. For as your great misery is your separation and estrangement from him, so your happiness or last end is your return again to him. And because there is no coming to God but by Christ's righteousness, and no Christ to be had but by faith, and no faith without humiliation or sense of your misery, hence therefore let all your prayers and tears be that God would first humble you, that so you may fly by faith to Christ and come by Christ to God.

Letter from Rev. Thomas Shepard to his son, in *Publications of the Colonial Society of Massachusetts*, XIV (Boston, 1913), pp. 192–198.

II. Remember the end of this turn of your life, viz. your coming into the College: it is to fit you for the most glorious work which God can call you to, viz. the holy ministry, [so] that you may declare the name of God to the conversion and salvation of souls. For this end your father has set you apart with many tears and hath given you up unto God, that He may accept of you, and that He would delight in you.

III. Remember therefore that God looks for and calls for much holiness from you; I had rather see you buried in your grave than grow light, loose, wanton, or profane. God's secrets in the holy scriptures, which are left to instruct ministers, are never made known to common and profane spirits. And therefore be sure you begin and end every day wherein you study with earnest prayer to God, lamenting after the favor of God, reading some part of the Scriptures daily, and setting apart some time every day (though but one quarter of an hour) for meditation of the things of God.

IV. Remember therefore that though you have spent your time in the vanity of childhood sports and mirth, little minding better things, yet that now, when come to this ripeness of admission to the College, that now God and man expect you should put away childish things. Now is the time come wherein you are to be serious and to learn sobriety and wisdom in all your ways which concern God and man.

V. Remember that these are times and days of much light and knowledge, and that therefore you had as good be no scholar as not excel in knowledge and learning. Abhor therefore one hour of idleness as you would be ashamed of one hour of drunkenness. Look that you lose not your precious time by falling in with idle companions, or by growing weary of your studies, or by love of any filthy lust, or by discouragement of heart that you shall never attain to any excellency of knowledge, or by thinking too well of yourself, that you have got as much as is needful for you when you have got as much as your equals in the same year. No, verily, the spirit of God will not communicate much to you in a way of idleness, but will curse your soul, while this sin is nourished which hath spoiled so many hopeful youths in their first blossoming in the College. And therefore, though I would not have you neglect seasons of recreation a little before and after meals (and although I would not have you study late in the night usually, yet look that you rise early and lose not your morning thoughts when your mind is most fresh and fit for study), be no wicked example all the day to any of your fellows in spending your time idly. And do not content yourself to do as much as your tutor sets you about, but know that you will never excel in learning unless you do somewhat else in private hours wherein his care cannot reach you. And do not think that idling away your time is no great sin, if so be you think you can hide it from the eyes of others; but consider that God, who always sees you and observes how you spend your time, will be provoked for every hour of that precious time you now misspend, which you are like never to find the like to this in the College [in] all your life after.

VI. Remember that in ordering your studies you make them as pleasant as may be and as fruitful as possibly you are able, that so you may not be weary in the work God sets you about, and for this end remember these rules, viz.

1. Single out two or three scholars [who are] most godly, learned, and studious, and whom you can most love and who love you best, to be helps to you in your studies. Get therefore into the acquaintance of some of your equals, to spend some time with them often in discoursing and disputing about the things you hear and read and learn; as also grow acquainted with some that are your superiors, of whom you may often ask questions and from whom you may learn more than by your equals only.

2. Mark every man's disputations and conferences, and study to get some good by every thing. And if your memory be not very strong, commit every notion this way gained unto paper as soon as you get into your study.

3. Let your studies be so ordered as to have variety of studies before you, ⌊so⌋ that when you are weary of one book you may take pleasure (through this variety) in another. And for this end read some histories often, which (they say) make men wise as poets make witty; both [of] which are pleasant things in the midst of more difficult studies.

4. Let not your studies be prosecuted in an immethodical or disorderly way; but (for the generality) keep a fixed order of studies suited to your own genius and circumstances of things—which in each year at least, notwithstanding, there will be occasion of some variation of. Fix your course and the season for each kind of study, and suffer no other matters or persons needlessly to interrupt you or take you off therefrom.

5. Let difficult studies have the strength and flower of your time and thoughts; and therein suffer no difficulty to pass unresolved, but either by your own labor, or by inquiry of others, or by both, master it before you pass from it. Pass not cursorily or heedlessly over such things (rivet the knottiest place you meet with). 'Tis not so much *multa lectio sed sedula et attenta* that makes a scholar, as our phrase speaks.

153

6. Come to your studies with an appetite, and weary not your body, mind, or eyes with long poring on your book, but break off and meditate on what you have read, and then [go] to it again. Or (if it be in fit season) recreate yourself a little, and so [return] to your work afresh. Let your recreation be such as may stir the body chiefly, yet not violent; and, whether such or sedentary, let it be never more than may serve to make your spirit the more free and lively in your studies.

7. Such books as it is proper to read over, if they are very choice and not overlarge, read them over oftener than once. If it be not your own and [if it seems] that you are not like[ly] to procure it, then collect out of such book what is worthy to be noted therein—in which collections take these directions: (1) Write not in loose papers but in a fair paper-book, paged throughout. (2) Write faithfully the words of your author. (3) Set down in your paper-book the name of your author with the title of his book, and the page where you find the collection. (4) Allow a margin to your paper-book no broader than wherein you may write the letters, a, b, c, d, e, f, etc., viz. at the beginning of each observable collection, if you have more collections than two or three in a side. (5) When you have written out such a book being marked with some distinguishing character (as 1, 2, 3, 4, etc. or α, β, γ, δ, etc.), prepare another of the same dimensions as near as you can, and improve that as the former, and so onwards; which book may be (as the merchant's journal is to his principal ledger) preparatory for your commonplace book, as your reason and fancy will easily suggest how, by short reference of any subject to be handled, [it may be] found in (suppose) the paper-book, β, page 10, margin f. Suppose the subject be "Faith," you need only write in your commonplace book "Faith," *vide* β, 10, f; if the subject be "Hope," write "Hope," γ, 10, d., which signifies that there is some description of that subject "Hope," or some sentence about hope that is observable, or some story concerning that virtue and the like, in the third paper-book marked with γ and in the tenth page of the book, begun in the margin at the letter d. As you have leisure read over your paper-books wherein you have written your collections at large. The frequent perusal thereof will [in] many ways be useful to you, as your experiences will in time witness.

8. Choose rather to confess your ignorance in any matter of learning [so] that you may [be] instructed by your tutor or another as there may be occasion for it, than to pass from it and so continue in your ignorance thereof or in any error about it; *malo te doctum esse quam haberi.*

9. Suffer not too much to be spent and broken away in visits (visiting

or being visited). Let them be such as may be a whet to you in your studies and for your profit in learning some way or other, so that you be imparting to others, or imparted to from them, or both, in some notion or other, upon all such occasions.

10. Study the art of reducing all you read to practice in your orations, etc., turning and improving elegantly [the] words and notions and fancy of your author to set off quite another subject, a delicate example whereof you have in your *Christiados*, whereof Ross is the author, causing Virgil to evangelize. And as in your orations, so in all you do, labor for exactness and accuracy. Let not crude, lame, bungling stuff come out of your study; and for that end see that you neither play nor sleep nor idle away a moment's time within your study door, but remember your study is your work-house only and place of prayer.

11. So frame and order your studies that the one may be a furtherance to the other (the tongues to the arts and the arts to the tongues), and endeavor that your first year's studies may become a clue to lead you on the more clearly, strongly, profitably, and cheerfully to the studies of the years following, making all still useful and subservient to divinity; and so will your profiting in all be the more perspicuous and methodical.

12. Be sparing in your diet as to meat and drink, that so after any repast your body may be a servant to your mind, and not a clog and burden.

13. Take pains in, and time for, preparing in private for your recitations, declamations, disputations, and such other exercises as you are called to attend before your tutor or others. Do not hurry them off indigestly—no, not under pretence of studying some other matter first. But first (I say in the first place) attend those (straiten not your self in time for the thorough dispatch thereof), and then afterwards you may apply yourself as aforesaid to your private and more proper studies; in all [of] which, mind that reading without meditation will be in a great measure unprofitable, and rawness and forgetfulness will be the event, but meditation without reading will be barren soon. Therefore read much that so you may have plenty of matter for meditation to work upon. And here I would not have you forget a speech of your precious grandfather to a scholar that complained to him of a bad memory, which did discourage him from reading much in history or other books. His answer was, *"Lege! lege! aliquid haerebit."* So I say to you, read! read! something will stick in the mind; be diligent and good will come of it: and that sentence in Prov., 14:23 deserves to be written in letters of gold upon your study-table—"in all labor there is profit," etc. Yet also know that

reading and meditation, without prayer, will in the end be both blasted by the holy God. And therefore,

VII. Remember that not only heavenly and spiritual and supernatural knowledge descends from God, but also all natural and humane learning and abilities; and therefore pray much, not only for the one but also for the other, from the Father of lights and mercies. And remember that prayer at Christ's feet for all the learning you want shall fetch you in more in an hour than possibly you may get by all the books and helps you have otherwise in many years.

VIII. Remember to be grave (not childish) and amiable and loving toward all the scholars, that you may win their hearts and honor.

IX. Remember now to be watchful against the two great sins of many scholars. The first is youthful lusts, speculative wantoness, and secret filthiness, which God sees in the dark, and for which God hardens and blinds young men's hearts, His holy spirit departing from such unclean sties. The second is malignancy and secret distaste of holiness and the power of Godliness and the professors of it. Both these sins you will fall quickly into, unto your own perdition, if you be not careful of your company; for there are and will be such in every scholastical society, for the most part, as will teach you how to be filthy and how to jest and scorn at Godliness and the professors thereof, whose company I charge you to fly from as from the Devil and [to] abhor; and [in order] that you may be kept from these read often that scripture, Prov., 2, 10, 11, 12, 16.

X. Remember to intreat God with tears before you come to hear any sermon, that thereby God would powerfully speak to your heart and make His truth precious to you. Neglect not to write after the preacher always, and write not in loose sheets but in handsome paper-books; and be careful to preserve and peruse the same. And upon the Sabbath days make exceeding conscience of sanctifications. Mix not your other studies, much less idleness or vain and casual discourses, with the duties of that holy day; but remember that command [in] Lev., 19:30, "Ye shall keep my Sabbaths and reverence my Sanctuary; I am the Lord."

XI. Remember that whensoever you read, hear, or conceive of any divine truth, you study to affect your heart with it and the goodness of it. Take heed of receiving truth into your head without the love of it in your heart, lest God give you up to strong delusions to believe lies, and [lest you find] that in the conclusion all your learning shall make you more fit to deceive yourself and others. Take heed lest by seeing things with a form of knowledge the Lord do not bind you by that knowledge the more, [so] that in seeing you shall not see. If therefore God revealeth any truth to you at any time, be sure you be humbly and deeply thankful; and when He hides any truth from you, be sure you lie down and loathe yourself, and be humble. The first degree of wisdom is to know and feel your own folly.

2 Tim., 2:7. "Consider what I say and the Lord give thee understanding in all things."

Prov., 23:15. "My Son, if thine heart be wise, my heart shall rejoice, even mine."

Pater tuus,
T. Shepard

Advice to My Daughters

(circa 1740)

Solomon Williams

The care of a married woman is to please. And let it be your first and daily care to please God by a conscientious endeavor in all things to obey him, acting for his glory, with a strict eye to his laws and careful observance of all his admonitions [?], in public, in the family, and in secret. . . .

The next care is to please your husbands, in order to which be inviolably faithful to your conjugal banns. And with strict modesty avoid everything that carries any suspicion of disaffection to him or lightness. Don't affect finery but always neatness. Let your persons be ever neat, and your house and the affairs of it cleanly. Be always pleasant, good-humored, and agreeable in your carriages. Maintain as far as you can the humor of your husbands. Be blind to their failings. If anything falls out disagreeable to you, show not anger or resentment. Bear it with patience, and take the most seasonable opportunity, when you can do it without offence, to intimate your desires in such a way as will make him esteem your prudence and value more your love and tenderness. Never let him think you suspect his judgement [?] or think your own

Ms. original of this document in the Lyme Historical Society, Old Lyme, Conn. Used with permission. I should like to thank Jane Kamensky for helping me to decipher the nearly illegible script.

157

superior, but [rather] that his mistakes spring from want of more time for thought or the common infirmities of mortal man. Be careful to retain his affection. Don't depend on it that because he has sworn to love you he has and will continue to do so, however you behave. But remember the flame of love is to be kept alive by love, the practice of virtue, and your patience, fidelity, neatness, and care to please. When a woman once loses the affection of her husband, or lets him think she has no concern about it, 'tis hard to recover it; and their state will be very indifferent, if not very unhappy.

Treat your husband's friends and such as he values with a frankness and kindness that may discover [?] you are pleased with what pleases him (supposing they be persons of virtue). For if he should be so unhappy as to have other friends, it will [be necessary] for his and your heart to endeavor the best measures and [illegible words] to disengage him from them.

In the economy of your house, never be covetous but always thrifty and prudent. 'Tis not expected that a woman can increase the estate by her labor so much as by her prudent and sensible [?] economy.

If you have children, receive them as God's gift. Love them more for God's sake than your own. And remember your business is to nurse and bring them up for God. Take prudent care for the health of their bodies, that [they] may be sound and robust and employed in such business and exercise as is suitable for them. But take more care of their minds, that they may be formed from their infancy to virtue, religion, and usefulness in the world. Their pride, passions, and wills must be early and always kept under prudent, steady government and restraint. Never let your fondness for them indulge sin, pride, or self-will in them. You will find the best method to effect them will be by careful instruction, diligent employment, a calm, affectionate, dispassionate, steady exercise of your just authority and worthy example. Commit them to God in your daily prayers. If you have servants, treat them justly and kindly. . . . Expect no more of them than is reasonable. Their infirmities and lesser faults 'tis best not to see. Their obstinacy, willfulness, and wickedness fail not to correct and restrain. If from these they will not be reformed, endeavor that they may not dwell in your house. Be courteous to your neighbors. And to your ability be kind to the poor. Be just to all you are concerned with; be forgiving to your enemies, good to your friends, and let the law of kindness be in your heart and lips. By modesty, virtue [illegible word] piety maintain the dignity of your place. Live in a constant hatred and contempt of the idols of the world and lust of the flesh, lust of the eye, and the pride of life, i.e. sensuality, covetousness, and ambition. Love one another. Love your brethren. And love and thank God in all. . . .

I commend these hints to you, hoping by the blessing [that] they be of use to you. . . . I am your affectionate father, Solomon Williams.

Petitions of Richard Preston and His Servants
to the Provincial Court

(Calvert County, Maryland, 1663)

At a Provincial Court held at St. Leonard's in Calvert County, this 31 March, 1663.

Present:

Charles Calvert Esq., *Governor*	Mr. Baker Brooke	
Philip Calvert Esq., *Chancellor*	Mr. John Bateman	*Councillors*
Henry Sewall Esq., *Secretary*		

To the honorable the Governor and Council of Maryland:

The humble petition of Richard Preston showeth:

That your petitioner's servants did, upon the 5th day of the last week, called Thursday, peremptorily and positively refuse to go and do their ordinary labor upon the account (as they then alleged) that if they had not flesh, they would not work. Your suppliant's answer then was to them, that if they would not go to work unless they had flesh, I could not help it; for I had not flesh then to give them (your suppliant's business calling him that day abroad). And at night returning home, [he] found that his said servants had not been at work upon the account of not having that day some meat, although until that time they have not wanted for the most part, since the crop of tobacco was in, to have meat three times in the week and at least twice, they having other provision by them at all times to dress and eat when they will. And they continuing still in that obstinate rebellious condition, although I have instead of

---

The case of Richard Preston vs. his servants, in J. Hall Pleasants, ed., *Archives of Maryland*, XLIX (Baltimore, 1932), pp. 8–10. I am grateful to the Maryland Historical Society for permission to reprint this document.

flesh for the present provided sugar, fish, oil, and vinegar for them, [I] am constrained to address myself to this court, [in order] that according to equity and their demerits they may receive such censure as shall be judged equal for such perverse servants, lest a worse evil by their example should ensue by encouraging other servants to do the like. And though by the sheriff they were summoned to this court upon the 6th day last, yet since I have proferred them, if yet they will be contented with such as I can possibly provide for them, [that] there should be no further proceeding publicly in the thing. Moreover, I did offer them to give them a note from under my hand for three or four of them to take my boat and to spend a week's time or more, to see if they could buy any provision of flesh or anything else, and I would pay for it, though never so dear bought. Yet notwithstanding they still continue in their obstinate condition and would come to the court, although I have sundry times told them that I was loath to bring them or myself to appear publicly in the thing.

Richard Preston

To the honorable the Governor and Council:

The humble Petition of John Smith, Richard Gibbs, Samuel Coplen, Samuel Styles, etc., servants to Mr. Richard Preston, showeth:

That Mr. Preston doth not allow your petitioners sufficient provisions for the enablement to our work, but straitens us so far that we are brought so weak [that] we are not able to perform the employments he puts us upon. We desire but so much as is sufficient, but he will allow us nothing but beans and bread. These premises seriously considered, your petitioners humbly address themselves unto your honors to relieve our wants and provide that our master may afford us such sustenance as may enable us to go through with our labors for the future; and your petitioners shall as in duty bound ever pray, etc.

Upon these petitions of Mr. Richard Preston and his servants, and upon examination of the said servants present in court: the court, taking the same into serious consideration, ordered that these servants now petitioning, viz., John Smith, Richard Gibbs, Samuel Coplen, Samuel Styles, Henry Gorslett, and Thomas Broxam, be forthwith whipped with 30 lashes each. Then the court further ordered that two of the mildest (not so refractory as the others) should be pardoned and that those two so pardoned should inflict the censure or punishment on their other companions. And thereupon the said servants, kneeling on their knees, asking and craving forgiveness of their master and the court for their former misdemeanor and promising all compliance and obedience hereafter, their penalty is remitted or suspended at present. But they are to be of good behavior towards their said master ever hereafter (upon their promise of amendment as aforesaid). And so to be certified from court to court.

16

Courtship and Marriage

It was widely believed in the colonial period that courtship and marriage should be governed by certain "prudent" considerations. Love must be there, to begin with, but a couple should also evince a "fitness" of spiritual and material estate. And in assessing these matters, the families on both sides would play a major role. In fact, these norms were not invariably honored. Particularly among the less fortunate some courtships were carried on, and some marriages were made, without regard to the opinions of any except the two persons directly involved.

But this was unlikely in wealthly families, when a substantial inheritance hung in the balance. Thus when Elizabeth Winthrop, daughter of John Winthrop, Jr., became engaged to the Reverend Antipas Newman, there was much consultation and debate within her family. Some of this can be glimpsed in a letter from her father to her brother, Fitz-John, written in September 1658, when the latter was visiting for a time in England.

When Michael Wigglesworth proposed to Mrs. Samuel Avery in 1691, there was no occasion for widening the circle of deliberation, since both parties were past middle age and had been previously married and widowed. But Wigglesworth's list of "considerations"—designed to bring Mrs. Avery to a favorable response—reveal assumptions that were broadly operative.

The economic foundation of marriage was often declared in a contract between the parents of the prospective bride and groom. The couple would receive from the groom's family land, housing, tools, and cattle, and from the bride's family certain domestic furnishings and cash. The deed of Jacob Mygatt of Hartford, Connecticut, is a fairly typical example.

The feelings—the affections—of the bridal couple are least of all likely to appear in the historical record. Yet in rare cases they do come through. One example is a page of handwritten jottings—poems, anagrams, and acrostics—by and about Stephen Williams (groom) and Abigail Davenport (bride) of Longmeadow, Massachusetts (1718).

The specific forms of the wedding ceremony varied among the different religious groups. Puritans, for example, treated marriage as a civil ordinance (and thus as the responsibility of magistrates, not ministers), whereas for orthodox Anglicans it was still a church affair. But among people of every persuasion there was also a lighter side to weddings. An extract from the diary of Jonathan Holmes of Middletown, New Jersey, makes the point clearly enough.

The marriage of widowed persons raised some special problems. The woman, in particular, might wish to protect the properties that she retained from her earlier marriage. Sometimes this protection was assured by formal "articles of agreement," like those drawn up just before the wedding of Margaret Preston and William Berry of Maryland. These agreements had no exact precedent in English law, and they suggest therefore a significant improvement in the position of colonial women.

Inevitably, too, there were problems *within* marriage; Puritans, no less than other people of every time and place, sometimes fell far short of wedded bliss. An admittedly extreme case of stress and strife is found in the manuscript diary of a Connecticut clergyman named Jacob Eliot. The diary is, indeed, a virtually unbroken chronicle of marriage gone awry; only an extract is presented here. Because divorce was rarely obtainable—and never for what we would call incompatibility—the Eliots remained together through many unhappy years.

Letter of John Winthrop, Jr., to Fitz-John Winthrop

(1658)

Boston, Sept. 9, 1658

Son Fitz,

I received your letters of the 12th of April last and do bless God to hear of your safe arrival and [the] continuance of your health, wherein all your friends here rejoice and cannot but take notice of the special providence and favor of the Almighty in ordering things so that you did not go in the other ship. You have great cause to admire and adore the goodness of the Lord toward you in disposing things so, by His foreseeing providence for your good and safety, that you escaped that danger—for which you have great cause to praise and magnify His glorious name,

Letter of John Winthrop, Jr., to Fitz-John Winthrop, September 9, 1658, in *Collections of the Massachusetts Historical Society*, Fifth Series, VIII (Boston, 1882), pp. 45–49.

and no less for those many deliverances in that ship wherein you went, of which I perceive by your relation in your letters you were very sensible, as you had just cause. I beseech the Lord to give you a heart to glorify Him, who hath done so great things for you, and to devote yourself to His service and fear, to which I beseech the Lord to incline your heart. Be earnest with the Lord in prayer, that, having delivered you from those great dangers upon the seas, so He would preserve your soul and body from eternal death, and [from] all those snares and temptations and allurements of Satan, sin, and the world, that might plunge your soul into perdition. Be careful to avoid all evil and vain company, which are so great instruments of Satan to draw and entice [men] to evil and to allure the simple into the snares of destruction, as the bird is taken in the evil net; whoso[ever] is wise will beware of them. Be not drawn upon any motion or pretense whatsoever into taverns or alehouses or any houses or company of evil fame. I have often forewarned you and persuaded you against wine and strong drink—which, if it were only for your health, you should carefully shun, yea, the very moderate use thereof. The often use of such things, though very moderately taken, is [the] origin of great diseases and distempers; it never agrees with the constitution and lungs of any of our family; [and] it is more dangerous in those parts than here, especially to breed coughs, catarrhs, consumption, and burning fevers and such like.

I am much grieved at the dangerous sickness of your uncle which you write of; but some hopes of some abatement of the disease which you mentioned in the sequel of your letter did give us longing expectation of hearing the desired news of his recovery, which I hope by Mr. Lock to be informed of your letters. But [I] have not received any intelligence by any letters or other ways from you but a sad report which is spread abroad in all the plantations, which, I understand, cometh from a letter of Captain Leverett to his son, who writes, as I am by many informed, that God hath taken him out of this life, which makes me sadly to bewail the loss of so dear a friend and brother. But I cannot see that letter yet, but if it can be found he promiseth I shall see it to my better information, for I am but newly come to this town. I have yet some hopes that there may be some mistake or misreport about the same; but I wonder much that I should have no letters from you by Mr. Lock's ship which arrived here about three weeks since, by which I have yet received no letters from any, neither hath Mr. Amos Richardson received any, or any other intelligence save only by that letter from Captain Leverett. You should omit no opportunity of writing; your mother will also be troubled that most others that have relations here have written to their friends, and she cannot hear of any from you. You should write by every way that offers, either by Barbados, Virginia, or other opportunity, though never so briefly, where you are, and how you are in health, and our friends near you or further off. We shall be glad, by all occasions, to hear of your welfare: your letters, if any be sent by way of Barbados or other ports, must be enclosed to some known, settled person there that is also known here; but every direct passage I hope you will not fail.

Your mother and sisters were very glad of those letters from you and have all of them written to you; they were all in good health when I came from there about 14 days since. They are all at Hartford; but I heard since that your sister Elisabeth was ill of her head last week and was taking physic the morning when the last messenger came [from] thence. She was very near death last winter when she was sick of the measles, but it pleased the Lord to deliver [her] from the very doors of death, when we had but little hopes of her recovery. All the rest also had the measles, your cousin Martha also, and your brother in the Bay; but it pleased the Lord to recover them all without much illness.

Your mother informs me that in your letter to herself and in your letter to your sister, you still dissuade from that proceeding with Mr. Newman, which if you do out of care of your sister and love to her, as I doubt not you do, you do well. But those expressions which it seems you used of not owning him, etc., but that they are taken as proceeding from your earnest desire of dissuading her for her good, or otherwise, would seem to be too harsh. There is no such disproportion betwixt him and yourself as should occasion such expressions. Scholars are well esteemed everywhere, and the more if they have answerable parts. Whether that proceed or not, you know he is not a despicable man; and I find he is now very much esteemed and beloved of all in those places and here also. I have not heard more esteem of any where he is known; and in that regard your arguments and persuasions about that matter are less valid, except you had propounded another more fit, which upon very serious consideration and advice we find would be very doubtful and un-certain to be pitched upon, there being so little choice of such as might be suitable in all respects; which considerations hath made us, with many other friends, upon a late renewed motion, to have serious thoughts whether there be not some special providence in it (which we could not see before) for her future good. We looked at the business as at an end before you went away, and so all winter, and till of late; but he hath now lately so earnestly renewed his motion that we are now seriously advising with friends here about the same, being desirous to attend [to] council and advice in so weighty a case, to submit to the wise hand of Providence and the overruling will and pleasure of the Lord, who disposeth of hearts and affections and ordereth all such things as He pleaseth.

As for your sister, although her inclination was rather that way than any other that presenteth, yet her constant professions and resolutions have been to do nothing without our approbation; and so [she] hath been very well contented hitherto to submit to such [a] condition as we should see providence directing us to consent to for her future good and comfort. Therefore, what way soever is taken by us concerning her, you must continue the same endeared affection towards her as at any times before, and [towards] him also if the Lord shall please to put him in that relation to us. We have not yet fully resolved what to do in that business; but our friends here and those that were opposite before do not only now consent and approve, but persuade [us] to it, as [well as] very many others, yea, all that speak about it; so that your mother is very well satisfied in such things as were formerly objected against it. Your brother also and sister do now consent willingly to it; so as, though there be no conclusion yet, I rather think if [there is approval from] such further council which I am now advising with, and whose advice I have purposed to look at as a satisfactory issue in the case (having commended it to the Lord and hoping for His blessed guidance in the same), [we] will conclude for a speedy proceeding except some just impediment should appear.

His father hath purchased a very convenient house and land near the place where he is—I think in the plantation itself in Wenham—which is let for twenty pounds a year and can constantly be let for that price at least. And if there be a proceeding, that will for present be assured her; and the people there do proffer very largely for so small a people if he will continue with them, but it is not resolved whether he shall follow that employment. He may easily fall into other, if it be thought best for him. The plantation of Pequot, which is now called New London (that name being established by order of the General Court), hath been very earnest with him to be there—Mr. Blinman having left them, who is at present settled in New Haven and likely to continue there. He lives in Mr. Hook's house there. Those people at New London have been very earnest to have Mr. Newman, but the others of Wenham are not willing to hear of his removal from them; and in respect of the conveniences of nearness to the plantations in the Bay, it may be most likely for this continuance there, if he follow that employment. I hope the Lord will direct for the best. I am sorry there is a house and a very good orchard upon the land which he reserves and doth not let out.

[From John Winthrop, Jr.]

Letter of the Reverend Michael Wigglesworth
to Mrs. Avery
(1691)

Mrs. Avery, and my very kind friend.

I heartily salute you in the Lord, with many thanks for your kind entertainment when I was with you March 2nd. I have made bold once more to visit you by [means of] a few lines in the enclosed paper, not to prevent a personal visit but rather to make way for it, which I fully intend [for] the beginning of the next week if weather and health prevent not, craving the favor that you will not be [away] from home at that time; yet if your occasions cannot comply with that time, I shall endeavor to wait upon you at any other time that may suit you better. Not further to trouble you at this time, but only to present the enclosed to your serious thoughts, I commend both it and you to the Lord and wait for an answer from Heaven in due season. Meanwhile I am and shall remain,

Your true friend
and well wisher,
Michael Wigglesworth

Malden March 23, 1691

I make bold to spread before you these following considerations, which possibly may help to clear up your way before you return an answer unto the motion which I have made to you. I hope you will take them in good part, and ponder them seriously.

1st. I have a great persuasion that the motion is of God, for diverse reasons: [such] as, first, that I should get a little acquaintance with you by a short and transient visit, having been altogether a stranger to you before, and that so little acquaintance should leave such impressions behind it as neither length of time, distance of place, nor any other objects

Letter of Rev. Michael Wigglesworth to Mrs. Samuel Avery, March 23, 1691, in *New England Historical and Genealogical Register*, XVII (1863), pp. 140–142.

could wear off, but that my thoughts and heart have been toward you ever since.

2ly. That upon serious, earnest, and frequent seeking of God for guidance and direction in so weighty a matter, my thoughts have still been determined unto and fixed upon yourself as the most suitable person for me.

3ly. In that I have not been led hereunto by fancy (as too many are in like cases) but by sound reason and judgment, principally loving and desiring you for those gifts and graces [that] God hath bestowed upon you, and propounding the glory of God, the adorning and furtherance of the Gosepl, the spiritual as well as outward good of myself and [my] family, together with the good of yourself and [your] children, as my ends inducing me hereunto.

2ly. Be pleased to consider, that although you may peradventure have offers made you by persons more eligible, yet you can hardly meet with one that can love you better, or whose love is built upon a surer foundation, or that may be capable of doing more for you in some respects than myself. But let this be spoken with all humility, and without ostentation. I can never think meanly enough of myself.

3ly. Whether there be not a great suitableness in it for one that hath been a physician's wife to match with a physician. By this means you may, in some things and at some times, afford more help than another, and in like manner receive help, get an increase of skill, and become capable of doing more that way hereafter, if need should be.

4ly. Whether God doth not now invite you to the doing of some more eminent service for Him, than you are capable of doing in your present private capacity? And whether those many emptyings from vessel to vessel and great afflictions that have befallen you might not be sent with a design to fit you for further service, and to loosen you from the place and way you have been in?

5ly. Whether the enjoyment of Christ in all His ordinances (which at present cannot be had where you are) be not a thing of that weight that may render this motion at this time somewhat more considerable?

6ly. Consider, if you should continue where you are, whether the looking after and managing of your outward business and affairs may not be too hard for you, and hazard your health again?

7ly. If God should exercise you with sickness again, whether it were not more comfortable and safe to have a near and dear friend to take care of you and yours at such a time, especially now when your dear mother is gone to Heaven?

8ly. This following summer is likely to be full of troubles (unless God prevent, beyond the expectation of man) by reason of our Indian and French enemies: now, whether it may not be more comfortable and safe to get nearer the heart of the country than to continue where you are and to live as you do?

9ly. The consideration of the many afflictions, losses, and bereavements which have befallen you, as it hath affected my heart with deep sympathy, so it hath been no small inducement to me to make this motion—hoping that, if God should give it acceptance with you, I might be a friend and a comforter to you instead of your many lost relations; and I hope upon trial you would find it so.

10ly. As my late wife was a means under God of my recovering a better state of health; so who knows but God may make you instrumental to preserve and prolong my health and life to do Him service.

Obj. As to that main objection in respect to my age, I can say nothing to that but [that] my times are in the hands of God, who, as He hath restored my health beyond expectation, can also if He please prolong it while He hath any service for me to do for His name. And in the meantime, if God shall please and yourself be willing to put me in that capacity, I hope I shall do you as much good in a little time as it is possible for me to do; and [I will] use some endeavors also to provide for your future, as well as present, welfare, as God's bounty shall enable me; for true love cannot be idle.

Obj. And for the other objections from the number of my children and [the] difficulty of guiding such a family.

1st. The number may be lessened if there be need of it.

2ly. I shall gladly improve my authority to strengthen yours (if God shall so persuade your heart) [and] to do what lieth in me to make the burden as light and comfortable as may be. And I am persuaded there would be a great suitableness in our tempers, spirits, principles, and consequently a sweet and harmonious agreement in those matters (and in all other matters) betwixt us; and indeed this persuasion is a principal thing which hath induced me to make this motion to yourself and to no other.

Finally, [hoping] that I be not over tedious, I have great hope that if God shall persuade you to close with this motion the consequence will be for the furtherance of the Gospel [and] for the comfort of us both and of both our families, and that the Lord will make us mutual helpers and blessings to each other, and that we shall enjoy much of God together in such a relation, without which no relation can be truly sweet.

Marriage Contract for Jacob Mygatt and Sarah Whiting
(Hartford, Connecticut, 1654)

Whereas I, Joseph Mygatt, of Hartford upon the River and in the jurisdiction of Connecticut in New England, have in the behalf of my son Jacob and at his request made a motion to Mrs. Susanna Fitch, in reference to her daughter Sarah Whiting, that my said son Jacob might with her good liking have free liberty to endeavor the gaining of her said daughter Sarah's affection towards himself in a way of marriage: now this present writing showeth that the said Mrs. Susanna Fitch having consented thereunto, I do hereby promise and engage that if God, in the wide disposition of His providence, shall so order it that my son Jacob and her daughter Sarah shall be contracted together in reference to marriage, I will pay thereupon unto my said son as his marriage portion the full sum of two hundred pounds sterling, upon a just valuation in such pay as shall be to the reasonable satisfaction of the said Mrs. Fitch, and so much more as shall fully equalize the estate or portion belonging to her said daughter Sarah. And I do further engage for the present to build a comfortable dwelling house for my said son and her daughter to live in by themselves, as shall upon a true account cost me fifty pounds sterling. And [I] will also give them therewith near the said house one acre of ground planted with apple trees and other fruit trees, which said house, land, and trees shall be and remain to my said son as an addition to his marriage portion, before mentioned, and to his heirs forever. And I do also further promise and engage that at the day of my death I shall and will leave unto him my said son and his heirs so much estate besides the dwelling house, ground, and trees, before given and engaged, as shall make the two hundred pounds, before engaged and to be paid [at] present, more than double the portion of the said Sarah Whiting. And for the true and sure performance hereof I do hereby engage and bind over my dwelling house and all my lands and buildings in Hartford, with whatsoever estate in any kind is therein and thereupon. And I do further engage that my daughter Mary's portion of one hundred pounds being first paid to her, I will leave to my said son and his heirs forever my whole estate at the day of my death, whatsoever it shall amount unto, and in what way, kind, or place soever it lies, he paying to my wife during her natural life twelve pounds a year, and allowing to her a dwelling entire to herself

Marriage settlement of Jacob Mygatt, of Hartford, Connecticut, in *Collections of the Connecticut Historical Society*, XIV (Hartford, Conn., 1912), pp. 558–560.

in the two upper rooms and cellar belonging to my now dwelling house, with the going of half the poultry and a pig for her comfort in each year during her said life; also allowing her the use of half the household stuff during her life, which she shall have power to dispose of to Jacob or Mary at her death, as she shall see cause. And I do further engage that the portion my said son shall have with her daughter Sarah shall (with the good liking of the said Mrs. Susanna Fitch and such friends as she shall advise with) be laid out wholly upon a farm for the sole use and benefit of my said son, her daughter, and their heirs forever. And upon the contraction in reference to marriage I do engage to jointure her said daughter Sarah in the whole estate or portion my son hath with her, laid out or to be laid out in a farm as aforesaid or otherwise, and in the thirds of his whole estate otherwise, to be to her sole and proper use and benefit during her life and after her death to their heirs forever. And lastly I do engage that the sole benefit of the Indian trade shall be to the sole advantage of my son Jacob, and do promise that I will during my life be [an] assistant and helpful to my said son in the best ways I can, both in his trading with the Indians, his stilling, and otherwise, for his comfort and advantage which I will never bring to any account with him; only I do explain myself and engage that in case my son Jacob shall depart this life before her daughter Sarah, and leave no issue of their bodies, then her said daughter Sarah shall have the full value of her portion left to her, not only for her life as before, but to her as her property to dispose of at her death as she shall see cause, and her thirds in all his other estate for her life, as is before expressed. It being also agreed and consented to that my wife after my decease and during her natural life shall have the use of two milch cows which my son Jacob shall provide for her, she paying the charge of their wintering and summering out of her annuity of twelve pounds a year. In witness whereunto, and to every particular on this and the other side, I have subscribed my name, this 27th of November, 1654.

Witnesses hereunto
John Webster
John Cullick
John Tallcott

The mark of
J M
Joseph Mygatt

Courtship Poems, Stephen and Abigail Williams
(1718)

A short word in way of congratulation of the happy meeting & uniting of those worthy names, viz. of the Reverend Mr. Stephen Williams, Pastor of the Church of Christ in Longmeadow, and the pious & very desirable young gentlewoman Mrs. Abigail Davenport, daughter of the Reverend Mr. John Davenport, pastor to the Church of Christ in Stamford, whose honorable marriage was religiously performed in Stamford, July the 17 day 1718.

How happily two names are met
Two names of note & of renown.
The foremost here in order set
Is Stephen which denotes a crown.
The other name is Abigail
A father's joy it signifies.
Which twain conjoining will not fail
Of sounding forth sweet harmonies.

Anagram: Stephen Williams
I small when I step—
I safest am when I am small.
And when I do not step too high.
When great and lofty men do fall,
They most endangered are thereby.

Another Anagram: Stephen Williams
In will he stamps—
When my husband for me doth call,
Or stamps, I'll run his will to know.
And say, my dear, I hope I shall
To you, my head, due honor show.
Your pleasure, sir, when understood
With readiness I shall obey
In all things lawful, as I should,
Yea, instantly, without delay.

Ms. original in Longmeadow Historical Society, Longmeadow, Mass. Used with permission.

Chapter 16

Anagram: Stephen Williams
She will stamp in—
Alas, how she doth stamp and cry,
Like one whose will is sorely crossed,
Or one in pain and agony,
Or one that hath all comfort lost

The last thing mentioned is my case.
It's that which doth my passions move.
I want to see ye lovely face
Of him whose worth commands my love.

I hear thy voice, thou mourning dove.
Is thy soul so distressed for me?
Come, take ye pledges of my love.
Let mine embraces comfort thee.

Now sighs and fears are passed away.
Serenity steps in their room.
Arise, my soul, and do not stay.
Go forth to meet with thy bridegroom.

Anagram: Abigail Williams
A Abigail I'll Swim—
A Abigail, think well of him
Who for thy sake can be most free
To suffer much. Yea, I could swim
Through seas of troubles to please thee.

I such contentment take in thee
I shall begrudge no pains or cost,
Whereby thy life may happy be.
I hope with us no love is lost.

Acrostick
S irs, I have found that rare good thing
T hat Solomon commanded much.
E ven a wife, a choice blessing,
P icked out for me, a quite none such.
H ow bountiful is God to me.
E nough I can't His grace admire,
N or as I ought so thankful be,

W ithout more grace, which I desire.
I am well suited to my mind.
L ikewise, I hope, so is my wife.
L ove doth increase, and we do find
I t admits peace, and excludes strife.
A h, what are these, our pleasant things?
M ors, when it comes, a period brings.
S weet comforts fade, yea, fly with wings.
    Why, then, should we dote on such things?
                              S W

Acrostick
A las, dear sir, you boast too much,
B efore you had much proof of me.
I am by you miscalled "none such".
G reatly mistaken you may be.
A loving and a loyal wife
I hope that I may be to you.
L iving in love's a pleasant life.
W e both have tried and found it true.
I beg of God wisdom and grace.
L end me also your helping hand.
L earn well ye duty of my place
I hope I shall at God's command.
A as you well noted, so would I
M ind this, we should, as all must die.
S o death must part my dear and I.
    God fit us for eternity. Amen
                            A W

Extract from the Diary of Jonathan Holmes

(Middletown, New Jersey, 1737)

June 12: Sabbath: I tarried at home. Toward evening John Stanley and
Grace Maunder was married by John Bowne Esq. John Bray, his wife,
and second daughter was at our house until the event was almost passed

Extract from the diary of Jonathan Holmes of Middletown, N.J., for June 12, 1737,
in John E. Stilwell, ed., *Historical and Genealogical Miscellany,* III (New York, 1914), p. 370.

and did not know of such an intent. Just after they went away it passed. Mrs. Bray, as I heard, said she would send them as much company as she could, and several came from that way, Brays and others. At night when the bride was to be put to bed, she would not let any put or see her to bed. I answered that she ought not to talk, for I would throw the stocking. At that she stepped into her room and shut the door and said, "then John shall not come to bed tonight." And then [she] shut the door and locked it. After some time the groom came and knocked at the door, and she opened it, though she had sat in the dark long enough to have undressed herself. And other [people] slipped in with the groom, and she said, "it signified nothing: you shall not see me abed tonight; I'll sit up all night first." Some time after [she said] she would run away and go somewhere else for to lodge; but being prevented, then she said she would jump out of the window. I answered, "aye, jump out you will, and he may get another." After pestering them I took down one of the casements of the room and pinned up a cloth to keep out the wind. Then [we] let them shut the door and said that we would come in at the window, which occasioned them (as we thought) to sit and lay all night with their clothes on, which occasioned much laughter. Next day we had much mirth about their manner of bedding.

Articles of Agreement between William Berry and Margaret Preston

(Calvert County, Maryland, 1669)

Articles of agreement, made and agreed upon between William Berry of the one part and Margaret Preston, both of Patuxent River in the County of Calvert, of the other part, witnesseth that the abovesaid Margaret Preston and William Berry have fully and perfectly concluded and agreed, that the said Margaret doth reserve for her own proper use and behoof, before she doth engage herself in marriage to the said William Berry, the value of one hundred pounds sterling, to be at her the said Margaret's own disposal, in such goods as shall be hereafter mentioned: viz.

Plate, to the value and worth of forty pounds sterling.

Articles of agreement between William Berry and Margaret Preston of Calvert County, Maryland, January 8, 1669, in J. Hall Pleasants, ed., *Archives of Maryland*, LVII (Baltimore, 1940), pp. 468–469. I am grateful to the Maryland Historical Society for permission to reprint this document.

The little Negro girl called Sarah, born in Richard Preston's house, valued to ten pounds sterling. If the said girl should die, the said William Berry [agreed] to make the same good to the said Margaret by another Negro or the value.

A good mare to ride on, value seven pounds sterling.

A chamber or room to be well furnished with bedding and furniture, with other household stuff to the value of forty-three pounds sterling.

And for a further testimony that the above mentioned articles are fully and perfectly concluded and agreed upon by the parties aforesaid, the said William Berry both binds himself, his heirs, executors, and administrators to the true performance of all and every [one] of the above mentioned articles, to the full value as is aforementioned, whensoever the said Margaret Preston shall make demand of the same for her own proper use. But if it shall be so ordered after the aforementioned William Berry and Margaret Preston be married that the said William shall die first, that then the abovesaid goods (or the value) do remain firm to and for the said Margaret's own proper use, as she shall think fit to bestow, over and above her proportion of the estate which by the said William Berry shall be left her. For the true performance of this agreement the abovesaid William Berry hath hereunto set his hand and seal this ninth day of the tenth month, called December, in the year one thousand, six hundred, sixty, and nine.

William Berry (sealed)

Signed and Sealed
in presence of
  George Deulins
  Wm. Jones

Recorded at the instance and request of the abovenamed William Berry, January the 8th, 1669.

Extract from the Diary of the Reverend Jacob Eliot

(Lebanon, Connecticut, 1763)

Nov. 24. Another V. quarrel, after having plagued my heart out all the morning, in directing and dictating about all my affairs, charging me with,

Ms. original in the Woodward Papers, Connecticut Historical Society, Hartford, Conn. Used with permission.

and often twitting me for, being too honest, neglecting my business much, trusting too much to other folks, not overseeing my own business, nor foreseeing things, events, and dangers as I might and ought, and reflecting as if [I were] incapable of it, etc., till I could bear no longer. I showed some heat and anger (God forgive me) and earnestly begged of her to forbear and not insist upon them things anymore, for it was more than flesh and blood could bear. Or, if she did not, I would complain to her friends and expose her—upon which she flew into the utmost rage and fury again, calling me a cursed Devil, kicked at me, and struck me with her fist again, and took up a powder horn to strike me over the head with. But, defending myself, I warded off the blows, etc. But she protested she would expose me to all the parish, have nothing more to do with me, nor hear me again, as long as she lived, etc. But after a while, on my tamely submitting to hear all the bad stories about first wife, Betty Higley [?] etc., and crying with her, and not carrying to her as before, ever since I saw her etc., and bearing the greatest insults from her, her passion at last subsided.

Decem. 3. Another venged quarrel for nothing but jesting with her about getting her a calico gown in spring, in a cheerly manner suggesting it was a good while to spring, and hadn't she calico gowns enough etc. She took me in earnest and flew into a violent passion and protested [that] she would never ask me for anything again, but would get what she wanted without being beholden to me, that my first wife might have anything she asked for, or my mistress Mrs. Robinson, Betty Higley, or the widow Kellogg. [She] would not go to breakfast with me. (When courted, and the sugar pot offered to take sugar for coffee, [she] refused, saying no, I set it away from her as far as I could at other times, she had long observed, and therefore she would not touch it now.) And when I offered to put sugar in her dish (declaring I was only in jest before, and crying out shame upon her) she said she would not drink any of it if I did, and, further, that if it was from a young man she could take a jest, but not from such a covetous old man as I. And she knew I was in earnest, and that soon after we were married, when she asked me for a few yards of ferret [?] for binding for her riding hood, I refused to let her have it and said she might stay till she had earned it first etc., which was made out of the whole cloth and as D—h a lie as ever told with tongue, unless I was asleep, or drunk and knew not what I said. At last [she] seemed to get over her passion, but remained muggy a good while.

Decem. 19. Another most V. Q., after long preaching to me upon the old score about doing nothing about settling with Jacob and 1000 bugbears raised about her and Josie being left destitute etc. etc. till I could bear no longer (and it is marvelous I have borne so much). I with some zeal earnestly begged and entreated her to forbear and not trouble me and herself with those things—I intended to take care about them as soon as I could conveniently etc.—on which she flew into her usual, most violent, and uncurbed passion, and with utmost rage and fury and malice cried out "God damn you, leave your devilling, begone out of the house or I will." Upon which I said, "you may go, and you will for I shan't." This she took in a great dudgeon, flung the child into my arms, and went quick out of the room. Patty went after her, but could not find her for a while [and] at last found her in the study closet. Then she came in again, and after Jacob and Patty were gone to bed, protested she would never lie with me again as long as she lived. (Though before they went off, [she] asked Patty for the key of the little chamber, to lie there; I said she should not have it.) Then [we] had a long parley, whether she or I should lie up-chamber. I said I would not and she should not, but earnestly advised her out of compassion to herself and the child, if she had none for me, to go to bed in the study, and I offered to warm it for her, or she might warm it herself, but she refused. And so we sat debating the case for an hour or two, except [for a] great part of the time she, as sullen and surly as a mad bull, would say nothing at all. At last she said that if I would give her my word that I would not come to bed at all to her, she would go to bed (for if I did she would get out again, for she would never have anything more to do with me, for I was no husband to her etc.), to which I (like a fool, for peace sake) consented and submitted, and accordingly warmed the bed for her, and she went to bed in state with the child. And poor Pill Garlick was forced to sit by the fire and expected to do it all night to watch her (tho' were it not for fear she would do herself, or the child, mischief, I would have sent her to Jericho before I would have done it). However, I tamely yielded and built up a good fire for that end. After I sat a while, she bid me go and sit in the kitchen. I told her I hoped she would allow me the liberty of my own fire and not be so cruel to the poor old man as to make him sit in the kitchen such a cold night (and as cold as almost ever known) without fire (for that was raked up), and I would not disturb her. After we had then sat silent a while, she with sovereign authority said, "I command you to go and lie up-chamber." At which I laughed and replied that she had expressly inverted the sacred text now and read it (as the woman did to her blind husband), "Husbands obey your wives."

178

After profound silence again for a while, I at last very lovingly said, "My dear, if you will make up so far as to admit me to bed with you tonight, then if we can't make up matters between ourselves, and you think it worthwhile, we'll refer the case between us to any one indifferent person whom you please on the morrow," to which she faintly consented. Then I raked up the fire and went to bed. She was muggy a while and said she meant I should go to bed up-chamber. [She] advised me to turn my back and not my face to her, but at last partially made up the matter, and we lay peaceably till the morning when we wholly finished the matter and got pretty well reconciled. (Though she had before said she never would be reconciled again, but [would] expose me to the whole parish and go home, and after [being] abed got up twice in her smock to look after me, going into the closet and into the kitchen.) And so the controversy ended for that time.

17

The Elderly

There is some reason to think that life in the New World was particularly hard on the elderly. Since society was more fluid and personal relationships were inherently less secure than in the mother country, old people were sometimes left without the support of friends and relatives when they needed it most. The correspondence between two brothers, Thomas and William Leeds of New Jersey, suggests vividly some aspects of this predicament; the will of the Presbyterian minister, John Lawrence, tells a similar story—though with a happier ending. Some elderly persons, however, had the means and the ingenuity to obtain protection for themselves. The "articles of agreement" between Jared Speck and Thomas Burr of Connecticut record a bargain that was a direct response to the problems of old age.

Correspondence of Thomas Leeds and William Leeds

(New Jersey, 1736–1737)

Brother:

I received yours some time in Christmas by chance. I hear J. Grover will be at Solomon Smith's at night or tomorrow; therefore I take the opportunity to write, hoping this will find you in health. As for myself, I am recovering of a bad looseness. It had carried [elements] of some other distempers, for I am very crazy, disconsolate, and childish; the latter I have always [been]. [It] was so as I have been played upon all my life, but I hope my time in this world is short. I have still a mind. did [?] Revell Elton but I cannot sell to my mind. I had nobody this last sickness to tend me because it [would] have cost 12 shillings a week.

Correspondence of Thomas Leeds and William Leeds, of Monmouth County, N.J., in John E. Stilwell, ed., *Historical and Genealogical Miscellany*, III (New York, 1914), p. 450–452.

Some [people] scare me by telling me I shall live 20 years longer, but [I] hope I shall not, for I am weary already and shall be except I get some [more] comfortable way of living than at present, the which I doubt will never be. I am very poorly on many accounts. I am fallen backward 30 pounds in repairs [needed] in [my] house lot, wool shop, clothes, and bedding, and other things, which makes me afraid I shall outlive my estate. For I cannot work but contrive not to spend too fast but pinch when I can. I did not think I should live so long. I would have you to make inquiry when I am dead [as to] what I have left, you and Daniel, and get it into your own hands as soon as you can. My spirits are exceedingly low with this sickness. If my clothes were not so bad, I should have a mind to come and see you this spring. Here some of our kindred would be glad to see you here, Cousin Ann especially. 'Tis very well you have a minister—if he preaches so, by precept and practice, so as he reforms the people. That will be a blessing to the country and people. As for a separate Governor I think [that] will prove a bubble (it all to me in them cases of Governor [?]). I shall still be a miserable creature as folks told me before I was 14 years old, but now am much worse. Old age is come on me. No more at present, but [with] my love to you and your wife and brother Daniel, so I rest,

Your Brother,
Thomas Leeds

Brother:

I received yours May the 4th, after John Shaw was gone. I did not see him at all when he was last here. As for the gloves I know nothing about them. The house I do not like to go to; [the] reasons you may guess. You may employ John Shaw and send money by him, for I shall not undertake it for some reasons. I sent home a letter by Will Curles last week; I would have you get it if you can. This I send by a woman, my near neighbor, hoping it will find yours in better health than I am. For the distemper is very bad at times. When I get a little cold, then I think I am going to die. I do think it will kill me at last. I am willing to die as soon as God pleases. I do remember my best desires to you and my love to your wife and all my friends. I am troubled with the swelling of my legs. I have not been able to work since you was here. I am afraid I shall never be, but am in expectation of death's last stroke, but how it will fall out I cannot tell. Sometimes I think I should not be sick, were not I dejected in my mind, but I cannot be sure 'tis so.

[I] know I am melancholy by living so alone. I got one swelled knee, but I hope it won't continue long, but [will] be better; and farewell from your brother,

Thomas Leeds

April 20, 1737

I think this will be the last letter. It is a week since I sent the other.

Brother Thomas:

Last summer I was taken with a little hard swelling about as big as a swanshot, full of little red pimples, in my private parts. In August it got as big as an Indian corn. Then I applied myself to a doctor, and to another, but they cannot stop its increasing; and of late it is very troublesome or else I should have come myself. Our mother, when she gave that piece of gold to Jonathan, left a great charge that he and we should be careful of it and said it might be of some benefit if any of us got a bad sore; and particularly she said she was afraid I should. So that she had [a] belief [that] it might do me some good. Her belief causes me to request this favor of you—to send me that piece of gold by the bearer James Rice, and I shall be careful of it, and return it to you again. And I have sent you security for [the] performance [thereof] and rest your loving

brother,
William Leeds

Brother William:

I ventured to send the piece of gold you sent for, doubting I shall ever see it again. I was ready to think at first 'twas one of your old tricks, but thought 'twas best to let [it] go, hoping God will take care for me as He has done heretofore. I have a dreadful cough so I cannot write, which cough I do expect will keep with me as long as I live. [As to] your desiring my prayers, I cannot tell whether the removal of your affliction will be good for you. It may be sent to you to bring you to a sense of your wickedness of your life and all your wicked contrivances and bring all your evil deeds to judgment, those to me and others, and make restitution to those you wronged. The more you think on your evil deeds with indignation, the lighter will be your punishment. I am [feeling] very poorly and have nobody to do nothing for me. I have thought myself a-going several times, but am alive still and may be thus several years. Yet I cannot tell how long I can last on this principle of what I have. Whether I seek the [???] of your contrivances at this time I cannot tell.

I would have you go to Master Grover and ask him [about] the German doctor who cured the swelling on his throat. Perhaps the same may help you. If you die before me, you ought to leave me something to live on for reasons you and I know; for what I have wastes fast. I cannot work.

The piece of gold is as much mine as the coat on my back, for my sister bought it dear of Jonathan and [I] bought it again for 17s. 6d. new money from Sister Elizabeth Jong's mother. For Sister Mary did give it to nephew John when she died. There is a woman in West Jersey that has had such a cough [as mine] 40 years and [is] yet alive, which makes me think I may live a great while, for it purges me.

The piece of gold would have fetched 20s. two years ago. I am forced to live meanly because what I have wastes so fast that I am afraid. If you send 20s., you may have your bond.

　　　　　　[Letter not signed, but is evidently from Thomas Leeds]

Will of the Reverend John Lawrence

(Virginia, 1684)

At Virginia, in the County of Lower Norfolk, in Little Creek, at the house of Nicholas Huggings, I, John Lawrence, master of arts, being very sick and weak of body, but, blessed be God, of sound and perfect memory, do revoke all manner of former wills by me made, and do declare this only instrument of writing to be my last will and testament, in manner and form as followeth. *Imprimis*, I give and bequeath my soul to God that gave it and my body to the earth from whence it came, to be decently and Christianly buried; and as for my worldly goods, [I] give and bequeath them as followeth. Secondly, I do declare that I am the eldest lawful son of John and Dorothy Lawrence and was born [and] baptised at the Wormlyberry house, in the parish of Wormly in Hartfordshire, and [that] I am now possessed of six tenements situated in the parish of St. Giles in the Fields, in Church Lane, which I was resolved to give to Cary Lawrence, the eldest son of Andrew Lawrence, my brother's son. But now my resolution is altered; and resolving with myself, I thought fit to come to Virginia to a sister which I had living there, expecting to find comfort by her. But not finding that entertainment which I did expect, I did not tarry long with her, but went and lived in Maryland

Last will and testament of Rev. John Lawrence, in *Virginia Magazine of History and Biography*, II (1895), pp. 176–177.

three years, where I preached the gospel to the comfort of many thousands, but could not be endured by the Roman Catholics. And afterwards I was persuaded to go for Carolina, which persuasions I did embrace. And to that effect I took a boat at Potomac River on purpose to transport myself to Carolina. And coming to Point Comfort, I did meet with a good friend aboard a ship bound for that same place where I was bound, aboard of which ship I did put myself with my chest and clothes. But I was so weak and feeble, being taken with the griping of the guts, being occasioned by the long passage of two weeks aboard the aforesaid boat being hardly in a condition to swim. And, meeting with this good friend, by name Mrs. Mary Benson, widow, who, being of a tender heart, had compassion on me, [and] the ship being full of passengers, she did lay me upon her own bed and in her own cabin, and did attend upon me both night and day for five months to the admiration of all the people that heard or knew of it, I being aged three score and fifteen years. And by God's good providence it was my good fortune to meet with this tender and compassionate-hearted gentlewoman, after my long passage in the said boat and my said sickness occasioned thereby. And being bound and obliged in all equity and reason to recompense her so far as possible I am able, I do therefore alter my former resolution and do leave the aforesaid six tenements to the said Mrs. Mary Benson, widow, her heirs, executors, administrators, and assignees. And I do hereby ordain and appoint them my full and sole executrix of this my last will and testament—revoking hereby all former deeds of gifts, jointures, and all other writs, wills, and testaments made by me. And I do hereby leave to her and to her [heirs] aforesaid all my jewelry, rings, gold, silver, and all whatsoever I have; and also I appoint and ordain the aforesaid Mrs. Mary Benson, widow, and her [heirs] aforesaid to uplift and receive seven years' rent of the said six tenements at 36 pounds sterling per year, allowing 50 pounds sterling which I received by me. And it is to be deducted out of the aforesaid seven years' rent. And I do leave the same to her heirs, executors, administrators, and assignees forever, forever, and forever. And finally this I ordain to be my testament and latter will inviolable, and for the confirming thereof I have hereunto affixed my hand and seal, this 26th day of September, Anno Domini 1684.

John Lawrence and seal

Signed, sealed, and delivered in the presence of us:
  Jacob Johnson
  John Coe
  George Smart

Proved, County Court of Lower Norfolk, the 15th October 1684, by the oaths of all the evidence.

Articles of Agreement between
Jared Speck and Thomas Burr
(Connecticut, 1686)

Hartford, February 22, 1686. Articles of agreement between Jared Speck and Thomas Burr, both of Hartford in the colony of Connecticut in New England, witnesseth that the abovesaid Thomas Burr doth for himself, his heirs, executors, administrators, or assignees covenant to and with the above said Jared Speck that he will from the day of the date hereof, so long as he shall live in this present world, maintain him the said Speck with sufficient meat, drink, washing, and lodging, and clothing, and house room, and all other necessaries comely and convenient for such an ancient person, both in sickness and health, and at his decease to be at the charge of a comely burial according to the custom of this place. And for the conditions above expressed and the love I bear to him and his wife and other considerations me hereunto moving, I have therefore fully, clearly, and absolutely given, granted, and confirmed, and do by these presents fully, wholly, clearly, and absolutely give, grant, and confirm unto him, the said Thomas Burr, his heirs, executors, administrators, or assignees all the estate that I now stand seized of (except so much as will defray my just debts which are now due from me at the date hereof) and, in particular, besides my moveables, my house, and barn, and home lot situated in Hartford aforesaid. The land is about two acres, be it more or less. All that was mine I give and grant to him for the abovesaid Thomas Burr, his heirs, executors, administrators, or assignees to have; and to hold, possess, and enjoy the abovesaid estate with all the profits and privileges thence arising or thereunto belonging, from the day of the date hereof forever, without any eviction, ejection, or molestation whatsoever from or by any person or persons claiming or that may claim the same or any part thereof by virtue or color of any lawful right or title any ways derived from me—warranting hereby that at the signing and sealing hereof the abovesaid estate was free of and from all other alienations whatsoever. And I do hereby grant to [the] said Thomas Burr

Articles of agreement between Jared Speck and Thomas Burr of Hartford, Conn., February 22, 1686, in *Collections of the Connecticut Historical Society*, XIV (Hartford, Conn., 1912), pp. 166–167.

full power and lawful authority to record the promises to himself and his heirs or assignees forever. For confirmation hereof we have set to our hands and seals, this day and year above expressed.

Jared Speck and seal
the mark of Thomas Burr and seal

Signed, sealed, and delivered in presence of us,
  Thomas Olcott, Robert Sandford

18

Death

Every society tends to maintain a distinctive pattern of response to death, and the study of funerals, styles of grieving, and behavior toward the mortally ill can therefore be very informative. Among the colonists, of course, religion suffused all forms of thinking and feeling about death. Both the dying person and the bereaved survivors viewed the event as an entrance to the afterlife of the spirit. All concerned sought to find "assurance" that it would, in fact, be a happy "translation," a fulfillment of the salvation that God had promised to His chosen followers. It seems, however, that this sense of assurance was not always quite secure, and that the terrors of hell could not be put entirely out of mind. People awaited death with no less anxiety than they do now —and perhaps with more.

The following group of documents contains accounts of two separate deathbed scenes. The first (taken from the diary of the Reverend Ebenezer Parkman of Westborough, Massachusetts) illuminates the roles of the minister and the relatives in attendance at such times. The second (a narrative of the passing of a Baptist woman in New Jersey) focuses more directly on the feelings of the dying person. There is also a letter of condolence from the Reverend John Cotton of Plymouth to one of his parishioners, which presents an affecting combination of formalized piety with deep personal warmth.

Another kind of document concludes this unit: the gravestone. In the first of the examples presented here the stone-cutter has depicted an hourglass, along with imps shooting darts into a skull—images, clearly, of time and death. At the same time, the wings on either side of the skull, and the panels below with their fruits and flowers, connote spiritual renewal and the life to come. The second example is a triple-stone, with separate panels for each of three infant siblings who died within a few years of one another. It reminds us that death often came, to early Americans, very early—and in clusters.

Extract from the Diary of the Reverend Ebenezer Parkman

(Westborough, Massachusetts, 1727)

[April 21:]
Sometime after sundown Lieutenant Forbush came and requested me to go down to see his wife, who, they thought, was drawing near her end and wanted to see me. I went down. When I entered I said, "Mrs. Forbush, I am sorry to see you so ill. I am come at your desire. Which way can I become the most serviceable to you?" She replied [that] she was under apprehension of the approach of death and she could not but be under fears on so great an occasion. Upon which I proceeded to enquire into the grounds of her fears, telling [her] withal that I should endeavor to remove them; and (receiving some very general answers) to promote the matter the more readily I began to say something concerning true repentance, universal obedience, and the unfeigned love of God and to the people of God—which, finding [it] in her, might show to her the truth of grace to be wrought in her, which being demonstrated must necessarily make all things bright and clear and comfortable. But this process I managed in such an easy and familiar manner as this following.

1. "I am hoping (Mrs. Forbush) you have freely repented of any sin that you have known yourself guilty of." She answered that she trusted she had, and was heartily willing to [repent] of all that she had been chargeable with that she had not particularly known of, etc.

2. "You have told me heretofore that you have used your utmost to keep the commands of God universally; but especially now, since you have openly dedicated yourself to God and joined yourself to the communion of the Lord's people and waited upon Christ's table, I conclude you have much ground for satisfaction and comfort. (You should have if you have sincerely and uprightly done your duty)." To which she [said], "it has indeed been a comfort to me, and I am now glad that I have not that work to reproach myself with the commission of; (or in these words) I am glad [I] haven't that work to do now." (Having some reference, I believe, to the trouble that many have been in at such an hour [over the realization] that they had never obeyed the command of Christ.) etc., etc., etc.

Extract from the diary of Rev. Ebenezer Parkman of Westborough, Mass., for April 21, 1727, ed. by Francis G. Wallett, *Proceedings of the American Antiquarian Society*, LXXI (Worcester, Mass., 1962), pp. 186–191. I am grateful to the American Antiquarian Society for permission to reprint this document.

3. "Well, Mrs. Forbush, but to let you see things more plainly still, let us a little further enquire. Don't you find in you such a love to God as has made you both repent of sin and obey His commands from a desire of His glory?" etc. etc.

"But to find out some further proof of all this and to have some stronger evidence of your love to God and Christ, have you a pure love to the Godly? Do you love the disciples of Christ, those that you think bear the image of God unfeignedly?"

She: "I hope really that I do."

N.B. Mr. Thomas Forbush and [his] wife, Captain Byles and [his] wife, and Jedediah How were in the room, besides the family. But the person being looked upon as near expiring, I thought not to thrust those persons so well acquainted with the woman—as nearer [relatives] she has not (except one)—out of the room, and seeing [that] my discourse was general and what anyone might hear. Yet when under any of those heads any particular private matters have occurred, it has then been usual with me to desire the company to withdraw. But here I apprehended would be such things spoken as might be very profitable and suitable for all that heard, as I concluded these near relatives were gratified not a little by them. However, upon some account or other it seems old Mr. Forbush is displeased; and though [it was] at the most awful time, when every thought was profoundly serious and solemn, yet he thinks fit to [break in] upon us in a sad, passionate manner upon the last sentence, spoken thus. "Sir, we are grown folks." I turned about in great surprise and, calmly looking upon him and then as calmly speaking, asked him what he had said. He repeated the same words as before. I asked him, "What then?" (Now raising myself up in my chair) "Why then," says he, "we understand these things already; [we] have read in the Bible and some other books and ourselves know these things, being grown folks and come into years." Here up I spoke the words following (his wife, his sisters, especially the apprehended dying person, besought him not to open his mouth any further, they being astonished as well as I, and the woman declaring it much to her comfort and benefit that I had proceeded as I had and that it was the end of her sending for me, etc.), "Mr. Forbush, I am astonished at such interruption at such a season, when I come upon my commission and charge to minister in the name of God to a servant of His ready to leave the world," etc., etc. Says he, "if I had been in your place, I would not have asked such questions." I replied in defense of them. He said Mr. Breck would not ask such. I answered I was not now to enquire what Mr. Breck would ask, but I was able to affirm that the most learned, the most pious, and the most judicious ministers would. I therewith prayed him to say which [questions] were improper and wherein. He appeared not able to tell so much as what any one question was that I had asked. "Well," said I, "seeing you won't or can't tell me which," etc., "I'll endeavor to recollect all that I have said, though I did not study before I came down what I should say, nor had I time; neither did I confine myself strictly to any method but said what I thought of the greatest weight in the case before me." I then recapitulated and demanded as I went along what exceptions he had to make and wherein they were go grossly injudicious as to be foundation enough for his so strange interposition.

1. He supposed she had repented before now and she had examined herself before this time of day often and often, no doubt. And then I had lived in the house and knew the woman long ago, so that I had no need to ask questions now. Besides I had or should have asked her when she was admitted into the church. "Truly," said he, "if it was my wife, you should not have asked her whether she had repented of her sins. We hope she has done it long ago." To which I said, "this person I knew so well as that I saw no danger from my asking general questions. She has had nothing scandalous in all her life that I know of, neither could anyone think that I desired to rake into all the particulars of her past conversation in the world and managements in the family." (Not but that if I had made such enquiries she might, I believe, have produced what would have been very instructing.) "Were I examining a person that had been notoriously vicious and demanding a particular confession and before so many witnesses, it had been another thing; but I have been endeavoring to assist this person in preparing actually to give up her account to the great Judge. And though she may have viewed it numberless times and we may have reviewed and examined it together, yet now at the awful juncture before delivering it into His hands we act most wisely to look all over as carefully as possible to find out whatever escapes or flaws there may be, since it can never be done [here]after throughout Eternity, and Eternity depends upon this account. Mr. Forbush, those questions appear injudicious to you; yet they are so far from being a reflection upon your sister that the most advanced Christian that is on earth won't scruple to ask them, and they are the very questions therefore that the gravest and profoundest divines in the Christian Church do put in these cases," etc., etc.

2. "You ask," said he, "whether she had not comfort in her having been at the Sacrament. How needless [is] that question. What do you

think she went to it for, sir?" "I admire at you Mr. Forbush. Your sister's end was to testify her obedience to the command of Christ, and to obtain of her Lord divine grace and support under all troubles and difficulties, to engage God's merciful presence in a time of extremity, especially when death approaches. She has been, I say, [striving] for these great and important things; and now when she needs them most of all I ask whether she has got her errand and how she is sure she has these things; and [you say] this is impertinent," etc., etc.

3. "And you asked whether she loved the Godly? What a question that is! I know what you mean, whether she loves all that appear professedly to be Christians. I haven't a charity for everybody because they make a profession. There is some that I know of that I won't have a charity for though they have joined to the Church." To which I rejoined, "Mr. Forbush, in trying whether true Grace be in the heart, love to Christ's disciples is always inquired into. I doubted not but your sister doth [carry herself] so, yet it is asked to make all things as clear as possible. By Christ's disciples I mean the same as Saint John doth by the Brethren, by which are understood all that [in] any way bear the image and resemblance of Christ. And Mr. Forbush, notwithstanding what you have last said as to your charity, I'll tell you mine is so extensive that there is not a person in all Westborough but I would charitably hope he may be a subject for the Divine Grace to work upon." Well, he would not, etc. It was time I should do what I could for the woman. I told him he had prevented me and unfitted me, etc., but I turned about and went on. Mr. Forbush asked [that] I'd forgive him if he had said anything wrong, but he thought he would not ask such questions; so that I so far lost my labor with him. I told him if he was so much disturbed about them, I would submit them to the judgment of whatsoever ministers in the country he should choose. I prayed him to consider his sister. He was willing withal, saying that he knew not how soon he should need me on the same account and therefore again desired me to forgive his bluntness; but yet he could not desire me if ever I should to ask him such sorts of questions. Thus did he in a strange manner keep up the flame by throwing in oil when he pretended to cast in water to quench it. "No, Mr. Forbush," said I with some earnestness, "I'm afraid you would not care that I should deal feelingly with your soul." I now told him of my being obliged in conscience to do my utmost for persons when, as his sister, etc. I shall take no further notice of the strange reply he made [to] me nor the long discourse he further occasioned. I was grieved heartily to see so much of his ignorance and passions. It grew very late.

It was well [that] the woman (it may be through her fright) was revived. We came into so amicable a composition as to go to prayer and we parted friends. But both my head and heart were full. It was twelve when I got home. Sister Ruth discerned my trouble. I went to bed but could not sleep for a long time. I beseeched God to quicken me hereby in my work, and make me more diligent to accomplish myself lest I meet with worse trials than this. I remember and would take notice of it that the suddenness and lateness of the Lieutenant's coming for me prevented my usual address to heaven before such ministrations. I would be humbled for my sin and take the punishment God inflicted for it.

"The Triumphant Christian": A Record of the Death of Sarah Lippet

(Middletown, New Jersey, 1767)

Or Faith's Victory over Death and the Grave, exemplified in the last, expiring, and dying words of Sarah Lippet of Middletown in East Jersey, who had been a member of the Baptist Church in the said place for many years. She departed this life the first day of October, 1767, aged sixty-one years, nine months, and twenty days. She was ailing six months before she died, but kept her bed [only] four days. Her last words and dying behavior is the subject of the following narrative.

The first morning that she was so exceeding ill she said, "my breath is short, and all the time I have I pray [that] I have patience to bear what the Lord pleases to lay on me. I have had comfort, a little before, and now am willing that His will should be done." At her request one [person] read the third chapter of Habakkuk; said she, "I will say as Habakkuk did—let it be with one as it will, yet I will serve the Lord." She desired to hear the sufferings of Christ read, whereupon she said, "What great love He had for sinners, to lay down His life for them. Scarcely for a righteous man will one die; yet He died for sinners, and for me shed His precious blood, and for all them that believe in Him; and [He] is now at the right hand of God, an intercessor. All my lifetime I have been in fears and doubts, but now am delivered. He hath delivered them who through fear of death were all their lifetime subject to bondage. For the love I have for Christ I am willing to part with all my friends

"The Triumphant Christian," in John E. Stilwell, ed., *Historical and Genealogical Miscellany*, III (New York, 1964), pp. 465–466.

to be with Him, for I love Him above all; yet it is nothing in me, for I know if I had my desert I should be in Hell. I believe in Christ, and I know that I put my whole trust in Him, and he that believeth in Him shall not be ashamed nor be confounded." At her request she had the second chapter of the first epistle of Peter read, and often would mention these words, "Who Himself bore our sins in His own body on the tree."

The second night of her being so very ill, about one o'clock, it was thought she would have instantly expired. People coming into the room, she said, "they think I am dying, but I know I am not, and think I shall not die this night. Yet I have no expectation of getting up, and am to go, yea, rather go than stay." About an hour [later] she revived and slumbered, then awoke with these words, "it is all calm. I have no terrifying thoughts in my mind, [but] a great calm." About eight o'clock that morning she said, "whether it be today or tonight, I am ready and willing; don't mourn for me, but for yourselves and [your] children." One of her friends came in to take leave of her [and] asked her how she did. She said, "I am just departing, and have been kept all my life time in doubt and fears, but now am delivered. I am free and willing [that] the Lord's will should be done in me. I hope to see you in Heaven, for I shall never see you here again." Her friends coming in, she perceived their concern [and] said, "why do you mourn when I rejoice? You should not; it is no more for me to die and leave my friends for the great love I have for Christ than for me to go to sleep. I have no fears of death in my mind. Christ has the keys of death and hell, and blessed are the dead that die in the Lord. I can't bear to see a tear shed. You should not mourn as [for] those which have no hope." Some she advised to seek for an interest in Christ, and said, "when all things else leave you, that will not; for what advantage will it be to gain the whole world and lose your soul?"

The morning before she died one of her friends came in to see her, to whom she said, "I am just going, I am right free and willing to go. I had rather a great deal go than stay, if I had my choice, for I love Christ above all; yet if it is the Lord's will [that] I should stay, I am willing. I have no fear on my mind; death is no terror to me. Yet it is nothing in me; I know if I had my desert, I should be in the hottest Hell. I believe in Christ and His blood cleanseth from all sin. I see that the Lord's afflicting me so lightly at first and so long hath been for my good. This [past] three months I have been resigning myself up to the Lord day and night, for my death has been revealed." [She said] to one [person that] she desired him with her, and said in Sampson's words,

"Oh, that the Lord would strengthen me this once, though I want to be strengthened many times; but now, if it is His will to strengthen me, [I ask you] to hear this prayer which was adopted to the desire of friends." Then she said, "I have been strengthened to hear and know [that] your prayer was heard. For I saw the Lord Jesus look down from Heaven and smile on me. I am now on a dying bed and I know not but a dying hour, for I feel one of my eyestrings broke and [I] don't expect to see the light of another day. It is true I see Jesus, by an eye of faith, look down from Heaven and smile on me."

About two that afternoon she was sensible of a very great alteration in herself, although she continued till past one o'clock that night. One [person] asked her if she did not long for that hour; to which she said, "I await the Lord's pleasure. It don't seem like dying to me but going [on] a long journey. I can seem to see how it will be with me when I am in Heaven. I am going to a world of spirits, and death is no terror to me; all tears shall be wiped from their eyes."

In the time of her illness, when they took [their] leave, her answers would be, "the Lord's will be done." That evening before she died she desired one [person] to pray with her, for she was very sensible [that] it would be the last time. Said she, "my friends, you must all lie on a dying bed as you see me now, and I have nothing to do but to die. Don't mourn for me when I am dead, for I shall rejoice." After some time she said, "I must bid you all farewell." She said, "how impatient I am, I now long for the hour; come quickly, Lord Jesus." She died very hard [and] said, "I never asked the Lord for an easy passage, or else I believe I should have had it granted—come quickly, Lord Jesus, and receive my soul." Then [she] slumbered for a few minutes. When she awoke they thought she would [have] gone off then. She said, "don't let me go asleep again, for I want to know when I die." Then one [person] asked her if her faith was strong yet. "Oh yes, I tell what I see and feel; my breath is short." She bid them ask her when they see her going; "then," said she, "you will know I am not deceived." She then broke out in these words, "Lord, leave me not, nor forsake me; but be with [me] and let thy holy angels guard my soul to Heaven and my body lie in the grave till the Resurrection. Lord, leave me, nor forsake me [not] in this hour of death, not an hour of darkness, in this hour of trial." Then said she, "I see the lights; Lord Jesus, receive my soul and body. I commit into thy care, Lord Jesus, my spirit." And so she died with a smile on her lips.

FINIS

Letter of John Cotton to Mary Hinckley

(Plymouth, 1683)

Honored and dear friend,

A due sympathy [of] one with another in affliction is a gospel duty. God's bowels yearn towards his [people] in distress; and, could we show ourselves [to be] the children of God by bowels of affection to the distressed, it would well become our Christian profession. I am not able to do or say what my heart is willing to express in this case; but, hearing that you are deeply dejected under the late bereaving stroke of God's hand in your family, I cannot but, in conscience of my duty to God and in compassion to you—whom my blessed father loved, and whom I much respect in the Lord—speak a few words, that may by divine blessing tend to allay that excessive grief that hath taken hold of you. Consider, I beseech you, what is done and who hath done it and why is it done. You have lost a dear grandchild by an ordinary disease. What is there in this more than the common portion of the children of men—yea, and of the children of God? You are not the first afflicted in this kind. My own dear mother, besides the death of her own [children], passed under this rod in the death of a pleasant grandchild of eight years old, on whom her heart was exceedingly set. If God deals with you as with a child, you have hereby an evidence of your adoption. You will not be cast down because God seals His fatherly love to your soul by this correction. God hath done what is done, and He did you no wrong. His right was greater to that little one than yours. It was covenant-seed, and God hath made haste to accomplish all covenant-mercy to it. I hope this will not grieve you. A babe embraced in the arms of Jesus Christ, the redeemer and shepherd of these lambs, lies safer and more comfortably than in the bosom of the most tender-hearted grandmother. Will this grieve you? What did you intend in the keeping of this child, if it had lived? Certainly you meant, while it was with you, to train it up for the Lord; and did you not often pray for it, that its soul might be accepted in the covenant of grace? All your good purposes, desires, and prayers are answered in this, that it is safe in Heaven. Your work is rewarded to the utmost of the wishes of your heart; and who can tell (but He that knows all our hearts) how much you needed this affliction, and how much spiritual good God intends to your soul hereby? Weaning dispensa-

Letter of John Cotton to Mary Hinckley, January 10, 1683, in *Collections of the Massachusetts Historical Society*, Fourth Series, V (Boston, 1861), pp. 113–115.

tions are very merciful to a child of God. Our hearts cleave too close to earthly enjoyment. God, who is well worthy, would have more of our affections; and happy is that affliction that is sanctified to cause the heart to be more in love with God. Upon my thoughts of your present visitations, I thought of Psalm 30; and [I] see no reason but to think that good David, when he came into his new house, had a dangerous fit of sickness, which God sent to season his heart with more ardency, life, and strength of grace and holiness, to dedicate himself and [his] house unto the Lord. And I am verily persuaded that is the worst harm [that] God intends [for] you by your present trials; and when tried, you shall come forth as gold. I pray, pardon my boldness with you. From you and your mate I have been comforted and directed in an evil day; and therefore I own myself your debtor, though unable to discharge it. Think of Psalm 42, last. The Father of mercies be your comforter and supporter!

So prays yours, affectionately, in our Lord Jesus,

John Cotton

Gravestones: The Iconography of Death

Gravestone of Elias Row, Phipps Street Burial Ground, Charlestown, Mass.

Gravestone of the Neal children, Old Granary Burial Ground, Boston, Mass.
Photograph by Moira Demos.

19

Inheritance

In most human cultures inheritance is tightly bound up with the life of the family. Indeed, families have always been the primary agency for maintaining and redistributing the ownership of property. This circumstance is, if anything, more pervasive in preindustrial communities, where the most valuable resource is land.

In colonial America the interplay between family and property was extremely complex. Within the broad framework of English common law there was room for infinite variation in detail. But certain underlying tendencies can be discerned. On the one hand, a common stake in property served to bind families together into tight cooperative units. On the other hand, questions of inheritance sometimes uncovered deep tensions within the family. The critical issue was the actual transmission of property from one generation to the next—its manner and its timing. Some men conveyed substantial "gifts" as soon as their children became adult. Others waited until the occasion of marriage. And still others retained final title to most or all of their properties until the day of their own death. Examples of each pattern can be found in the following set of documents: a "deed of gift," and two wills.

Often enough wills and deeds did not prevent dispute among inheriting survivors. And sometimes the result was a full-blown court case. The last of the documents included here is an extract from the record of such a case, in early Virginia, where a local planter describes the human and legal *sequelae* to the deaths of one Richard Charlton and his daughter Elizabeth.

Though centrally about inheritance, these materials touch on other matters as well. They are suggestive about the spatial arrangements of colonial communities. They offer—at least in the wills—yet another vantage-point on religious belief and values. They evince, in one instance, the workings of the charitable impulse. And, in the Charlton case, they tell an affecting personal story of a fatherless child apparently preyed on by scheming fortune-hunters.

Deed of Gift from William Almy to His Son
(Portsmouth, Rhode Island, 1659)

Know, all men, by these presents, that I, William Almy, inhabitant of the town of Portsmouth in the Colony of Providence Plantation in New England, do freely give unto my son, John Almy, dwelling [?] with me, a part of my farm whereon I now dwell, on the south side thereof, the said parcel of land lying next unto the farm belonging to Richard Barden; the breadth thereof being on the front of my farm thirty-eight rods wide, as also thirty-eight rods wide at the seaside from the said Richard Barden's farm northward; and so to run upon a straight line on the north side from the front down to the sea, the said land being about fifty acres more or less. I say I, William Almy, have given my said son, John Almy, the aforesaid parcel of land with all the privileges therein containing, to him and his heirs forever, upon such tenure as followeth *videlicet*, that the said land shall successively belong unto my said son John [and] his heir male; but in case he hath no heir male at his death, then it shall be [passed] to my son Christopher or his heir male, if he hath any, or otherwise to the next brother; but [in] case there be no heir male, then it shall return to the first heir female. I say I have given the said land unto my said son, John Almy, upon the terms aforesaid, together with this injunction: that in case we cannot agree together to make use of the whole farm in common, the same my said son is to maintain the whole fence betwixt us. I say I, William Almy, aforesaid, have freely given unto my said son, John Almy, the aforesaid parcel of land and to the heirs successively, according to the tenure expressed in the premises; and in witness of this, my act and deed, I have hereunto set my hand and seal, this seventeenth of October, Anno Domini 1659.

William Almy

Signed, sealed, and delivered
  in presence of us,
  John Greene
    her mark
  Adrey Almy

A true copy by me, Tho. Cornell, Town Clerk

Deed of gift, from William Almy to John Almy, October 17, 1659, in *The Early Records of the Town of Portsmouth, Rhode Island* (Providence, R.I., 1901), p. 372.

Will of Edward Garfield
(Watertown, Massachusetts, 1668)

I, Edward Garfield of Watertown, being sick in body yet through God's goodness sound in my memory, do declare this to be my last will and testament as followeth:

Imprimis: I give and bequeath unto my son, Samuel Garfield, ten pounds, to be paid in corn or cattle within one year after my decease; and forty acres of my land, lying on the side of Prospect Hill; and a piece of meadow containing about two acres and a half and being on the east side of Stony Brook (the same piece of meadow which the said Samuel have made use [of] already for diverse years with my allowance)— provided the same Samuel allows a cartway through the said piece of meadow to my meadow on the other side of Stony Brook. Also I give unto the said Samuel all my wearing clothes and my great Bible. Now the reason why I give no more to my said son Samuel is because (he marrying many years ago) I have formerly given him both land and other estate.

Secondly, I give unto my son, Joseph Garfield, the house and land which he now lives in, the land containing about nine and twenty acres. Also I give unto the said Joseph ten acres of meadow, lying on the farther side of Chester's Brook, westward, commonly called plain meadow. Also I give unto the said Joseph my farm, as also a mare colt of about a year old.

Thirdly, I give unto my daughter, Rebecca Mixter, twenty pounds, to be paid her in corn or cattle within two years after my decease; as also two pewter platters.

Fourthly, I give unto my daughter, Abigail Garfield, twenty pounds, ten pounds to be paid at the time of her marriage and ten pounds to be paid two years after; but if the said Abigail shall die unmarried, then my will [is] that the said twenty pounds be equally divided to Samuel Garfield, my son, and Joseph Garfield, my son, and Benjamin Garfield, my son, and Rebecca Mixter, my daughter; and if the said Abigail do live unmarried [I declare] that then my will is [that] she shall be allowed five and twenty shillings a year so long as she lives unmarried. Also I give unto the said Abigail a feather bed and bolster, with a rug and two blankets and one pewter platter.

Will of Edward Garfield, of Watertown, Mass., December 30, 1668, in *Proceedings of the Massachusetts Historical Society*, XIX (Boston, 1882), pp. 93–94.

Fifthly, I give unto my grandchild, Sarah Parkhurst, one ewe sheep and an ewe lamb.

Sixthly, I give unto Sarah Garfield, my grandchild, seven pounds, provided she serves out her time; but if she serves not out her time, then my will is that she shall have but fifty shillings only.

Seventhly, I give unto Ephraim Garfield, my grandchild, two cows, to be paid within three years after my decease.

Eighthly, I give and bequeath unto my beloved wife a cow, which my said wife shall have liberty to choose [from] among all my cattle. Also I allow unto my said wife five pounds a year as long as she lives, for which my wife had a bond of me before marriage. The said five pounds [is] to be paid in wheat and peas and rye and Indian [corn], by equal proportion (if my executor have them growing), at country price at such [a] place in Cambridge as my said wife shall appoint. Also my will is that my said wife shall, if she please, continue in my house. She shall have the new bedchamber for her use, with all the furniture in it, for space of seven months, as also a sufficiency of firewood for her own particular burning. Also my will is that my beloved wife abovesaid and my daughter Abigail abovesaid and my maid Ann should enjoy the benefit of what flax or hemp or wool there shall be in my house at my decease; and also that they are to live at the charge of my estate for the space of seven months as abovesaid.

As an addition to my beloved wife's legacy, my will is that she shall enjoy a feather bed and bolster and two little pillows which were of her own making; also a woolen wheel and a linen wheel.

Also I do nominate and appoint my loving son, Benjamin Garfield, executor to this my will and testament—to receive all [that is] due to me, and to pay all my just debts.

Thus resigning my spirit to God that gave it and my body to the dust from whence it was taken, I declare this to be my last will and testament, and do hereunto set my hand [on] this thirtieth day of December, one thousand, six hundred, sixty and eight—desiring my loving friends, Nathan Fiske, senior, and William Bond, senior, to see that this my will be performed.

Edward Garfield did own this to be his
will and did subscribe to it on the day
and year abovesaid, as testifieth
Nathan Fiske   William Bond

The mark of
Edward Garfield

Taken upon oath 11, 5, 1672 [by]
Wm. Bond & Nathan Fiske,
before Capt. Daniel Gookin
and Thomas Danforth.

Will of John Moon

(Isle of Wight County, Virginia, 1655)

In the name of God, amen. I, Captain John Moon, of the Isle of Wight
County in Virginia, and born at Berry near Gosport in the parish of
Stoak in Hampshire in England, being in health and good memory (praised
be God for it) do make this my last will and testament, in [the] manner
as followeth.

Oh Lord, I have waited for Thy salvation, and now, oh Lord, into
Thy hands I commit my soul or spirit; for Thou hast redeemed it, oh
Lord, thou god of Truth, and [I commit] my body unto the earth to
be interred in [a] decent manner, being fully assured of its resurrection
and [the] reuniting of it together again in that great day of God's power.
And all my worldly goods I give and bequeathe as is hereafter expressed.

Imprimis: I give and bequeathe unto my loving and well-beloved wife,
Prudence Moon, (my debts being paid) one-fourth part of all my movable
estate, that is to say, the same to be equally divided between my wife
and my three daughters, Sarah, Susannah, and Mary Moon. And [as]
for my land and houses, I dispose of [them] as followeth. I give and
bequeathe unto my oldest daughter, Sarah Moon, and to her heirs of
her body lawfully begotten, forever, my dwelling house now named Bethlehem, with all of [the] land and houses from Pagan Creek and joining
upon Henry Watt's land, unto the easterly side of the reedy swamp and
to the mouth of the creek by the dwelling house. And unto my second
daughter, Susannah Moon, I give and bequeathe all the land and houses
from the reedy swamp to the westerly side of the land that Samuel Nichols
now liveth upon, on the easterly side of Bethlehem Creek, that land
now [being] named Bethsaida, to belong to her, the said Susannah and
to the heirs of her body lawfully begotten, forever. And to my daughter,
Mary Moon, I give and bequeathe all the land and houses that lyeth
on Red Point side, now named Bethany, with that which Dennis Syllivant

Will of John Moon, of Isle of Wight County, Va., August, 12, 1655, in *Virginia Magazine
of History and Biography*, VI (1899), pp. 33–36.

liveth upon, and the land belonging to the Poplar Neck that lyeth by
the King of All Places, all [of] which [is] to belong to the said Mary
and to the heirs of her body lawfully begotten, forever. Now my intent
and will is that if my daughter Sarah [should] depart this life without
heirs as abovesaid, that then Bethlehem, her inheritance, shall belong
to my daughter, Susannah Moon, and her heirs as abovesaid, forever;
and that then half [of] Bethsaida, which is my daughter Susannah's inheritance, shall belong to my daughter Mary and her heirs as abovesaid,
forever, and half [of] Sarah's moveables. Also, my intent and will is that
if Susannah [should] depart this life without heirs as abovesaid before
Sarah or Mary, that then her inheritance [shall] belong wholly to Mary
Moon and her heirs as abovesaid, forever. As also, if Mary [should] depart
this life without heir as abovesaid before Sarah or Susannah Moon, [my
will is] that then her inheritance [is] to belong wholly unto Susannah
Moon and her heirs as abovesaid, forever.

And also, if Sarah Moon and Susannah Moon [should] depart this
life without heirs as abovesaid, [my will is] that then both of their inheritances are to belong unto Sarah and her heirs as abovesaid, forever; and
so accordingly; and [as to] all other things herein given and bequeathed,
my intent and will is that it shall belong unto the survivor of them and
her heirs as abovesaid, accordingly, forever. And also, my intent and
will is that my loving wife, Prudence Moon, shall be in, and abide and
dwell in, my now dwelling house called Bethlehem House, with my
daughter Sarah Moon or Susannah Moon or Mary Moon or either [of]
their heirs, for and during the widowhood of my well-beloved wife after
my decease; as also [she will have] so much land as is necessary for her
own particular use for planting and pasture during the time abovesaid.
And [as] for my children, I charge you all before God and the Lord
Jesus Christ, who shall judge the quick and the dead, that you demean
yourselves loving, obedient, [and] comfortable unto your mother all the
days of her life. And I charge you, my beloved wife, that you provoke
not your children to wrath, lest they be discouraged; but bring them
up in the nurture and admonition of the Lord and live peaceably and
lovingly together, and the God of love and peace will be with you. And
the Lord direct your ways in all things and make you all to increase and
abound in love one towards another and towards all men, and establish
your hearts unblameable in holiness before God, even our Father, at the
coming of the Lord Jesus Christ with all His Saints.

And my will is that my brew house and [the] land belonging to it
at Jamestown be sold toward the payment of my debts. Also, there is

a certificate already granted for seven hundred acres of land and rights for two hundred more—which nine hundred acres of land, my will is that it should be taken up in some convenient place. And when it is taken up, I give and bequeathe three hundred acres of it unto my wife, Prudence Moon, and her heirs forever, and the other six hundred acres [are] to be equally divided between my three daughters, Sarah, Susannah, and Mary Moon, and their heirs forever, in [the same] manner and form as [for] those other inheritances aforesaid is expressed. Also, I give and bequeathe unto Joan Garland, my wife's daughter, four female cattle and two hogsheads of tobacco, to be delivered, if she be living, or to her child if living, the year after my decease. Also, I give and bequeathe unto William Wilson, my wife's son, two female cattle and two hogsheads of tobacco, to be delivered, if he be living, the year after my decease. Also, I give and bequeathe unto Peter Garland, my wife's son-in-law, one hogshead of tobacco, the produce whereof [is] to be laid out in plate and kept in remembrance of me, and if living the tobacco to be delivered as abovesaid. And further, [as] for my land in England lying at Berry and Alverstoak in Hampshire near Gosport and Portsmouth—the which, when I was last in England, I mortgaged unto Mr. Owen Jennings of Portsmouth for two hundred pounds sterling money—my will is that if you cannot redeem it, that then it be sold outright and the money to be equally divided between my three daughters, Sarah, Susannah, and Mary Moon, in [the same] manner as is abovesaid; only, [as for] ten pounds sterling of the money that it is sold for, I give and bequeathe unto the poor of Berry five pounds of it, and the other five pounds I give unto the poor of Alverstoak, which money is to be delivered into the hands of the overseers for the poor in each place, to remain for a stock for the poor to let out, and the interest thereof [is] to be given to the poor in each place yearly. Also, there is due to me seven pounds odd money from Mr. Jennings, which he (being my attorney) received for me for rent due before the mortgage took place, and three rundletts of tobacco of about a hundred pounds weight that I left with him to sell for my use (but I have not received anything from him since); this also [is] to be divided as abovesaid. Also, I give and bequeathe four female cattle to remain for a stock forever for poor, fatherless children that hath nothing left them to bring them up, and for old people past their labor, or lame people that are destitute in the lower parish of the Isle of Wight county—the females from time to time to be disposed to those that do keep such persons to have the milk, provided that those that have them be careful of those they receive and of their increase. My will is that all the female increase from time to time be and remain for a stock for their use, and the male cattle and old cows [are] to be disposed of for clothing and schooling and the like necessities for such persons in [such a] condition as is before expressed; and the overseers of [the] poor, with [the] consent of my children, from time to time are to see this my will in this particular really performed, as it is in my will expressed, and not otherwise.

Recordatur, 12 August, 1655
    Examined and truly transcribed.

Teste.   Jas. Baker, Cl. Cur.

Extract, Records of the Northampton County Court, Virginia, February 19, 1663: Paper Submitted by Colonel Edmund Scarborough, Commissioner

Gentlemen: This case between Isaac Foxcroft, on behalf of Bridget Charlton, and John Gething hath enforced me to an unusual intendment of writing, which I speak that this may stand for affadavit to persons who are most concerned, and for whose sake I count myself chiefly obliged to vindicate truth and justice, which must prevail or the world perish.

The case in question I take thus: whether John Gething shall have the estate he claimeth in right of Elizabeth Charlton [late wife of Gething, and] second daughter to Stephen Charlton, deceased, or not, or whether Isaac Foxcroft, in right of Bridget [wife of Foxcroft, and] oldest daughter of the said Stephen Charlton, hath any right thereunto, or not.

The better to resolve this question, we are to consider by what pretended right the plaintiff in either case doth lay his claim, which requires the review of old Charlton and his disposures of the estate for which he labored long to enjoy little and to complete that folly [which] the wise man condemns in getting goods and cannot tell for whom. We see him now in his care for his children, contriving, devising, and securing estates for his two daughters.

That which concerns my present occasion is a deed of gift to his daughter Elizabeth, dated 27 October 1654, in which I have noted carefully Charlton gave his second daughter Elizabeth land and chattels personal. The land, in case of the said Elizabeth's decease in her minority, he wills

Quoted in Ralph T. Whitelaw, *Virginia's Eastern Shore* (Richmond, Va., 1951), pp. 427–430.

to his eldest daughter. The personal chattels he determined not, but is therein mute. And the better to secure what was intended, he appoints two feofees in trust until his said daughter Elizabeth attained to fourteen years of age, who are to take care of and improve the estate until the time designed by the donor. Here we leave this article, until occasion reassumes the further inquiry.

Now, the more clearly to demonstrate this case, we must track the progress of Charlton's affairs. Charlton soon after this deed aforesaid dieth and made a will—the contents and issues whereof is so well known to this court as needs not to be recited. Only [it] is to be noted [that] he deviseth something more to his said daughter Elizabeth.

Anno 1661. About the month of August John Severn, by clandestine means, procures Elizabeth to go from Captain Jones's house where she was in care for education, and carries her to John Gething, where a marriage was endeavored with the said Elizabeth Charlton, being a child about twelve years of age.

September 4th. Upon complaint made, a special court condemns the said John Severn for stealing the said Elizabeth from school, and engageth him to return her thither and answer the abuse [at the] next court. About the same time several endeavors were used to procure a license from the Honorable Governor's substitute, that John Gething might be married with Elizabeth Charlton—which failing, the said John Severn and John Gething went out of this county and illegally procured a license by misinforming Colonel Yeo, and so [Gething and Charlton] were married.

September 29. John Gething supplicates the court of Northampton County to be possessed of the estate that he claimed in right of Elizabeth, his wife, wherein the court proceeds with order for security to save the court harmless for delivering the estate before the said Elizabeth was at age according to the will of her father Charlton.

Anno 1662. About midsummer Elizabeth Charlton dieth, and soon after John Gething obtaineth letters of administration upon the estate of Elizabeth Charlton.

And now we are come to this present time, where Foxcroft complains that he hath petitioned this court for justice and cannot be heard nor have his petition read—of which imputation to acquit myself and the worshipful commissioners and the due administration of justice, we both hear the plea and proceed.

Isaac Foxcroft, in right of Bridget Charlton, his wife, lays claim to all that Elizabeth had a possibility unto, for that she died before she attained to fourteen years of age, and doth challenge law for just claim.

And herein I am much to seek, [this] being a science I may not pretend unto. Indeed it is a great study, and much knowledge [is] required which I could never read [that] any age can determine without contradiction. Sometimes the questions of right and wrong call in for their support statute law, precedents, and equity. And when those lie not in a direct line to secure the occasion, analogy must come in. And where a case is cloudy or mysterious (and sometimes where it is most obvious), wit and interest are not vainly additional. But to shun Scylla and pass by Charibdis, I shall call on your aid for conduct and desire [that] you improve reason, the basis of all law, by which scale I shall measure the case and propose this question: if you would not think yourselves much injured that your own estates should not be at your own disposal? Doubtless the question is resolved as soon as heard.

Then why should not Charlton dispose [of] his own according to his own will? If Charlton put an estate for his daughter Elizabeth into the hands of feofees in trust, to be improved and delivered at fourteen years of age to the said Elizabeth, will it seem reasonable to take this estate out of the hands of those entrusted by Charlton and deliver [it] to John Gething, a person scarcely thought on by old Charlton?

I am sure it is reason [that] the estate should proceed accordingly to the will of the donor. What law there is against it I cannot tell.

Neither should I presume to question the judgment of this worshipful court, but speak my own mind: That I should not have altered any part of Charlton's will or deed of gift, nor delivered [to] Elizabeth Charlton —much less John Gething—that estate which was laid up with feofees until Elizabeth [should] attain 14 years of age. And [that] I should have fortified this resolve from the reason of the order of Court of the 4th of September 1662, which condemned and questioned John Severn for suggesting the match with John Gething—whereby, I judge, five of the Council and Burgesses together with the whole court censured the intention of marriage as unfit. And how that fact which was in September condemned should in November following be approved by ordering the estate to be delivered to John Gething seems to me most preposterous. But, gentlemen, your (by me) unquestionable judgments have thought it fit, and that discretion which guided [you] will undoubtedly guard the action.

Nor did it seem necessary to me to grant J. Gething administration on his wife's estate, for I take it to be a kindness, giving him what he had before, by reason [that] what estate was his wife's he was invested with in marriage, and what she had a possibility unto, and had not attained thereto, could not be his by administration.

Gentlemen, give me leave further to presume on your patience and put the case [that if] Elizabeth Charlton had continued unmarried and died before she attained 14 years of age, who should then have had the estate, when the donor is mute? I suppose none will say John Gething. I have said before [that] I pretend not to the law and knowledge thereof, but I think it reason [that] it should return to the donor and his heirs, which I take to be Charlton's widow and eldest daughter—not John Gething.

And now here comes another material point into my thoughts: That the marriage of John Gething with Elizabeth Charlton was after an unlawful manner, for these reasons:

First, that the said Elizabeth Charlton was a child of about twelve years of age.

2ly, that she was stolen from Captain Jones's house, where she was at school.

3ly, for that she was detained after five of the Council and Burgesses and the whole court of Accomack had ordered her return.

4ly, for that they were denied a license in the county where they dwelt.

5ly, for that they went over the bay, and misinformed Colonel Yeo to procure license.

6ly, for that the license was not procured according to the act of [the] Assembly.

7ly, for that neither the court, intrusted by her father, nor her feofees in trust, nor the keeper and interests of the child, knew of or gave consent to the marriage.

And it seems reasonable to me that no unlawful means can attain a lawful end.

Consider what I have said and take the consequence with you, wherein I appeal to physicians, knowing men, and motherly women whether this early match with a child of about twelve years of age might not reasonably be supposed the occasion of her untimely death. Let us look back to Sarah Douglas, a child of the same years, who expired in haste because she was matched too soon.

There is none of you gentlemen but have children. Your toil and care is for their future support. Where learned clerks and council is wanting to devise your estates expressly to your nearest concerns, would you not have the best construction made for the advantage of yours? Would any of you think John Gething nearer to you (perhaps for accidentally killing your child) than your surviving child or children? Do you think old Charlton intended that deed of gift to John Gething, rather than his daughter Bridget or [his] widow? The Golden Rule prompts me to do as I would be done unto, and I doubt not the same spirit is amongst you all.

Consider [that] you have children and a wise man may be wanting to devise your last wills; would you [wish] that a stranger should enjoy your estates rather than your child? Before your eyes this day is the miscarriage of Elizabeth Charlton; do you know whose turn is next?

Gentlemen, you are zealous to do justice. Do it in the name of God. Think now of your wives, your children, and posterity. I supplicate your tender care of this case, that he which labors may work in hope for him or his to reap the harvest of all his toils.

Reason hath dictated this discourse, and many arguments too tedious to recite confirm me, though express words are wanting, that the best construction of the donor's intent is to be received. And thereby Bridget, the daughter of Stephen Charlton, and [his] widow, not John Gething, ought to have the estate Elizabeth Charlton had [the] possibility to enjoy, had she lived to fourteen years of age.

That this is my judgement, but still submitting to better reason, I fix my hand, in open court, this 28th day of January 1662/63.

—Edmund Scarborough

Upon debating the case above stated, the court were pleased to declare their construction of [their] former orders concerning the estate of Elizabeth Charlton, alias Gething. And [they] did resolve [that] they never intended, nor did at all dispose of, any part of the estate granted by deed or gift from Stephen Charlton to his daughter Elizabeth. But [they] are so far from averring the same that they have ordered the feofee Samson Robbins to be brought by summons to the next court and there to give an account of the estate and [the] proceeds which was given to the said Elizabeth. For the county's vindication and repute of justice [this] is put on record, with the former [writing] by Edmund Scarborough.

20

The Passage of Generations

The word "family" is subject to two different sorts of meaning. Most frequently, perhaps, it designates kinfolk in their arrangement through space—for example, the household as constituted more or less at one given moment. But there is also the family in its extension through time —one's ancestry and descendants, the whole lineal progression of kindred over many generations.

The next document projects vividly this second meaning of family. It is a chronicle, written by several hands, of the fortunes and vicissitudes of the descendants of Tobias Payne, over more than a century of American colonial history. The Paynes should be regarded as typical not of the colonists at large, but of a certain "elite" group: people of high status, substantial wealth, and broadly cosmopolitan connections. Though somewhat disjointed and confusing as presented here, their story more than repays a careful reading. There is material for the economic historian, the demographer, the genealogist, and the student of social mores. Most striking overall is the impression of mobility, of far-flung enterprise, and of enormously varied experience. In the final analysis the Paynes emerge less as a Massachusetts family, or even an American family, than as a transatlantic family with a membership scattered all around the English-speaking world. They were, moreover, joined in marriage and economic partnership to many other families of a similar character. All this is a salutary antidote to certain long-familiar stereotypes of colonial society and a reminder that there was much fluidity and change in the lives of at least some of our ancestors.

History of the Family and Descendants of Tobias Payne

"A Short Abstract of the Course of My Life," by Tobias Payne

I was born in the parish of Fownhope in the county of Hereford, my father being named William Payne and my grandfather Tobias Payne, who lived in the parish of Kingscaple in the said county but was born at Berkeley in the county of Gloucester where his ancestors had lived. In the year 1640 I was put to school to learn English, and there continued until 1645, when I spent some time [attempting] to learn the rudiments of Latin and to cipher; after which time until the year 1648 I remained with my grandfather. But God Almighty at that time taking him out of this world, I returned to my father at Fownhope, where I remained until the later end of the year 1649. But having no employment [I] was not satisfied with that course of life, so [I] desired him to place me in London, whereupon he sent me there with an instruction so to do; but that failing, I returned into the country again. However, the next year, anno 1650, I went to London again and applied myself to my uncle Richard Bridges, with hopes to find out some place, but could not do it to our content. However, rather than be idle, he let me remain with his uncle, alderman Adams, from whom I might depart at pleasure; so [I] betook myself under him to receive his rents, keep his cash, etc.

In the year 1651 the alderman departed with his family for Elsenham in Essex where we lived that summer, and returned against the winter to London again. Having remained with the alderman three years, viz. until the end of the year 1653 (in which time I studied French and made a beginning in Spanish, as also [I] bettered myself in writing and arithmetic), I understood from his son-in-law, Mr. William Christmas, that his factor, Mr. Richard Twyford, in Hamburg, had occasion for an apprentice. I thereupon acquainted Mr. Christmas that I was not minded to remain any longer with the alderman and had likewise a desire to see foreign parts. So, with the help of my uncle Bridges, [I] agreed with him, viz. to pay the said Mr. Twyford £200 sterling ready money, and to serve him eight years, as also that my uncle should stand security in a bond of 1000 pounds for my faithful service. So in the beginning of January, 1654, I took leave of the alderman etc. and set forward [on]

History of the Payne family, in *Proceedings of the Massachusetts Historical Society*, XIII (Boston, 1875), pp. 405–418. Note: Some of the place names mentioned in the early part of the narrative cannot be positively identified. In all such cases the original spelling has been retained. In all other cases the spelling has been changed to conform to current English usage.

my journey for Hamburg—first for Gravesend, thence with the packet boat for Dunkirk, and so through Flanders, Brabant, Zeeland, Holland, East and West Friesland, [the] Dukedom of Oldenburg, [the] Bishopric of Bremen and Holstein. And so, through God's mercy, I arrived safe at Hamburg in the latter end of the said month of January, in which [journey] I saw these cities and places following, viz. Dunkirk, Mardike, Ostend, Veurne, Bruges, the Fort St. Danasin, Sluce, Flushing, Middleburg, Trevees, Dort, Rotterdam, Delft, Leyden, Amsterdam, Harlingen, Leeuwarden, Groningen, Delfzijl, Emden, Apen, Oldenburg, Delmenhorst, Bremen and Stade.

So, coming to Hamburg, I applied myself to my master, and was presently bound to him (the 200 pounds being paid by his order to Mr. Robert Christmas, and the bond for my faithful service [being] entered into by my uncle); whereupon I entered his service, and was in [a] few days after sent by him out into the country to Hanover, to learn the High Dutch or German language, where, after I had remained four months and made an indifferent progress, [I] was (in regard of business) called home again; in which journey the only noted things I saw were the Prince of Hanover and Prince of Zell's Courts.

Returning to Hamburg, I betook me to my employment; and the ensuing winter, my master having occasion for England, [he] departed thither and left me alone in the business, which I managed till his return about three months after, and then delivered him all things to his good content. Not long after I was sent to Bremen to get in some old debts, and returned thence in six weeks, continuing in my business until March '56, at which time I received the sorrowful news of my father's decease. So [I] desired leave of my master to return into England for [the purpose of trying] to settle something that was fallen into me by his decease, which I obtained; and in the month of May [I] departed home in our company's ship, Captain Edmund Green [being] master. And [I] had a very sudden passage for London, from whence after a short stay I departed into the country, where, dispatching my business, I returned again for London. And [I] took my passage in [the ship of] Captain James Talbot, one of our company ships, for Dordrecht in Holland, where by God's mercy we arrived in few days.

From thence I went over land for Hamburg, viz. through Gelderland, Westphalia, etc. and saw in my journey, Haarlem, Nareden, Amersfoort, Zwolle, Lingen, Wildeshausen, Bremervorde and Hornburg, etc. So, returning to Hamburg, [I] thanked God for his continual preservation of me and fell again to my business, in which I remained until the year

1657—when, understanding from my friends that my presence in England was very needful, as to the disposing of some lands fallen unto me by the death of my father, I obtained again leave of my master to return thither. And in the month of August [I] set forward by land for Holland, in which passage, besides what [I] formerly mentioned, I saw these following places; Doemin, Bolsward, Workum, Enkhuizen (where I had the honor to sup with two of the States gentlemen, viz. mynheer Marode and mynheer de Vett) and Armuyen. At Flushing, with some other passengers, I hired a small vessel, and in 24 hours we arrived through God's mercy in safety at Gravesend; and from thence [I went] to London, where I found the company ship, [with] Captain Edmund Green, in a readiness to depart for Hamburg.

So, after 14 days stay in the city, I departed into the country and remained there three weeks, in which time I effected my business and returned again for London, where I understood that Captain Green lay wind-bound in Guinborough road. So I presently departed [from] London in [a boat with] a pair of oars, and after much danger came aboard of him there; and in a day or two after [we] had a fair wind, which brought us in a short time to Hamburg.

Coming thither, I fell again to my business, in which I remained until the year 1658. And then in February [I] was sent out by my master to get in some debts in the country, in which I passed through the dominions of the dukes of Braunschweig and Luneburg, as also of the Elector of Brandenburg and Bishop of Collen, and saw (besides what [I have] formerly mentioned) the following places: Braunschweig, Luneburg, Hildesheim, Bochum, Saltsdetford, and Lambspringe, a monastery of English Benedictines where I was most civilly entertained for the space of two or three days by the Lord Abbot Placidius Gascon and the rest. So returning to Hamburg [I] fell again to my business. In the month of November in this year 1658, my master's business calling him again for England, he departed thither and left me the management of his affairs here, which I performed to his content until his return, which was in the month of March, 1659. In the month of July following I was again sent into the country to gather in monies, and saw (besides what [was] formerly mentioned) Minden, Lemgo, Vlotho, Nienburg, Verden, Verden Sconce, Jeance and Neustadt. So, [I] returning to Hamburg in November afterwards, my master presently departed for England and left me again alone in the business, which I managed until his return, which was in May following (Anno 1660), and then delivered him all things to his content. In the month of January, 1662, my master went again for England and left me [for] the last time in his business; about the latter end of March he returned again. So, my time being expired, I delivered him all things to his content, and with satisfaction on both sides departed his services, receiving of him the bond of £1000 which my uncle had entered into for my fidelity, which I returned for London cancelled, with due acknowledgement for his love.

Hereupon I began the management of my own affairs and the serving of some friends in commission, in which employment I continued until the year 1664. And then upon the 20th of April I left Hamburg and departed by land for England, in which journey I saw, besides what [was] formerly mentioned, these cities and places following, viz. Hinlopen, Molguern, Standen, Hoorn, Edam, Mopiskedam, Tertolen, Antwerpen, Brussels, Aalst, Ghent, Ostend, the miraculous church of our Lady of the Lake by Brussels, the Prince of Orange's house of Risewick and in the Bush by the Hague, Wininbergen, Burburg, Gravelines, and Calais, from when I took my passage in the packetboat for Dover, and the 24th of May arrived, God be thanked, in safety at London. I saw also in this journey (which [places] are omitted above) Mauritius fort, Nassau fort, Salter fort, Klunder fort, Hogerwerft fort, the small city of Sandfliet, Frederick Henry fort, Hulst, Bergen-up-some, Lillo fort, Gentz fort, Lieskineo hock fort, all belonging to the Hollanders upon the frontiers of Brabant; as also the Philip fort, the Mary fort, the Perle fort, St. John's fort, Isabella fort (belonging to the Spaniards by Antwerp), together with the Nassau and Orange forts there belonging to the States.

Arrived at London as aforesaid, I applied myself to some members of the royal company who had invited me over to undertake an employment in their service—which, after two or three treaties, were concluded upon, viz. to go first to Barbados, and there to reside in commission with Mr. Peter Collison and Mr. Thomas Modyford until Mr. Reid arrived there, and then to go down into Jamaica in commission with Sir Thomas Modyford, etc. So upon the lst of September, 1664 I departed from London for Gravesend where I lay till the 5th; and then [I] embarked myself upon the *Concord*, Captain James Strutt [being] master, for the Barbados, lying then in the Hope, [with] 14 guns, 250 tons, 22 seamen and about 65 passengers. On the 6th in the name of God we weighed anchor thence. . . .

[The log of the voyage is omitted. On Sept. 14 they lost sight of England, and they arrived in Barbados Oct. 16]

The 16th in the morning we were hard by the land and about 8:00

cast anchor in Carlisle Bay, and so went on shore at the Indian Bridge
(or St. Michael's town), giving God thanks for our prosperous passage
and His merciful preservation of us. Our voyage from the Downs was
32 days, in which time we sailed by computation, comparing the log
and observations, about 4000 miles.

Some time after I had resided in Barbados, I had a balance and inventory
of the royal company's concerns delivered unto me, which I posted into
a new pair of books, and sent them copies of all unto my delivering
over the said books unto Mr. Thomas Colleton and Mr. John Reid, which
was in the month of December, 1665. And then, receiving a letter from
the company with orders for my going down to Jamaica, I embarked
[at] the first opportunity, which was the *Oporto*, merchantman, Captain
James Alford commander, designed thither with 500 Negroes. In which
ship I embarked myself [on] the 21st [of] December, being Thursday. . . .

[The log of this voyage is omitted also.]

January, 1665–6. Friday, the 5th, about 3:00 in the afternoon, we
came to an anchor in the harbor of Port Royal; for which God be praised.
Our voyage was 16 days and very troublesome, in regard [of the fact
that] we were pestered with so many Negroes and feared an insurrection.
The next day I waited upon his Excellency, Sir Thomas Modyford, Governor at St. Jago de la Vega, and so fell to assisting in the company's business;
wherein I continued until the beginning of October, 1666, at which time
the company ordered Sir Thomas (in regard the contract with the Spaniards went not forward) to reduce the factory to two persons only. So
he was pleased to make choice of Mr. Hendee Molesworth and myself,
ousting Mr. Lewis and Mr. Reid. But presently after [this] it pleased God
to visit me with sickness, and the advice of my doctor was that in case
I removed not to another climate [I] might run a great risk of death
or a tedious sickness.

So I petitioned Sir Thomas that he would discharge me of the company's service, which he accordingly did under his hand; whereupon I delivered up and cleared my accounts, and [on] the 12th of September set
sail from Jamaica in the *Friendship Catch*, burden 25 tons, Thomas Jenner
commander, bound for New England. . . . .

[The log of this voyage is omitted also; the vessel had many passengers,
and was poorly supplied with provisions, but arrived safely October 22.]

October the 21st we made Cape Cod and met with a ketch outward-
bound, but could not speak with her, having a calm. We saw hereabouts

many whales, penguins, and other sea-fowl. The 22nd we came in sight
of the islands before Boston, but the wind veering to NW [we] were
forced back and put into Plymouth.

The 23rd [of] October we went on shore there and hired horses for
Boston, being 40 miles off, where we arrived the 25th—for which blessed
be Almighty God who hath been pleased to preserve me hitherto out
of all known and unknown dangers, *and to a good wife.*

[Here the record ceases; and another hand takes the pen, and continues
thus:]

William Payne, the only child, was born January 22nd, 1669 on a
Friday morning, and after schooling went to college, anno 1685, where
I remained four years, [and] then lived with my stepfather, Richard Middlecott, two years, to keep his warehouse. Anno 1692 I went for England
and returned the next year to merchandise. But, meeting with continued
losses, I got my Lord Bellomont's commission for the impost, anno 1698,
[and] for Duty Collector [in] 1699, in which post I continued to the
year 1710. [In] Oct. 1694 I was married to Mrs. Mary Taylor by whom
I had four children:

William Payne, born Nov. 25,   1695
Tobias Payne, born June 25,   1697
Sarah Payne, born Jan.—,   1699
Mary Payne, born Jan. 6,   1700

On the same day, January 6th, 1700, my wife died in childbed, and
on May 12, 1703 I was again married, to Margaret Stuart, by whom
I have the following:

Sarah Payne,	born June 15, 1704
William Payne,	" Sept. 19, 1706
William Payne,	" Jan. 26, 1708
Edward Payne,	" Mar. 17, 1709
Ann Payne,	" June 8, 1711
John Payne,	" Feb. 9, 1713
Edward Payne,	" Oct. 1, 1714
Margaret Payne,	" May 22, 1716
Richard Payne,	" Apr. 4, 1718
Thomas Payne,	" Apr. 23, 1720
Edward Payne,	" Feb. 4, 1722
Jane Payne,	" Feb. 17, 1724

[The last three names and dates were added later, by the son Edward.]

[A new writing begins here, that of Deacon Edward Payne, grandson of the emigrant.]

The foregoing account of my grandfather's life and family [is] continued down to this day, by Edward Payne.

Tobias Payne, my grandfather, arrived at Boston from Jamaica the 26th [of] Oct., 1666, from whence he intended to proceed (as soon as he had recovered his health) to the island of Madeira; but finding this place so encouraging to trade, he soon resolved to tarry here. Accordingly, in November following he was married to Mrs. Sarah Standish, widow of Captain Miles Standish (to whom she was married in 16—, and with whom she lived about —months). She had no children by him; he sailed hence for England and was never heard of.

Her maiden name was Winslow, daughter of Mr. John Winslow of Boston, merchant. She had five brothers and four sisters, viz.

John Winslow
Edward Winslow
Samuel Winslow
Isaac Winslow
Joseph Winslow

Her eldest sister was married to Mr. Laitham; another was married to Mr. Grey, whose daughter married Mr. Leblone. A third [was] married to Mr. Southward; a fourth was married to Mr. Little.

My grandfather had one child by her, viz. my father William Payne. He was born the 22nd [of] Jan., 1668; after which my grandfather lived but about 8 months, and on the 12th [of] Sept., 1669 he departed this life.

Anno 1672, my grandmother was again married to Mr. Richard Middlecott, merchant, son of Mr. Middlecott of Warminster in England. He lived with a merchant in Bristol; after his time was expired he came to New England and settled here as a merchant. She had four children by him:

Mary Middlecott,	born 1673
Sarah Middlecott,	" 1678
Edward Middlecott,	" 1680
Jane Middlecott,	" 1682

[On] June 13, 1704 Mr. Middlecott died, and left her again a widow (with five children), which she continued until her decease, being the 10th [of] June, 1726.

Mary Middlecott, her eldest daughter, was married about anno 1696 to Mr. Henry Gibbs, son of Councillor Gibbs of Barbados, by whom she had 3 children born here, viz.

Sarah Gibbs
John Gibbs
Henry Gibbs

After which, anno ——, Mr. Gibbs went to Barbados to settle his affairs there, and intended to return and settle here; but his father dying while he was there prevented it. He sent for his wife to come there to him, which she did, but left her two eldest children behind with my father. Soon after her arrival there Mr. Gibbs died. Anno 1702, she was again married at Barbados to Othaniel Haggat, Esq., by whom she had four children born at Barbados, viz.

Othaniel Haggat
Nathaniel Haggat
Mary Haggat
William Haggat

She lived at Barbados till June, 1718, when Mr. Haggat, his wife, and the three youngest children took their passage with Capt. Spencer for Boston, to visit her relations here. But she was deprived of that pleasure, for about eight days before their arrival she died, in the 45th year of her age. The next year Mr. Haggat returned to Barbados, and took with him:

Sarah Gibbs
John Gibbs
Mary Haggat

Anno 1702, Sarah Middlecott was married to Mr. Lewis Boucher, who came from ——— in France, and settled here as a merchant, by whom she had six children, viz.

Ann Boucher,   born April, 1703
Sarah Boucher,   "   Sept., 1705
Mary Boucher,   "   1708⎫ these three
Mary Boucher,   "   1710⎬ all died
Lewis Boucher,   "   1713⎭ very young
Jane Boucher,   "   May, 1716

He sailed hence for England, anno 1715, and was never heard of [any] more.

Edward Middlecott lived with his father to learn merchandising till anno ——, then went for England where he purchased his father's life in an estate at Warminster of £300 per annum which was entailed to him by his uncle. He married the only daughter of ——, anno ——, by whom he had one child, viz. Edward Middlecott, born at Warminster, anno ——.

Jane Middlecott was married, anno 1702, to Elisha Cooke, Esq., of Boston, by whom she had 10 children, viz.

Elisha, born 1703, died young
Middlecott, born 1705
Elisha ⎫
Elisha ⎬ these four died very young
Jane ⎪
Jane ⎭
Elizabeth, Feb., 1708
Sarah,   Apr., 1711
Jane,   died young
Mary,   1723

Anno 1737, August 24, Mr. Cooke departed this life, aged 59. Sept., 1743, my aunt Cooke departed this life, aged 61.

Sarah Gibbs, my cousin, went from here to Barbados with her step-father, Mr. Haggat, anno 1719, where she married Mr. Scott.

My cousin, John Gibbs, continued with my father till anno ——, after which he lived with Mr. Jeffries to learn merchants' accounts till anno 1717 or 1718, and in 1719 he went to Barbados with his father-in-law, Mr. Haggat, where he ended his days, anno 1720, [as] a bachelor.

His brother, Henry Gibbs, went to Barbados with his mother, anno —— and in a few years returned to my father to be educated here. He also lived with Mr. Jeffries to learn merchants' accounts till anno ——; then he went to Barbados where he married Mrs. —— by whom he had —— children. He died there, anno ——.

My cousin, Othaniel Haggat, went from Barbados for England, in anno 1717, to be brought up in the university there; after which he returned to Barbados and married his mother-in-law's eldest daughter, by whom he had —— children. [He] was one of the judges of the island. He died there, anno ——.

My cousin, Nathaniel Haggat, came to Boston with his father, anno

1718, and continued here with my father til anno ———. Then [he] went for England in [a ship commanded by] Capt. Durell, and from thence to the university at Dublin, where he continued till anno ———, after which he went to Barbados, and married his stepmother's youngest daughter, by whom he has several children, and with whom he now lives at Barbados where he is one of the judges.

My cousin, Mary Haggat, returned to Barbados with her father, and from thence went to her Aunt ——— at Bristol, where she now lives [as] a maiden.

My cousin, William Haggat, came to Boston with his father [in] 1718 and continued here till anno ———, when he went for England with his brother Nathaniel, and from thence to Dublin; after which he entered into Holy Orders, is settled at Barbados where he now lives, and is married to ———.

My cousin, Ann Boucher, daughter of my Aunt Sarah Middlecott, was married in Sept., 1721, to Mr. Nathaniel Cunningham of Boston, merchant, by whom she had eight children, viz.

Nathaniel, 10 April, 1725
Ann
Ruth,   15 Jan.,   1728
Sarah,   6 Sept.,   1731
Timothy

She departed this life, the 31st [of] March, 1736.

Sarah Boucher was married in Oct., 1729, to Mr. John Foye of Charlestown, merchant, by whom she had six children, viz.

Sarah Foye, born 2 January, 1731
Ann,   Sept.,   1733
John,   Sept.,   1734
Elizabeth,   Dec.,   1735
Ann,   April,   1737
Lewis,   January, 1739

Jane Boucher now lives [as] a maiden.

Middlecott Cooke, son of Jane Middlecott, my aunt, now lives [as] a bachelor.

Sarah Cooke, daughter of Jane Middlecott, was married in May, 1733 to Mr. John Phillips of Boston, merchant, by whom she had five children, viz.

Elisha Cooke, Sept., 1733
John,   Apr.,   1735
William,   Aug.,   1736
Thomas,   Oct.,   1737; died Feb. 1741
Mary,   May,   1739; died Oct. 1741

She departed this life [on the] 11th [of] July, 1740.

Mary Cooke, the youngest daughter, was married, the 3rd [of] July, 1744, to Richard Saltonstall, Esq., of Haverhill.

The foregoing account of my grandmother's children by Mr. Middlecott being completed, as far as it's necessary for my purpose, I shall now say something of my own father, William Payne, the only child of my grandfather Tobias Payne.

He was born, the 22nd [of] January, 1668, about eight months before his father's death. In 1685 he went to college, where he continued until 1689; after which he lived with his stepfather, Mr. Richard Middlecott, to learn merchants' accounts, till 1691. He went for England in 1692 and returned the next year to merchandise; but, meeting with continual loss, he applied himself to public business, and in 1698 received a commission from Gov. Stoughton for the impost. In 1699 [he] received a commission from my Lord Bellomont for collector, in which office he continued till 1710. In 1714 he had a commission from the Council for Sheriff of the County of Suffolk. In 1715 he had a commission from Governor Tailer for the same. In 1716 he was Commissioner of the Excise, after which he was in no business at all, but lived on the income of his estate until his decease, which was [on] the 10th of June, 1735, in the 66th year of his age—leaving a widow, three sons, five daughters, one daughter-in-law, a widow, and five grandchildren, all living.

In October, 1694 he was married to Mrs. Mary Taylor, daughter of James Taylor, Esq., of Boston, who died in childbed, the 6th of January, 1700. By her he had four children, viz.

William, born Nov. 25, 1695
Tobias, born June 25, 1697
Sarah, born   Jan.,   1699
Mary, born   Jan. 6,   1700

In May, 1703, he was married again to Mrs. Margaret Stuart, an orphan, the only child of William and Margaret Stuart of Ipswich. Her mother was the daughter of a dissenting minister in Yorkshire in the reign of King Charles the Second, whose father and mother died when she was young, which occasioned her going to live with her sister in Limerick, where she was married to my grandfather, Mr. William Stuart, of whom I can give no further account than that he was a Scotchman and a good liver. They both came to New England in 1684 and settled at Ipswich, where my grandfather kept a shop till his decease, which was in August, 1693. By him my grandmother had one child, viz. my mother, Margaret Stuart, born in Limerick, in May, 1683. After my grandfather's decease my grandmother was again married to Colonel Gedney of Salem, anno 1696, with whom she lived till her decease, being the 15th of October, 1697.

By her my father had eight sons and four daughters.

Sarah,   born June 15, 1704, dec'd 1705
William,   "   Sept. 19, 1706, died
William,   "   Jan. 26, 1708
Edward,   "   Mar. 17, 1709, died
Ann,   "   June   8, 1711
John,   "   Feb.   9, 1713
Edward,   "   Oct.   7, 1714, died
Margaret,   "   May   22, 1716
Richard,   "   Apr.   4, 1718
Thomas,   "   Apr. 23, 1720
Edward,   "   Feb.   4, 1722
Jane,   "   Feb. 17, 1724

My eldest brother, William Payne [was] born 25 Nov., 1695 [and] deceased Feb., 1705.

My brother, Tobias Payne, lived with my father till he was 18 years of age; then [he] went to sea with his uncle, Capt. Christopher Taylor, with whom he sailed about a year, and was taken by the pirates; after which he resided some time at Barbados, where my uncle Haggat put him in [as] master of the sloop. Some time after he returned to New England and married Mrs. Sarah Winslow, daughter of Kenelm Winslow of Marshfield, by whom he had one child, viz.

Mary Payne, born ——
He sailed hence as captain of a ship, till his decease about the Virgin Islands, anno 1733.

Sarah Payne.

Mary Payne was married in October, 1724 to Mr. Jonathan Sewall, a merchant, son of Major Sewall of Salem, with whom she lived till his decease, being in November, 1731, and had six children by him, viz.

Margaret Sewall, 6 Oct., 1725

———

———

Jonathan Sewall,   Aug., 1728

———

Jane Sewall,   Nov., 1731

My sister, Sarah Payne, was married the 26th of December, 1734, to Mr. John Colman, Jr., a distiller, son of John Colman, Esquire, of Boston, with whom she now lives and has had five children, viz.

Sarah Colman,   July,   1736
John Colman, 18 Jan.,   1738
William Colman,   Aug.,   1739
Benjamin Colman, July,   1748
William Colman,   Aug.,   1744

My brother, William Payne [was] deceased May,———.

My sister, Ann Payne, now lives a maiden.

My brother, John Payne, lived two years as an apprentice to Mr. Jonathan Sewall, viz., till his decease; then he wrote in the Registrar's office with Mr. Boydell till his decease (being [in] 1740); after which he continued in said office under Mr. Jonathan Belcher while he held said office (being ———); then under Mr. Auchmuty while he held the said office (being ———); then under Mr. Belcher again, in which place he continues at this day.

My brother, Edward Payne, deceased June, ———.

My sister, Margaret Payne, was married the 7th [of] October, 1741, to Mr. John Phillips of Boston, who was formerly married to my cousin, Sarah Cooke, with whom she now lives and has no children.

My brother, Richard Payne, served seven years as an apprentice to Mr. Joseph Sherburne, to learn the brazier's trade.

My brother Thomas died [as] a child.

Sister Jane now lives [as] a maiden.

Edward, the youngest son, born the 4th [of] Feb., 1722, lived as an apprentice with Mr. Benjamin Colman, merchant, in Boston, from April, 1736 to May, 1743. In August following [he] opened a store on the Long Wharf at the desire of Brother John Phillips, who proposed to put a stock into my hands to trade with on our joint accounts; but, his stock being chiefly employed in a distilling house with Brother Colman, he could not furnish me with the stock I expected.

In November, 1745, I engaged in the distilling business with Brother Colman, who was then separated from Mr. Phillips, but, finding [that] our stock was not sufficient to carry on the business to advantage and that Brother Colman did not manage the distilling as I expected, I determined to quit that business, and proceed on a voyage to Gibraltar. In April, 1746, I purchased a vessel in company with Mr. John Mascarene and others, which we loaded with rum, fish, flour, etc., and in June I sailed for Gibraltar, where I arrived the 24th [of] July, and soon after dispatched the vessel back to Boston with a cargo of prize goods, wine, and fruit; but [I] remained there myself to dispose of the cargo and [to] purchase another against her return. This vessel, called the ———, [with] Davenport Walker [as] master, on her return to Gibraltar with another cargo had the misfortune to be taken as she entered the straits. I then purchased a brig called the *Zant*, put Capt. Phillip Payne in [as] master, took some prize goods, and proceeded in her to Villa Nova in Portugal, where I loaded her with salt and some fruit and returned to Boston, where I arrived safe [on the] 22nd [of] April, 1747.

In May, 1748, Mr. Peter Chardon put 1000 pounds sterling into my hands to be employed in the English trade, for which I was to have one-third of the profit in said stock and to have liberty to do my own business; but, money growing scarce and that trade being dull, I did not continue long in it, and in Feb., 1752 I finished [with] that concern and parted amicably.

In March, 1752, I entered into copartnership with Mr. James Perkins of Boston, and engaged to settle at Gloucester and to carry on a trade there in the fishery on our joint account. He put in a stock of 1000 pounds sterling, and I [was] to put in 500 pounds sterling. The 22nd of this month I removed there, built a store and a number of fishing vessels, and carried on that business; also a foreign trade in which I succeeded beyond my expectation, built a wharf and fish flakes. In this business I continued to mutual satisfaction until July, 1761, when we closed our copartnership and divided the stock to the satisfaction of both parties. And on the 1st [of] Oct., 1761, I returned to Boston after nine years' residence at Gloucester, which I esteem as the pleasantest part of my life, being advantageously employed in business and enjoying a set of agreeable acquaintances.

During my abode at Gloucester I was married to Rebecca Amory of

Boston (daughter of Thomas and Rebecca Amory), born the 25th of June, 1725, by whom I had three children born in Gloucester, viz.

Mary
Sarah } twins, born Dec.   1, 1757
Rebecca,   born Aug. 28, 1759

The last five years I lived at Gloucester we were at war with France, during which [time] I had two vessels taken in Europe on which I had no insurance, and two in the West Indies that were partly insured. In the course of the war Louisburg was taken a second time, [and] Quebec and all Canada surrendered to the English [on] the 8th [of] Sept., 1760.

Part Four
The Community

21

A Social Contract

The process of settlement in new lands was, of course, the great dramatic theme of colonial history. It began with Columbus, with the Jamestown settlers, with the Pilgrims at Plymouth, and was developed and redeveloped until long after the Revolution. It was a theme as grand as the American continent itself—but it was also as delimited, as concrete, as the smallest band of pioneers. Each push westward, each new community engaged specific human lives in a tangle of difficult, often unanticipated problems.

Among these problems none was more fundamental than the establishment of an enduring system of authority. Sometimes authority came ready-made, as when the "patroons" of New York brought tenants to their wilderness estates, or the General Court of Massachusetts appointed certain men as "proprietors" to oversee the founding of new towns. But on many other occasions the settlers arrived more or less independently and only afterward joined together to establish "wholesome laws and government." At such times they created, and put down on paper, a simple form of "social contract"; in doing so they followed instinct and common sense, rather than inherited philosophical traditions or known precedents from their own personal experience. The Mayflower Compact is the most famous American document of this type, and justifiably so; but it is unique only in the sense that it came first in time.

The settlers of the town of Exeter, in what was then the province of Massachusetts Bay (and is now New Hampshire), were among the many people who created government where none had existed before. They were, so far as one can tell, average people of their time: farmers, artisans, and perhaps a few persons of "gentle" birth. (It is worth noting, in this connection, that 40 percent of this group signed the compact with only a "mark"—and no doubt some of the others who signed their names could write little else.) The initial instruments of their government consisted of three parts: the compact itself, plus a "rulers' oath," and an "oath of the people."

Agreement among the Settlers

(Exeter, New Hampshire, 1639)

Whereas it hath pleased the Lord to move the heart of our dread sovereign Charles, by the grace of God, King of England, Scotland, France, and Ireland, to grant license and liberty to sundry of his subjects to plant themselves in the western parts of America: We, his loyal subjects, brethren of the church of Exeter, situated and lying upon the river of Piscataqua, with other inhabitants there, considering with ourselves the holy will of God and our own necessity, that we should not live without wholesome laws and government amongst us, of which we are altogether destitute, do in the name of Christ and in the sight of God combine ourselves together to erect and set up amongst us such government as shall be to our best discerning agreeable to the will of God, professing ourselves subjects to our sovereign lord King Charles, according to the liberties of our English colony of Massachusetts, and binding ourselves solemnly by the grace and help of Christ and in his name and fear to submit ourselves to such Godly and Christian laws as are established in the realm of England to our best knowledge, and to all other such laws which shall upon good grounds, be made and enacted amongst us according to God, that we may live quietly and peaceably together, in all godliness and honesty.

Mon., 5th day, 4th [month], 1639

John Wheelright	his mark:
Augustin Storre	Darby X Field
Henry Elkins	his mark:
his mark:	Robert X Reid
George X Walton	Edward Rishworth
Samuel Walker	his mark:
Thomas Pettit	Francis X Matthews
Henry Roby	Ralph Hall
William Wenbourn	his mark:
his mark:	Robert X Soward
Thomas X Crawley	Richard Bullgar
Chr. Helme	Christopher Lawson
Thomas Wight	

Compact and oaths of the settlers of Exeter, 1639, in Nathaniel Bouton, ed., *Documents and Records Relating to the Province of New Hampshire,* I (Concord, N.H., 1867), pp. 132–134.

William Wentworth
  his mark:
George X Barlow
Richard Morris
Nicholas Needham
Thomas Wilson
  his mark:
George X Ruobon
  his mark:
William X Coole

  his mark:
James X Walles
Thomas Levvit
Edmond Littlefield
  his mark:
John X Crane
  his mark:
Godfrey X Dearborne
Philamon Pormort
Thomas Wardell
  his mark:
Robert X Smith

The following are the forms of oath taken by the Elders and the People:
  The Elders' or Rulers' Oath.

You shall swear by the great and dreadful name of the High God, Maker and Governor of Heaven and Earth and by the Lord Jesus Christ, the Prince of the Kings and rulers of the earth, that in His name and fear you will rule and govern His people according to the righteous will of God, ministering justice and judgement on the workers of iniquity, and ministering due encouragement and countenance to well-doers, protecting of the people, so far as in you lyeth, by the help of God from foreign annoyance and inward disturbance, that they may live a quiet and peaceable life in all godliness and honesty. So God be helpful and gracious to you and yours in Christ Jesus.

  The Oath of the People

We do swear by the great and dreadful name of the High God, Maker and Governor of Heaven and Earth, and by the Lord Jesus Christ, the King and Savior of His people, that in His name and fear we will submit ourselves to be ruled and governed according to the will and word of God and such wholesome laws and ordinances as shall be derived therefrom by our honored rulers and the lawful assistants with the consent of the people, and that we will be ready to assist them by the help of God in the administration of justice and preservation of the peace with our bodies and goods and best endeavors, according to God. So God protect and save us and ours in Jesus Christ.

22

The Framework of Town Government

It was one thing to "combine . . . together to erect and set up . . . such government as shall be . . . agreeable to the will of God"; it was something else to fashion the multiple instruments of effective local administration. Yet no task was more pressing, none more fraught with immediate, everyday significance. From the standpoint of the average settler, the higher centers of power—provincial governor and councilors, or courtiers and bureaucrats across the ocean—were extremely remote. What counted were the decisions made in one's own village. What is one's fair share in the common lands? How much must one pay as rates (taxes)? Where will one's corn be ground? These were questions for local government—whatever its specific shape and substance.

In designing their institutions of local government, the colonists turned naturally to the experience of their English forebears. There were, in fact, various precedents from which to choose, and, not surprisingly, people in different parts of the colonies evolved different institutional structures. In Virginia, for example, the English county system was firmly transplanted by the middle of the seventeenth century. The county court, with its small circle of commissioners, became the chief focus of authority.

Farther north, in New England, the celebrated town meeting was rapidly taking root. There were models for this system, too, in the administrative practice of certain English parishes. Furthermore, the congregational forms of church governance, so dear to the New England settlers, seemed to suggest a similar pattern in civil affairs. Thus by 1640 many of these communities were being administered by regular meetings of most, or all, of the resident male householders.

But these gatherings seemed inherently unwieldy, and sometimes downright unruly. "Disorderly jarring," "janglings," "intemperate clashings" occurred all too frequently for people who regarded harmony and "peaceableness" as prime standards of value. They sought therefore to modify the openness and liberality of the town meeting with additional administrative devices. They constructed an elaborate network of town offices and committees to deal with such regular tasks as fence viewing, highway construction, and "overseeing the poor." And, to insure the smooth functioning of the whole system, they chose selectmen —a board of leading citizens with broad supervisory powers. In many communities the selectmen became in time a powerful counterweight to the democracy of the meeting itself.

The concerns, the values, the inherited traditions that helped shape this system are evident in the following excerpt from the town records of Dorchester, Massachusetts.

Bylaws of Town Meeting

(Dorchester, Massachusetts, 1645)

24th [day], 10th month, 1645

We, the present inhabitants of Dorchester, being provoked and excited hereunto by the godly and religious request of some among us that have laid to heart the disorders that too often fall out among us, and not the least or seldomest in our town meetings, and the slighting of the orders for the orderly carrying on of our prudential business and affairs in the town of Dorchester aforesaid, as also being heartily sorry for and ashamed of the premises and desiring to manifest the same for the time to come, and also according to the charge that lies over us in many respects to provide for peace and the flourishing in our own times and in our children's, have thought good upon mature and deliberate consideration to compose these few lines following as a platform or an abridgment of such orders which by the blessing of God both we and our selectmen from year to year will endeavor to walk in, to the honor of God and Jesus Christ whose name we profess. (Amen)

First of all, we do bind ourselves that upon the first day of the second month, yearly, about nine or ten o'clock, we will come together, warning being given upon some lecture day (or other meeting before), which shall be the charge of the selectmen for the time being to see it done, for these uses following: viz., [1] to elect seven or so many of our most

Platform of government, Dorchester, Mass., 1645, in *Fourth Report of the Boston, Massachusetts, Record Commissioners*, Document No. 9 (Boston, 1880), pp. 289–293.

grave, moderate, and prudent brethren as shall then be thought meet for the managing of the prudential affairs of the town for that year; (2) and also [to elect] all other officers as may be useful for the carrying on of the town affairs, viz., bailiff, supervisors, raters, etc., (and [we decree] that all our elections be by papers and not propounded by their predecessors); (3) that day [is] to be a day of liberty for orderly agitation for the redressing of any grievance that may be discovered; (4) or [a day of liberty] for the adding or detracting to or from these rules or anything concerning the whole town's liberty and power.

Secondly, we do give [to the seven selectmen], upon confidence of their careful and prudential improvement, full power and liberty of ordering all our prudential affairs within the town of Dorchester, with these limitations and cautions: (1) that they shall not meddle with the giving or disposing of any of the town land without the consent and good will of the town first obtained; (2) neither shall they take upon them to alter any parcel of land from the present improvement without the consent of proprietors. (Or the proprietors shall do it themselves by the major vote, being fairly proceeded in, in two or three peaceable agitations before the seven men.) Nevertheless, we do give them all accustomed liberty concerning common lands in fence, [and] also our town lots, that they shall have power to enjoin the several proprietors to make and repair such fence as is due unto them by proportion, and upon default therein to charge such penalty upon them as they see meet. *Item:* [we require] that they order the ringing and yoking of hogs, the keeping of our cows in the pen, stinting the cow's walk, barring the woods in season, and that they carefully provide for the safety of our Commons in wood and timber.

Thirdly, we do require that the seven men shall faithfully and prudently oversee all the business of the town or [disputes] between party and party that are committed to them and carefully and peaceably issue them seasonably; as also that they shall take care of all inferior officers, [seeing to it] that they discharge their places faithfully, and take accounts from them and thereof to make faithful and punctual record in their town book that so satisfaction may be given in any doubt upon demand; as also that all delinquencies and overplus in rates taxed upon the town by the General Court or otherwise may be discovered and condignly dealt with; as also that the seven men for the time being do tenderly and prudently provide that all abuses [which] hitherto have been grievous and justly offensive unto many in the disorderly jarring of our meetings, and the intemperate clashings, and hasty, undigested, and rash votes may be prevented, viz., that votes of any concernment be first drawn up in meeting and then deliberately published two or three times, and [that] liberty [be] given for any to speak his mind moderately and meekly, and then the sign to be required, and things more orderly carried [on] and dispatched; and also that care be taken that such remainders of rates as are unpaid and expose the town to blame or any engaged for the town (for now payment be according to their best light [what] they can get) be inquired after and reformed, and we do give them full liberty and power to impose upon the offenders in this case or the like such penalty as they find cause [for], provided they exceed not five shillings for the first offense to be levied by distress; and furthermore we do by these presents declare our intent to be that the seven men from time to time shall have power to relieve any person or persons that the town doth require to transact any business for [them] or [in] any way to become engaged for them and afterwards fails them to their damage and discredit (provided they do their utmost to find out the delinquents [in order] that the innocent suffer not).

Fourthly, we require that our seven men shall be careful to meet eight times in the year, viz., the second Monday of every month in the year except the second, fifth, sixth, and eighth [months] at some place which shall be certainly known unto all the town, and there to be resident from nine o'clock in the forenoon unto three o'clock in the afternoon; that, so, all such as have any complaints or requests to make or any information to give or anything whatsoever to do with them may certainly find all, or five of them at least, upon pain of five shillings for the first default, and also that [they suffer] displacement if good account be not rendered upon demand. And [we require] further that they kindly receive all complaints, requests, informations as [there] shall be, and speedily and seasonably apply themselves to their best prudence and ability to issue all such business in a fair, peaceable, and quiet manner, and thereof to make a fair and plain record in the town book, [in order] that, in case any prove contentious and will not be satisfied, there may be a testimony for the wronged party. And we allow them twelve pence apiece for their dinners at the ordinary or elsewhere upon the town charge. Also we do give them power to charge the town with such sum or sums of money from time to time as they shall have need of for the prudent and orderly managing of such things as fall out in their times, provided that one rate be not above 20 pounds and that they make faithful collection and also disbursement thereof, to be recorded before another rate be made. And we require that all their orders about town business be seasonably drawn up in writing and published upon some meeting and also fixed upon some observable place, that so the offenders may have no excuse or pretense.

Fifthly, forasmuch as hitherto it hath been upon sad experience seen that whatsoever good orders have been made have come to nothing by reason of want of execution, we, the freemen of Dorchester, desiring the reformation therof for the time to come, have ordered as follows, viz., that upon the day of election, according to the premises, we submit ourselves unto the election by papers of the major parts, [and] to be at the seven men's appointment in the point of execution of all their orders and [to be] taking distraints by commission from them for one year. And, further, we order that such a one so chosen shall not be blamed by any for his faithful execution, but for his encouragment shall have all due respect and freedom from all other town offices that year, and also such recompense as the seven men shall judge meet out of the distraints or otherwise; and every one refusing shall forfeit for the first offense thirteen shillings, four pence to be levied by distress.

Sixthly, for our seven men's encouragment we, the freemen of Dorchester, do agree that it shall not be lawful for any of Dorchester whosoever to slight either the persons or orders of the seven men for the time being, but that all their orders for prudential order shall stand ratified from the liberty aforegiven; and whosoever shall offend in the premises we will require of him a sum beside such penalty as his offense shall deserve.

Seventhly, we, the freemen of Dorchester, do unto the premises assent and agree, and heartily and truly by the help of God will endeavor the inviolable observation of the same. And for the confirmation of the premises according to our usual manner we have solemnly given our vote and also chosen and entreated our brother, John Wiswall, this 24th of the tenth month, 1645, to record the same to be a rule for ourselves and [our] successors, except God shall put into our or their hearts some more profitable, prudent way; and we do further profess that we intend no neglect or contempt of the General Court or the wholesome laws from thence established.

The 27th of the 11th month, 1645: An order for the ordering of our town meetings.

Forasmuch as the intemperate clashings in our town meetings, as also the unorderly departings of sundry before other brethren and neighbors, and the undigested and importunate motives by diverse divulged, have been not only grievous but justly offensive unto diverse, as also great occasion of misspent precious time and an hindrance [such] that good orders and other business have not succeeded as otherwise probably they might have done—the premises being taken into consideration, it hath pleased the freemen and brethren of Dorchester to commend the care of the redress unto the seven men for the time being. These are therefore to declare unto all our loving brethren and neighbors of Dorchester that, according to the care commended unto us and by the authority conferred on us, it is ordered, first, that whensoever the seven men shall have occasion of the assembling of the town or freemen thereof [we] shall give due notice and cognizance unto them. And we account this to be due notice, viz., that if it be on a lecture day that so many as are present shall take it for notice; or if it be by sending a special messenger from house to house, that if notice be left at the house with wife or child above the age of twelve years, the husband or father not being within or not at home, if he come home before the day appointed and not repair to the seven men, or four of them, to give in his excuse or appear upon the day of meeting, so many as shall have such notice and cognizance and attend not nor give in some valuable excuse unto the seven men shall forfeit six pence for the first offense.

Secondly, when the company is assembled as aforesaid, it is ordered that all men shall attend unto what is propounded by the seven men and thereunto afford their best help as shall be required in due order, avoiding all janglings by two or three in several companies, as also [avoiding] to speak unorderly or unseasonably—[from] which nevertheless is this to be construed that we intend not the least infringement of any brother or neighbor's liberty, nor [in] any way to suppress the abilities of any, nor to quench the smoking flax, but [we expect] that all in due time and order may communicate and contribute such help as they may have opportunity to do; but [we intend] only that confusion may be avoided and business [be] more orderly dispatched. For the ends before mentioned we, the seven men, have appointed one of us to be our moderator to propound and also to order our meetings; and [we require] that all the assembly shall address and direct their speech unto him and shall be attentive unto the business of the assembly.

Thirdly, [we order] that no motions be divulged or propounded but such as the seven men shall have seasonable knowledge of, and they [are] to propound the same; which is thus to be understood, that in case the seven men shall refuse to propound any man's motion, the party shall after some competent times of patience and forbearance have liberty to propound his own cause for hearing at some meeting, provided all disturbance and confusion be avoided.

Fourthly, [we require] that no man shall depart the assembly without giving due notice unto the moderator and declaring such occasion [of his departure] as shall be approved by the seven men, upon pain of twelve pence for the first offense.

23

Community Life:
The Spatial Dimension

The use and arrangement of space in early America varied dramatically from one region to the next. In the southern colonies population was widely dispersed, with individual plantations and farmsteads strung out across the landscape. In the middle colonies there was at least a degree of clustering. And in New England nuclear towns and villages were quite fully developed.

An old plan of Deerfield, Massachusetts, shows the typical pattern (for New England). The numbers at the lower right specify "homelots" (where settlers would indeed build their dwellings). The much larger plots, above and to the left, are field strips in the meadow and pasture lands outside the village center. Each town proprietor would have a share in these—and in other sections not represented here.

The larger colonial towns, modest as they were, offered something more like an urban setting. Boston was initially the largest—and most urban—of these. An illustration, prepared some years ago to represent the Boston Town House (as described in the original builder's contract), suggests the look of life in that community at an early stage. The Town House served as both a marketplace and a center of local goverance —and (one suspects) as a focus of sociability, too.

Plan of Deerfield, Massachusetts

(circa 1671)

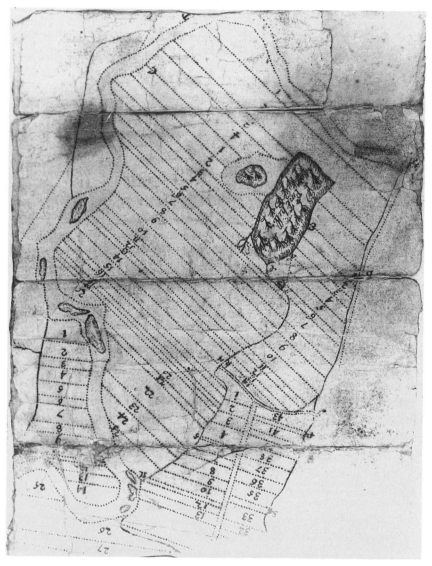

Ms. original in Pocumtuck Valley Memorial Association Library, Deerfield, Mass. Photograph by Amelia F. Miller. Used with permission.

The Boston Town House: Conjectural Drawing

(1657)

The Boston Town House, as drawn from the original specifications for Thomas
Joy and Bartholomew Bernard (1657); photograph from The Bostonian Society,
Old State House. Used with permission.

24

Profile of a Village Economy

The customary term for taxes, in colonial parlance, was the "rate." Every community had to find revenues with which to undertake a variety of regular tasks—for instance, to pay the minister, or repair public buildings, or support the local poor. Accordingly, each householder was assessed for the sum of his tangible possessions and ordered to pay a proportionate share.

The "rate lists" on which such assessments were recorded yield much valuable information for the historian. They provide, in effect, a precise economic profile of many early American communities: the distribution of lands, the range of property differences, and in some cases the size of households. The list for Midwout (Flatbush), New York, in 1683 is a fairly typical case. Of its thirteen columns, the first shows the number of adult males present in the household; the second through the eleventh deal with domestic animals; the twelfth refers to land acreage; and the last records the total value of all assets in pounds. The scale of value for each type of property is shown in parentheses along the top.

Chapter 24

Profile of a Village Economy

Rate List of Midwout (Flatbush), New York

(1683)

	Polls (18 lb)	Horses (12 lb)	3 years (8 lb)	2 years (5 lb)	yearling (3 lb)	Oxen (6 lb)	Cows (5 lb)	3 years (4 lb)	2 years (50 sh)	yearling (30 sh)	Hogs (1 lb)	Acres (1 lb)	£	s.
Nys Teunisen	1	1					4					50	100	
Loffert Pietersen	1	2				2	7	3	6	3		54	174	10
Cornelis Berryen	1	3					10	2	2	7		152	279	10
Laurens Cornelis	1	2					2		3	1		36	97	
Reynier Arens	2	3					7	1	3	5		44	166	
Pieter Guilliams	1	4			3		7		2	2		160	287	
Theodorus Polhemius	1	2					5	1	2	2			79	
Jan van Ditmersen	2	3					12	3	7	9		129	295	
Dirk Hooglant	2	2					1			2		52	120	
Jacop Hendricks	1	4					4	1	1	1		46	140	
Willem Guilliams	2	4	1	1			6	1		5		144	277	
Pieter Lot	2	4	1				6	7	6	4		140	308	
Harmen Key	1	1					3		2	1		44	95	10
Lowys Jans	1	1					2		1	1			44	
Jan Auke	1	2					4	1		1	1	46	114	10
Adrian Reyerse	2	2					5	3	4	3		70	197	
Titus Zirachz	1	3	1	1	1		8		3	2		50	159	10
Jan Rems	2	2	1				4	2	2	3		38	135	10
Hendrick Rycke	1	2	2				4	3	3	3		38	140	
Dirck van der Vlier	2	2			1		3	1	3	2		36	130	
Hendrick Willems	1	4					7	2	2	2		100	217	
Jan Vlier	1	2					2		2			60	117	
Cornelius van der Veer	2	4					11		5	4		100	257	10
Cornelius Barents	1	4	1				8	4	1	5		100	240	
Willem Jacops	2	3			1		9	2	2	3		60	197	
Gerrit Lubbers	1	3					8	2		2		60	165	

Rate List of Midwout (Flatbush), N.Y., 1683, in E. B. O'Callaghan, ed., *The Documentary History of the State of New York,* II (Albany, N.Y., 1849), pp. 504–507.

	Polls (18 lb)	Horses (12 lb)	3 years (8 lb)	2 years (5 lb)	yearling (3 lb)	Oxen (6 lb)	Cows (5 lb)	3 years (4 lb)	2 years (50 sh)	yearling (30 sh)	Hogs (1 lb)	Acres (1 lb)	£	s.
Auke Jans van Nuys	2	3					5	1		3		48	153	10
Rem Remse	1	3	1				5		3	4		60	157	10
Gerrit Snedeker	2	3	1				10	2	2	2		90	236	
Jacop Larzilier	1	3	1				6	1	1	1	4	60	160	
Pieter Cornelissen												54	54	
Cornilis Pieterse	1	2					4		3	2		84	156	10
Gerrit Strycker	1	2					3	2	1			60	127	10
Stoffel Probasco	1	2					6		4	3		60	146	10
Lymen Hanse	2	3	1				5	3	3	1			125	
Jan Barensen	1	1					2			1		60	101	10
Joost Casperse	1	2					3		1			30	89	10
Claes Barens	1	2					2					30	82	
Jan Strycker	1	2					7	3	5	2		72	176	10
Mr. Tomes Barker	1	3					2		2		2	40	111	
Mr. Maris	1	3					6		3	6		110	210	10
Catryna Hegemans	3	3	1	2			9	2	3	4	1	132	300	10
Jacop Janse	1	1					5					32	87	
Hendrick Hegeman	1	2										60	102	
Adriaen Hendricks	2	2					4	1	2			28	102	
Pieter Strycker	1	3					8		2	5		50	156	10
Adriaen Andriessen	2	4					3	1				30	131	
Aris Janse	1	3				3	6	4	5	3		108	243	
												lb 7757	10

25

College Life and Social Place

The importance of "station"—or "status," as we might put it—was implicit in virtually all the social arrangements of colonial America. In some contexts, moreover, it was rendered quite visible and concrete. Terms of address were linked to social rank: "Mr." and "Mrs." were restricted to gentlemen and their ladies, whereas "goodman" and "goodwife" served for the "middling sorts." The assignment of seats in churches was made according to status—the closer to the front, the more distinguished the occupant. And wearing apparel reflected similar consideration. (Indeed, in Massachusetts there was actual legislation designed to prevent average people from dressing "above their station.")

The next two documents illustrate the theme of status in still another setting: the colonial college. At both Harvard and Yale students were "placed" each year in an "Order of Seniority." At first, it seems, these rankings were based on academic achievement, but by the end of the seventeenth century they had come to reflect pedigree alone. The statement written by General John Winslow to President Holyoke of Harvard reveals the system at work in a specific case. (Winslow's son Pelham had just gained admission to Harvard.)

Under special circumstances the college authorities would demote a student from his rightful place on the list as a form of punishment. The letter from Samuel Melyen to Cotton Mather, recording precisely this situation, reminds us that status is especially important to those who have lost it.

Letter of John Winslow to President Edward Holyoke

(Boston, 1749)

Reverend and Honored Sir,   Boston, Oct. 20th, 1749

As I am bound to sea, and rank in our way is looked upon as a sacred thing, and it is generally allowed that the sons of the New England Cambridge are placed according to the degrees of their ancestors, I have therefore put in my pretensions for my son, beginning with the country in which we breathe, and [as] for genealogy [I] say:

That Edward Winslow, my great grandfather, was the eldest of the name in England and of five brothers [who were] first settlers of what is now this province; and that the said Edward was one of the first planters and in the first ship of what was lately the colony of Plymouth, and [was] some time Governor thereof, and [was] one of the Grand Commissioners in the unhappy expedition against Hispaniola and died at the taking of Jamaica, leaving one son (Josiah), who in his day was [for] many years Governor of said colony and Captain General of the United Forces of New England in the memorable Indian war called King Philip's War, in which he got his death, leaving one son (named Isaac, my father), who had the honor to have the first place in both civil and military affairs in the County of Plymouth for many years, and [who] until he resigned was President of the Council of this province. And [I say further] that in the year 1738 he died, leaving two sons, of which I am the eldest. And [I] have to say for myself that from my early days I have been entrusted in the public affairs of the county and province, until 1740, when I had a company in the unfortunate expedition against Cartagena; and [I] have had since two commissions of the same rank under His Majesty and [have been] entrusted with the command of the second garrison in North America, which is my present station. Pardon my saying thus much; [I] offer these things as facts and leave the events to the honorable and reverend body to and for whom I have the greatest regard. And at all times with the utmost respect [I] shall take leave to subscribe yours and their very humble servant,

J. Winslow

To the Honored and Reverend
Edward Holyoke Esq., President
of the College to be [line unfinished]

Letter from John Winslow to President Edward Holyoke, 1749, in *Proceedings of the Massachusetts Historical Society,* Second Series, IX (1894–1895), p. 6.

Letter of Samuel Melyen to Cotton Mather

(Massachusetts, 1698)

Mr. Mather,   May 19th Anno 1698
    Reverend Sir:
After my respects are paid to yourself and the Lady [who is] your worthy consort, this is come to inform you that I have not as yet finished your book, but intend by the last day of this week (God willing) to put a conclusion thereunto. Sir, I hope you will not impute my tardiness to anything of unwillingness, but [rather] partly to the license you sent me when you last sent the original, and partly to my intervening business. Pray, sir, be assured by this that I am not only willing and ready to serve you as far as in me lies, but esteem it an honor to be in your service —wherefore, sir, I hope you will not decline your imposing it upon me at any time when your occasions call for it.

One favor, worthy sir, I should be exceedingly rejoiced to obtain at your benign hands, if it may not engage yourself in too great a trouble, which I will manifest after I have premised that towards the end of our sophomoreship, by my audaciously calling freshmen at the door of the worthy Mr. Brattle in a way of contempt, the venerable and reverend President with my tutor, the well-deserving Mr. Leverett, saw it convenient to place me the lowest in the class, whereas before I was placed between Sir Remington and Sir Whitman.

Now, sir, my humble request is (seeing the catalogue has not since been printed, and is before the ensuing commencement to be printed) that you would be pleased to [make a] motion to the Reverend President that I may be reduced into my former station. Nothing, sir, can be more grateful to my father and mother, nor anything more encouraging to me. I am very sorry (and desire to be very penitent) that in that, as well as in many other things, I have displeased so worthy a gentleman as the President and so kind a tutor as Mr. Leverett with the Rev. Mr. Brattle, [and I am] hoping that the remainder of my days may be so managed that glory may redound to God, and [that] thereby some satisfaction may be made for the wrong I offered them. I lie at their feet and humbly beg their pardon (praying the Lord to forgive me in and through His Son, Jesus Christ), hoping they will henceforth pretermit the offenses of my former life and grant me this favor, which will much

Letter from Samuel Melyen to Cotton Mather, 1698, in *Proceedings of the Massachusetts Historical Society*, First Series, VIII (1864–1865), p. 34.

encourage me in my labor and lay me under fresh obligations to serve them and your noble self in anything that I may or can. Had I, sir, been placed at first inferior to the rest, I should have been contented and thought it my place (wherefore, sir, I hope you will not conjecture that pride is the impulsive cause of this, my petition); but it being after such a nature as it was makes me very desirous of reducement. Sir, all our class that were placed at first beneath me, have voluntarily manifested unto me that they were very willing [that] I should enjoy my ancient standing. Thus, sir, hoping you will do your endeavor and pardon my boldness, I shall at present beg leave to conclude myself your

humble petitioner and hearty servant,
Samuel Melyen

These to the
Reverend Mr. Cotton Mather
with my hearty respects,
presented
per Bishop Elliott

26

A Colonial Confidence Man

In an abstract sense the mentality of status was universal among the colonists, but real circumstances sometimes told a different story. In fact, some aspects of life in the New World seemed quite uncongenial to the preservation of social distinctions. The empty land, the freedom of movement, the remoteness from Europe: here were the ingredients of a corrosive mix that would gradually undermine the delicate supports of traditional culture.

In part, the situation could be viewed as a problem of identification. It was often difficult to *place* people in a reliable framework of time and space. In forming a relationship with another, one sometimes had to accept on faith the other's own account of personal past history and present circumstances. There was no independent check, no objective record of performance in a stable community. All this was deeply disturbing to people of a conservative temperament, for it made them feel vulnerable to various kinds of charlatanism. Some would surely be tempted to make inflated claims for themselves—and, worse still, they might well be believed.

The testimony of a Boston couple named Atkinson, in reference to the career of one Thomas Rumsey, describes a graphic case in point. It should only be added that Mr. Edward Rawson was a leading merchant of Boston and for many years was secretary to the General Court of the Bay Colony. To have successfully wooed his daughter was a feat of no mean consequence.

Testimony about Thomas Rumsey

(Massachusetts, 1680)

The testimony of Theodore Atkinson and Mary, his wife, inhabitants of Boston in New England, sayeth:

That about the third month in the year 1678 Thomas Rumsey came to me and tendered his service to me for one year to work with me. And he told me he was a Kentishman, and that his father lived near Canterbury, and that his father was a yeoman and had an estate [of] about four hundred [pounds] a year, and also that his father died when he was but young, and that his father's estate did fall to him at his stepmother's decease. And also he pretended that he came over to New England upon the account of religion; and, further, he hired himself with me for a year, for to attend my business, and to keep my book of accounts, and for gathering in of my debts. But when he had been about a month with me he pretended he was one that had been highly bred, but he would not say further what he was. But about five months after he came to me, then he told me his father was a Knight and Baronet, and that his stepmother was a Lady. So he lived and carried himself, pretending he was highly bred, that I, the said Atkinson, did not set him on work because he promised me he would satisfy me for what charges and expenses I was out about him. But a little time after he came to me he began to discover himself, so as his religion did seem to wear away; and before the year was expired he changed his name, and said his name was Hailes, and professed he had been a great traveler in the Straits for about two and twenty months; and [said] that his mother was called the Lady Hailes, and paid him his money by bills of exchange from time to time; [and] that she was a lady that had three hundred pounds annually of her own that she brought with her, and that his father had about eight hundred a year and a vast estate which he durst not nor would mention lest he should be laughed at and not be believed; [and] that all his father's estate after his mother's decease was his—those, and such like unheard-of stories as those, in which there is not the least shadow of truth (as the deponents are informed), and as [the ones which] the deponents now perceive he made use of as a delusion to put a cheat on Mr. Edward Rawson of Boston aforesaid, to accomplish his abominable villainy and deceive him of his daughter, Mistress Rebecca Rawson, whom

Testimony of Theodore and Mary Atkinson, 1680, in *New England Historical and Genealogical Register*, XV (1861), p. 60.

he was married unto by a minister of the Gospel on the first day of July in the year of our Lord one thousand, six hundred and seventy nine, in the presence of near forty witnesses.

27

Order in Human Relationships

Ours is not the first era in which the length and style of men's hair have become a matter of public controversy. During the latter part of the seventeenth century, especially in New England, there was frequent discussion of this topic. Some men were starting to use wigs fairly regularly—following a fashion trend that was already well established in England. But others decried this as a sign of decadence, another symptom of the steady erosion of old ways and values.

The following essay, by the Reverend Nicholas Noyes, is an extended example of the criticism leveled against the new trend. In some respects it reads like the plaint of conservative people in all ages when confronted with the inexorable facts of social change. But this is also a distinctively "Puritan" document, in its extreme reliance on Scripture, its insistence on literal meanings, and its devotion above all else to the value of orderliness. Its interest for us lies just here—and not on the trivial surface of its overt subject matter. In fact, it lays bare a whole cast of mind that was fundamental not only to Puritans, but in varying degrees to all English people of the seventeenth century. From hair style the argument plunges immediately into questions that lie right at the heart of human culture. What is the proper relationship between the old and the young? Between men and women? Between humankind and the animals? The discussion proceeds almost entirely on this level.

Nicholas Noyes (1647–1717) was for many years the pastor at Salem, Massachusetts. He is, incidentally, best known to history as one of the leaders in the prosecution of witches during the notorious events of 1692–1693.

An Essay against Periwigs
Nicholas Noyes

REASONS AGAINST WEARING OF PERIWIGS, ESPECIALLY AGAINST MEN'S WEAR-
ING OF PERIWIGS MADE OF WOMEN'S HAIR, AS THE CUSTOM NOW IS, DEDUCED
FROM SCRIPTURE AND REASON

It removeth one notable distinction, or means of distinguishing one man
from another. For so is a man's own hair—one man differing from another
in hair, as to color, thickness, thinness, straightness, curledness. A man
with his hair cut off, and another's put on, looketh not as he did before
—especially if before of light-colored hair [and] now dark, or before dark,
now light, before, thin straight hair, now bushy and curled and longer
than before, or other the like difference, which is most familiarly made
by those that wear periwigs. So that he that wears a periwig doth in
effect put on a vizzard and disguise himself. And the same man ordinarily
keepeth diverse periwigs differing one from another in length, color, curls,
or the like, sometime wearing one, sometimes another, so that such a
one is strangely inconsistent with himself, and unlike today to what he
was yesterday, and so less liable to be known. Now to affect a disguise
is not the guise of a good man, but of a bad one. (*Job*, 24: 14, 15,
17) It is recorded of Saul and Ahab and Jeroboam's wife that they disguised
themselves, which gives no credit to the cause if their persons and cases
be duly considered. But it may be said that Jacob disguised himself. And
it may be answered [that] it was with goat's hair and not with women's,
and he did not cut off his own. But the special answer is that it was
in him evidently a particular lie and a cheat, and was fruit of unbelief,
done in sin and followed with sorrow. If it be said that Josiah disguised
himself and went into the battle, it may be answered [that] this instance
availeth but little unless it had succeeded better with him, for it fared
with him as it did with Ahab. And Jehosaphat escaped better in his kingly
equipage and royal apparel. Yet if it be lawful for a man to disguise in
battle, is it therefore in peace? If upon extraordinary occasion, is it in
ordinary? But Josiah should not have engaged in that battle, and disguising
himself did not preserve him (2 *Chron.*, 35: 22, etc.) If it be said [that]
one of the sons of the prophets disguised himself (1 *Kings*, 20: 38), it

Nicholas Noyes, "Reasons Against Wearing of Periwigs," in *Publications of the Colonial
Society of Massachusetts*, XX (1917–1919), pp. 120–128. I am grateful to the Colonial Society
of Massachusetts for permission to reprint this document.

may be answered [that] it was on a particular occasion, and for a short time, and to make him look like a soldier for an advantage to his office, that his reproof might take the more effect upon a hard-hearted king. It was to make him look like himself, and unlike a prophet, or a son of a prophet. But he did not ordinarily go in a disguise as in the case in hand. And supposing it lawful on extraordinary occasions, that is far from proving it lawful on ordinary [ones]; that it rather proveth the contrary. And as for this [use] of periwigs, they are many times used for disguise by the worst of men, as by shaven-crowned popish priests, highway robbers, etc. Dr. Annesly, when by the iniquity of the times he was forced to abscond and conceal himself in the day, went abroad in the evening to take the air, and then put on a periwig. When he called for it, he used to say (as his son-in-law told me), "Give me my rogue" —implying that when he had a periwig on he did not look like himself nor like an honest man.

2. It removeth one notable, visible distinction of sex; for so is hair, as is [made] evident by 1 *Cor.*, 11: 6, 7, 14, 15. And it is obvious to everyone that men's hair and women's hair are not ordinarily alike. And if they were, there would be no temptation to make periwigs of women's hair for men; and so diverse just prejudices against the periwigs in use would be removed. Nay, men might ordinarily make them of their own hair, which would yet be less offensive; whereas now women are shaven or shorn, and so in that respect are more like men—being, when shorn, really unlike what they were before, and unlike other modest and honest women that would not be shorn or shaven on any temptation. And men, putting on their hair, have hair like women and not like men, as is noted of the locusts, those harpies of hell (*Rev.*, 9: 8). They had hair as the hair of women, plainly implying that men's hair and women's hair is not alike. Now this transmutation of the visible tokens and distinctions of sex is not lawful, as is undeniably proved by *Deut.*, 22: 5. It is manifest that the hair of periwigs ordinarily pertains to women—growing on women's heads, [and] having been their glory and covering for many years —and therefore must needs be unlawful for men to wear. And if a man for this reason, viz. distinction of sex, might not wear a woman's habit, much less might he wear a woman's hair. The words in *Deut.*, 22: 5 are very plain and very terrible: The woman shall not wear that which pertaineth to a man; neither shall a man put on a woman's garment; for all that do so are [an] abomination to the Lord thy God.

3. It removeth one notable distinction of age, which is necessary to be known because of some duties depending on it: (1) in respect of men's

selves. The frequent sight of gray hairs is a lecture to men against levity, vanity, and youthful vagaries and lusts. It calls for a gracious, grave, and majestical deportment, lest they defile the gray hairs with youthful folly and lusts. It puts men in mind of their mortality, as the flourishing of the almond tree doth of the approaching summer (*Eccles.*, 12: 5). Whence when gray hairs are removed out of sight, and youthful ones in stead thereof [are] in view (as it is oftentimes in the case of periwigs), it hath a natural tendency to make men forget that they stand upon the edge of the grave and on the brink of Eternity. Gray hairs are here and there upon them; and they are not aware of it (*Hosea*, 7: 9). And indeed how should they be aware of it, when they are removed out of their sight? For, out of sight, out of mind, as sayeth the proverb. (2) In respect of others: Others are obliged to rise up before and honor the old man, the demonstrative token of which is his gray hairs. But strangers to old men cannot so well distinguish of the age of those they converse with, when youthful hairs are grafted on a gray head, as is often times [true] in the case of periwigs. Are we bound to rise up before the youthful hair of girls and young women? (*Levit.*, 19: 32). Thou shalt rise up before the hoary head and honor the face of the old man. It is evident by that text that an old man's face should ordinarily be accompanied by gray hairs. And when periwigged men are known to be old, though they do their utmost to conceal their age, yet such levity and vanity appears in their affecting youthful shows as renders them contemptible and is in itself ridiculous. And so the old man comes to be despised, contrary to the law of God and good of human societies; and the young men [are] led into temptation to this evil, by old men's appearing on the stage without the badge of their age and honor, which would challenge respect. The beauty of old men is the gray head. (*Prov.*, 20: 29) (3) In respect to God Himself, relating to some of His divine perfections, particularly His majesty and eternity—which are in some respects shadowed forth in old men when they wear their gray hairs, the livery of their old age, especially when a gracious heart is adorned with a gray head. (*Prov.*, 16: 31) The hoary head is a crown of glory, if it be found in the way of righteousness. And therefore, when God's majesty and eternity are set forth in Scripture, it is with white hair, denoting that He is indeed the Ancient of Days. (*Dan.*, 7: 9; *Rev.*, 1: 14) His head and His hairs were white like wool, as white as snow. It is not therefore merely good manners to honor the old man, but religion—such a one bearing the image of God in those respects more than they that are younger. (*Levit.*, 19: 32) Thou shalt rise up before the hoary head, and honor the face of the old man, and fear thy God; implying that they want the fear of God, as well as good manners, that don't rise up before the hoary head. So that when aged persons dissimulate their age by putting off their gray hairs and by putting on youthful looking hair, they do it not only in their own wrong, to the loss of some degrees of due honor, but also to the wrong of those they lead into temptation to despise old men; which is contrary to the law of God. Moreover they do wrong to God Himself, whose fear is promoted by the reverence due to gray hairs.

4. Wearing periwigs proceeds many times from a discontent at God's workmanship. He that likes not his hair because of color, etc., doth in effect say to his Maker, why hast Thou made me thus? (contrary to *Rom.*, 9: 20; *Isa.*, 45: 9)—which were it but to an earthly father is enough to bring a woe. (*Isa.*, 49: 10) Woe to him that sayeth to his father, what begettest thou? or to the woman, what hast thou brought forth? For such [as] bring discontent with their hair and looks do thereupon affect, and effect, to change it. And although they themselves cannot make one hair white or black, yet [they] are so bold with Him that could and did make it of that color that offends them, suppose white, or black, or red, etc. And this is undeniably a breach of the Tenth Commandment, for a man to be discontented with his own hair which God made for him and gave to him, and to covet another's which God made for another and gave to another. To covet another's hair is a sin of the same kind with coveting our neighbor's house or his wife. For the same Commandment forbids coveting anything that is thy neighbor's (*Exod.*, 20: 17)

5. Wearing of periwigs evidently marreth the workmanship of God, and so defaceth His image. For God and Nature, or God in Nature, hath suited man's complexion and hair; and in Nature they are suited, as naturalists observe. *"Pilorum enim differentia est pro qualitate cutis Animalium,"* as Aristotle observed [in] *Lib. de gener.* And this is evident in diverse instances. When the constitution is hale and flourishing, the hair is so; and as the consitution gradually declines and changeth, so doth the hair. (*Prov.*, 20: 29) The glory of young men is their strength; but the beauty of old men is the gray head. Therefore it deforms an old man to put on him a young person's hair, as it would deform a young man to put on him gray hairs, which is the beauty of old men, not of young. And the hair, for the most part at least, is colored and qualified according to natural causes in the constitution. Such as is the predominant element, such is the predominant temperament, such is the predominant humor in the body; and according to that, the flesh and skin; and according to all these, the hair, as physicians know and show, and [as] is observable

to every observing eye. So that between the periwig hair and the complexion of him that wears it there is ordinarily a manifest incongruity; so that he that hath skill in physiognomy shall be able to know that this hair could not grow upon that head, no more than salt-marsh can grow upon a hill. And for this reason there is, for the most part, an incongruity between a man's hair and a woman's complexion, the hair of women being suitable to their soft, moist, cold constitution, but not to the masculine, hot, and dry constitution. And consequently in the case in hand there must needs be an unnatural incongruity between the complexion and hair, when the complexion and constitution is masculine and the hair feminine. (Rev., 9: 7, 8) Their faces were as the faces of men; and they had hair as the hair of women. Now if this were not unnatural and incongruous and a kind of monstrosity, to see things so heterogenous linked together, I see no reason for such description. Note other parts of the description together with these: man-faced, woman-haired, lion-toothed, scorpion-tailed, horse-shaped, etc.; and it describes such a medley going to make up a locust, as we call neither fish, nor flesh, nor good red herring. And [note] what the poet said of the mermaid, "Desinet in piscem mulier formosa superne." And in the case of periwigs we may say, "Desinet inque vium mulier formosa superne." So also to put black hair on the flesh and skin that naturally produceth red, yellow, or light-colored hair is unnatural and incongruous; so likewise to put red hair, or yellow, or light-colored on flesh and skin that naturally produceth black. So youthful hair, and sunk eyes, deaf ears, wrinkled faces and palsied heads, etc. are not more suitable than the blossoming of apple trees in autumn when the leaves are falling off. And thus Nature teacheth that periwigs are undecent and unsuitable on this very score, the trimming not being suitable to the cloth nor the crop to the soil.

6. It seems to be unlawful and most foolish and absurd for a woman to part with her hair to adorn a man. And if it be so, it must needs be unlawful for men to desire it, and buy it, or beg it, or use it in periwigs. (1) It is a glory to a woman to have long hair (1 Cor., 11: 15) and therefore a shame to her to part with it by being shorn or shaven. (1 Cor., 11: 6) Because if it be a shame to a woman to be shorn or shaven, it is indisputably an argument taken ad absurdo and therefore a foolish and absurd thing for a woman to be shorn or shaven—which yet is ordinarily done in order to furnish periwigs. But such consult their own shame. (2) Her hair is given her for a covering to herself, not to another. (1 Cor., 11: 15) So then the end God gave it [to] her for is perverted. And their brains are exposed to reproach and damage who thus uncover their

own barns, to thatch others anew; which surely none would do unless their own barns were empty, seeing the recompence is, instead of well-set hair, to have baldness —which in Scripture is accounted a curse. (*Isa.*, 3: 24) (3) It seems a disorder in religious worship, that offends the angels, for a woman to pray shaven or shorn. (1 *Cor.*, 11: 5, 6, 10, 13) Judge in yourselves: is it comely that a woman pray unto God uncovered? Yet in the sense of that text and context, she that is shaven or shorn prays unto God uncovered, if she prayeth at all to God; for her hair was given to her for a glory and for a covering, as is there manifest. And if by reason of other covering men see not their bald crowns, yet the angels of God see them; and they cannot be hid from the all-seeing eye of God, who seeth how ungratefully she hath parted with her glory and covering which He gave her. (4) A woman degrades herself unto the rank and quality of a beast, when she submits to be shorn as the beasts are to cover others with their hair. What a shame is it to women to be content to be made such fools of by men, that when some men's periwigs are made of the hair of a horse's tail, and others' of a goat's beard, they should voluntarily suffer themselves to be so abused as to part with their hair to make periwigs also! And women's hair and goat's hair many times go into the same periwigs, as if they were *eiusdem farinae*, or birds of a feather. Nay the woman, of the two, that parted with her hair voluntarily, is more goatish, or at least foolish, than the goat, that parteth with his involuntarily; though it be so honorably matched as to be hanged cheek-by-jowl with a woman's hair. What a mad world would it be, if women should take the same affection to wearing of men's beards as men do to women's hair? Would they not be accounted mere viragos or virile housewives? And by the same reason, why should it not be accounted effeminacy in men to covet women's hair, which is a token of women's subjection when they wear it themselves for a covering, and to have it cut off a token of immodesty? Moreover, what mad work would it make with womankind, if they were bound to supply all mankind with periwig stuff? For the sheep to be dumb before the shearer is admired patience; and yet that is, comparatively, no wonder to this, because God gave her her wool for that end. And the sheep is so subject to man that he may at his pleasure cut her throat, as well as her wool, and eat her flesh, and tan and wear her skin as well as her wool. But God hath not so subjected women to men. But as Virgil said of sheep, *"Sic vos non vobis vellera fertis oves,"* so it may be now said of women, *"Sic vos non vobis mulieres crinificatis."* If the hair of women be so necessary and useful, as it is pretended in this age, for periwigs, perhaps the next age may find a way to spin it and make cloth of it. And their skins, well-tanned, may make good leather; and at length they will become very profitable creatures to men.

7. The folly and absurdity of men's periwigging themselves with women's hair appears in many particulars. (1) It is a shame for a man to wear long hair; but periwigs are usually long hair. And if Nature teacheth that it is a shame for a man to wear long hair though his own, Nature must teach that it is much more shameful to wear long hair of another body's, and especially of women's. It was no shame for men to wear their own short hair; it must needs therefore be shameful to part with it for that which it is a shame for man to wear, viz. women's long hair. (2) Women's hair, when on their own heads, is a token of subjection—how comes it to cease to be a token of subjection when men wear it? It was made for a token of subjection in the wearer, and is no more a token of superiority in men than wearing the breeches is a token of subjection in women. (1 Cor., 11: 3,4,5,6,7, etc.) (3) To be beholden to another without cause is ignominious in a high degree, for the borrower is servant to the lender, at least in some degree. It was an abatement of Solomon's glory that it was not genuine and connatural, as the lilies' glory was. Sin exposed men to this shame and misery, to be beholden to some of the creatures for clothing and covering. But in the case of hair there is no such need, seeing God and Nature provided for every man hair of his own. In cases of extraordinary casualty when the head is left bare, other supply may be made by periwigs made of the hair of other creatures. There is no need to rob Peter to pay Paul, and to make one bald that ought to be covered [in order] that another may be covered that might be conveniently covered some other way. (4) For a man to pray covered is absurd and shameful and dishonors Christ. But so do men when periwigged. For the woman's hair is given for a covering, and is so to whomsoever wears it in that length and abundance that is usual in periwigs; and consequently such dishonor Christ. (1 Cor., 11: 4) (5) It is a foolish exchange, to exchange the living for the dead. In this case, as well as in others, a living dog is better than a dead lion. A mean head of hair, living, sweet, lively-colored, and brisk, through its constant derivation of its natural juice from the soil where it first sprung up, is to be preferred before the most flourishing periwig that is lopped off from the root and derives no more vital sap, but is always withering and decaying and needs artificial oil and perfumes to keep it from putrefaction. (6) A good man would set the more price upon his own natural hair because Christ said, "the hairs of your head are all numbered." (Mat., 10: 30) And [He also

said] that a hair on their head shall not perish. (*Luke,* 21: 18) That God will have the same regard to begged, or borrowed, or bought periwigged hair we have no security. When the three children were cast into the fire, not a hair of their head was singed; if they had worn perwigs, it had been well if they had escaped so. If Samson had thought to have thatched his shaven crown and mended his broken vow with a periwig of Delilah's hair, though it might have been longer than it was before and much longer than it was grown to at the time he made the Philistines' sport, I question whether he had had such an extraordinary assistance as he had when he pulled down the house on the Philistines' heads. If the baldness of Elisha's head had come by a voluntary shaving of his head to make room for a periwig made of women's hair, the children that laughed at his bald head might, for ought that I know, have done well enough for all the bears. For it had been a ridiculous thing for the old prophet to have voluntarily laid aside his gray hairs, for to make way for a more florid appearance in a borrowed dress in some foolish youthful woman's hair. (7) There is manifest pride, levity, vanity, affectation in periwigs. For they are not made in imitation of men's hair, as it naturally groweth; whereas Art should imitate Nature, where it pretends to mend the accidental defects or decays of Nature. Let all the world judge (whose periwig locks don't hang in their eyes) whether the periwig part of mankind, as to hair, look like them that go in their own hair. Whereas the periwigs might as easily be made to imitate the honest guise of those Christians that wear their own hair, if men desired to have them so, and would be less offensive than they are now. (8) It will not be an easy thing to account with God for so much needless cost and expense as is now laid out on periwigs. And much more would the expense be if the fashion should prevail among the generality. Alas, that men should be so prodigal and profuse this way in an age so barren and fruitless as to good works, and when they are so much needed for the maintaining [of] the government in order and honor, and for building forts, and maintaining soldiers to defend the plantation against the enemies that will take off the scalp, both skin and hair, if we fall into their hands. They that do little or nothing for relieving the poor, and are backward in maintaining the worship of God, and make poverty their excuse, and yet might bear all the cost of periwigs, as well as the paring of their nails, will be found ill stewards of the estates which God hath given them. (9) If all the foregoing arguments prove no more than that there is an appearance of evil in it, yet that is enough to prove that periwigs of women's hair should not be worn by Christian men, seeing [that] Christians are required to abstain from all appearance of evil. Neither should we for so small a temptation run the venture of living in a course of sin, and of being exemplary to others in what is doubtful and very many good men think sinful—[men who] are offended and grieved at the sight of Christians that have faces like men and hair like the hair of women, and [who] are especially grieved when they see [that] magistrates and ministers, that are in reputation for wisdom, honor, and office, and ought to be examples to others in what is good, are, in their opinion, become examples in what is evil.

FINIS.

28

A Sinner Cast Out

Among the first residents of Boston were a certain Mr. and Mrs. William Hibbens. Mr. Hibbens was wealthy (from various forms of mercantile enterprise), socially prominent (witness the honorific "Mr."), and politically influential (as a magistrate and councilor in the government of the Massachusetts Bay Colony). From all one can tell, he was an important and exemplary member of his community. But his wife, evidently, was a somewhat different sort. A writer from the period speaks of her reputation for "natural crabbedness of temper," and there is little doubt that she was often in trouble with her neighbors.

In 1640 she became embroiled in a bitter quarrel with a joiner (that is, carpenter) named Crabtree, over some work that he had performed in her house. She accused him of overcharging her and refused to accept the contrary opinion of neutral parties (in particular, a certain "brother Davis," also a joiner) called in to arbitrate the case. The upshot was a series of proceedings against Mrs. Hibbens in the Boston church. There was, first, on September 13, 1640, a long discussion of her conduct—in which new sins were also added to her charge. At the end she was "admonished" to mend her ways or face further, more serious action. Then, five months later, the whole business was thrashed out once more, since the culprit seemed still unrepentant. The final result was a decision for full excommunication, the most dire penalty that a New England church could inflict. Luckily for us, all of these proceedings were recorded in detail by another member of the church, Robert Keayne. The interplay of charge and countercharge, the strategies of attack and defense, the whole effort of the other church members to compel submission from the errant "sister": here are the ingredients of an affecting personal drama.

Mrs. Hibbens does not appear again in the historical record for more than a decade. But in 1654 her husband died, and with him, one suspects, went a personal influence that had long shielded her from the full weight of her neighbors' hatred. For, in 1656 she was indicted, tried, and convicted in a major criminal proceeding before the General Court. The charge was witchcraft. And the sentence was death.

Proceedings of Excommunication against Mistress Ann Hibbens of Boston

(1640)

[From Sept. 13, 1640 (afternoon), after Rev. John Cotton's exposition on *Luke*, chapter 7.]

The sermon, prayer, sacrament of baptism, and contribution [being] ended, Mrs. Hibbens was to be called into question for some offence which she had given to some brethren and [about which she] would not be convinced. It was now to be told to the church [in order] that they may judge of it.

Brother Davis. The offence was between Mrs. Hibbens and myself and some others. That which I have to lay to her charge was an untruth, or a lie or two, that she told, as also that she accused me of a combination and said that the timbers of the room would cry for judgment against me; and yet she did not deal with me according to the rule of the Word, and this day in the morning she desired me to give her a meeting, and instead of satisfaction she did more unsatisfy me. And further my offence is that she hath broken covenant with me in accusing of me and yet not dealing with me in the name of Christ.

Mr. Cotton [the teacher]. Brother, she sayeth that once or twice she did speak to you to reverse what you had done, believing you were mistaken; but your carriage and backwardness was such in it that she was discouraged to proceed farther with you, the which was her fault. Besides, she sayeth that she sent our Brother John Leveret to you to the same purpose, but you used him so roughly that she was discouraged to proceed.

Brother Davis. She said my sin was so great that if she should not speak

Proceedings against Mrs. Ann Hibbens, First Church of Boston, 1640, in Robert Keayne, "Notes on John Cotton's Sermons," ms. in the Massachusetts Historical Society, Boston. I am grateful to the Society and to Mrs. Helle M. Alpert of Tufts University for permission to use portions of this most valuable document. Mrs. Alpert is currently preparing a complete edition of the "Notes." Most of all, I am grateful to Anita Rutman for making available to me her excellent transcription of this nearly illegible document.

the timber of the room would cry out for judgment against me; and yet she never dealt with me. Besides, our Brother Leveret never dealt with me about it.

Mr. Hibbens. I desire to speak one thing to the congregation, wherein I would now lay aside the other relation and speak as a brother. And this I can testify, that in one thing our Brother Davis did receive satisfaction from my wife, and such satisfaction that he did bless God that had so much humbled her spirit, she confessing her error with tears. Therefore how seasonable it is, or according to rule, for our Brother to make mention of this publicly, and to tell the church of it.

Brother Davis. I refer myself to the church. The thing was public; and therefore, though I may be satisfied, yet the church may call for satisfaction.

Brother Huchison. I, asking my Brother Davis about it, he told me [that] in that particular he had received satisfaction, if other things had concurred. But other things not concurring wherein she was guilty, he seemed to me to be unsatisfied. And my question is whether our Brother might take one confession for satisfaction, when there is other heinous evils that lie upon her which she gives no satisfaction in.

Brother Button. Our Brother Davis did tell me he was not satisfied because her satisfaction was constrained and not free; and we heard today that there [are] four sorts of hypocritical humiliation, and this was one of them—[a] constrained acknowledgment and not voluntary.

Brother Davis. My other offence against her was about the chimney piece, in which she told a lie, as [she said] that she would have her bed according to the chimney piece, and yet afterwards she denied it. And there are two or three witnesses to prove it. And another lie was this: that she called to have her bed done, and the work fashionably [done]; and after[-ward] she found fault with them as toys and gewgaws.

Pastor [Rev. John Wilson]. Indeed we had witnesses of this; and when the matter was in question before us, it did seem to us that she did contradict herself.

Mr. Colborn. I must needs say that when I dealt with our Sister Hibbens I did find that she did contradict herself and [that] some guilts did lie upon her; and at first God did begin kindly to melt her spirit. As I am witness to this turning, therefore I am sorry to hear so much spoken in her excuse and to mitigate her offence, for I hope she will more kindly melt and come off than you are aware of.

Pastor. Sister Hibbens, I speak to you in the name of Christ, that you would give a plain and direct answer to this lie that is laid to your charge —and [to] the charging of our Brother with a confederacy, and divulging and publishing it all abroad to ministers, magistrates, neighbors and others, [in order] to lay infamy, disgrace, and reproach upon this our Brother.

[No answer from her at this point]

Brother Penn. I marvel [that] she shows so much contempt to the church as to sit when the elders speak and when she is in dealing with [them].

Brother Button. It is a great offence to us that she shows so much disrespect to our elders and [that she dares] not to attend to what is spoken.

Pastor. It may be [that] some bodily infirmity is upon her, and therefore we leave her to her liberty.

[Speaker not identified on behalf of] Mrs. Hibbens. She is not resolved yet that it is lawful for her to speak in the church and therefore desires [that] she may be spared till the next Lord's Day; and she hopes that God may help her then to answer more fully and to give more free satisfaction — this she propounded by a Brother.

Mr. Cotton. Indeed, Sister, when the Pastor shall speak to you in the name of Christ and you are in the presence of God, [you] therefore ought humbly to stand upon your feet, and not to sit, and to hearken [to] what the Lord hath to speak to you, and not to turn your ear any way, or speak to any other, when the Pastor of the church is speaking to you.

Brother Penn. Her carriage hath been so proud and contemptuous and irreverent in the church, when the church is dealing with her, that it is intolerable. Therefore I think she ought first to be dealt with for this, and some admonition [ought] to be passed upon her for this, before the church proceeds any further with her.

Pastor. Sister Hibbens, in the fear of God, with reverence and submission, give answer to the church for the offence that is taken at you. Hath God convinced you or begun to melt your spirit for this contempt that you have shown to ordinances of Jesus Christ in your irreverent carriage and turning aside to talk with this Brother or that Sister when the Elders are speaking to you in the name of Jesus Christ? Do you see it to be a sin in you?

Brother Fairbank. I desire to propound this to [the] church, seeing [that] our Sister hath a scruple and is unsatisfied in the lawfulness of a woman's speaking in the church: whether it may not be a salve to her to be put to give a present answer, for if she should speak she should contradict herself or else be drawn to speak against her conscience; or whether it will not be more meet to put it off to the next Lord's Day, in which time her scruple may be removed.

Pastor. It hath been answered already by our teacher that it is lawful for a woman to speak when she is asked a question.

Mr. Winthrop. Seeing it is now late and that all the things objected against our Sister cannot now be gone through, it would not be amiss to defer it till the next Lord's Day.

Pastor. It is now late, and the sun is set; and therefore let us defer it, and pray to God to give our Sister a humble heart and kindly to melt and to lay down her pride and veil her pomp and any thoughts of herself, and to submit herself to the church and the power of Christ over her, and to take all shame and confusion to her own face, both of her lies that she hath spoken and [of] other offences given, that all the glory may come to Christ Jesus.

[20 Sept., 1640, afternoon; after Cotton's exposition on *Luke*, chapter 8.] The sermon and sacrament of baptism, the first prayer, and contributions being ended, the church proceeded with Mrs. Hibbens and called her to answer.

Mr. Hibbens. I humbly crave leave to speak a word.

Pastor. Make silence in the church, that everyone may hear what now is to be spoken to the matter in hand which was begun the last Lord's Day.

Mr. Hibbens. Some of my godly Brethren watching over me when I spake the last day in that case wherein I opened my mouth, they put me in mind of an expression that I used in calling one of my Brethren "sir" instead of "brother." How it fell from me I know not; but it was an expression unsuitable to the convenant I am in, and the more unsuitable for myself because the title of brother is such a phrase that I have found my heart many times enlarged when in the use of it. And therefore my Brethren telling me of it, with their advice and the free consent of my own heart I desire that the Brother to which I spake it would pardon it; and so I desire of all the rest of my Brethren.

Pastor. I hope the Brethen do take satisfaction in this acknowledgment, and let me say this to you in relation to your yoke-fellow and companion. And therefore let me say this to you, dear Sister: seeing your husband hath been readily moved to make so ingenious an acknowledgment of so small a matter that it may be few or none in the congregation observed [it] except one—and that one, it may be, [was] not much offended —let it be an example to yourself from your husband to abase yourself, and take shame to your own face, and freely and openly and readily confess the faults and sins and offences. Now you are like to be called forth [by] his ingenious example, his meekness of spirit in humbling himself and taking any shame to himself rather than offend his Brother. Therefore, in the fear of God be ready and forward to acknowledge your faults and sins wherein you have given offence, and I doubt not but the church will be as ready to forgive you as your husband. And remember that one example, that hath been so much pressed upon you this afternoon, of Mary Magdalene, that having sinned and given great offence she doth abase and humble herself; and the more penitent she was, the more honorable esteem she had in the heart of Jesus Christ, and she was preferred and honored above other women more honorable in their places.

Mrs. Hibbens. Observing my carriage, I must needs confess [that] there was sin on both parts; but leaving others and coming to myself, [I must confess] that [as] for my carriage and the mistake thereof I desire to be humbled for it. And though there was no sin intended, yet there was such an appearance of evil as might give offence to others; and therefore I desire to be heartily sorry, so as [I] may give satisfaction to such as was offended.

Brother Penn. I desire to know whether this confession she now makes hath respect to the business in hand between our Brother Davis and she, or the offence she gave the last day to the church in her carriage.

Mrs. Hibbens. I have only [spoken in] respect to the last, and would give a reason why I did then sit if it be desired.

Pastor. I suppose your reasons will not be desired if you can say in the presence of God that this was not your reason, that you did it in contempt of God, His church, and ordinances, or in contempt of those that were dealing with you.

Mrs. Hibbens. I can speak it in the presence of God, that it was not out of any contempt to God or His ordinances.

Elder Leveret. Then you may proceed to that which follows, and to give answer to such things as were objected against you the last day.

Mrs. Hibbens. I desire you all to take notice of my fall that you may stand, and to take heed of sleeping while you hear and of sleeping while you seem to hear, as it hath been my own fault. Take heed of the miscarriage of the congregation in not walking according to the rule and [in being ready] to make ourselves guilty of sin in receiving false reports, or [not?] believing true reports, and so to hate our brother in our hearts. (She desires the help of the prayers of the church) because I know not how far the Lord hath withdrawn Himself from me. And lest the Lord should not stand by me to assist me in giving satisfaction or in speaking to the satisfaction of the church, [I desire] that the church would give me leave to express myself in writing to the church; and so it may be read. And if it may be allowed, then I desire that I may be respited to the next Lord's Day to bring it in.

Pastor. Then the sum of your speech is this: that for the present God hath not yet convinced you of your sin in telling a lie, or of your accusation against the Brethren of a combination against you, or of the unrighteousness of your cause; and therefore you would clear it in your writings, that so you may speak the less yourself.

Mrs. Hibbens. Yes, that is my meaning.

Pastor. Then the church is to consider whether they consent to her motion; if so, then we will draw to a conclusion.

Mr. Winthrop. I think in this case your self should direct the church whether it be meet to be granted or no; and as you shall advise, I think the church will consent.

Mr. Cotton. The practice of writing is uncouth in the church and we have no precedent for it in Scripture, except in extraordinary cases of absence and sickness, or when God's servants have been in prison; then they have written and their writings have been read in the church, but not in these cases. Therefore, Sister, you shall do well to express yourself, for the thing laid to your charge is [a] matter of crime and sin; and that may either be acknowledged or cleared, and by writing things would be drawn on to a further length, when the Brethren hath been too long already delayed in the answer and the chruch hath many other business —[such] as to proceed with our Brethren at the island, which we would willingly do the next Lord's Day.

Mrs. Hibbens. My motion of writing was not with any unwillingness to speak or thereby to excuse myself in anything wherein I may justly accuse myself of.

Pastor. What say you then to the lies that you were accused of; do you acknowledge it or no?

Mrs. Hibbens. I cannot accuse myself of any lies [at the time] when I did speak it; I did think it to be so as then I spake.

Pastor. But, Sister, there is two witnesses, one a Brother of the congregation, and the other one which we have no exception against; and they both accuse you of a lie.

Mrs. Hibbens. If the congregation please to assist me with their prayers and to lift up their hearts to God for me that He would keep me from lying and assist me to speak nothing but truth, I shall declare unto you the ground that hath made me stir so much in it as I did, and declare in speech what I made account to write.

Pastor. Pray go on; and speak nothing but that which is pertinent to the matters objected against you.

Mrs. Hibbens. [Keayne's notes to himself rather than the direct speech] She relates the beginning of the argument and the proceedings of the whole bargain with Goodman Crabtree, whom she accuseth of deceitfulness in his work and slight doing of it, and breach of his promise, and neglecting his work after he began it.

Mrs. Leveret. I desire to crave leave for a word to the congregation. It is offensive to many that these things which have been agitated again and again in private—that [they] should take up so much time on this day, to relate over the things again.

Pastor. For my part, I think the same—they [in] nothing tending to clear herself in those things that are objected against her, but tend[ing] to lay aspersions upon others.

Mrs. Hibbens. I desire to proceed, that I may clear myself [from] those many aspersions that have been laid upon me in this business. Things have proceeded to great offence; for whereas my bargain with Goodman Crabtree was for forty shillings, which he [ended by] taking 13 lb. for —I thought [this] was so great that I could not tell how to put it up.

Brother Gridly. Many of the Brethren are much unsatisfied with this discourse.

Brother Lyall. I think we should prefer the honor and glory of God before our own honor. It is very grievous for us to stay so long to hear such unprofitable discourse.

Mrs. Hibbens. I now come to that which you aim at. I might have omitted some of that I began withal, but I have almost done.

Mr. Ting. I desire to know whether the church's motion is not to be hearkened to, that our Sister should be limited or cut short in this impertinent discourse; and [I] desire her to draw her speech directly to that which is laid against her.

Pastor. All this that you now relate is only to excuse yourself, and lessen your own fault, and lay blame upon others. And therefore you have in an unsatisfied way sent from workman to workman and from one to another to view the work and to appraise it. And when the elders and others, that met at your own house about this, did see reason that you should be satisfied, yet you have been so suspicious and used such speeches to accuse our Brother Davis and other workmen when they would not speak as you do, yet you have continued still to be so unsatisfied, that you have caused more expense of time than all your work is worth. And when our teacher and the elders and myself, upon due search and examination of the matter, did not find that there was any great wrong done to you, or if it were a wrong yet we thought you ought to have been satisfied and to stir no more in it, such hath been the unquiet frame of your spirits that you would take no warning nor hearken to our council and exhortation, but have still been stirring to the offence of many of the congregation whose names and credits you have defamed, and we are unsatisfied also. Therefore consider whether this hath been according to the rule of Christian love; and therefore if you cannot give a better answer, you must expect the farther proceedings of the church against you, as shall be most wholesome for your soul.

Elder Oliver. Sister, I think [of] the last meeting we had about this business, when there was ten of us together, five for you and five for our Brother Davis, and many witnesses [were] examined, and the joiners [were] professing as in the presence of God that they had rated it as low as ever as they could—and so low as we can get no other joiners in this town to do the like. And they brought it to ten pounds or thereabouts; and therefore methinks you should be satisfied and speak no more.

Mrs. Hibbens. There was a joiner from Salem and some others that saw it that did not reckon it above half the price of what he took for it.

Brother Penn. All that our Sister hath spoken tends not to any measure of repentance or sorrow for her sin, but to her further justification and [the] excusing of herself and casting blame upon others, which savors of great pride of spirit and a heart altogether untouched by any of those means that hath been used with her.

Sergeant Savidge. I think if all other offences were passed by that hath been mentioned, yet she hath shed forth one sin in the face of the congregation worthy of reproof: and that is transgressing the rule of the Apostle in usurping authority over him whom God hath made her head and husband, and in taking the power and authority which God hath given to him out of his hands. And when he was satisfied and sits down contented, she is unsatisfied and will not be content, but will stir in it—as if she were able to manage it better than her husband, which is a plain breach of the rule of Christ.

Pastor. That indeed is observed in her by diverse [persons] as a great aggravation of her sin, in so much that some do think she doth but make a wisp of her husband. Yet this she alleged for herself: that her husband did give her leave to order and carry on this business to her own satisfaction.

Brother Corser. It is thought by many that it is an untruth which she speaks, and that it will be proved on oath that her husband would have had her [be] contented and rest satisfied, and she would not.

Brother Hibbens. At the first, I did give my wife leave to argue with the joiner and to order the business with him as she thought good; yet I must needs say in faithfulness to the church that when difference did arise about the work, my wife told me she had agreed with him to do it for 40s., which I cannot affirm having no witness but my wife's own affirmation, [and] which he denied from the first. And therefore, conceiving that the work was too much for the price, I told him when it was done [that] what[ever] it came to more I would give him as two men should judge it worth. And I chose my Brother Davis, of whose faithfulness I am well satisfied, and [I] was very willing to stand to that agreement he made, and did persuade my wife, and could have wished with all my heart [that] she had been willing to have done the same, and I have had some exercise of spirit with her, that she hath not done so.

Brother Scott. I desire to speak a word or two to this woman, our Sister, to help on the work of humiliation upon her heart, if God so please, which I fear He hath left to a great measure of hardness. And I would have her [try] to look at it as a just hand of God against [her] that she, who hath been so uncharitable against her Brethren, not believing anything they have spoken—except [when] they spake to her mind—when an oath is appointed of God to end controversy, [and who] now when Brethren affirm in the presence of God that they do judge of things and speak according to the best of their skill and judgement which is no less than an oath, yet she will not believe them but contends still it is just with God [—truly it is a just hand of God against her] that Brethren now should have as hard thoughts of her and hardly to believe her in anything she speaks.

Mr. Colborn. I desire to help on the work of humiliation upon the heart of our Sister, and sorry I am to see what I do at this time, that she should altogether justify herself and hide her sin. She was in a better frame of spirit a week ago and seemed to melt under her conviction. I desire [that] she would take notice of the frame of her own spirit, and [consider] whether she did not use some indirect means to make men undervalue the work by stirring them up to judge it before they have well viewed it or considered the extent and manner of it—yea, sometimes obscuring the work and speaking disgracefully and slightly of it, as she did to myself. And when men have judged it as low as they could, yet she would lay it upon their consciences as if they spoke partially, which savors not only of uncharitableness but of a covetous frame of spirit, as that she would have work done, and that with some cost of curiosity, and yet would not allow the worth of it.

Mrs. Hibbens. The Lord knoweth that in all this I have but only desired to find out the truth of a thing and to do them good with whom I had to deal. For there being a general complaint of oppression in work and workmen, and I finding this to exceed all reason, in so much that some cried out of the excess of it and advised me to complain of it in the court, and because the truth of it would hardly be found out by the joiners of this town, I was councilled to seek out two others in some other town—that would speak the truth and, when they had spoken it, would not be afraid to stand to it—which I did. And because I feared that some such thing might be objected, that I did it for lucre of gain, [though] I might lawfully take that [which] is my own—yet to prevent that objection, though I found he had taken more by half than the work was worth, yet I resolved not to purse one penny of it, but to dispose [of] it to some other use.

Pastor. It is now late and we must draw to a conclusion, and therefore the church is to express themselves [as to] whether we shall proceed to pass some censure upon her [such] as that of admonition, for the further melting and humbling of her soul, if God so please—or, if He leave her to obstinacy and impenitence, it may make way to the more speedy and final cutting of her off by that great censure of excommunication.

Brother Penn. If she hath told a lie, as it seems is testified against her by two witnesses, and more than one lie is laid to her charge besides other notorious crimes, then I desire to know how the church can put her off only with an admonition, and not proceed to cut her off by excommunication.

Pastor. Though there be two witnesses that testify [to] that which carries the sound and appearance of a lie (and indeed it seems too probable), yet she hath some excuse and defense for it, and sayeth she understood it one way and they another. They testify she said so, but they cannot testify she meant so; she sayeth she did not mean as they would understand it. Therefore let us proceed to that which is plain and admonish her first for that; and if any other thing can be proved against her, or this lie can be made more manifest, it will [not?] hinder the church's further proceeding with her. Therefore if it be your mind, we shall proceed to admonition. We shall take your silence for consent herein.

Pastor. Then attend to your censure.

Mrs. Hibbens. I desire that you would not do so, though I shall be willing to submit to this censure as an ordinance of Christ; yet I pray God not to lay the blood of this act to the charge.

Pastor. To whose charge? then it seems [that] you lay the blame upon the whole church and put if off from yourself. But you should remember

what our teacher taught the last day, that it is possible [that] a church
may err and may mistake, but is it likely that God should so far leave
His church wherein He useth to bestow His presence, and that you in
your own cause should be more upright than all they? Therefore, for
your contempt and pride of spirit, and for exalting yourself against your
guide and head—your husband I mean—when you should have submitted
yourself; and because you have rejected the advice of Brethren and Sisters
and the council and exhortation of your Elders, when they persuaded,
advised, and earnestly exhorted you to be quiet and to sit down satisfied,
and did express their own judgments that having heard all things and
the full examination of all matters and witnesses they did not find you
much wronged nor them much to blame, but yourself rather in more;
and though some have dealt with you alone and many together, yet such
hath been the pride and unquiet frame of your spirit that, contrary to
all these councils and exhortations and pains that hath been taken with
you, you have been stirring and have uttered words tending to the disgrace
and defamation of your Brethren, as if they had combined together to
deal unjustly, when by covenant you ought to have a better opinion of
[them]: therefore for these and many other [of] your grievous sins and
offenses I do admonish you, in the name and fear of Jesus Christ and
His church, and for the pulling down [of] the pride and height of your
spirit, and for the mortification of your lusts and covetous distempers,
[and in order] that you would speedily seek to God that He would make
you sensible of your sins and come to a holy confession of them and
humiliation for them before the Lord and His church. Or else, if you
shall delay to give the church satisfaction and out of the pride and obstinacy of your heart shall refuse so to do, it will make the church more
speedy in calling you to a further account for such things as remain,
and proceed[ing] more speedily to cut you off by the great sentence of
excommunication, and delivering you up to Satan for the further destruction of your unmortified flesh, if not to the perdition of your soul—
if God give you not a heart to repent and turn to Him. Therefore as
you desire to avoid the second censure, let it appear speedily what work
this first ordinance of the Lord hath upon your soul.

[A middle section of the proceedings against Mrs. Hibbens has been left
out here, owing to limitations of space. The omitted material comprises
the first part of Keayne's notes on the church's deliberations of February
24, 1641. On that day the entire membership met by special appointment
for the sole purpose of reopening the case. Mrs. Hibbens's misdeeds were

described in detail once again. Particular emphasis was given to her wrongful accusations against the joiners, her lack of due respect for her husband, and—a new charge—her complaint that the church itself had dealt unfairly with her at its earlier meeting. Mrs. Hibbens still declined to display full "penitence" and "humiliation" before her offended brethren. The church moved at length to a formal sentence of excommunication, at which point our *verbatim* transcript resumes.]

Pastor. We see [that] the Lord hath not yet broken her spirit, nor there is nothing [which] comes from her that tends to satisfaction; therefore we must propound it to the church what is further to be done—whether they be satisfied or what course they shall judge meet to be further taken herein. Therefore pray, Brethren, consider whether it will be meet to give her further time, or to pass a second admonition upon her, or to proceed to some further censure.

Brother Button. For my own part I do not see how the church can be satisfied with an admonition. The former hath not wrought upon her in all this time. She hath now given no satisfaction, but all her speeches hath tended to excuse herself and to lay all the blame upon others— as upon our honored magistrate Mr. Winthrop, upon our own Elders and the revered elders of other churches—to hide her sin, as if they had advised her or drawn her into these miscarriages. She sees nothing amiss in herself; therefore I think the church cannot but proceed to the uttermost censure of excommunication.

Mr. Winthrop. For my own part I do not see of what use a second admonition should be, nor [do I see any reason] to give her longer time. Indeed if it had been [a] matter of opinion or error, then a second admonition might have followed the former; but this is a matter of fact which is plain and manifest to every eye. Therefore I see no rule for that, nor use of it.

Pastor. For my own part I am of the same mind. Yet seeing [that] the former admonition hath had no better fruit, some sharper corsie had need be applied to search in to the bottom of the sore—though I would not be against any lenity the church should think meet to show.

Mr. Hutchison. I desire our teacher to help us [as to] whether that place whereof the Apostle, in speaking of a heretic, sayeth that after once or twice [trying] admonition, reject him—whether that place doth not hold over a liberty to the church for a second admonition if they see cause.

275

I do but only propose it, not intending to oppose but to join with the church in what[ever] they shall determine and conclude herein.

Mr. Cotton. That place doth not speak of the admonition of the church, as I conceive, but rather of private admonition, after which we may reject them from having society and communion with them; and it is such a one as is condemned in his own conscience. Secondly, our honored magistrate hath well answered that already: if it had been for heresy or an error in judgement, some further patience might have been used to see if she might have been convinced and brought to the truth; but this is matter of fact and practice and that which any by the light of nature may see to be evil, as it is in the case of other gross sins. Therefore, though if the church had seen fit to have afforded longer patience and [to] have tried [to see] what a second admonition would have done, I should have gone that way and for my own part could have desired it, yet [the case is] not but that I think she deserves a further and sharper censure; and if the mind of the church shall carry it that way I will not hinder [them] but can freely join with them in that censure and have no scruple against it.

Brother Fairbank. I had thought to have joined with our Brother Stoddard in the same motion he was about to make to the church; but the greatness, hardness, and averseness of our Sister's spirit in all the pains and council that hath been given her this day hath much discouraged me, and I fear God hath withheld repentance from Her. Yet I shall propose one place of Scripture to the church's consideration, [as to] whether it may not be a rule to us for some further patience. The words are: (Esa., 57: 17,18) "for his wicked covetousness I was wroth and smote him and hid me and was wroth, and he went on forwardly in the way of his heart; I have seen his ways and will heal him, I will lead him also and restore comforts to him and his mourners." This place may somewhat suit our Sister's condition. The Lord hath been angry with her and hath smote her for the iniquity of her covetousness, and it seems God hath hid Himself from her, as appears by the great obdurateness of her heart this day, which I speak [of] with grief; and though God hath smote her, yet she goes on in her sin stubbornly and forwardly. Yet the Lord may have mercy upon her as follows in the verse: "I have seen his ways and will heal him, and I will restore comfort to him and his mourners though he was very wicked." Yet God promiseth to heal him—[I question] whether this may not give warrant for longer patience in imitation to God. I shall leave it to the church. I only propose it, but shall willingly go along with the church in that [course which] they shall determine of.

Captain Gibbens. This Sister of ours hath held forth many sins this day in the face of the congregation, the least whereof deserves a sharp censure. She hath accused diverse of the Brethren falsely, when no such thing appears, and so hath borne false witness against the rule of the Word. She hath taken away their names and credits (what in her lies) which is as precious as life itself. She hath accused others to justify herself. She hath sat in the throne of God Himself, as hath been shown in her judging the consciences and hearts of her Brethren. She hath usurped authority over her guide and head, whom she should have obeyed and unto whom God hath put her in subjection; yet she hath exalted her own wit and will and way above his, to the great dishonor of God and of him. She hath committed one of those seven sins which Solomon sayeth God hates, that is, to sow sedition and strife amongst Brethren; and she hath been eminent this way not only amongst Brethren, but she hath done her endeavor to sow discord between churches and to set them at variance and to hatch jealousies between them. And indeed I do not know what sin she is not guilty of. And all these [offences] are accompanied with impenitency and obstinacy. And therefore I think the church should be unfaithful to her soul if they should not proceed to a further and sharper censure, and to cast her out from that society which she hath had so slight an esteem of. Only I should propose this to the church: whether it were not more meet to refer the passing of the censure upon her till the next Lord's Day, when all the Brethren and church will be present and [when there will be] a full assembly, which will admit more authority and solemnity to the ordinance.

Sergeant Oliver. For my own part I look at the case of this Sister of ours to be somewhat like that of Miriam's, who rose up against Moses and Aaron [and] whose leprosy appeared in the face of the congregation. And there was a law for lepers that the priest should search and view them; and if upon the search they found leprosy appearing, the priest was to pronounce them lepers, and then they were to be thrust out for a time till they were healed of that disease for the [sake of the] congregation and the society of God's people. As this Sister hath been diligently searched and viewed and upon the search she is found leprous and diverse spots are risen and do manifestly appear to the congregation, therefore, according to the law of God, I think she ought to be pronounced unclean and as a leprous person to be put out from amongst us; and it appearing so plainly, I know not how with safety or without danger of infecting others we may keep her one week longer amongst us. It hath been too long forborne already, and there is danger that many hath been infected by the church's delaying so long. And how safely we may dispense with the law and rule of God's word any longer, seeing the leprosy appears so plainly to every eye, I know not. And if our Sister should go home and God should strike her sick or lay any other judgement upon her or should take her away before the next Lord's Day, I know not how the church should answer it before God; but [I think] that the blood of her soul would be required at our hands for neglecting to apply that remedy which God hath appointed for the healing of her sin and [for the] recovering her of her disease. Therefore I think the censure ought speedily to be applied to cast her out of the church as leprous.

Mr. Hibbens. I humbly crave leave for a word or two of the congregation, in regard of that relation that is between us. I am sorry that I should have any occasion to speak, yet it is not to hinder the church in their proceedings; but what[ever] they shall conclude of I shall sit down contented with. Only I would humbly propose one place to your wise consideration, if it may be of any use to your direction, and to crave a little more patience and leniency—that the Lord may sanctify that to my dear wife, if the Lord shall see it good. And that is what the Lord sayeth concerning Ephraim and Israel: "How shall I give thee up, Ephraim? how shall I deliver thee, Israel? how shall I make thee as Admah? how shall I set thee as Zeboim? My heart is turned within me; my repentings are rolled together; I will not execute the fierceness of my displeasure; I will not return to destroy Ephraim. For I am God and not man, the holy one in the midst of thee, and I will not enter into the city." Wherein we see [that] though God was highly provoked at Israel, yet His bowels pitied them and He promised to spare them and not to deliver them up. So if the church would show their bowels of pity in sparing or respiting her censure for a time, the Lord may so bow the heart of my wife that she may give the church full satisfaction, which would be the rising of my soul. I shall wholly leave it with you.

Sergeant Oliver. I desire to speak one word to this dear Brother in answer to the place he mentioneth. That delivery which the Lord there speaks of was a delivering of them up to destruction; but this delivery of the church is not to destruction but for salvation, that the sin may be destroyed and mortified [and] that the soul may be saved in the day of the Lord. Therefore thus to deliver her up is the best pity the church can show to her; and not to deliver her up were not to spare her but to destroy her.

Pastor. It grows now very late, and we must put it to [illegible], therefore, if it be the mind of the church that we shall proceed to pass the sentence of excommunication upon this Sister. We shall take your silence for your consent and approbation thereto; if any of the church be of another mind, he hath liberty to express himself. [Silence.] We perceive by the universal silence of the church that with one consent it is your mind [that] we should proceed. And therefore let us first seek unto God for His direction and for a sanctified use of this His ordinance, and [in order] that we may proceed not out of bitterness or envy but out of tender love to her soul, and that God would give her a sight of her great and many evils and break her heart by kindly repentance [so] that she may the more speedily return to God and the church again, as now she is cast out.

The prayer being ended, the church proceeded to [the] sentence of ex-communication.

Elder Leveret. Mrs. Hibbens, stand up and attend to the censure which the church hath determined to pass upon you for your sins and offences.

Pastor. Then you are to know that for your many and gross sins and offences that this day hath been proved against you by many witnesses:

For your slandering and raising up an evil report of your Brethren and spreading of it to the disgrace of the gospel and of them (which you could not prove, but the contrary appears).

And for your uncharitable thoughts of them, setting yourself in the place and throne of God, judging their hearts and consciences when they have cleared themselves by solemn protestations and oaths in the presence of God and His church that they have dealt justly and conscientiously with you, doing as they would be done by in the things that were referred to their judgment and arbitration; yet you, out of a covetous and greedy desire to keep from workmen that which justly appears to be due to them, against the advice of your husband whose council you ought to have hearkened to, and against the advice and council of your Elders, of our honored magistrates and diverse other Brethren and friends, you have not sat down satisfied; but with a restless and discontented spirit you have gone from person to person, from house to house, and from place to place, not only in this town but to diverse other towns and persons not of this congregation; and [you] have vented your slanders and evil reports, and have not spared to threaten vengeance against them and to affirm that the timbers of your house would cry for vengeance against them, when you have more cause to fear that those timbers will cry to God for vengeance upon yourself for your wicked covetousness and sinful carriage, if you prevent it not by speedy repentance.

And for your suffering these Brethren to lie in so great and grievous sins as you apprehended and [you] did not labor to bring them to repentance in a right way according to the rule of God's word.

And for your several lies and untruths which you have told.

And for your stopping your ears and hardening your heart against the former admonition of the church and against the council and advice of diverse [persons], both of the Brethren and Sisters, that have taken pains with you in private—which, though at some time you gave some small hope of yielding and coming on to repentance, yet you have turned with the dog to his vomit, and you have sent them away with grief in their hearts instead of comforting their spirits.

And for [the reason] that, though your memory hath appeared to be very good in declaring anything that may make for your own turn and purpose, yet, for things produced against you, you cannot, or rather will not, remember any of those things, though they have been spoken at several times to several persons and [are] proved against you by many sufficient witnesses.

And for your want of subjection to so wise [and] discreet a head that we [need to] say no more, which God hath set to be your guide, whose council you should have followed, unto whom you ought to have been obedient in the Lord; yet against the institution of God and the rule of the Apostle, and [to] the evil example of diverse other wives, you have against nature usurped authority over him, grieved his spirit, and carried yourself as if he was a nobody, as if his wisdom were not to be compared to yours; and [you have continued] to harden yourself in a way of disobedience, to the evil example and unquietness of the family. (You have not only done so, but expressed it to be your judgement that husbands must hearken to their wives and be guided by them in all things, which corrupt opinion you have gone about to father on our teacher.)

As also for your sowing of discord and jealousies, not only between Brethren but between our church and others, our Elders and others— had not the wise providence of God prevented [this] by bringing some of them amongst us this day, who have been witnesses of our proceedings with you, and who have been patient to hear the offences on both sides laid open and are gone home fully satisfied, being very sorry (as they have expressed to you) that they were so inclinable to hearken to you and to entertain the least thought of jealousy against our church or any member in it.

And also for your accusing of the church of unrighteous proceeding against you, with whose censures you ought to have sat down satisfied, as with the act of Jesus Christ, and [ought] not to report that you were cast out or censured for laboring to find out sin in others when you were censured, for the sin was found out in yourself.

For these and many more foul and sinful transgressions, I do here, in the name of the whole church and in the name of the Lord Jesus Christ and by the virtue of that power and authority which He hath given to His church, pronounce you to be a leprous and unclean person; and I do cast you out and cut you off from the enjoyment of all those blessed privileges and ordinances which God hath entrusted His church withal, which you have so long abused. And because you have scorned council and refused instruction and have like filthy swine trampled those pearls under your feet, I do now in the name of Jesus Christ deprive you of them and take them from you [in order] that you may learn better to prize them by the want of them. And I do exclude you not only from the fellowship of the church in all the public ordinances of the same, but also from all private fellowship and communion with any of the servants of God in this church, except only in those relations in your own family—to your husband, children and servants. And for the greater terror and amazing of you, I do here, in the name of Christ Jesus and His Church, deliver you up to Satan and to his power and working, that you who would not be guided by the council of God may be terrified and hampered by the snares and power of Satan—for the destruction of your proud flesh [and] for the humbling of your soul, that your spirit may be saved in the day of the Lord Jesus, if it be His blessed will. And so as an unclean beast and unfit for the society of God's people, I do from this time forward pronounce you an excommunicated person from God and His people.

Elder Leveret. Then, Mrs. Hibbens, you are to depart the congregation as one deprived worthily of all the holy things of God.

Pastor. Let us now seek to God by prayer and call upon Him for a blesssing upon this ordinance.

Mr. Hibbens. I desire leave to speak one word before the congregation be dismissed.

Pastor. Speak on.

Mr. Hibbens. It is my humble and earnest request to the congregation, first to our reverend Elders and then to every Brother and Sister in the congregation, that both in public and private they would remember my afflicted condition before the Lord and earnestly pray to God that this ordinance of His may be sanctified to my wife for the good of her soul and for the returning of her back again—first to Himself and then unto you—and that is all I have to say.

29

Confrontation Politics, Colonial Style

The psychologist Erik Erikson has remarked that the human personality "can best be studied in the state of conflict." The same point could be made for the study of communities as well. Every individual must develop a way of handling aggressive impulses, and all societies provide channels for—and barriers against—the expression of such impulses. Styles of conflict are, then, culturally determined in part, and there is always much to be learned from observing how people fight.

In fact, the resolution of conflict was a particularly sensitive problem in many of the early American settlements. Court records are the best source of information here; when taken altogether, they reveal an extraordinary degree of litigiousness among the colonists. But this general impression needs to be refined somewhat in order to become truly meaningful. On the one hand, the records show relatively few episodes of violent crime: murder, rape, or even ordinary assault. Yet, on the other hand, they report literally countless suits for debt, trespass, wrongful withholding of property, slander, and the like. Moreover, in many cases where details are available, it seems clear that considerable feeling was invested in the matter at issue, from all sides. Hostility was, then, controlled beyond a certain point (where life and limb might be threatened), but was rampant in a host of lesser, everyday contexts.

The following set of depositions from an eighteenth-century court case in North Carolina exemplifies the common pattern. The case is atypical only in respect to the social position of the principals. The plaintiff was the governor of the colony, and the defendant was his immediate predecessor in office. The various testimonies offered serve to underline the vividly personal character of life in the culture of colonial America. Virtually all human transactions—from the most trivial affairs of ordinary citizens to the dealings between men who deployed the greatest measure of political and economic power—were conducted on a face-to-face basis. It seems incredible that the leaders of a colony could actually express their differences by routing one another from bed for a shouting confrontation in the middle of the night. But this is only a measure of the distance between their world and ours.

Attack by Ex-Governor George Burrington
on Governor Richard Everard and Others
(Edenton, North Carolina, 1725)

The information of the Honorable Sir Richard Everard, Baronet, Governor, and Commander in Chief, etc., taken upon oath before us, Christopher Gale, Esq., Chief Justice, and John Lovick and Henry Clayton, Esqrs., Justices of the Peace, this third day of December, Anno Domini 1725. [He] sayeth that on the second of this instant December, about three or four of the clock in the morning, Mr. Burrington, the late Governor, with several ruffians in company, came to the back door of his house; and having made a violent knocking for some time, he called out, "open the door"— which he repeated several times. But Sir Richard, knowing his voice, as did his servant who told him it was Mr. Burrington, Sir Richard advised him to go about his business or it would be worse for him; upon which Mr. Burrington replied after a rude and threatening manner, "come out; I want satisfaction of you for saying you would send me to England in irons. Therefore come out and give it [to] me, you Everard, you a Knight, you a Baronet, you a Governor. You are a Sancho Panza, and I'll take care of you, numbskull head." And upon Sir Richard's threatening him that if he offered to break into the house he would shoot him, or that if he did not go away quietly he would have him punished, he replied, "you have not an officer [who would] dare speak to me or look me in the face." And so, defying Sir Richard and his authority, he went away, calling Sir Richard "scoundrel" and several other abusive names.

Jurat Coram Nobis, 3rd Day, December, 1725.

  C. Gale   J. Lovick   Richard Everard

The examination of Richard Everard, Esq., aged about sixteen years, taken upon oath this third day of December, 1725.

Depositions in the case of Gov. Richard Everard vs. Ex-Gov. James Burrington, Edenton, N.C., 1725, in *North Carolina Historical and Genealogical Register*, III (1903), pp. 229–236.

The examinant sayeth that on the second of this instant December about three or four of the clock in the morning, [he] being in bed was wakened by his father's servant. And as he came downstairs he heard Mr. Burrington scurrilously abusing the Governor, Sir Richard Everard, saying, "you send me to England in irons, you be damned. I will make your heart ache before I have done with you." And then Mr. Burrington demanded whether the Governor would send him home to England or no; upon which the Governor desired him to go home, adding that he should see all things done in time, at which Mr. Burrington made a jest crying, "ah! ah! ah! I am come to turn up my Cape Fair —————— to you, before it goes to take its leave of you, Dick D——, you, you a sorry fellow. I'll scalp your damned thick skull." Whereupon the Governor again bid him depart, and soon after he went away, drumming against the window-shutters and weather-boards of the house.

Jurat Coram Me 3 tio Die.

Richard Everard

December, 1725
   C. Gale, C. J.

The examination of Mrs. Susanna Parris, wife of Mr. Thomas Parris of Edenton, taken upon oath this third day of December, Anno Domini 1725.

This examinant sayeth that on the second day of this instant December, in the morning a long time before day, Mr. Burrington, the late Governor, came to the door of their house in Edenton aforesaid and knocked violently; upon which one of their servants (all of the family being in bed) called to know who was there and he answered, "open the door," to which the servant answered, "I am coming." And upon a second knocking and the servant asking who it was, he commanded the servant to open the door or he would break every pane of glass in the windows, to which the servant answered that they dared not open the door, their Master and Mistress being in bed. And immediately upon it this examinant heard a stuzza and the outer door of their house was broken open. And Mr. Burrington came into the house and to the door of the room where this examinant was in bed with her husband whom he called for. And Mr. Parris, asking who was there, was answered, "a friend"; and being asked him how he got into the house he answered that he came in at the window. Mr. Parris made answer [that it] was not customary for friends to come in at the window, to which Mr. Burrington answered, "Damn you, Tom, get up; what, have you a mind to be licked?" And this examinant hearing

Mr. Burrington threaten her husband, she said something concerning his rude behavior in coming into their house at such an unseasonable hour and abusing her husband, when immediately Mr. Burrington began to give this examinant all manner of abusive language, calling her ———— and talking after so obscene a manner that it is not to be repeated.

And Mr. Parris, having dressed himself, went out to him. And whilst he went to light a candle, this examinant heard Mr. Burrington endeavoring to set a ruffianly fellow that came in his company, named Cornelius Harnett, to beat her husband and abuse him, which made her get up. But [she] was so ill treated by Mr. Burrington that she ran out of the house to call assistance to rescue her husband from them, for fear of worse consequences.

Jurat Coram me

                                                  Susanna Parris

    C. Gale, C. J.

The examination of James Potter of Edenton, being of full age, taken upon oath before John Lovick, Esq., one of his Majesty's Justices of the Peace, the eighth day of December, Anno Domini 1725.

This examinant sayeth that on Thursday, being the second of this instant December, about three or four of the clock in the morning, as he lay in his bed at Mr. Thomas Cook's house in Edenton opposite to the house of Joseph Young, he heard a noise at the said Young's house and somebody calling to have the door opened, threatening that if they did not immediately open the doors they would pull down one side of the house to get in. And thereupon, hearing several strokes made either against the doors or windows, this examinant got up and went over to Mr. Young's. And as he was going, he heard Mr. Young, who was then constable for the said town, commanding the peace. And making all the haste he could, he found Mr. Burrington, the late Governor, and one Cornelius Harnett in the house. And this examinant was immediately seized by the throat by the said Harnett, who told Mr. Burrington whom it was, to which Mr. Burrington replied, "———— he [would] run that villain Potter through," but this examinant, disengaging himself with some difficulty from Harnett, went immediately to the Governor's house, where he understood Mr. Burrington had been with his ruffians in company committing disorders.

Sworn to before me [on] the day and year above written

                                                  J. Lovick, Just. Pac.

The examination of Mrs. Young, the wife of Joseph Young of Edenton, taken upon oath before John Lovick, Esq., one of his Majesty's Justices of the Peace, on the eighth day of December, Anno Domini 1725; who, having heard the examination of Mr. James Potter read to her, remembers the particulars to be true as to what was done in their house. And [she] further sayeth that after Mr. Potter went away, Mr. Burrington and Harnett made endeavors to break into this examinant's chamber to search for James Potter; and Mr. Burrington declared that if he had known sooner that it was Mr. Potter, he would certainly have run him through. But this examinant, not being dressed, used all her endeavors as well as her husband to keep them from coming into her chamber, for which Mr. Burrington gave ill language and called her several names and struck her husband. And this examinant further sayeth that by the cold she got in being forced out of her bed and the fright she was put in, she has been so very ill ever since that she has kept her bed most of the time —which she believes to be entirely owing to Mr. Burrington's behavior in her house.

Sworn to before me [on]

J. Lovick, Just. Pac

the day and year above written

[Note: It appears from the following affidavits that the episode on December 2, 1725, was a continuation of earlier trouble begun Nov. 15, 1725.]

The deposition of Mrs. Susanna Parris, wife of Mr. Thomas Parris of Edenton and Burgess for said town, who, being of full age and sworn on the holy evangelists, sayeth:

That on Monday, the fifteenth day of this instant November, about three of the clock in the morning, as she was in bed, she heard a knocking at the outer door of the house; and her husband, inquiring who was there, was answered, "damn you, get up." But he not immediately rising, the person at the door swore he would break into the house, if the doors were not immediately opened; upon which her husband opened the door and found it was Mr. Burrington, the late Governor, who immediately went to the door of Mr. Cockburne's room where the said Cockburne lay sick and speechless in bed. And upon Mrs. Cockburne inquiring who was there, this deponent heard Mr. Burrington answer [that] it was a doctor come to Mr. Cockburne, which gained him admittance into the room where he lay. And upon this deponent's afterwards asking Mrs. Cockburne what his business was with her husband, she told this deponent that he had very much abused Mr. Cockburne as he lay in that condition, giving all manner of abusive language and threatening to cut off his ears. And this deponent further sayeth that after he came out of Mr. Cockburne's room she heard Mr. Burrington speaking to her husband. [He] said "―――― are all you country men such fools as Sir Richard Everard? He is a noodle, an ape," and several other epithets. And further [he] said that he (the said Richard Everard meaning) was not more fit to be a governor than a hog in the woods. Soon after Mr. Burrington, directing his discourse to one James Winwright, a person that he had previously made Provost Marshal, he swore to him that before nine months he would make him Provost Marshal again; and [he] offered to lay five thousand pounds that he the said Burrington should be Governor again by that time. And then a health was drunk by the company to Governor Burrington. And this deponent further remembers that, in the midst of his speeches and abusive language of the Governor Sir Richard, she heard him mention Judge Gale, whom he called "a perjured old rogue," and swore he should never be easy till he had cut his ears off, which sort of language about the Judge she has heard him several times repeat since Colonel Gale came last from England.

Susanna Parris

Taken and sworn before me,
   the 23rd day of November, 1725.
   J. Lovick, Just. Pac.

   The information of Dorothy, the wife of Adam Cockburne, Esq., Collector of [His] Majesty's Customs for the port of Rappahannock in the Dominion of Virginia, taken upon oath before Christopher Gale, Chief Justice of the said province, sayeth,

   That on Monday morning, the fifteenth of this instant November [illegible] the house of Mr. Thomas Parris in Edenton within this province, where she then lodged with her said husband, who then lay sick without either speech or senses (and had been so for a day or two before that time) in an inner room of the said house. And to gain admittance into the house, he pretended to be a doctor come to see Mr. Cockburne. As soon as he got into the house he directly came through two other rooms to that where the said Cockburne lay sick. And coming to the bed where he lay, he asked the said Mrs. Cockburne whether she knew him (being in an unusual dress), and taking hold of her arm was pulling her from out of the bed; but she thereupon got up. Then he placed himself in a chair on that side of the bed where her husband Mr. Cockburne lay, and took hold of him, and, as she imagined, was designing to pull him out of the bed; for at the same time he called him "rogue," "villain," and many other scandalous names, threatening to cut off his ears, and at the same time felt in his pockets (as she thought) for a pen-knife or some other instrument to do it with. Whereupon she went to him and asked him how he could be so barbarous and inhuman to treat a person in his condition after such a manner. He answered, she might be sure he was likely to die, for it would be a greater sorrow for her to see how barbarously he would torture him, and if he had not met with him here, he should have followed him elsewhere to use him so. And further she, the said Mrs. Cockburne, sayeth that Mr. Burrington told her that not only her husband but also his brother, one of the Lords of the Admiralty, were both removed from their offices by his means for their villainy to him, and two of his friends succeeded them, or words to that effect; and [he uttered] much more abusive language against them both, which by reason of the surprise she was then in she does not remember. And [she sayeth] further that she was obliged to sit up so long as he stayed in the house, to prevent him from further or other insults against her said husband; for he continued in the house in a riotous manner for a considerable time thereafter.

Dorothy Cockburne

Taken and sworn to before me,
this 23rd day of November, Anno Domini 1725.

C. Gale, C. J.

30

The Militia in Training

The colonists would never abandon the struggle to maintain traditional norms of order and pattern in their lives, in spite of an environment that seemed generally inhospitable to such efforts. In some instances their behavior was so highly formalized, so completely irrelevant to their practical needs and circumstances, as to be incomprehensible except as a kind of ritual enactment. Consider, for example, the following set of orders for a training exercise and sham fight to be conducted by the militia of Boston in the summer of 1686. And consider at the same time the actual manner of fighting in the New World—as revealed in Mrs. Rowlandson's narrative (see below) or any of a hundred comparable accounts. In fact, the colonists were obliged to learn a style of combat that could be roughly translated, in modern terms, as "guerilla warfare"; and on the whole they learned well. They retained the memory, however, and to some extent the practice, of a different military tradition—useless for fighting Indians, but presumably still important for ceremonial reasons.

Directions for a General Training Exercise
of the Boston Militia

(1686)

August 30, 1686: 8 Companies and 4 troops of horse.

Viz. Capt. Paige, C. Prentis; Capt. Wade, C. Thaxter.

In the forenoon every company to be apart at their usual stations, to settle themselves in order to afternoon exercise.

To be at the parade in the market place at one of the clock; to draw up six deep; and place themselves so as to march out by succession:

Directions for a General Training of the Boston Militia, August 30, 1686, in *Proceedings of the Massachusetts Historical Society*, Second Series, XIII (Boston, 1900), pp. 328–330.

viz., Capt. Sewall on the right wing, leaving space for the Major's Companies on the right of him, and for Capt. Heywood next before Capt. Dummer, who is to bring up the rear.

Thus to march into the Common, there to draw up in an even front according to dignity: viz., the major on the right wing, Capt. Sewall on the left, the rest of the Captains in their proper places.

Then wheel the front into a circle (viz., all face outward and wheel), closing the ring to that place which was the first front.

Then the 8 Lieutenants attended by 8 drums. 16 Sergeants to go to Mr. Usher's (where the president is desired to be) and wait on the president, etc. conducting him into the ring at the place of closing.

Then the Captains, being at the head of their respective companies, at the beat of drums (observing the drum major) to fire at once, presenting into the air.

The president may have opportunity to give commissions and install all that desire it. Then face outward and fire three times.

Then wheel of this ring into an even front.

And form the regiment into two grand divisions: viz., musketeers face about and march down 12 feet clear of the rear, and face to the front; then close files outward to order of each arms; then subdivide each division of musketeers, move them up to flank each body of pikes. Maintain interval of 12 feet between the two divisions.

Then prepare for a charge of the horse, encircling the front rear and both flanks of both divisions with pikes. Viz., command: the 2 outmost files of each division of pikes move and flank your musketeers. Half files of pikes face about to the right, pikes move clear of the standing part of the body. Musketeers of each division close to the right and left inward to order. Files of pikes rank to the right and left outward.

Then (having given notice to the Commander-in-Chief of the horse, before, [of] your intention of a skirmish) your drums are to beat a challenge, colors flying. The horse to charge one troop at a time, or half a troop, who wheeling round the body of foot, are to draw up again on their own ground (which is to be the lower end of the Common near the fence), and so successively till all have fired over. Then the whole body of horse to charge in four or six or eight files abreast, as they see cause. And after once wheeling about the foot, to draw off at a convenient distance that their rear may be clear of the foot, they are to charge again in the front of the foot where, between the two grand divisions, a sign shall be made (by a handerchief on a halberd) where

they shall break through and pass out at the rear, and wheeling about
to the right and left draw up on their own ground again. The pikes charging to the horse and firing to front, rear, and both flanks successively as
the horse come on, and half files of musketeers facing to the rear and
fire as the horse wheel about.

Reducement: The 2 outmost files of pikes of each division stand; the
rest of the pikes file three to the right and left inward. Musketeers move
outward from the center of each division, ten paces. Pikes of each division
face to the center, march, and close your divisions. Face all to your leader.

Command: The whole body face to the right about and move. The
right wing perform; but the left wing, led forward by the first Capt.,
notwithstanding all commands of the Commander-in-Chief, move away
and draw up at 100 paces distance, and each division face one another
as enemies. The major sends a drum to know the reason of this disobedience; they answer want of pay, etc. It is returned their complaint is without cause, etc., and [the command] requires their present quiet return
to their station; otherwise they must expect to be reduced by force. They
answer they will oppose force with force. Then both parties send to
the horse for assistance; who supply both; and both armies are winged
with horse, and prepare for battle. The major's drums beat a preparative,
colors fly, and trumpets sound; they answer with the like.

The fight begins, first by the horse skirmishing each other, two or
three files from each wing at a time, till all have fired over; rallying themselves in the rear of their foot.

The the foot engage, first by forlorns. Viz., first six files from each
wing, led out by 2 sergeants to each company, meet the enemy with
as many, and within 20 paces fire once over reducing in their own rear
and returning; 6 files more from each wing do the like till all have fired
over. Then 2 files from each flank led out by a sergeant meet with the
opposite party within 20 paces, fire at once, rankwise and return. Other
two files from each flank, move forward and fire in the same manner,
till they have gone through the body. Then fire once over rankwise,
one rank at a time moving forward to convenient distance and firing,
reducing in their own rear. The whole body now move forward and approaching within 50 paces, trail their pikes, still moving slowly forward;
and begin to fire, first by two files from each flank ranking before the
body, reducing themselves next the pikes; then rankwise, the whole body
moving up and pikes charging, sometimes one retreating and then the
other as the drums give notice, but none approaching nearer than ten
paces of both arms. In the heat of which all the horse, joining together,

interpose; and drums beat a retreat on all hands, face about, and move to a convenient distance; drums beat a triumph, colors flourishing; then (if any minister be there) draw together as before and so into a circle as before, and pray.

Then every Capt. receiveth his own company, marcheth home, and lodgeth his colors.

31

A Model Economy

It is widely assumed in our own day that a good economy is a growing one, that the potentialities for development and expansion of the productive system are (or should be) virtually without limit. Everyone can hope for a bigger piece of the pie, because the pie itself can be continually enlarged.

The colonists, like all people of their time, assumed no such thing. On the contrary, they believed that wealth was essentially a fixed quantity, and that economic activity should be governed by principles of orderliness and stability. Since the size of the total pie was unalterable, one person's gain would necessarily be another's loss. If changes of any sort occurred on a large scale, the result might be a major social upheaval. It was, indeed, the right and duty of the state to head off such possibilities by direct intervention in the economy. In practical terms, this meant that the state would act to hold both wages and prices within certain "just" limits, would enforce equable standards of weight and measure, and would require that all able-bodied men work (or, conversely, that everyone's job be protected from sudden arbitrary termination). These were the main ingredients of the "equilibrium" model that underlay the theory and practice of economics almost everywhere before the nineteenth century.

Of course, the system never worked to perfection, but in the Old World it seemed for the most part to correspond with social reality. In the colonies, however, it was subjected at once to certain severe strains. Two factors, peculiar to the American setting, seemed particularly disruptive: a chronic shortage of labor, and the ready availability of empty land. For most people the situation was dramatized by a steady rise in both wages and prices. The result, in experiential terms, was a profound sense of loss of balance.

From our distant vantage-point these trends are observed most clearly with reference to New England, for it was there that the strongest efforts were made to combat them. The next document is a good case in point.

It consists of a set of proposals for the regulation of economic transactions, introduced as a bill in the General Court of Massachusetts Bay in May 1670. Ultimately, the bill was rejected—perhaps because of its unusually sweeping character. (Certainly, piecemeal legislation of a similar type was enacted on many occasions, both earlier and later on.) It stands, in any case, as an accurate epitome of the "problem" of economic instability, and of the "solutions" the people of this culture would find appropriate.

Bill of Wages and Price Legislation

(Massachusetts, 1670)

This Court, considering the great difficulty and discouragement that at present lies pressing upon many inhabitants of this jurisdiction, especially upon such as whose callings are in husbandry, not only by reason of the afflicting hand of God upon them [for] several years in blasting their principal grain and abating their increase in other corn, and [the] slowness of [the] market and [the] exceeding low price for that [which] the husbandman can raise (unto whose afflicting hand all ought to submit and humble themselves, and yet with the prophet confess, "Thou, Lord, hast afflicted us less than we deserve"), but also [by reason of the] difficulty and discouragement [that] is yet heaped and increasing upon them and others by reason of the excessive dearness of labor by artificers, laborers, and servants, contrary to reason and equity, to the great prejudice of many householders and their families, and tending to their utter ruin and undoing; and [also considering that] the produce thereof is by many spent to maintain such bravery in apparel which is altogether unbecoming [to] their place and rank, and in idleness of life, and a great part spent viciously in taverns and alehouses and other sinful practices, much to the dishonor of God, scandal of religion, and great offence and grief to sober and godly people amongst us—all [of] which timely to prevent, this Court account it their duty carefully by all good means to provide, and therefore do order as follows.

It is therefore ordered by this Court and the authority thereof that no person within this jurisdiction, directly or indirectly, shall hereafter either pay or receive for work, labor, or commodity, more or above than

Bill of Wages and Price Legislation, Submitted to the General Court, Massachusetts Bay Colony, May 17, 1670, in the Archives of Massachusetts, Vol. CXIX, folios 28–29.

is in this present order appointed—and that upon the penalties therein hereafter expressed.

	s.	d.	
Imprimis Laborers by the day, from the end of September to the end of March, dieting themselves:	1	3	per day
From the end of March to the end of June:	1	8	
From the end of June to the end of September, they working 10 hours in the day beside repast:	2	0	

	s.	d.	
2. Task work. One acre of salt marsh, and one acre of English grass, well mown:	2	0	per acre
One acre of wheat, well reaped:	4	0	
One acre of rye, well reaped:	3	0	
One acre of barley, and one acre of oats, each well mown:	1	0	
One acre of peas, cutting:	3	0	
One acre of wood, cutting and well cording:	1	3	

This wage is allowed, as above, to workmen dieting themselves.

3. Carpenter and masons and stonelayers, from 1 March to 10 of October:	2	0	per day

And all work taken by the great or piece by carpenters, masons, joiners, or shinglers is to be apportioned according to the equity of the value of a day's work as above, they dieting themselves.

4. Master taylors, and such as are fully workmen of that trade, for one day's work of 12 hours:	1	8
Apprentices to that trade [during] the first 4 years, the like day:	1	0

And all weavers, for their work at 12 hours per day, are to have the like wages as tailors.

5. [This section, which evidently dealt with the tanning of hides, is crossed out in the original.]

6. All men and women servants shall in their respective wages be moderated according to the proportion of labor above limited.

7. No person shall pay, neither shall any shoemaker receive, more than 5s for men's shoes of elevens or twelves; nor for women's shoes of sevens or eights, more than 3s., 8d.
And all boots and shoes of other sizes proportionable to the rates abovesaid.

8. Coopers shall not receive, nor any person pay, for a tight barrel of 32 gallons above 2s.,8d.; and other cooper's work proportionable in price to barrels.

9. Smiths shall not take, nor any person pay, for great work, as for ships, mills, plough irons, all irons for cart wheels well laid upon the wheels, and other the like great work, above 5d. per lb. For smaller work [such] as chains and other the like sold by weight, not above 6d. per lb. For the largest horse shoe, well set with seven nails, not above 6d. per shoe. For removing a horseshoe, 2d. For an ordinary felling axe, 3s., 6d. For one broad axe, 5s., 6d.; one broad hoe, 3s.; all being good and well steeled, and all other smith's work not named to be proportioned according to the prices abovesaid.

10. And whereas it appears that glovers, sadlers, hatters, and several other artificers do at present greatly exceed the rules of equity in their prices, they are all required to moderate the same according to the rules prescribed to others, or know that in neglect thereof they are liable to presentment and [to be] proceeded against according to the law—title, "Oppression."

Innkeepers and ordinary keepers are required to attend the duty of them expected according to law—title, "Innkeepers," Sect. 11—which order ought more carefully and strictly to be executed for the prevention of oppression in [the] selling of wine; and as for selling beer they are to attend the law that orders what quantity of malt is to be put into each hogshead of beer, and that when malt is under 4s. per bushell then to sell no less than one quart for 1s., 1/2d.; and for the entertainment of horses in summer [they are] not to take more than 4d. for one day and night, and in winter not to exceed 6d. for the like time.

All these payments are to be made in merchantable corn at the price from year to year set by the General Court, provided that when the materials are brought from the market by the artificer, as [in the case of] shoemakers, smiths, and the like, allowance may be made for that charge by the buyer according to what the transportation may be.

If any person shall pay or receive more than according to the rates above expressed, he or they, both buyer and seller, shall forfeit the full treble value of what shall be paid or received, one-half to the informer and the other half to the Treasurer of the several County Courts.

The President of every County Court shall at every such court give in [a] charge to the Grand Jury to enquire into the breach of this order in every particular thereof.

And all Grand Jurymen are required upon their oath to present all offences against this law; and if it shall appear to the Court of the County, at any time within one year after the offence is committed, that any Juryman have knowingly neglected his duty herein, he shall upon conviction before the Court be fined ten times so much as the offenders should have paid whom he ought to have presented.

32

The Problem of Slavery

The precise origins of slavery in British North America are obscure. The first Africans arrived as early as 1619 and may initially have been held only to limited terms of servitude. By the 1660s and 1670s, however, the legal and statutory foundations of racial bondage-for-life were firmly in place throughout the colonies. In the eighteenth century slavery became massively important, especially in the Chesapeake and further south.

Unfortunately, there is no way to study this subject from the inside —that is, from the vantage-point of the slaves themselves. The historical record does not allow them to speak in their own words; instead, all that we know of them comes "filtered" through their white peers and masters.

Three documentary specimens are presented here. One is a brief, general description of Virginia slaves in the early eighteenth century, written by Hugh Jones, an itinerant English clergyman. Jones was closely attuned to the interests (and viewpoint) of the slaveowners—some of whom, indeed, acted as his patrons.

Another sort of evidence is provided by short notices—in effect, "classifieds"—from owners seeking the return of slave runaways. Newspapers in every major city published such material quite routinely; it affords information about numerous individual slaves that cannot be obtained by any other means.

Some slaves resisted their lot in ways more direct, and more violent, than simple escape. Occasionally, they joined together in "conspiracies" against their masters. A particularly sensational instance occurred in New York City during the spring of 1741. A string of suspicious fires led to the arrest of dozens of slaves and several alleged associates in the white community. The resultant trials uncovered much bizarre evidence of a local underworld (centered on the tavern of an Irishman named Hughson). Convictions were followed by wholesale executions, though the facts—as read today—suggest more hysteria on the part of the whites than actual plotting by the blacks. The trials were carefully recorded by a magistrate named Daniel Horsmanden; his transcript is the source of our third document. It includes the prosecutor's summation against two accused ringleaders (Quack and Cuffee), their obviously coerced confessions, and a short account of the execution procedure itself.

The Present State of Virginia: Excerpts

(1724)

Hugh Jones

The Negroes live in small cottages called quarters, in about six in a gang, under the direction of an overseer or bailiff; who takes care that they tend such land as the owner allots and orders, upon which they raise hogs and cattle, and plant Indian corn (or maize) and tobacco for the use of their master; out of which the overseer has a dividend (or share) in proportion to the number of hands including himself; this with several privileges in his salary, and is an ample recompence for his pains, and encouragement of his industrious care, as to the labour, health, and provision of the Negroes.

The Negroes are very numerous, some gentlemen having hundreds of them of all sorts, to whom they bring great profit; for the sake of which they are obliged to keep them well, and not overwork, starve, or famish them, besides other inducements to favour them; which is done in a great degree, to such especially that are laborious, careful, and honest; though indeed some masters, careless of their own interest or reputation, are too cruel and negligent.

The Negroes are not only increased by fresh supplies from Africa and the West India Islands, but also are very prolific among themselves, and they that are born there talk good English, and affect our language, habits, and customs; and though they be naturally of a barbarous and cruel temper, yet are they kept under by severe discipline upon occasion, and by good laws are prevented from running away, injuring the English, or neglecting their business.

Their work (or chimerical hard slavery) is not very laborious; their

Hugh Jones, *The Present State of Virginia, From Whence Is Inferred a Short View of Maryland and North Carolina*, ed. Richard L. Morton (Chapel Hill, N.C., 1956), pp. 74–76.

greatest hardship consisting in that they and their posterity are not at their own liberty or disposal, but are the property of their owners; and when they are free, they know not how to provide so well for themselves generally; neither did they live so plentifully nor (many of them) so easily in their own country, where they are made slaves to one another, or taken captive by their enemies.

The children belong to the master of the woman that bears them; and such as are born of a Negro and an European are called Molattoes; but such as are born of an Indian and Negro are called Mustees.

Their work is to take care of the stock, and plant corn, tobacco, fruits, etc. which is not harder than thrashing, hedging, or ditching; besides, though they are out in the violent heat, wherein they delight, yet in wet or cold weather there is little occasion for their working in the fields, in which few will let them be abroad, lest by this means they might get sick or die, which would prove a great loss to their owners, a good Negro being sometimes worth three (nay four) score pounds sterling, if he be a tradesman; so that upon this (if upon no other account) they are obliged not to overwork them, but to cloath and feed them sufficiently, and take care of their health.

Several of them are taught to be sawyers, carpenters, smiths, coopers, etc. and though for the most part they be none of the aptest or nicest; yet they are by nature cut out for hard labour and fatigue, and will perform tolerably well; though they fall much short of an Indian, that has learned and seen the same things; and those Negroes make the best servants, that have been slaves in their own country; for they that have been kings and great men there are generally lazy, haughty, and obstinate; whereas the others are sharper, better humoured, and more laborious.

The languages of the new Negroes are various harsh jargons, and their religions and customs such as are best described by Mr. Bosman in his book intitled (I think) *A Description of the Coasts of Africa*.

Runaway Slaves: Advertisements

Ran away from his Master Eleazer Tyng, Esq. at Dunstable, on the 26th May past, a Negro Man Servant Call'd Robbin, almost of the complexion of an Indian, [a] short thick square shoulder'd Fellow, [with] a very short

Excerpts from Eileen Southern, ed., *Readings in Black American Music* (New York, 1982), p. 33.

neck, and thick legs, about 28 Years old, talks good English, can read and write, and plays on the Fiddle; he was born at Dunstable and it is thought he has been entic'd to enlist into the service, or to go to Philadelphia. Had on when he went away, a strip'd cotton and Linen, blue and white Jacket, red Breeches with Brass Buttons, blue Yarn Stockings, a fine Shirt, and took another of a meaner Sort, a red Cap, a Beaver Hat with a mourning Weed in it, and sometimes wears a Wig. Whoever will apprehend said Negro and secure him, so that his Master may have him again, or bring him to the Ware House of Messieurs Alford and Tyng, in Boston, shall have a reward of Ten Pounds, old Tenor, and all reasonable Charges.

N. B. And all Masters of Vessels or others are hereby cautioned against harbouring, concealing or carrying off said Servant, on Penalty of the Law.

[*New York Gazette Revived in the Weekly Post-Boy*, July 18, 1748]

RUN AWAY from the subscriber in Hanover about the middle of December last a likely Negro man named Damon, about 5 feet 9 or 10 inches high, has a scar on his forehead and cheek, is a brisk lively fellow, speaks good English, was born in the West Indies, beats the drum tolerably well, which he is very fond of, and loves liquor; had on when he went away Negro cotton clothes, and an old hat bound round with linen.

Sara Gist

Whoevery takes up the said Negro and contrives him to me, shall have 3 lb. reward.

[*Virginia Gazette*, April 17, 1766]

The New York Conspiracy: Trial Records

Friday, May 29 (1741)

The particular remarks on the testimony of the witnesses to the several points before mentioned, are here omitted for the sake of brevity, and because the substance of the evidence is before related. Then concluded,

Thus, gentlemen, I have distinguished the several points of the evidence against the prisoners, and have repeated the substance of what each witness

Excerpts from Thomas J. Davis, ed., *The New York Conspiracy* (Boston, 1971), pp. 104–114.

has said to each point, and shall leave it to you to determine whether the prisoners are guilty or not. I have endeavoured to lay no more weight upon any part of the evidence, than it will well bear; and I hope I have not urged any consequence which the fact proved will not fairly warrant.

Gentlemen, the prisoners have been indulged with the same kind of trial as is due to free men, though they might have been proceeded against in a more summary and less favourable way. The negro evidence, in the manner in which it has been produced is warranted by the act of assembly that has been read to you; the law requires no oath to be administered to them, and indeed it would seem to be a profanation of it, to administer it to a heathen in the legal form. You have seen that the court has put them under the most solemn caution, that their small knowledge of religion can render them capable of. The being and perfections of an Almighty, all knowing, and just God, and the terrors of an eternal world, have been plainly laid before them, and strongly pressed upon them. Unless they were professed Christians, and had taken upon them the bonds and obligations of that religion, their word, with the cautions that have been used, I suppose will be thought by you, as satisfactory as any oath that could have been devised. But, gentlemen, the court has no power to administer an oath, but in the common form, and if Pagan negroes could not be received as witnesses against each other, without an oath in legal form, it is easy to perceive that the greatest villanies would often pass with impunity.

Before I conclude, I cannot help observing to you, gentlemen, that by divers parts of the evidence, it appears that this horrid scene of iniquity has been chiefly contrived and promoted at meetings of negroes in great numbers on Sundays. This instructive circumstance may teach us many lessons, both of reproof and caution, which I only hint at, and shall leave the deduction of the particulars to every one's reflection.

Gentlemen, the monstrous ingratitude of this black tribe, is what exceedingly aggravates their guilt. Their slavery among us is generally softened with great indulgence; they live without care, and are commonly better fed and clothed, and put to less labour, than the poor of most Christian countries. They are indeed slaves, but under the protection of the law, none can hurt them with impunity; they are really more happy in this place, than in the midst of the continual plunder, cruelty, and rapine of their native countries; but notwithstanding all the kindness and tenderness with which they have been treated amongst us, yet this is the second attempt of the same kind, that this brutish and bloody species of mankind have made within one age. That justice that was provoked by former fires, and the innocent blood that was spilt in your streets, should have been a perpetual terror to the negroes that survived the vengeance of that day, and should have been a warning to all that had come after them. But I fear, gentlemen, that we shall never be quite safe, till that wicked race are under more restraint, or their number greatly reduced within this city.

But I shall not insist further, but refer you, gentlemen, to the direction of the court; and if the evidence against these prisoners proves sufficient in your judgment to convict them, I make no doubt but you will bring in a verdict accordingly, and do what in you lies to rid this country of some of the vilest creatures in it.

Then the jury were charged, and a constable was sworn to attend them as usual; and they withdrew; and being soon returned, found the prisoners guilty of both indictments.

The prisoners were asked, what they had to offer in arrest of judgment, why they should not receive sentence of death? and they offering nothing but repetitions of protestations of their innocence, the third justice proceeded to sentence, as followeth:

Quack and Cuffee, the criminals at the bar,
    You both now stand convicted of one of the most horrid and detestable pieces of villainy, that ever satan instilled into the heart of human creatures to put in practice; ye, and the rest of your colour, though you are called slaves in this country, yet are you all far from the condition of other slaves in other countries; nay, your lot is superior to that of thousands of white people. You are furnished with all the necessaries of life, meat, drink, and clothing, without care, in a much better manner than you could provide for yourselves, were you at liberty; as the miserable condition of many free people here of your complexion might abundantly convince you. What then could prompt you to undertake so vile, so wicked, so monstrous, so execrable and hellish a scheme, as to murder and destroy your own masters and benefactors? nay, to destroy, root and branch, all the white people of this place, and to lay the whole town in ashes.
    I know not which is the more astonishing, the extreme folly, or wickedness, of so base and shocking a conspiracy; for as to any view of liberty or government you could propose to yourselves, upon the success of burning the city, robbing, butchering, and destroying the inhabitants, what could it be expected to end in, in the account of any rational and considerate person among you, but your own destruction? And as [to] the wickedness of it, you might well have reflected, you that have sense, that there is a God above, who has always a clear view of all your actions, who sees into the utmost recesses of the heart, and knoweth all your thoughts; shall he not, do ye think, for all this bring you into judgment, at that final and great day of account, the day of judgment, when the most secret treachery will be disclosed, and laid open to the view, and every one will be rewarded according to their deeds, and their use of that degree of reason which God-Almighty has entrusted them with?
    Ye that were for destroying us without mercy, ye abject wretches, the outcasts of the nations of the earth, are treated here with tenderness and humanity; and, I wish I could not say, with too great indulgence also;

304

for you have grown wanton with excess of liberty, and your idleness has proved your ruin, having given you the opportunities of forming this villain-ous and detestable conspiracy; a scheme compounded of the blackest and foulest vices, treachery, blood-thirstiness, and ingratitude. But be not de-ceived, God Almighty only can and will proportion punishments to men's offences; ye that have shewn no mercy here, and have been for destroying all about ye, and involving them in one general massacre and ruin, what hopes can ye have of mercy in the other world? For shall not the judge of all the earth do right? Let me in compassion advise ye then; there are but a few moments between ye and eternity; ye ought therefore seri-ously to lay to heart these things; earnestly and sorrowfully to bewail your monstrous and crying sins, in this your extremity; and if ye would reasonably entertain any hopes of mercy at the hands of God, ye must shew mercy here yourselves, and make what amends ye can before ye leave us, for the mischief you have already done, by preventing any more being done. Do not flatter yourselves, for the same measure which you give us here, will be measured to you again in the other world; ye must confess your whole guilt, as to the offences of which ye stand convicted, and for which ye will presently receive judgment; ye must discover the whole scene of iniquity which has been contrived in this monstrous confed-eracy, the chief authors and actors, and all and every [one of] the parties concerned, aiding and assisting therein, that by your means a full stop may be put to this horrible and devilish undertaking. And these are the only means left ye to shew mercy; and the only reasonable ground ye can go upon, to entertain any hopes of mercy at the hands of God, before whose judgment seat ye are so soon to appear.

Ye cannot be so stupid, surely, as to imagine, that when ye leave this world, when your souls put off these bodies of clay, ye shall become like the beasts that perish, that your spirits shall only vanish into the soft air and cease to be. No, your souls are immortal, they will live forever, either to be eternally happy, or eternally miserable in the other world, where you are now going.

If ye sincerely and in earnest repent you of your abominable sins, and implore the divine assistance at this critical juncture, in working out the great and momentous article of the salvation of your souls; upon your making all the amends, and giving all the satisfaction which is in each of your powers, by a full and complete discovery of the conspiracy, and of the several persons concerned in it, as I have observed to ye before, then and only upon these conditions can ye reasonably expect mercy at the hands of God Almighty for your poor, wretched and miserable souls.

Here ye must have justice, for the justice of human laws has at length overtaken ye, and we ought to be very thankful, and esteem it a most merciful and wondrous act of Providence that your treacheries and villanies have been discovered; that your plot and contrivances, your hidden works of darkness have been brought to light, and stopped in their career; that in the same net which you have hid so privily for others your own feet are taken: that the same mischief which you have contrived for others, and have in part executed, is at length fallen upon your own pates, whereby the sentence which I am now to pronounce will be justified against ye; which is,

That you and each of you be carried from hence to the place from whence you came, and from thence to the place of execution, where you and each of you shall be chained to a stake, and burnt to death; and the lord have mercy upon your poor, wretched souls.

Ordered, that the execution of the said Quack and Cuffee be on Saturday the 30th of this instant, between the hours of one and seven o'clock in the afternoon of the same day.

The court adjourned till Tuesday the 2d of June next, ten o'clock in the morning.

Saturday, May 30

This day Quack and Cuffee were executed at the stake according to sentence.

The spectators at this execution were very numerous; about three o'clock the criminals were brought to the stake, surrounded with piles of wood ready for setting fire to, which the people were very impatient to have done, their resentment being raised to the utmost pitch against them, and no wonder. The criminals shewed great terror in their countenances, and looked as if they would gladly have discovered all they knew of this accursed scheme, could they have had an encouragement to hope for a reprieve. But as the case was, they might flatter themselves with hopes: they both seemed inclinable to make some confession; the only difficulty between them at last being, who should speak first. Mr. Moore, the deputy secretary, undertook singly to examine them both, endeavouring to persuade them to confess their guilt, and all they knew of the matter, without effect; till at length Mr. Roosevelt came up to him, and said he would undertake Quack, whilst Mr. Moore examined Cuffee; but before they could proceed to the purpose, each of them was obliged to flatter his respective criminal that his fellow sufferer had begun, which stratagem prevailed: Mr. Roosevelt stuck to Quack altogether, and Mr. Moore took Cuff's confession, and sometimes also minutes of what each said; and afterwards upon drawing up their confessions in form from their minutes, they therefore intermixed what came from each.

Quack's confession at the stake. He said,

1. "That Hughson was the first contriver of the whole plot, and promoter of it; which was to burn the houses of the town; Cuffee said, to kill the people.
2. "That Hughson brought in first Caesar (Vaarck's); then Prince (Auboyneau's); Cuffee (Philipse's); and others, amongst whom were old Kip's negro; Robin (Chambers's); Cuffee (Gomez's); Jack (Codweis's) and another short negro, that cooks for him.
3. "That he Quack did fire the fort, that it was by a lighted stick taken out of the servants' hall, about eight o'clock at night, that he went up the back stairs with it and so through Barbara's room, and put it near the gutter, betwixt the shingles, and the roof of the house.
4. "That on a Sunday afternoon, a month before the firing of the fort, over a bowl of punch, the confederates [were] at Hughson's amongst whom were the confederates above named, Albany, and Tickle, alias Will, Jack and Cook (Comfort's); old Butchell; Caesar, and Guy (Horsfield's); Tom (Van Rants's); Caesar (Peck's); Worcester, and others voted him Quack, as having a wife in the fort, to be the person who should fire the fort, Sandy, and Jack (Codweis's); Caesar, and Guy (Horsfield's); were to assist him in it.
5. "That Hughson desired the negroes to bring to his house, what they could get from the fire, and Hughson was to bring down country people in his boat to further the business, and would bring in other negroes.
6. "That forty or fifty to his knowledge were concerned, but their names he could not recollect (the mob pressing and interrupting).
7. "That Cuffee (Gomez's); and Caesar (Peck's), fired Van Zant's storehouse.
8. "That Mary Burton had spoke the truth, and could name many more.
9. "Fortune (Wilkins's), and Sandy, had done the same; and Sandy could name the Spaniards, and say much more, which Cuffee particularly confirmed.
10. "Being asked what view Hughson had in acting in this manner? He answered, to make himself rich.
11. "That after the fire was over, Quack was at Hughson's house, Jack (Comfort's), a leading man, Hughson, wife and daughter present, and said, the job was done, meaning the fire; that he went frequently to Hughson's house, and met there Tickle and Albany.
12. "Quack said his wife was no ways concerned, for he never would trust her with it, and that Denby knew nothing about the matter.
13. "Jamaica (Ellis's) not concerned that he knew of, but was frequently at Hughson's with his fiddle.
14. "Said he was not sworn by Hughson, but others were."

McDonald (the witness against Quack upon the trial) at the stake desired Mr. Pinhorne to ask Quack, whether he had wronged him in what he had said of him at court? He answered no; it was true he did pass him at the fort gate, about eleven o'clock that morning.

The witness then went up to him himself, and asked him the same question; and he answered the same as to Mr. Pinhorne, that he had not wronged him, and further, "that he, Quack, thought the fort would have been on fire the night before; for that he had taken a firebrand out of the servants' hall, and carried it up into the garret, on the seventeenth at night (St. Patrick's) and when he came up the next morning into the garret, he found the brand alight, and blew it, and then went away again."

Cuffee's confession at the stake.—He said,

1. "That Hughson was the first contriver of all, and pressed him to it: that he Cuffee was one of the first concerned.
2. "The fire was intended to begin at Comfort's shingles, and so through the town.
3. "Old Kip's negro; Robin (Chambers's); Jack (Comfort's); and Cuffee (Gomez's); were of the conspirators: Albany and Tickle were concerned.
4. "That he was sworn, and Caesar and Prince also, by Hughson.
5. "That Cuffee (Gomez's); and Caesar (Peck's); burnt Van Zant's storehouse.
6. "That Sandy set fire to Mr. Machado's house; Niblet's negro wench can tell it, and Becker's Bess knows it.
7. "That he set fire to the storehouse as sworn against him, that when his master went to the Coffee-House, he ran out of the other door, and went the back way into the storehouse, having lighted charcoal in his pocket between two oyster shells, he put the fire between the ropes and the boards, and leaving it on fire, went home.
8. "That Hughson's people were to raise a mob to favour the design.
9. "That the evidence that Peterson did see him was true; that Fortune did see him the night before.
10. "That Fortune knew and was as deeply concerned as he; and Sandy was concerned, and knew the Spaniards.—And (being asked) did confess there was a design to kill the people, but not told to all. And said,
11. "There was about fifty concerned; and that all were concerned that a constable who stood by had seen all at Hughson's house."

After the confessions were minuted down (which were taken in the midst of great noise and confusion) Mr. Moore desired the sheriff to delay the execution until the governor be acquainted therewith, and his pleasure known touching their reprieve; which, could it have been effected, it was thought might have been means of producing great discoveries; but from the disposition observed in the spectators, it was much to be apprehended, there would have been great difficulty, if not danger in an attempt to take the criminals back. All this was represented to his honour; and before Mr. Moore could return from him to the place of execution, he met the sheriff upon the common, who declared his opinion, that the carrying the negroes back would be impracticable; and if that was his honour's order it could not be attempted without a strong guard, which could not be got time enough; and his honour's directions for the reprieve being conditional and discretionary, for these reasons the execution proceeded.

Part Five
Indians

33

Noble Savage (?)

No aspect of American colonization was more compelling than the encounter with new racial and cultural types. From a European standpoint, Indians seemed endlessly perplexing, troubling—and fascinating: how to understand such peculiar beings and their connection to "us"?

Some colonists (and travelers to the colonies) sought to fit them to ancient prototypes of humanity. One persistent favorite was the "noble savage," a type less sophisticated than European counterparts but admirably endowed with moral virtues. Others omitted the "noble" aspect and drew out the darker implications of the "savage." Some suggested links to the Ten Lost Tribes of Israel; others found a likeness to classical (Greek and Roman) people.

John White, governor of the ill-fated "lost colony" at Roanoke (in what is today North Carolina), was the first English person to paint native Americans. His depiction of "an ageed manne, in his winter garment" was initially done in watercolors and was subsequently published as one of a series of engravings in an early travel memoir. White, in effect, introduced his English contemporaries to the inhabitants of the New World.

An Ageed Manne in His Winter Garment
John White

First published in Thomas Hariot, *A Briefe and True Report of the New Found Land of Virginia* (London, 1590); reprinted in Paul Hulton, *America 1585: The Complete Drawings of John White* (Chapel Hill, N.C., 1984), figure 13. Used with permission.

34

Indians at Home

Alongside their fascination with native physique, the colonists maintained a lively interest in native culture. This, too, could be either "noble" or "savage"—or both. The Indians' technology seemed grossly deficient, and they were ignorant, too, of what Europeans called "true religion." On the other hand, they were notably generous, hospitable, and orderly in their social relations.

The positive side of these reactions was perhaps strongest in the early "contact" phase. It shows up quite clearly in another image by John White—this one depicting the shape of an entire village.

Algonquian Indian Village
Theodore DeBry

(A) Tomb of chieftains	(F) Watchman guarding corn
(B) Place of assembly for prayer	(G) Green corn, between rows of ripe corn
(C) Ceremonial dance	(H) Squash (I) Pumpkins
(D) Feast (E) Tobacco	(K) Ceremonial fire (L) Body of water

Algonquian Indian Village, engraving by Theodore DeBry, after a painting by John White, in Thomas Hariot, *A Briefe and True Report of the New Found Land of Virginia* (London, 1590): reprinted with legend in Richard L. Morton, *Colonial Virginia* (Chapel Hill, N.C., 1960), p. 16. Used with permission.

35

Intermarriage: John Rolfe and Pocahontas

For all their evident curiosity about Indians, the settlers rarely revealed the emotional side of the contact experience. We should like to know more than they usually allow us to see about their inner feelings when confronting, for the first time in most of their lives, a people entirely "strange."

The next document—a personal letter—does provide some insight into this aspect of their situation. Its writer, John Rolfe, was among the first planters of Virginia and a man of considerable ingenuity and resourcefulness. His most signal contribution to the early history of the colony was his successful experimentation with tobacco growing. But Rolfe was best known to his contemporaries as the first Englishman of any prominence to take an Indian wife. The woman in question was none other than Pocahontas, a local princess and the reputed savior on an earlier occasion of Captain John Smith. Pocahontas had been captured by the Virginians in 1613, and in the following year Rolfe determined to marry her. But it was not an easy thing to arrange. Rolfe was obliged to seek approval from the authorities in England, and in this connection he sought the support of Thomas Dale, then governor of Virginia. His remarks to Dale show clearly that the match had aroused widespread comment, much of it adverse. Here, as always in the field of race relations, people perceived the question of intermarriage as especially critical.

But the marriage was consummated nonetheless, and Pocahontas was formally converted to Christianity. In 1616 the couple traveled to England and were ceremoniously received at the court of King James I. Everywhere they went, Pocahontas was viewed as a living argument for the effort to "civilize" the Indians. Her sudden and tragic death in 1617, just as she and her husband were preparing to return to Virginia, set in motion a special campaign to found a college for Virginia's Indians.

317

Rolfe returned alone to the colony later in the same year. Ironically, he met his own death in battle on March 22, 1622—at the hands of his late wife's fellow tribesmen.

Letter of John Rolfe to Sir Thomas Dale

(Virginia, 1614)

The copy of the gentleman's letters to Sir Thomas Dale, that after[ward] married Powhatan's daughter, containing the reasons moving him thereunto.

Honorable Sir, and most worthy Governor:

When your leisure shall best serve you to peruse these lines, I trust in God the beginning will not strike you into a greater admiration than the end will give you good content. It is a matter of no small moment, concerning my own particular, which here I impart unto you, and which toucheth me so nearly as the tenderness of my salvation. How be it, I freely subject myself to your grave and mature judgement, deliberation, approbation, and determination, assuring myself of your zealous admonitions and godly comforts, either persuading me to desist or encouraging me to persist therein, with a religious fear and godly care—for which (from the very instant that this began to root itself within the secret bosom of my breast) my daily and earnest prayers have been, still are, and ever shall be produced forth with as sincere a godly zeal as I possibly may, to be directed, aided, and governed in all my thoughts, words, and deeds, to the glory of God, and for my eternal consolation. To persevere wherein I never had more need, nor (till now) could [I] ever imagine to have been moved with the like occasion.

But (my case standing as it doth) what better worldly refuge can I here seek than to shelter myself under the safety of your favorable protection? And did not my ease proceed from an unspotted conscience, I should not dare to offer to your view and approved judgement these passions of my troubled soul, so full of fear and trembling is hypocrisy and dissimulation. But knowing my own innocence and godly fervor in the whole prosecution hereof, I doubt not of your benign acceptance and clement construction. As for malicious depravers and turbulent spirits, to whom

Letter of John Rolfe to Sir Thomas Dale, in Lyon G. Tyler, ed., *Narratives of Early Virginia* (New York, 1907), pp. 239–244.

nothing is tasteful but what pleaseth their unsavory palate, I pass not for them, being well assured in my persuasion (by the often trial and proving of myself, in my holiest meditations and prayers) that I am called hereunto by the spirit of God; and it shall be sufficient for me to be protected by yourself in all virtuous and pious endeavors. And for my more happy proceeding herein, my daily oblations shall ever be addressed to bring to pass so good effects that your self and all the world may truly say: this is the work of God, and it is marvelous in our eyes.

But to avoid tedious preambles and to come nearer the matter: first suffer me, with your patience, to sweep and make clean the way wherein I walk from all suspicions and doubts which may be covered therein, and faithfully to reveal unto you what should move me hereunto.

Let therefore this, my well-advised protestation, which here I make between God and my own conscience, be a sufficient witness at the dreadful Day of Judgement (when the secret of all men's hearts shall be opened) to condemn me herein, if my chiefest intent and purpose be not to strive with all my power of body and mind in the undertaking of so mighty a matter—[in] no way led (so far forth as man's weakness may permit) with the unbridled desire of carnal affection, but [striving] for the good of this plantation, for the honor of our country, for the glory of God, for my own salvation, and for the converting to the true knowledge of God and Jesus Christ [of] an unbelieving creature, namely Pocahontas, to whom my hearty and best thoughts are, and have [for] a long time been, so entangled, and enthralled in so intricate a labyrinth, that I was even wearied to unwind myself thereout. But Almighty God, who never faileth His [followers] that truly invoke His Holy Name, hath opened the gate and led me by the hand [so] that I might plainly see and discern the safe paths wherein to tread.

To you, therefore, most noble Sir, the patron and father of us in this country, do I utter the effects of this my settled and long-continued affection (which hath made a mighty war in my meditations); and here I do truly relate to what issue this dangerous combat is come unto, wherein I have not only examined but thoroughly tried and pared my thoughts even to the quick, before I could find any fit, wholesome, and apt applications to cure so dangerous an ulcer. I never failed to offer my daily and faithful prayers to God for His sacred and holy assistance. I forgot not to set before mine eyes the frailty of mankind, his proneness to evil, his indulgence of wicked thoughts, with many other imperfections wherein man is daily ensnared and oftentimes overthrown, and them compared to my present estate. Nor was I ignorant of the heavy displeasure which Almighty God conceived against the sons of Levi and Israel for marrying strange wives, nor of the inconveniences which may thereby arise, with other the like good motions which made me look about warily and with good circumspection into the grounds and principal agitations which thus should provoke me to be in love with one whose education hath been rude, her manners barbarous, her generation accursed, and so discrepant in all nurture from myself that oftentimes with fear and trembling I have ended my private controversy with this [thought]: surely these are wicked instigations, hatched by him who seeketh and delighteth in man's destruction. And so, with fervent prayers to be ever preserved from such diabolical assaults (as I took those to be), I have taken some rest.

Thus, when I had thought [that] I had obtained my peace and quietness, behold, another but more gracious temptation hath made breaches into my holiest and strongest meditations, with which I have been put to a new trial in a straighter manner than the former. For besides the many passions and sufferings which I have daily, hourly, yea, and in my sleep endured, even awaking me to astonishment, taxing me with remissness and carelessness, [with] refusing and neglecting to perform the duty of a good Christian, pulling me by the ear and crying, "why dost not thou endeavor to make her a Christian?" (and these have happened, to my greater wonder, even when she hath been furthest separated from me, which in common reason, were it not an undoubted work of God, might breed forgetfulness of a far more worthy creature)—besides, I say, the holy spirit of God hath often demanded of me, why I was created, if not for transitory pleasures and worldly vanities, but to labor in the Lord's vineyard, there to sow and plant, to nourish and increase the fruits thereof, daily adding with the good husband in the gospel somewhat to the talent, [so] that in the end the fruits may be reaped, to the comfort of the laborer in this life and his salvation in the world to come? And if this be, as undoubtedly this is, the service Jesus Christ requireth of His best servant: woe unto him that hath these instruments of piety put into his hands and willfully despiseth to work with them. Likewise, adding hereunto her great appearance of love to me, her desire to be taught and instructed in the knowledge of God, her capableness of understanding, her aptness and willingness to receive any good impression; and also the spiritual, besides her own, incitements stirring me up hereunto.

What should I do? Shall I be of so untoward a disposition as to refuse to lead the blind into the right way? Shall I be so unnatural as not to give bread to the hungry? Or [so] uncharitable as not to cover the naked?

Shall I despise to actuate these pious duties of a Christian? Shall the base fear of displeasing the world overpower and withhold me from revealing unto man these spiritual works of the Lord, which in my meditations and prayers I have daily made known to Him? God forbid. I assuredly trust He hath thus dealt with me for my eternal felicity and for His glory; and I hope so to be guided by His heavenly grace that in the end, by my faithful pains and Christian-like labor, I shall attain to that blessed promise, pronounced by that holy prophet Daniel, unto the righteous that bring many unto the knowledge of God: namely, that they shall shine like the stars forever and ever. A sweeter comfort cannot be to a true Christian, nor a greater encouragement for him to labor all the days of his life in the performance thereof, nor a greater gain of consolation to be desired at the hour of death and in the Day of Judgement.

Again, by my reading and [by] conference with honest and religious persons have I received no small encouragement—besides *serena mea conscientia*, the clearness of my conscience clean from the filth of impurity, *quae est instar muri ahenei*, which is unto me as a brazen wall. If I should set down at large the perturbations and godly motions which have stricken within me, I should but make a tedious and unnecessary volume. But I doubt not [that] these shall be sufficient both to certify you of my true intents in [the] discharging of my duty to God and to yourself, to whose gracious providence I humbly submit myself, for His glory, your honor, our country's good, the benefit of this plantation, and for the converting of one unregenerate to regeneration; which I beseech God to grant, for His dear son Christ Jesus, His sake.

Now if the vulgar sort, who square all men's actions by the base rule of their own filthiness, shall tax or taunt me in this my Godly labor, let them know [that] it is not [from] any hungry appetite to gorge myself with incontinency. [To be] sure, (if I would, and were so sensually inclined), I might satisfy such desire—though not without a seared conscience, yet with Christians more pleasing to the eye and less fearful in the offence unlawfully committed. Nor am I in so desperate an estate that I regard not what becometh of me. Nor am I out of hope but one day to see my country; nor so void of friends, nor mean in birth, but there to obtain a match to my great content. Nor have I ignorantly passed over my hopes there; nor [do I] regardlessly seek to lose the love of my friends by taking this course. I know them all, and have not rashly overslipped any.

But shall it please God thus to dispose of me (which I earnestly desire

[in order] to fulfill my ends before set down), I will heartily accept of
it as a Godly task appointed [for] me. And I will never cease, (God assisting me), until I have accomplished and brought to perfection so holy
a work, in which I will daily pray God to bless me, to mine and her
eternal happiness. And thus desiring no longer to live, to enjoy the blessings of God, than this my resolution doth tend to such Godly ends as
are by me before declared, [and] not doubting of your favorable acceptance, I take my leave, beseeching Almighty God to rain down upon you
such plenitude of His heavenly graces as your heart can wish and desire.
And so I rest,

at your command, most willing
to be disposed of,
John Rolfe

36

Efforts of a Missionary

It is well known that the conversion of Indians to Christianity was one of the avowed purposes of settlement in the New World. Leaders in all the colonies periodically reaffirmed the pious goal of "bringing the light of the Gospel to the heathen." What seems less clear, however, is the amount of actual effort devoted to this goal. On the one hand, no missionary campaign of substantial proportions was ever mounted in British America, and the number of Indian converts seems always to have remained quite small. (The contrast to the labors of Catholic missionaries in New Spain is instructive here). On the other hand, detailed investigation of the lives of colonial ministers uncovers a surprising number who had at least some experience in trying to preach to Indians. Perhaps the safest conclusion about all this is that although the intention was often there, the knowledge and skills necessary for successful missionary work were sadly lacking.

The next document throws a vivid light on some aspects of the problem. Its author, William Treat, was an early graduate of Yale and sometime clergyman in several different New England communities. In 1734, with the encouragement of Governor Talcott of Connecticut, he spent several months working with a group of Wangunk Indians near Middletown. His subsequent "statement," submitted as part of a request for financial support, records the somewhat unhappy result of his mission.

Statement of the Reverend William Treat

(Connecticut, 1737)

In the fall of the year 1734, I, being at Boston, heard there that the Governor of that province had newly recommended to the Court (which was then sitting) their duty to take some further measures than had been

"Mr. Treat's Statement," in *Collections of the Connecticut Historical Society,* V (Hartford, Conn., 1896), pp. 479–484.

taken towards the reformation and conversion of the heathen in these American parts—which never was very agreeable with me. Whereupon, when I returned home, I went to that party of Indians at Middletown (hoping that, by reason of that good understanding there has formerly been between my predecessors and them, I might the better win upon them) to treat with them about their subjecting themselves to be instructed in things of a religious nature. And [I] offered them that if they would, I would do what I could that some meet person might be improved, in the first place, to learn them to read. [They] took the motion into consideration and after some considerable discourse among themselves told me that if I would come among them they would submit to my instructions. I told them that it would be something difficult for me by reason of my living so far distant from them; however, I would take the case into consideration. I should then immediately have waited upon his Honor, the Governor, for his advice and instructions in the affair, but it was so difficult passing the river at that season that I could not. Wherefore I advised with sundry ministers on that side of the river, who advised me to go as speedily as I could and begin to instruct them, particularly Mr. Woodbridge of Hartford, who told me that Mr. Joseph Pitkin had primers sent to him to distribute, in order to forward that business. I went to him, and he helped me to some; and accordingly I began to instruct them, Dec. 26th, 1734, and continued to do so until the river was passable, by which time I learned something more of their inclinations and readiness to receive instruction. Then [I] waited upon his Honor and informed him of what I had been doing, and what prospect I had of success; upon which act he discovered good satisfaction, and also directed and improved me to continue with them. Whereupon I continued to instruct their children, which were there then present to the number of about 12 or 14, and also maintained at least a weekly conference with them, thereby to lead them into a knowledge of the true God and of our obligations to approve ourselves in His service. Which service was very difficult, for they were such strangers to the written word of God that whatever I quoted from them had but little effect otherwise than as it was agreeable with those natural principles upon which I was obliged to proceed with them. And besides, it was very difficult to impart to them anything of this nature by reason of their brokenness of speech in the English dialect and their unacquaintedness with things, as also an aversion thereunto in some of them. I shall give one instance of the many that I might instance in to discover this. I took occasion to speak of the resurrection and judgment to come, etc., and either at that time or

soon after one of them (in a scoffing and ridiculing manner) asked me
(a pig then lying by the fire) whether that pig would rise again after it
was dead as well as we. It would not have done to have answered a
fool according to his folly, and yet he must be answered according thereunto; otherwise he would have been wise in his own conceit. And with
much ado I silenced him for that present, but it was a great while before
I could do it. Thus I continued daily to instruct them, except [for] a
few intervals which my then late remove obliged me unto, the whole
of which amounted to about the space of three weeks or a month. In
April I began to preach to them upon the Sabbath and continued so
to do till some time in June next following (except [for] two Sabbaths,
[on] one of which I was prevented by high water, and the other when
they were gone to the election), as well as to instruct them and answer
their objections and little sluffles as before hinted; and then [I] left them.

And the reason of my leaving them is as follows. Notwithstanding
the Governor, his sending to Boston (I suppose more than once) giving
an account of my service and what prospect I had of success, yet there
was no return that I thought I could in any measure depend upon as
an encouragement to my progress therein, and the necessities of my family
[were] then calling me to do something that might serve to their support.
However, as my occasions would allow and as I had opportunity, I did
all that summer what[ever] lay in my power to beget a good opinion
in them concerning their receiving instruction in things before spoken
of. There was one piece of service more which I did, and if your patience
will allow me I shall give an account of [it]. Some time in the latter
part of that summer they had a great dance, at which time I supposed
they would be together [so] that I might get an account of their number,
as directed unto by His Honor the Governor and [the] Commissioners
at Boston, which I had before endeavored to do but could not. They
met upon Friday in the afternoon, and upon Saturday I went upon the
business aforesaid, as also not knowing but what I might be a means
to prevent no little wickedness which they are commonly guilty of at
such times. When I came, I found them in a most forlorn condition,
singing, dancing, yelling, humming, etc., the like to which I have never
seen before, and so compelling the rest of their number. Some of them,
seeing me come there at that time, came to me and asked what I was
come there for, and told me I had no business there, and bid me begone.
I told them that others came to see them, and others did so, which
they allowed of; and [I] asked them why they were so affronted at my
coming there. One of them, with no little fury, told me that I was come

to see if I might not preach to them the next day, which he said I should not do. I replied that that was not my business there at that time; however, I was ready to do them all the service that lay in my power to do. I subjoined that seeing they were come together to take off their mourning clothes for one that was dead, I thought it was a proper season for them to do something to fit them for death; for others would put on their mourning clothes for them as they had done, and were then putting them off, for one that was dead. He told me that tomorrow was their day, and therefore I should not preach there. However, a number of Nahantick and Mohican Indians gathered together and told me [that] if I would come to a house adjacent they would come there and hear me preach the next day.

Accordingly, the next morning I went; but when I came to the house none of them were there, [for] they had other business to do. But understanding that one of the Indian children was there very sick, I thought I had a good excuse to go to them and so lay myself in the way of doing them some service. When I came I went to see the sick child, and [I] had not been there long before sundry of them came and did what[ever] they could (except violence) to drive me away. However, a number of them interposed and told me that if I would withdraw to a number of apple trees about ten or fifteen rods distant, they would speedily come to me and they would hear me preach. I withdrew thither— I had not been there long before they began the most doleful noise that can be thought of. It consisted of grunting, groaning, sighing, etc., which was caused by their smiting upon their breast. I cannot express the forlorn, dolorous noise that they then made. In short, I suppose they were in a pow-wow; and the reason of it was this, viz., the then lately-deceased Indian a little before his death had a quarrel with another Indian, and in the time of his sickness called for his gun to kill that Indian, which made them suspect that that same Indian had poisoned the deceased, which was the cause of his death; and they wanted to know of the devil whether it was so. I was at a great loss [as to] what to do at that time. However, I expected the devil would speedily make his appearance; and in short, if he had been incarnate in every one of them, I cannot think there could have been a much worse noise. However, in the midst of this I broke in among them and broke them up for that time. But I cannot express the rage some of them were in, and [it] seemed as though they would immediately fall upon and rid the world of me. But there were some that again interposed and told me that they desired that I would withdraw as before, and they would speedily come to me. I told them

I was afraid they would do as they had before done and return to their wickedness again; [but] they urged so much that I went as before. I had not been there but a few minutes before they began their infernal din as before. But then I presently broke in upon them again and broke them up a second time, and so from time to time till at last their hellish rout was broken up. And after [taking] some time to season them (for they were very unmeet) for divine service, I began divine service among them. They were very orderly and made no disturbance; and afterwards their neighbors told me there never was such a thing before among them, for the evening after the Sabbath there was but little if any noise, as [there] used to be at other times. The next morning they went off and dispersed, and I can't learn that they have ever been there since upon any like occasion.

Thus, I've given as short a narrative of my doings as I could, and yet I fear I have tired your patience. If I have, I ask pardon of this honorable Court and pray that you would consider my hard labor and toil in that service, and if it is worthy to recommend my request, [that] you would grant me according to what you shall think I ought in justice to have.

37

"A Dialogue," in Two Languages

The meager results of missionary work among the Indians may be attributed in large part to basic problems of communication. There is little in the historical record to suggest that the average colonist cared to learn Indian languages; in fact, the general expectation was quite clearly the reverse—that Indians would be induced to master English. This, in turn, reflected the broader unwillingness of the settlers to approach Indian culture on its own terms.

Of course, there were exceptional men and women among the colonists who did learn to speak to Indians in their own tongue. One of these was Josiah Cotton, a schoolmaster and minor public official in Plymouth, Massachusetts, and also an occasional preacher to the nearby Natick tribesmen. Sometime in the first decade of the eighteenth century Cotton wrote out an elaborate study of the Natick language. But this document reflects in its own way the unevenness, the suspicion, and the chronic misunderstanding implicit in the whole relation between the settlers and their native American neighbors. Consider, for example, the sample "dialogue" that Cotton included as part of his manuscript —and which may remind a modern reader of the "phrase books" so popular among tourists in our own time.

Vocabulary of the Massachusetts Indian Language: Extract
Josiah Cotton

A Dialogue

How does your wife, or husband do?	Toh unnuppomântum kummittŭmwus asuh kāsuk.

Josiah Cotton, *Vocabulary of the Massachusetts (or Natick) Indian Language* (Cambridge, Mass., 1829), pp. 94–99.

What is the matter that Indians very often no speak true?

Toh waj unnak Indiansog moochĕke nompe matta sampwe unnoowoо̄о̄о̄og.

Have you been at Squantam lately?

Sun Squantam kuppeyômus pāswe.

Do the soldiers go to Canada? No.

Sun aiyeuehteaenūog aūog Canada; matteag.

Then they will do no good, but a great deal of hurt.

Neit nag pish matta toh unné wunnesēog, qut moocheke woskeŭssēog.

Yes, they will put the country to a great deal of charge.

Nux, nag pish mishe, о̄adtehkontamwog wuttohkeо̄ngash.

Is not the fleet come ashore yet?

Sun chuppoonâog asq koppaemŭnnoo.

Do you think they will ever come?

Sun kuttenântam nash pish peyômо̄ooash.

It may be not.

Ammiate matteag.

Very likely not.

Ahche ogqueneunkquat matteag.

I believe they are gone to Spain.

Nuttinantam nag monchuk en Spain.

Why do you remove from Natick?

Tohwaj ontootāā wutche Natick.

You will get more money there than at Sandwich.

Woh kummoochke wuttehtīnum teagwas nâut onk Moskeehtŭkqut.

My family is sickly there.

Nutteashinnĭnnēonk wuttit mohchinnonāop.

And were they healthy at Sandwich? Yes.

Kah sun nag wunne pomantamwushanneg ut Moskeehtŭkqut. Nux.

Don't you owe a great deal of money there?

Sunnummatta kimmishontuk-quahwhuttĕhoh nâ utt.

Yes, but I hope to clear it quickly.

Nux, qut nuttannôos
nuttapoadtehkônat pāswēse.

What if they would put you in
prison?

Toh woh unni
kuppūshagkinukquēan.

Then they will hurt themselves
and me too.

Neit nag woh woskehheaog
wuhhogkāuh kah nen wonk.

It is very cold today.

Moochĕke tohkoi yeu kesukod.

Almost I freeze my ears and
fingers.

Nāhen togquttïnash
nuhtauōgwash kah
nuppoohkuhquānitchēgat.

Why don't you get a thick cap?

Tohwaj matta ahchuehteocōōu
kohpŏgkag kah onkquontŭpape.

Because I have no money.

Newutche matta nuttohtcoo
teagwash.

And why don't you work hard?

Kah tohwaj mat
menukânâkausēan.

So I would with all my heart,
but I am sickly.

Ne woh nuttussen nashpe
manŭsse nuttah, qut
nummōmohtehŭnam.

But it may be work will cure
you, if you would leave off
drinking too.

Qut ammiate woh anakausuonk
kukketeŏhhuk,
tohneit wonk ohksippamwēan.

I think you give good advice,
but let me work for you.

Nuttinântam kuttinunŭmah
wunne kogkahquttüonk
koowehquttumauish unnanumeh
kutanakausuehtauuununat.

How many years old are you?

Noh kutteăshe kodtum wōhkom.

Eighteen. And how old is that
boy, or girl?

Piog nishwosuk. Kah toh
unnukkoohquiyeu noh nonkomp
kah nonksq.

Why do boys of that age run
about and do nothing?

Tohwaj nonkompaog ne
anoohquiitcheg pumomashaōg,
kah matteag usseog.

You had better let me have him, and I will learn him to write and read.

An wunnegik kuttinninumiin kah pish nunnehtŭhpeh wussukqŭohamŭnat kah ogketamŭnat.

He shall want for nothing, neither meat, drink, clothing or drubbing.

Noh matteag pish quenauehhikkoo asuh metsuonk wuttattamooonk oglooonk asuh sasamitahwhuttuonk.

Idleness is the root of much evil.

Nanompanissūonk wutchappehk moocheke machuk.

Do you come, or else send him tomorrow early.

Pasoo asuh nekonchhuash saup nompoāe.

Don't forget your promise.

Wanantōhkon koonoowaonk.

I am glad to see you.

Noowekontam ne kenauŭnun.

Where have you been this long time? Hunting. And what did you find?

Tonoh koomūmus yeu qunnohquompi? Adchânat. Kah teagwas kenamiteoh?

A fox or two.

Wonkqŭssis asuh nees.

I believe so; these drams will ruin Indians and English.

Nuttinantāmun; yeush nukquttikkupsash pish papukquanhukqunoōash Indians kah Châh (quog).

A great deal of praise that Indian deserves that keeps himself sober.

Moochĕke wowenotuonk noh Indian woh ahto nanauehhēont wuhhoguh maninniyeuongānit.

I wish such an one would come and set down on my land; I would be kind to him as long as I have anything.

Nâpehnont neahhenissit peyont kah appit nuttohkēit. Woh nooneunneh tô sâhke ahtou nanwe teag.

Why do you deceive me so often?

Tohwaj wunnompuhkossēan ne tohshit.

I am forced to be worse than my word.

Nunnamhit nummatchiteo nukkuttooonk.

I am in debt. To who?	Nuttinohtukquāhwhut. Ut howaneg.
To a great many, and they force me to stay and work with them.	Ut monsog kah nag chekewe nukkogkanunūkquog anâkausuehtauōnat.
If it be not very much, I will pay it.	Tohneit matta wussômēnook kuttoadtehteanisish.
I am ashamed to tell you how much; it is above 40 pounds.	Nuttohkodch kūmishamauununate neatahshik; papaumēyeuooyauinchake poundyeuoo.
O strange! But Indians are not to be trusted anymore.	Mohchanitamwe! Qut Indiânog mat wonk woh unnohtŭkquohwhôun kooche.
So they say, and I don't care.	Ne unnoōwon kah matta nuttintupantamoōun.
Your house smokes, and so do I smoke when I can get tobacco.	Kek pŭkkuttāūo kah nen nuppukkutohteam uttuh annooh wuttoohpooomweonish.
Will you smoke it now?	Sun woh kootam eyeu.
Yes, and thank you too.	Nux, kah kuttabotômish wonk.
Why don't you ask for what you want?	Tohwaj matta wehquttomoōan uttah yeu quenauehhikquēan
Because I am afraid you will be angry.	Newutche noowabis kummosquantamŭnat.
Be very free always when you come to my house.	Moocheke nukkógkittāmwem payoaīnish nekit.
Well, what have you got for dinner?	Neit teagwa kuttohto wutch pohshâquôpoōonk.
Pray give me some drink.	Koowhequttumauish wuttattamwēhe.
Very much I want old coat and stockings.	Nukquenauĕhhik nukkonōgkoo kah muttāsash.

Why don't you come and preach every day?

Tohwaj mat nonche kuhkootumauweog nishnoh kesukod.

Your father came oftener than you do.

Kooshi moochikit peyāpan onk ken.

Because my father have [sic] a great deal more than I.

Newutche nooshi moocheke ahtōai onk nen.

I have five pounds less than others that don't preach so often.

Nunnōgkos ohtom napannatāshe poundyeuash onk onkatogig matta netāhshe kukkootumwehteahitteg.

Pray what is the reason for that?

Koowehquttumauish tohwaj ne ūnnag.

Will you help us husk tonight? I can't tell.

Mat noowahteooo. Sun woh kuppohkogquttanumiumin yeu nuhkon.

No, I am going to a wedding.

Mat, nuttomwetauwatuonganit.

Who is to be married?

Howan tohqunithitit.

Who married them?

Howan wuttohqunitheuh.

The Indian justice.

Indiane Nanuunuacnin.

How shall I learn Indian?

Uttuh woh nittinne nehtuhtaūan Indianne unnontoowaonk.

By talking with Indians, and minding their words and manner of pronouncing.

Nashpekeketookauāonk Indiansog kah kuhkināsinneat ukkittoonkānnoo kah wuttinnohquatumooonkānnoo.

Is not Indian a very hard language to learn?

Sun mat Indianne ūnnontoowaonk siogkod nehtuhtauūnat.

Yes, 'tis very difficult to get their tone.

Nux, ne ahche siogomomŭkquat ohtauūnat wuttinontoowaonkannoo.

333

What do you think about me?
Do you think I shall ever learn?

Toh kuttinantam wutche
(papaume) nen, sun kuttinantam
pish nunnehtuhtauun.

I am afraid not very well.

Nen noowabes mat papaneyeue.

Would it not be better to preach
to the Indians in English?

Sun ummat ayn-wanegig
kuhkootumauonau Indiansog ut
wadtohkōōne 'nontoowaonkanit.

Yes, much better than to preach
in broken Indian.

Nux, moocheke kooche
wunnegen onk neit
kuhkootumauonat ut
nannohtoohquatumooonkānit.

Can the Indians understand the
most that I say?

Sun woh Indiansog wahtamwog
uttuh annoowai asuh
unnontoowai.

Sometimes they can, and
sometimes they can't.

Momānĭsh woh watamwog kah
momanish woh mat
wahtomoowog.

What is the reason for that?

Tohwaj ne ŭnnage.

Because you have some of your
father's words, and he learnt
Indian at Nope, and because you
don't put the tone in the right
place.

Newutche kuttahto nawhutche
ukkuttooonkash kooshi kah noh
nehtuhtoup wuttinontoo-
waonkannooo Nope Indiansog,
kah mat kukkuhkenaŭwe
poomummcoo wuttinuhquatu-
mooonkānoo.

Did your father study Indian at
Nope?

Sun kooshi kod wahtamwus
Indianne 'nontoowaonk ut Nope.

So I hear.

Ne nuttinnehtamunap.

And what is the difference
between the language of the
Island, and the main[land]?

Kah uttuh unnuppencŏnat
wuttinnontoowaonk ne
munnohonk neit
kohtohkomukoouk.

334

I can't tell, or don't know; only this I know, that these Indians don't understand every word of them Indians.

Mat woh nummissohhamŏoun asuh matta noowahitoe webe yeu noowahteauun yeug Indiansog mat wahtanoog uag Indiansog ut nishnog kuttooonganit.

Pray tell me how to pronounce Indian right.

Noowehquttum missŏhhamunat samp-wohquatumunat Indian.

I will do what I can about it.

Uttuh annoohque tapenum nuttissen.

Well, friend, I am sorry you are going away, but I hope it will be for the best.

Netomp nunnooantam asuh kunnouskŏsseh nekummoncheonk, qut nuttannôoūs neanwanegig wutche ken.

I wish you may do and receive good where you are going, and I wish you a good journey.

Napehnont ussean kah attumunuman uttuh ayoan, napehnont wanegig kuppumwishaonk.

And I hope you will keep your self soberly and Christianly.

Kah nuttannoous pish kummaninnis kah Christiane kenanaueh kuhhog.

Try to keep yourselves from those vices to which Indians are given, and which will bring the wrath of God and men upon you, *viz*., drunkenness, falseness, idleness, and theft, etc.

Qutchétaûish kenanauehheŏn kuhhog wutche yeush Indiansog womantamwehhittichch ne woh patonkquĕan ummosquanta- mooonk God kah wosketompaog kenuhkukkonqŭnat, nahnane, kogkesippamoonk, assookekodteamooonk, nanompanissuonk, kumootooonk.

And God be with you, and bless you. Amen.

Kah God wetomŭkquish kah wunnanumŭkquish. Amen.

38

The Process of Negotiation

By the fifth decade of the eighteenth century a crisis was approaching in the long struggle between France and England for final domination of the North American continent. The English pushed steadily inland from their network of settlements near the Atlantic coast, while the French in Canada flung a chain of forts and trading posts through the Great Lakes and far down the Mississippi River. Naturally enough, each side sought the friendship and support of the various Indian tribes whose lands lay in between.

This was the backdrop for an important conference, held at Lancaster, Pennsylvania, in the summer of 1744 between representatives of three English colonies (Pennsylvania, Virginia, and Maryland) and chieftains from the famed Six Nations of the Iroquois Confederacy. The colonists came with three main purposes in mind: to renew an old but sometimes shaky alliance with one of the most powerful of all Indian peoples, to resolve certain conflicting claims to lands in Virginia and Maryland, and to settle an ugly quarrel between the Iroquois and other Indian tribes to the south (particularly, the Catawbas and the Cherokees). The Six Nations, who had their own interest in achieving each of these objectives, proclaimed as a further matter for discussion their desire to gain free access to a road passing south from their lands through Virginia.

The negotiations seem to have been a complete success and highly satisfying to all parties concerned. The English, in particular, were fortunate in securing such an important ally, at the start of almost twenty years of open warfare with the French. Much earlier James Logan of Pennsylvania, a man of long experience and sound judgment in these matters, had said, "If we lose the Iroquois, we are gone." And a recent scholar, impressed with the truth of this comment, has called the Lancaster Treaty "a turning point in colonial history."

But what concerns us here is not the long-range significance of the treaty itself, but rather the process of negotiation characteristic of many such episodes. The records kept at Lancaster were quite extensive, and the following excerpt represents only a small part of the whole. Nonetheless, it does offer some insight into the underlying assumptions, the tactics, the style, and tone of colonist-and-Indian diplomacy everywhere.

Certain of the leading protagonists should be briefly identified. Canasatego was the chief of the Onondaga tribe and leader of the entire Six Nations delegation. Gachradadow was chief of the Cayugas. Governor George Thomas of Pennsylvania was host to the conference and was ceremonially addressed by the Indians as "Onas." "Assaragoa," another name specially bestowed by the Iroquois as a mark of honor, referred to the governor of Virginia. Conrad Weiser, the official interpreter, was a Pennsylvanian of great reputation as a diplomatist—and friend—to the Indians.

Treaty Negotiations between the Commissioners of Virginia and Maryland and the Indians of the Six Nations, Held in Pennsylvania

(1744)

In the Court-House at Lancaster, June 28, 1744, P.M.
   The Honorable George Thomas, Esq., Governor.
   The Honorable the Commissioners of Virginia.
   The Honorable the Commissioners of Maryland.
   The Deputies of the Six Nations.
   Conrad Weiser, Interpreter.
The Commissioners of Virginia desired the interpreter to let the Indians know that their brother Assaragoa was now going to give his reply to their answer to his first speech, delivered [to] them the day before in the forenoon.

"Sachems and warriors of the united Six Nations, we are now come to answer what you said to us yesterday, since what we said to you before on the part of the Great King, our Father, has not been satisfactory. You have gone into old times, and so must we. It is true that the Great King holds Virginia by right of conquest, and the bounds of that conquest to the westward are the Great Sea.

A Treaty Held at the Town of Lancaster, in Pennsylvania, by the Honourable the Lieutenant-Governor of the Province and the Honourable the Commissioners of the Provinces of Virginia and Maryland with the Indians of the Six Nations, in June, 1744 (Philadelphia, 1744), reprinted in *Indian Treaties Printed by Benjamin Franklin* (Philadelphia, 1938), pp. 60–66. I am grateful to the Historical Society of Pennsylvania for permission to reprint from this document.

If the Six Nations have made any conquest over Indians that may at any time have lived on the west side of the Great Mountains of Virginia, yet they never possessed any lands there that we have ever heard of. That part was altogether deserted and free for any people to enter upon, as the people of Virginia have done by order of the Great King very justly, as well by an ancient right as by its being freed from the possession of any other and from any claim even of you the Six Nations, our brethren, until within these [past] eight years. The first treaty between the Great King, in behalf of his subjects of Virginia, and you, that we can find, was made at Albany by Colonel Henry Coursey seventy years since. This was a treaty of friendship, when the first covenant chain was made, when we and you became brethren.

The next treaty was also [made] at Albany, above fifty-eight years ago, by the Lord Howard, Governor of Virginia; then you declare yourselves subjects to the Great King, our Father, and give up to him all your lands for his protection. This you own in a treaty made by the Governor of New York with you at the same place in the year 1687; and you express yourselves in these words, 'Brethren, you tell us the King of England is a very great King; and why should not you join with us in a very just cause, when the French join with our enemies in an unjust cause? Oh, brethren, we see the reason of this; for the French would fain kill us all, and when that is done they would carry all the beaver trade to Canada, and the Great King of England would lose the land likewise. And therefore, Oh Great Sachem beyond the Great Lakes, awake and suffer not those poor Indians, that have given themselves and their lands under your protection, to be destroyed by the French without a cause.'

The last treaty we shall speak to you about is that made at Albany by Governor Spotswood, which you have not recited as it is. For the white people, your brethren of Virginia, are in no article of that treaty prohibited to pass and settle to the westward of the great mountains or to the southward of Cohongoroston. And you agree to this article in these words: "that the great river of Potomac, and the high ridge of mountains, which extend all along the frontiers of Virginia to the westward of the present settlements of that colony, shall be forever the established boundaries between the Indians subject to the dominions of Virginia and the Indians belonging and depending on the Five Nations; so that neither our Indians shall not on any pretence whatsoever pass to [the] northward or westward of the said boundaries without having to produce a passport under the hand and seal of the governor or commander-in-chief of Virginia, nor [are] your Indians [permitted] to pass

338

to the southward or eastward of the said boundaries without a pass
port in like manner from the governor or commander-in-chief of New
York.'

And what right can you have to lands that you have no right to walk
upon but upon certain conditions? It is true, you have not observed this
part of the treaty; and your brethren of Virginia have not insisted upon
it with a due strictness, which has occasioned some mischief.

This treaty has been sent to the Governor of Virginia by order of
the Great King, and is what we must rely on; and, being in writing,
[it] is more certain than your memory. That is the way the white people
have of preserving transactions of every kind and transmitting them down
to their children's children forever; and all disputes among them are settled
by this faithful kind of evidence, and [it] must be the rule between the
Great King and you. This treaty your sachems and warriors signed some
years after the same Governor Spotswood, in the right of the Great King,
had been with some people of Virginia in possession of these very lands
which you have set up your late claim to.

Brethren, this dispute is not between Virginia and you; it is setting
up your right against the Great King, under whose grants the people
you complain of are settled. Nothing but a command from the Great
King can remove them; they are too powerful to be removed by any
force of you, our brethren. And the Great King, as our common father,
will do equal justice to all his children; wherefore we do believe they
will be confirmed in their possession.

As to the road you mention: we intended to prevent any occasion
for it, by making a peace between you and the southern Indians a few
years since at a considerable expense to our Great King, which you confirmed at Albany. It seems, by your being at war with the Catawbas,
that it has not been long kept between you.

However, if you desire a road, we will agree to one on the terms
of the treaty you made with Colonel Spotswood; and your people, behaving themselves like friends and brethren, shall be used in their passage
through Virginia with the same kindness as they are when they pass
through the lands of your brother Onas. This, we hope, will be agreed
to by you, our brethren; and we will abide by the promise made to you
yesterday.

We may proceed to settle what we are to give you for any right you
may have, or have had, to all the lands to the southward and westward
of the lands of your brother, the Governor of Maryland, and of your
brother Onas; though we are informed that the southern Indians claim
these very lands that you do.

339

We are desirous to live with you, our brethren, according to the old chain of friendship, to settle all these matters fairly and honestly; and, as a pledge of our sincerity, we give you this belt of wampum."

Which was received with the usual ceremony.

[The meeting was adjourned at this point, and reconvened the following morning.]

In the Court-House Chamber at Lancaster, June 29, 1744, A.M.
    Present:
    The Honorable the Commissioners of Maryland.
    The Deputies of the Six Nations.
    Conrad Weiser, Interpreter.

Mr. Weiser informed the honorable Commissioners [that] the Indians were ready to give their answer to the speech made to them here yesterday morning by the Commissioners, whereupon Canassatego spoke as follows, looking on a deal-board where were some black lines describing the courses of [the] Potomac and Susquehanna [Rivers):

"Brethren, yesterday you spoke to us concerning the lands on this side [of the] Potomac River; and we have deliberately considered what you said to us on that matter, we are now very ready to settle the bounds of such lands and release our right and claim thereto.

We are willing to renounce all right to Lord Baltimore of all those lands lying two miles above the upper-most fork of [the] Potomac or Cohongoruton River, near which Thomas Cressap has a hunting or trading cabin, by a northline to the bounds of Pennsylvania. But in case such limits shall not include every settlement or inhabitant of Maryland, then [we accept] such other lines and courses from the said two miles above the forks to the outermost inhabitants or settlements as shall include every settlement and inhabitant in Maryland; and from thence, by a northline to the bounds of Pennsylvania, shall be the limits. And further, if any people already have or shall settle beyond the lands now described and bounded, they shall enjoy the same free from any disturbance whatever; and we do and shall accept these people for our brethren, and as such [shall] always treat them.

We earnestly desire to live with you as brethren, and hope you will show us all brotherly kindness; in token whereof we present you with a belt of wampum."

Which was received with the usual ceremony.

Soon after the Commissioners and Indians departed from the Court-House Chamber.

In the Court-House Chamber at Lancaster, June 30, 1744, A.M.

Present:

The Honorable the Commissioners of Virginia.

The Deputies of the Six Nations.

Conrad Weiser, Interpreter.

Gachradadow, speaker for the Indians in answer to the Commissioners' speech at the last meeting, with a strong voice and proper action spoke as follows:

"Brother Assaragoa, the world at the first was made on the other side of the Great Water different from what it is on this side, as may be known from the different colors of our skin and of our flesh; and that which you call justice may not be so amongst us. You have your laws and customs, and so have we. The Great King might send you over to conquer the Indians, but it looks to us that God did not approve of it. If he had, he would not have placed the sea where it is, as the limits between us and you.

Brother Assaragoa, though great things are well remembered among us, yet we don't remember that we were ever conquered by the Great King, or that we have been employed by that Great King to conquer others; if it was so, it is beyond our memory. We do remember [that] we were employed by Maryland to conquer the Conestogoes, and that the second time we were at war with them we carried them all off.

Brother Assaragoa, you charge us with not acting agreeable to our peace with the Catawbas; we will repeat to you truly what was done. The Governor of New York, at Albany, in behalf of Assaragoa, gave us several belts of wampum from the Cherokees and Catawbas; and we agreed to a peace if those nations would send some of their great men to us to confirm it face to face, and [to declare] that they would trade with us; and [we] desired that they would appoint a time to meet at Albany for that purpose, but they never came.

Brother Assaragoa, we then desired [that] a letter might be sent to the Catawbas and Cherokees, to desire them to come and confirm the peace. It was long before an answer came; but we met the Cherokees, and confirmed the peace, and sent some of our people to take care of them until they returned to their own country.

The Catawbas refused to come and sent us word that we were but women; that they were men, and double men, for they had two penises; that they could make women of us, and would be always at war with us. They are a deceitful people. Our brother Assaragoa is deceived by them; we don't blame him for it but are sorry he is deceived.

341

Brother Assaragoa, we have confirmed the peace with the Cherokees but not with the Catawbas. They have been treacherous, and [they] know it; so that the war must continue till one of us is destroyed. This we think proper to tell you, [so] that you may not be troubled at what we do to the Catawbas.

Brother Assaragoa, we will now speak to the point between us. You say that you will agree with us as to the road; we desire that may be the road which was last made (the wagon-road). It is always a custom among brethren or strangers to use each other kindly; [but] you have some very ill-natured people living up there. So that we desire [that] the persons in power may know that we are to have reasonable victuals when we are in want.

You know very well [that] when the white people came first here they were poor; but now they have got our lands and are by them become rich, and we are now poor. What little we have had for the land goes soon away, but the land lasts forever. You told us [that] you had brought with you a chest of goods, and that you have the key in your pockets; but we have never seen the chest nor the goods that are said to be in it. It may be small, and the goods few; we want to see them and are desirous to come to some conclusion. We have been sleeping here these ten days past and have not done anything to the purpose."

The Commissioners told them they should see the goods on Monday.

In the Court-House at Lancaster, June 30, 1744, P.M.
   Present:
   The Honorable George Thomas, Esq., Governor.
   The Honorable The Commissioners of Virginia.
   The Honorable the Commissioners of Maryland.
   The Deputies of the Six Nations.
   Conrad Weiser, Interpreter.

The three governments entertained the Indians and all the gentlemen in town with a handsome dinner. The Six Nations in their order having returned thanks with the usual solemnity of *Yo-ha-han*, the interpreter informed the Governor and the Commissioners that, as the Lord Proprietor and Governor of Maryland was not known to the Indians by any particular name, they had agreed in council to take the first opportunity of a large company to present him with one. And as this with them is deemed a matter of great consequence and attended with abundance of form, the several nations had drawn lots for the performance of the ceremony. And the lot falling on the Cayuga Nation, they had chosen Gachradadow, one of their chiefs, to be their speaker, and he desired leave to begin;

which being given, he, on an elevated part of the Court-House, with all the dignity of a warrior, the gesture of an orator, and in a very graceful posture, spoke as follows;

As the Governor of Maryland had invited them here to treat about their lands and brighten the chain of friendship, the United Nations thought themselves so much obliged to them that they had come to a resolution in council to give to the great man who is Proprietor of Maryland a particular name, by which they might hereafter correspond with him. And as it had fallen to the Cayugas' lot in Council to consider of a proper name for that chief man, they had agreed to give him the name of "Tocarry-hogan," denoting precedency, excellency, or living in the middle or honorable place betwixt Assaragoa and their brother Onas, by whom their treaties might be better carried on. And then, addressing himself to his Honor the Governor of Pennsylvania, the Honorable the Commissioners of Virginia and Maryland, and to the gentlemen then present, he proceeded:

"As there is a company of great men now assembled, we take this time and opportunity to publish this matter, that it may be known Tocarry-hogan is our friend, and that we are ready to honor him, and that by such name he may be always called and known among us. And we hope he will ever act towards us according to the excellency of the name we have now given him, and enjoy a long and happy life."

The Honorable the Governor and Commissioners, and all the company present, returned the compliment with three huzzahs; and, after drinking healths to our gracious King and the Six Nations, the Commissioners of Maryland proceeded to business in the Court-House chamber with the Indians, where Conrad Weiser, the interpreter, was present.

The Honorable the Commissioners ordered Mr. Weiser to tell the Indians that a deed released all their claim and title to certain lands lying in the province of Maryland, which by them was agreed to be given and executed for the use of the Lord Baron of Baltimore, Lord Proprietor of that province, was now on the table, and seals ready fixed thereto. The interpreter acquainted them therewith as desired, and then gave the deed to Canassatego, the speaker, who made his mark, and put his seal and delivered it; after which, thirteen other chiefs or sachems of the Six Nations executed it in the same manner, in the presence of the honorable the Commissioners of Virginia and diverse other gentlemen of that colony and of the provinces of Pennsylvania and Maryland.

39

War and Captivity

Intermarriage, missionary work, trade, and diplomacy: these were major points of contact between the colonist and the Indian. But surely the most vivid aspect of this long transcultural history was the recurrent resort to warfare. Here, all the misunderstanding and doubt and fear —on *both* sides—came together in moments of a very particular horror.

Some of that horror, and much else besides, is powerfully evoked for us in a unique literary genre that developed during the colonial period, the so-called captivity narratives. These accounts (mostly autobiographical) of the experience of various colonists as prisoners of war among the Indians found a very wide readership until well into the nineteenth century. As adventure stories (with blood, gore, and at least a hint of sex), as morality plays, as theological statements, the captivity narratives are among the most compelling indigenous products of the New World culture. At their best they succeed even as literature—with rich and varied imagery, sharp contrasts of character, and a certain measured cadence in the prose itself.

The most famous single example of the genre was *The Narrative of the Captivity and Restoration of Mrs. Mary Rowlandson*, first published in 1682 and reprinted many times thereafter. Mrs. Rowlandson, born to a family named White soon after the original settlement of Massachusetts Bay, was at the time of her capture the wife of a minister in the frontier town of Lancaster. The attack on Lancaster in February, 1676, with which her story begins, belongs to the middle phase of the bloody struggle that came to be known as King Philip's War.

Narrative of the Captivity and Restoration of
Mrs. Mary Rowlandson: Extracts
(1682)

On the tenth of February, 1675, came the Indians with great numbers upon Lancaster. Their first coming was about sun-rising; hearing the noise of some guns, we looked out; several houses were burning, and the smoke ascending to Heaven. There were five persons taken in one house; the father, and the mother, and a sucking child, they knocked on the head; the other two they took and carried away alive. There were two others who, being out of their garrison upon some occasion, were set upon; one was knocked on the head, the other escaped. Another there was who, running along, was shot and wounded and fell down; he begged of them his life, promising them money (as they told me), but they would not hearken to him, but knocked him in the head, and stripped him naked, and split open his bowels. Another, seeing many of the Indians about his barn, ventured and went out, but was quickly shot down. There were three others belonging to the same garrison who were killed; the Indians, getting up upon the roof of the barn, had advantage to shoot down upon them over their fortification. Thus those murderous wretches went on, burning and destroying before them.

At length they came and beset our own house, and quickly it was the dolefulest day that ever mine eyes saw. The house stood upon the edge of a hill. Some of the Indians got behind the hill, others into the barn, and others behind anything that could shelter them; from all [of] which places they shot against the house, so that the bullets seemed to fly like hail, and quickly they wounded one man among us, then another, and then a third. About two hours (according to my observation, in that amazing time) they had been about the house before they prevailed to fire it (which they did with flax and hemp which they brought out of the barn, and there being no defense about the house, only two flankers at two opposite corners and one of them not finished). They fired it once, and one ventured out and quenched it; but they quickly fired it again, and that took. Now is the dreadful hour come that I have often heard of (in time of war, as it was [in] the case of others), but now mine eyes see it. Some in our house were fighting for their lives, others wallowing in their blood, the house on fire over our heads, and the bloody

The Narrative of the Captivity and Restoration of Mrs. Mary Rowlandson, in Charles H. Lincoln, ed., *Narratives of the Indian Wars* (New York, 1913), pp. 112–133, 149–167.

heathen ready to knock us on the head if we stirred out. Now might we hear mothers and children crying out for themselves and one another, "Lord, what shall we do?"

Then I took my children (and one of my sisters, hers) to go forth and leave the house; but as soon as we came to the door and appeared, the Indians shot so thick that the bullets rattled against the house, as if one had taken a handful of stones and threw them, so that we were fain to give back. We had six stout dogs belonging to our garrison, but none of them would stir; though another time, if any Indian had come to the door, they were ready to fly upon him and tear him down. The Lord hereby would make us the more to acknowledge His hand and to see that our help is always in Him. But out we must go, the fire increasing and coming along behind us, roaring, and the Indians gaping before us with their guns, spears, and hatchets to devour us. No sooner were we out of the house but my brother-in-law (being before wounded, in defending the house, in or near the throat) fell down dead, whereat the Indians scornfully shouted and hallooed and were presently upon him, stripping off his clothes. The bullets flying thick, one went through my side, and the same (as would seem) through the bowels and hand of my dear child in my arms. One of my elder sister's children named William, had then his leg broken; which the Indians perceiving, they knocked him on the head. Thus were we butchered by those merciless heathen, standing amazed with the blood running down to our heels.

My eldest sister, being yet in the house and seeing those woeful sights —the infidels hauling mothers one way and children another, and some wallowing in their blood—and her elder son telling her that her son William was dead and myself was wounded, she said, "and, Lord, let me die with them"; which was no sooner said but she was struck with a bullet and fell down dead over the threshold. I hope she is reaping the fruit of her good labors, being faithful to the service of God in her place. In her younger years she lay under much trouble upon spiritual accounts, till it pleased God to make that precious scripture take hold of her heart, 2 Cor., 12: 9: *And He said unto me, my Grace is sufficient for thee.* More than twenty years after I have heard her tell how sweet and comfortable that place was to her. But to return: the Indians laid hold of us, pulling me one way and the children another, and said, "come, go along with us." I told them they would kill me; they answered [that] if I were willing to go along with them, they would not hurt me.

Oh, the doleful sight that now was to behold at this house! *Come, behold the works of the Lord, what desolations He has made in the earth.* Of thirty-seven persons who were in this one house none escaped either present death or a bitter captivity, save only one, who might say as he, *Job*, 1: 15, *And I only am escaped alone to tell the news.* There were twelve killed: some shot, some stabbed with their spears, some knocked down with their hatchets. When we are in prosperity, oh, the little that we think of such dreadful sights and to see our dear friends and relations lie bleeding out their heart-blood upon the ground. There was one who was chopped into the head with a hatchet and stripped naked, and yet was crawling up and down. It is a solemn sight to see so many Christians lying in their blood, some here and some there, like a company of sheep torn by wolves—all of them stripped naked by a company of hell-hounds, roaring, singing, ranting and insulting, as if they would have torn our very hearts out. Yet the Lord by His almighty power preserved a number of us from death, for there were twenty-four of us taken alive and carried captive.

I had often before this said that if the Indians should come I should choose rather to be killed by them than taken alive; but when it came to the trial my mind changed. Their glittering weapons so daunted my spirit that I chose rather to go along with those (as I may say) ravenous beasts than that moment to end my days. And, [in order] that I may the better declare what happened to me during that grievous captivity, I shall particularly speak of the several removes we had up and down the wilderness.

The First Remove

Now away we must go with those barbarous creatures, with our bodies wounded and bleeding and our hearts no less than our bodies. About a mile we went that night, up within sight of the town, where they intended to lodge. There was hard by a vacant house (deserted by the English before, for fear of the Indians). I asked them whether I might not lodge in the house that night; to which they answered, "What, will you love Englishmen still?" This was the dolefulest night that ever my eyes saw. Oh, the roaring and singing and dancing and yelling of those black creatures in the night, which made the place a lively resemblance of hell. And as miserable was the waste that was there made of horses, cattle, sheep, swine, calves, lambs, roasting pigs, and fowl (which they had plundered in the town), some roasting, some lying and burning, and some boiling, to feed our merciless enemies—who were joyful enough, though we were disconsolate.

To add to the dolefulness of the former day and the dismalness of the present night, my thoughts ran upon my losses and sad, bereaved condition. All was gone: my husband gone (at least separated from me, he being in the Bay—and to add to my grief the Indians told me they would kill him as he came homeward), my children gone, my relations and friends gone, our house and home and all our comforts within doors and without. All was gone except my life, and I knew not but the next moment that might go too. There remained nothing to me but one poor wounded babe, and it seemed at present worse than death that it was in such a pitiful condition, bespeaking compassion; and I had no refreshing for it nor suitable things to revive it. Little do many think what is the savageness and brutishness of this barbarous enemy —aye, even those that seem to profess more than others among them —when the English have fallen into their hands.

Those seven that were killed at Lancaster the summer before upon a Sabbath day, and the one that was afterward killed upon a week day, were slain and mangled in a barbarous manner by one-eyed John and Marlborough's praying Indians [i.e., Indians converted to Christianity] which Capt. Mosely brought to Boston, as the Indians told me.

The Second Remove

But now, the next morning, I must turn my back upon the town and travel with them into the vast and desolate wilderness, I knew not whither. It is not my tongue or pen [that] can express the sorrows of my heart and bitterness of my spirit, that I had at this departure; but God was with me in a wonderful manner, carrying me along and bearing up my spirit [so] that it did not quite fail. One of the Indians carried my poor wounded babe upon a horse; it went moaning all along, "I shall die, I shall die." I went on foot after it, with sorrow that cannot be expressed. At length I took it off the horse and carried it in my arms till my strength failed and I fell down with it. Then they set me upon a horse with my wounded child in my lap; and, there being no furniture upon the horse back, as we were going down a steep hill we both fell over the horse's head—at which they, like inhuman creatures, laughed and rejoiced to see it, though I thought we should there have ended our days, as overcome with so many difficulties. But the Lord renewed my strength still and carried me along [in order] that I might see more of His power—yea, so much that I could never have thought of, had I not experienced it.

After this it quickly began to snow, and when night came on they stopped. And now down I must sit in the snow, by a little fire and [with] a few boughs behind me, with my sick child in my lap and calling much for water, being now (through the wound) fallen into a violent fever. My own wound [was] also growing so stiff that I could scarcely sit down or rise up. Yet so it must be that I must sit all this cold, winter night upon the cold, snowy ground, with my sick child in my arms looking that every hour would be the last of its life, and having no Christian friend near me either to comfort or help me. Oh, I may see the wonderful power of God that my spirit did not utterly sink under my affliction; still the Lord upheld me with His gracious and merciful spirit, and we were both alive to see the light of the next morning.

The Third Remove

The morning being come, they prepared to go on their way. One of the Indians got up upon a horse, and they set me up behind him with my poor sick babe in my lap. A very wearisome and tedious day I had of it, what with my own wound, and my child's being so exceeding sick and in a lamentable condition with her wound. It may be easily judged what a poor, feeble condition we were in, there being not the least crumb of refreshing that came within either of our mouths from Wednesday night to Saturday night, except only a little cold water. This day in the afternoon, about an hour by sun, we came to the place where they intended, viz. an Indian town called Wenimesset, northward of Quabaug. When we were come, oh, the number of pagans (now merciless enemies) that there came about me—[so] that I may say as David, Psal., 27: 13, I had fainted unless I had believed, etc.

The next day was the Sabbath. I then remembered how careless I had been of God's holy time, how many Sabbaths I had lost and misspent, and how evilly I had walked in God's sight; which lay so close unto my spirit that it was easy for me to see how righteous it was with God to cut off the thread of my life and cast me out of His presence forever. Yet the Lord still showed mercy to me and upheld me; and as He wounded me with one hand, so He healed me with the other. This day there came to me one Robert Pepper (a man belonging to Roxbury), who was taken in Captain Beers' fight and had been now a considerable time with the Indians and [had gone] up with them almost as far as Albany to see King Philip, as he told me, and was now very lately come into these parts. Hearing, I say, that I was in this Indian town, he obtained leave to come and see me. He told me [that] he himself was wounded in the leg at Captain Beers' fight and was not able [for] some time to go. But as they carried him, and as he took oaken leaves and laid [them] to his wound, and through the blessing of God, he was able to travel again. Then I took oaken leaves and laid [them] to my side, and with the blessing of God it cured me also; yet before the cure was wrought I may say, as it is [expressed] in *Psal.*, 38: 5, 6: *My wounds stink and are corrupt; I am troubled, I am bowed down greatly, I go mourning all the day long.* I sat much alone with a poor, wounded child in my lap, which moaned night and day, having nothing to revive the body or cheer the spirits of her; but instead of that sometimes one Indian would come and tell me one hour that "Your master will knock your child in the head;" and then a second, and then a third, "Your master will quickly knock your child in the head."

This was the comfort I had from them—*miserable comforters are ye all,* as he [i.e. Job] said. Thus nine days I sat upon my knees with my babe in my lap, till my flesh was raw again. My child being even ready to depart this sorrowful world, they bade me carry it out to another wigwam (I suppose because they would not be troubled with such spectacles); whither I went with a very heavy heart, and down I sat with the picture of death in my lap. About two hours in the night my sweet babe like a lamb departed this life, on Feb. 18, 1675—it being about six years and five months old. It was nine days from the first wounding in this miserable condition, without any refreshing of one nature or other except a little cold water. I cannot but take notice how at another time I could not bear to be in the room where any dead person was; but now the case is changed—I must and could lie down by my dead babe, side by side, all the night after. I have thought since of the wonderful goodness of God to me, in preserving me in the use of my reason and senses in that distressed time, [so] that I did not use wicked and violent means to end my own miserable life. In the morning, when they understood that my child was dead, they sent for me [to come] home to my master's wigwam. (By my master in this writing must be understood Quanopin, who was a sagamore and married [to] King Philip's wife's sister. Not that he first took me, but I was sold to him by another Narragansett Indian who took me when I first came out of the garrison.) I went to take up my dead child in my arms to carry it with me, but they bid me let it alone; there was no resisting, but go I must and leave it. When I had been at my master's wigwam, I took the first opportunity I could get to go look after my dead child. When I came I asked them what they had done with it. They told me it was upon the hill. They went and showed me where it was, where I saw the ground was newly digged, and there they told me they had buried it. There I left that child in the wilderness, and must commit myself also in this wilderness-condition to Him who is above all.

God having taken away this dear child, I went to see my daughter Mary, who was at this same Indian town at a wigwam not very far off, though we had little liberty or opportunity to see one another. She was about ten years old, and [was] taken from the door at first by a praying Indian and afterward sold for a gun. When I came in sight she would fall a-weeping, at which they were provoked and would not let me come near her, but bade me begone—which was a heart-cutting word to me. I had one child dead, another in the wilderness I knew not where, the third they would not let me come near to: *Me* (as he said) *have ye bereaved of my children; Joseph is not, and Simeon is not, and ye will take Benjamin also; all these things are against me.*

I could not sit still in this condition, but kept walking from one place to another. And as I was going along my heart was even overwhelmed with the thoughts of my condition, and that I should have children and a nation which I knew not ruled over them. Whereupon I earnestly entreated the Lord that He would consider my low estate, and show me a token for good, and, if it were His blessed will, some sign and hope of some relief. And indeed quickly the Lord answered, in some measure, my poor prayers; for as I was going up and down mourning and lamenting my condition, my son came to me and asked me how I did. I had not seen him before, since the destruction of the town; and I knew not where he was till I was informed by himself that he was amongst a smaller parcel of Indians, whose place was about six miles off. With tears in his eyes he asked me whether his sister Sarah was dead, and told me he had seen his sister Mary, and prayed me that I would not be troubled in reference to himself. The occasion of his coming to see me at this time was this. There was, as I said, about six miles from us a small plantation of Indians, where it seems he had been during his captivity; and at this time there were some forces of the Indians gathered out of our company, and some also from them (among whom was my son's master), to go to assault and burn Medfield. In this time of the absence of his master his dame brought him to see me. I took this to be some gracious answer to my earnest and unfeigned desire.

The next day, *viz.* to this, the Indians returned from Medfield, all the company; for those that belonged to the other small company came through the town that now we were at. But before they came to us, oh! the outrageous roaring and whooping that there was. They began their din about a mile before they came to us. By their noise and whooping they signified how many they had destroyed (which was at that time twenty-three). Those that were with us at home were gathered together as soon as they heard the whooping, and every time that the other went over their number these at home gave a shout, [so] that the very earth rung again. And thus they continued till those that had been upon the expedition were come up to the sagamore's wigwam; and then, oh, the hideous insulting and triumphing that there was over some Englishmen's scalps that they had taken (as their manner is) and brought with them. I cannot but take notice of the wonderful mercy of God to me in those afflictions, in sending me a Bible. One of the Indians that came from [the] Medfield fight had brought some plunder, [and] came to me and asked me—if I would have a Bible, he had got one in his basket. I was glad of it, and asked him whether he thought the Indians would let me read. He answered, yes; so I took the Bible. And in that melancholy time it came into my mind to read first the 28th chapter of *Deut.* which I did; and when I had read it my dark heart wrought on this manner, that there was no mercy for me, that the blessings were gone and the curses come in their room, and that I had lost my opportunity. But the Lord helped me still to go on reading till I came to chapter 30, the seven first verses, where I found there was mercy promised again if we would return to Him by repentance; and though we were scattered from one end of the earth to the other, yet the Lord would gather us together and turn all those curses upon our enemies. I do not desire to live to forget this scripture, and what comfort it was to me.

Now the Indians began to talk of removing from this place, some one way and some another. There were now besides myself nine English captives in this place (all of them children, except one woman). I got an opportunity to go and take my leave of them, they being [ordered] to go one way and I another. I asked them whether they were earnest with God for deliverance, [and] they told me they did as they were able, and it was some comfort to me that the Lord stirred up children to look to Him. The woman, *viz.* Goodwife Joslin, told me [that] she should never see me again, and that she could find [it] in her heart to run away. I wished her not to run away by any means, for we were near thirty miles from any English town, and she [was] very big with child and had but one week to reckon, and [had] another child in her arms [of] two years old; and bad rivers there were to go over, and we were feeble, with our poor and coarse entertainment. I had my Bible with me, [and] I pulled it out and asked whether she would read. We opened the Bible and lighted on *Psal.* 27, in which psalm we especially took notice of that *ver. ult., Wait on the Lord, be of good courage, and He shall strengthen thine heart; wait, I say, on the Lord.*

The Fourth Remove

And now I must part with that little company I had. Here I parted from my daughter Mary (whom I never saw again till I saw her in Dorchester, returned from captivity) and from four little cousins and neighbors, some of which I never saw afterward; the Lord only knows the end of them. Amongst them also was that poor woman before mentioned, who came to a sad end, as some of the company told me in my travel. She having much grief upon her spirit about her miserable condition, being so near her time, she would be often asking the Indians to let her go home. They, not being willing to [do] that and yet vexed with her importunity, gathered a great company together about her and stripped her naked and set her in the midst of them; and when they had sung and danced about her (in their hellish manner) as long as they pleased, they knocked her on the head and the child in her arms with her. When they had done that, they made a fire and put them both into it, and told the other children that were with them that if they attempted to go home they would serve them in like manner. The children said she did not shed one tear, but prayed all the while. But to return to my own journey: we travelled about half a day or [a] little more, and came to a desolate place in the wilderness where there were no wigwams or inhabitants before. We came about the middle of the afternoon to this place, cold, and wet, and snowy, and hungry, and weary, and [with] no refreshing for man but the cold ground to sit on and our poor Indian cheer.

Heart-aching thoughts here I had about my poor children, who were scattered up and down among the wild beasts of the forest. My head was light and dizzy (either through hunger, or hard lodging, or trouble, or all together), my knees feeble, my body raw by sitting double night and day, [such] that I cannot express to man the affliction that lay upon my spirit, but the Lord helped me at that time to express it to Himself. I opened my Bible to read, and the Lord brought that precious scripture to me, *Jer.* 31: 16: *Thus saith the Lord, refrain thy voice from weeping, and thine eyes from tears, for thy work shall be rewarded, and they shall come again from the land of the enemy.* This was a sweet cordial to me when I was ready to faint; many and many a time have I sat down and wept sweetly over this scripture. At this place we continued about four days.

The Fifth Remove

The occasion (as I thought) of their moving at this time was the English army, it being near and following them. For they went as if they had gone for their lives, for some considerable way; and then they made a stop and chose some of their stoutest men and sent them back to hold the English army in play whilst the rest escaped. And then, like Jehu, they marched on furiously, with their old and with their young. Some carried their old decrepit mothers, some carried one, and some another. Four of them carried a great Indian upon a bier; but going through a thick wood with him they were hindered and could make no haste, whereupon they took him upon their backs and carried him, one at a time, till they came to Bacquaug River. Upon a Friday, a little after noon, we came to this river. When all the company was come up and were gathered together, I thought to count the number of them; but they were so many, and being somewhat in motion, it was beyond my skill. In this travel, because of my wound, I was somewhat favored in my load; I carried only my knitting work and two quarts of parched meal. Being very faint, I asked my mistress to give me one spoonful of the meal, but she would not give me a taste.

They quickly fell to cutting dry trees, to make rafts to carry them over the river; and soon my turn came to go over. By the advantage of some brush which they had laid upon the raft to sit upon I did not wet my foot (while many of themselves at the other end were mid-leg deep), which cannot but be acknowledged as a favor of God to my weakened body, it being a very cold time. I was not before acquainted with such kind of doing or dangers. *When thou passeth through the waters I will be with thee, and through the rivers they shall not overflow thee.* (Isai., 43: 2). A certain number of us got over the river that night, but it was the night after the Sabbath before all the company was got over. On the Saturday they boiled an old horse's leg which they had got, and so we drank of the broth as soon as they thought it was ready; and when it was almost all gone they filled it up again.

The first week of my being among them I hardly ate anything. The second week I found my stomach grow very faint for want of something; and yet it was very hard to get down their filthy trash. But the third week, though I could think how formerly my stomach would turn against this or that and I could starve and die before I could eat such things, yet they were sweet and savory to my taste. I was at this time knitting a pair of white, cotton stockings for my mistress, and had not yet wrought upon a Sabbath day; [but] when the Sabbath came they bade me to go to work. I told them it was the Sabbath day, and desired them to let me rest, and told them I would do as much more tomorrow; to which they answered me [that] they would break my face. And here I cannot but take notice of the strange providence of God in preserving the heathen. They were many hundreds, old and young, some sick and some lame, [and] many had papooses at their backs, [and] the greatest number at this time with us were squaws, and they travelled with all they had, bag and baggage, and yet they got over this river aforesaid. And on Monday they set their wigwams on fire, and away they went. On that very day came the English army after them to this river, and saw the smoke of their wigwams; and yet this river put a stop to them. God did not give them courage or activity to go over after us. We were not ready for so great a mercy as victory and deliverance —if we had been, God would have found out a way for the English to have passed this river, as well as for the Indians with their squaws and children and all their luggage. *Oh, that my people had hearkened to me, and Israel had walked in my ways; I should soon have subdued their enemies, and turned my hand against their adversaries.* (Psal., 81: 13, 14.)

The Sixth Remove

On Monday (as I said) they set their wigwams on fire and went away. It was a cold morning, and before us there was a great brook with ice on it. Some waded through it, up to the knees and higher; but others went till they came to a beaver dam, and I amongst them, where through the good providence of God I did not wet my foot. I went along that day, mourning and lamenting, leaving farther my own country, and traveling into the vast and howling wilderness; and I understood something of Lot's wife's temptation when she looked back. We came that day to a great swamp, by the side of which we took up our lodging that night. When I came to the brow of the hill that looked toward the swamp, I thought we had been come to a great Indian town (though there were none but our own company). The Indians were as thick as the trees; it seemed as if there had been a thousand hatchets going at once. If one looked before one there was nothing but Indians, and behind one nothing but Indians, and so [also] on either hand, [and] I myself in the midst, and no Christian soul near me—and yet how hath the Lord preserved me in safety! Oh the experience that I have had of the goodness of God to me and mine!

The Seventh Remove

After a restless and hungry night there we had a wearisome time of it the next day. The swamp by which we lay was, as it were, a deep dungeon; and [there was] an exceeding high and steep hill before it. Before I got to the top of the hill, I thought my heart and legs and all would have broken and failed me. What through faintness and soreness of body it was a grievous day of travel to me. As we went along I saw a place where English cattle had been, [and] that was [a] comfort to me, such as it was. Quickly after that we came to an English path, which so took with me that I thought I could have freely lain down in it and died. That day, a little after noon, we came to Squaukheag, where the Indians quickly spread themselves over the deserted English fields, gleaning what they could find. Some picked up ears of wheat that were crinkled down, some found ears of Indian corn, some found ground-nuts, and others [found] sheaves of wheat that were frozen together in the shock and went to threshing of them out. Myself got two ears of Indian corn; and whilst I did but turn my back one of them was stolen from me, which much troubled me. There came an Indian to them at that time with a basket of horse-liver. I asked him to give me a piece. "What," says he, "can you eat horse-liver?" I told him I would try if he would give a piece, which he did; and I laid it on the coals to roast. But before it was half ready they got half of it away from me, so that I was fain to take the rest and eat it as it was, with the blood about my mouth. And yet a savory bit it was to me, *For to the hungry soul every bitter thing is sweet.* A solemn sight methought it was to see fields of wheat and Indian corn forsaken and spoiled, and the remainders of them to be food for our merciless enemies. That night we had a mess of wheat for our supper.

[A portion of the narrative, covering the eighth through the eighteenth "removes," is here omitted. During this part of her ordeal, Mrs. Rowlandson was marched across the Connecticut River, northward into a region which today belongs to the state of Vermont, and thence back to Mount Wachusett in Princeton, Massachusetts. The total time elapsed was approximately seven weeks. The experiences recounted by the author are generally consistent with the rest of the narrative. Of special significance, however, was the receipt of a letter from the authorities at Boston, raising the prospect of negotiations for Mrs. Rowlandson's release. Though this initial overture was rejected by the Indians, subsequent efforts would succeed.]

The Nineteenth Remove

They said, when we went out, that we must travel to Wachusett this day. But a bitter, weary day I had of it, traveling now three days together, without resting any day between. At last, after many weary steps, I saw Wachusett Hills, but many miles off. Then we came to a great swamp, through which we traveled up to the knees in mud and water, which was heavy going to one tired before. Being almost spent, I thought I should have sunk down at last and never got out; but I may say, as in *Psal.*, 94:18, *When my foot slipped, thy mercy, O Lord, held me up.*

Going along, having indeed my life but little spirit, Philip, who was in the company, came up and took me by the hand and said, "Two weeks more and you shall be mistress again." I asked him if he spake true. He answered, "Yes, and quickly you shall come to your master again" (who had been gone from us three weeks). After many weary steps we came to Wachusett, where he was, and glad I was to see him. He asked me when I washed me. I told him not this month. Then he fetched me some water himself, and bid me wash, and gave me the glass to see how I looked, and bid his squaw give me something to eat. So she gave me a mess of beans and meat and a little ground-nut cake. I was wonderfully revived with this favor showed me. *Psal.*, 106: 46: *He made them also to be pitied of all those that carried them captives.*

My master had three squaws, living sometimes with one and sometimes with another one. One was this old squaw at whose wigwam I was, and with whom my master had been those three weeks. Another was Wettimore, with whom I had lived and served all this while. A severe and proud dame she was, bestowing every day in dressing herself near[ly] as much time as any of the gentry of the land; powdering her hair and painting her face, going with necklaces, with jewels in her ears and bracelets upon her hands. When she had dressed herself, her work was to make girdles of wampum and beads. The third squaw was a

younger one, by whom he had two papooses. By that time I was refreshed by the old squaw, with whom my master was, Wettimore's maid
came to call me home, at which I fell a-weeping. Then the old squaw
told me, to encourage me, that if I wanted victuals I should come to
her, and that I should lie there in her wigwam. Then I went with the
maid, and quickly came again and lodged there. The squaw laid a mat
under me and a good rug over me—the first time I had any such kindness showed me. I understood that Wettimore thought if she should let
me go and serve with the old squaw, she would be in danger to lose
not only my service but the redemption pay also. And I was not a little
glad to hear this, being by it raised in my hopes that in God's due time
there would be an end of this sorrowful hour.

Then came an Indian and asked me to knit him three pair of stockings, for which I had a hat and a silk handkerchief. Then another asked
me to make her a shift, for which she gave me an apron. Then came
Tom and Peter with the second letter from the Council about the captives. Though they were Indians, I took them by the hand and burst
out into tears; my heart was so full that I could not speak to them. But
recovering myself, I asked them how my husband did, and all my
friends and acquaintances. They said, "They are all very well but melancholy." They brought me two biscuits and a pound of tobacco. The
tobacco I quickly gave away. When it was all gone, one asked me to
give him a pipe of tobacco. I told him it was all gone. Then began
he to rant and threaten. I told him when my husband came I would
give him some. "Hang him, rogue," says he, "I will knock out his brains
if he comes here." And then again in the same breath they would say
that if there should come an hundred without guns they would do them
no hurt: so unstable and like mad men they were. So that, fearing the
worst, I durst not send to my husband, though there were some
thoughts of his coming to redeem and fetch me, not knowing what
might follow. For there was little more trust to them than to the master
they served.

When the letter was come, the sagamores met to consult about the
captives, and called me to them to inquire how much my husband
would give to redeem me. When I came I sat down among them, as
I was wont to do, as their manner is. Then they bade me stand up,
and said they were the "General Court." They bid me speak what I
thought he would give. Now knowing that all we had was destroyed
by the Indians, I was in a great strait. I thought if I should speak of
but a little, it would be slighted, and hinder the matter; if of a great

sum, I knew not where it would be procured. At a venture, I said "twenty pounds," yet desired them to take less. But they would not hear of that, but sent that message to Boston, that for twenty pounds I should be redeemed. It was a praying Indian that wrote their letter for them.

There was another praying Indian who told me that he had a brother that would not eat horse, his conscience was so tender and scrupulous (though as large as hell for the destruction of poor Christians). Then, he said, he read that scripture to him, 2 *Kings*, 6:25: *There was a great famine in Samaria; and, behold, they besieged it, until an ass's head was sold for fourscore pieces of silver, and the fourth part of a cab of dove's dung for five pieces of silver.* He expounded this place to his brother and showed him that it was lawful to eat that in a famine which is not [lawful] at another time. "And now," says he, "he will eat horse with any Indian of them all."

There was another praying Indian who, when he had done all the mischief that he could, betrayed his own father into the English hands, thereby to purchase his own life. Another praying Indian was at [the] Sudbury fight, though, as he deserved, he was afterward hanged for it. There was another praying Indian so wicked and cruel as to wear a string about his neck, strung with Christians' fingers. Another praying Indian, when they went to [the] Sudbury fight, went with them, and his squaw also with him, with her papoose at her back.

Before they went to that fight, they got a company together to powaw; the manner was as followeth. There was one that kneeled upon a deerskin, with the company round him in a ring, who all kneeled, striking upon the ground with their hands and with sticks, and muttering or humming with their mouths. Besides him who kneeled in the ring, there also stood one with a gun in his hand. Then he on the deerskin made a speech, and all manifested assent to it; and so they did many times together. They then bade him with the gun go out of the ring, which he did, but when he was out, they called him in again; but he seemed to make a stand. Then they called the more earnestly, till he returned again. Then they all sang. They gave him two guns, in either hand one. And so he on the deerskin began again; and at the end of every sentence in his speaking they all assented, humming or muttering with their mouths, and striking upon the ground with their hands. Then they bade him with the two guns go out of the ring again; which he did, a little way. Then they called him in again, but he made a stand, so they called him with greater earnestness; but he stood reeling and wavering, as if he knew not whether he should stand or fall, or which way to go. They called him with exceeding great vehemency, all of them, one and another. After a little while he turned in, staggering as he went, with his arms stretched out, in either hand a gun. As soon as he came in, they all sang and rejoiced exceedingly awhile. And then he upon the deerskin made another speech, unto which they all assented in a rejoicing manner; and so they ended their business, and forthwith went to [the] Sudbury fight.

To my thinking they went without any scruple but that they should prosper and gain the victory. And they went out not so rejoicing, but they came home with as great a victory. For they said they had killed two captains and almost an hundred men. One Englishman they brought along with them; and he said it was too true, for they had made sad work at Sudbury, as indeed it proved. Yet they came home without that rejoicing and triumphing over their victory which they were wont to show at other times, but rather like dogs (as they say) which have lost their ears. Yet I could not perceive that it was for their own loss of men. They said they had not lost above five or six, and I missed none, except in one wigwam. When they went, they acted as if the Devil had told them that they should gain the victory; and now they acted as if the Devil had told them they should have a fall. Whether it was so or no I cannot tell; but so it proved, for quickly they began to fall, and so it held on that summer, till they came to utter ruin. They came home on a Sabbath day, and the powaw that kneeled upon the deerskin came home (I may say, without abuse) as black as the Devil.

When my master came home, he came to me and bid me make a shirt for his papoose, of a Holland-lace pillowbere. About that time there came an Indian to me and bid me come to his wigwam at night and he would give me some pork and groundnuts. Which I did, and as I was eating, another Indian said to me, "He seems to be your good friend, but he killed two Englishmen at Sudbury, and there lie their clothes behind you." I looked behind me, and there I saw bloody clothes, with bullet holes in them; yet the Lord suffered not this wretch to do me any hurt. Yea, instead of that, he many times refreshed me; five or six times did he and his squaw refresh my feeble carcass. If I went to their wigwam at any time, they would always give me something, and yet they were strangers that I never saw before. Another squaw gave me a piece of fresh pork, and a little salt with it, and lent me her pan to fry it in; and I cannot but remember what a sweet, pleasant, and delightful relish that bit had to me, to this day. So little do we prize common mercies when we have them to the full.

The Twentieth Remove

It was their usual manner to remove when they had done any mischief, lest they should be found out; and so they did at this time. We went about three or four miles, and there they built a great wigwam, big enough to hold a hundred Indians, which they did in preparation to a great day of dancing. They would say now amongst themselves that the Governor would be so angry for his loss at Sudbury that he would send no more about the captives, which made me grieve and tremble. My sister, being not far from the place where we now were and hearing that I was here, desired her master to let her come and see me; and he was willing to [do] it, and would go with her. But she, being ready before him, told him she would go before, and was come within a mile or two of the place. Then he overtook her and began to rant as if he had been mad, and made her go back again in the rain, so that I never saw her till I saw her in Charlestown. But the Lord requited many of their ill-doings, for this Indian, her master, was hanged afterward at Boston. The Indians now began to come from all quarters, against their merry dancing day. Among some of them came one Goodwife Kettle. I told her my heart was so heavy that it was ready to break. "So is mine, too," said she; but yet [she] said, "I hope we shall hear some good news shortly." I could hear how earnestly my sister desired to see me, and I as earnestly desired to see her; and yet neither of us could get an opportunity. My daughter was also now about a mile off, and I had not seen her in nine or ten weeks, as I had not seen my sister since our first taking. I earnestly desired them to let me go and see them; yea, I entreated, begged, and persuaded them but to let me see my daughter. And yet so hard-hearted were they that they would not suffer it. They made use of their tyrannical power whilst they had it; but through the Lord's wonderful mercy their time was now but short.

On a Sabbath day, the sun being about an hour high in the afternoon, [there] came Mr. John Hoar (the Council permitting him, and his own forward spirit inclining him), together with the two aforementioned Indians, Tom and Peter, with their third letter from the Council. When they came near I was abroad. Though I saw them not, they presently called me in and bade me sit down and not stir. Then they

catched up their guns and away they ran, as if an enemy had been at
hand; and the guns went off apace. I manifested some great trouble,
and they asked what was the matter? I told them I thought they had
killed the Englishman (for they had in the mean time informed me that
an Englishman was come). They said: no, they shot over his horse and
under, and before his horse, and they pushed him this way and that
way at their pleasure, showing what they could do; then they let them
come to their wigwams. I begged of them to let me see the Englishman, but they would not. But there was I fain to sit [awaiting] their
pleasure. When they had talked their fill with him, they suffered me
to go to him. We asked each other of our welfare, and how my husband did and all my friends. He told me they were all well and would
be glad to see me. Amongst other things which my husband sent me
there came a pound of tobacco, which I sold for nine shillings in
money; for many of the Indians for want of tobacco smoked hemlock
and ground-ivy. It was a great mistake in any [person] who thought I
sent for tobacco; for through the favor of God that desire was overcome. I now asked them whether I should go home with Mr. Hoar.
They answered no, one and another of them; and it being night, we
lay down with that answer.

In the morning, Mr. Hoar invited the sagamores to dinner; but when
we went to get it ready, we found that they had stolen the greatest part
of the provision Mr. Hoar had brought, out of his bags, in the night.
And we may see the wonderful power of God in that one passage, in
that when there was such a great number of the Indians together, and
so greedy of a little good food, and no English [people] there but Mr.
Hoar and myself—that there they did not knock us in the head and
take what we had, there being not only some provision but also trading
cloth (a part of the twenty pounds agreed upon). But instead of doing
us any mischief they seemed to be ashamed of the fact, and said it were
some "matchit" Indian that did it. Oh, that we could believe that there
is no thing too hard for God! God showed His power over the heathen
in this, as He did over the hungry lions when Daniel was cast into the
den. Mr. Hoar called them betimes to dinner. But they ate very little,
they being so busy in dressing themselves and getting ready for their
dance, which was carried on by eight of them, four men and four
squaws, my master and mistress being two. He was dressed in his Holland shirt, with great laces sewed at the tail of it; he had his silver buttons [and] his white stockings; his garters were hung round with shillings, and he had girdles of wampum upon his head and shoulders. She

had a kersey coat, and [was] covered with girdles of wampum from the loins upward; her arms from her elbows to her hands were covered with bracelets; there were handfuls of necklaces about her neck and several sorts of jewels in her ears. She had fine red stockings and white shoes; her hair [was] powdered and [her] face painted red, that was always before black. And all the dancers were [dressed] after the same manner. There were two others singing and knocking on a kettle for their music. They kept hopping up and down, one after another, with a kettle of water in the midst, standing warm upon some embers, to drink of when they were dry. They held on till it was almost night throwing out wampum to their standers-by.

At night I asked them again if I should go home. They all as one said, no, except my husband would come for me. When we were lain down, my master went out of the wigwam, and by and by sent in an Indian called James the printer, who told Mr. Hoar that my master would let me go home tomorrow if he would let him have one pint of liquors. Then Mr. Hoar called his own Indians, Tom and Peter, and bade them go and see whether he would promise it before them three; and if he would, he should have it; which he did, and he had it. Then Philip, smelling the business, called me to him and asked me what I would give him, to tell me some good news and speak a good word for me. I told him [that] I could not tell what to give him, [and that] I would [give] anything I had, and asked him what he would have. He said: two coats, and twenty shillings in money, and half a bushel of seed corn, and some tobacco. I thanked him for his love; but I knew the good news as well as the crafty fox.

My master, after he had had his drink, quickly came ranting into the wigwam again, and called for Mr. Hoar, drinking to him and saying he was a good man. And then he would say, "Hang him, rogue!" Being almost drunk, he would drink to him, and yet presently say he should be hanged. Then he called for me. I trembled to hear him, yet I was fain to go to him; and he drank to me, showing no incivility. He was the first Indian I saw drunk all the while that I was amongst them. At last his squaw ran out, and he after her, round the wigwam, with his money jingling at his knees; but she escaped him. But having an old squaw he ran to her; and so through the Lord's mercy we were no more troubled that night. Yet I had not a comfortable night's rest; for I think I can say [that] I did not sleep for three nights together. The night before the letter came from the Council I could not rest, [because] I was so full of fears and troubles—God many times leaving us most in the dark, when deliverance is nearest. Yea, at this time I could not rest night nor day. The next night I was overjoyed, Mr. Hoar being come, and that with such good tidings. The third night I was even swallowed up with the thoughts of things, *viz.* that ever I should go home again, and that I must go, leaving my children behind me in the wilderness; so that sleep was now almost departed from mine eyes.

On Tuesday morning they called their General Court (as they call it) to consult and determine whether I should go home or no. And they all as one man did seemingly consent to it, that I should go home, except Philip who would not come among them.

But before I go any further, I would take leave to mention a few remarkable passages of providence, which I took special notice of in my afflicted time.

1. Of the fair opportunity lost in the long march, a little after the fort fight, when our English army was so numerous, and in pursuit of the enemy, and so near as to take several and destroy them—and the enemy in such distress for food that our men might track them by their rooting in the earth for ground-nuts, whilst they were flying for their lives. I say [it was remarkable] that then our army should want provision and be forced to leave their pursuit and return homeward; and the very next week the enemy came upon our town, like bears bereft of their whelps, or so many ravenous wolves, rending us and our lambs to death. But what shall I say? God seemed to leave His people to themselves, and [He] orders all things for His own holy ends. *Shall there be evil in the city and the Lord hath not done it? They are not grieved for the affliction of Joseph; therefore shall they go captive, with the first that go captive.* It is the Lord's doing, and it should be marvelous in our eyes.

2. I cannot but remember how the Indians derided the slowness and dullness of the English army, in its setting out. For after the desolations at Lancaster and Medfield, as I went along with them, they asked me when I thought the English army would come after them. I told them I could not tell. "It may be they will come in May," said they. Thus did they scoff at us, as if the English would be a quarter of a year getting ready.

3. Which also I have hinted before: when the English army with new supplies were sent forth to pursue after the enemy, and they, understanding it, fled before them till they came to Bacquaug River, where they forthwith went over safely, [it was remarkable] that that river should be impassable to the English. I can but admire to see the wonderful providence of God in preserving the heathen for further affliction

to our poor country. They could go in great numbers over, but the English must stop. God had an over-ruling hand in all those things.

4. It was thought if their corn were cut down, they would starve and die with hunger. And all their corn that could be found was destroyed, and they [were] driven from that little that they had in store into the woods in the midst of winter; and yet how to admiration did the Lord preserve them for His holy ends and the destruction of many still amongst the English! Strangely did the Lord provide for them, [so] that I did not see (all the time I was among them) one man, woman, or child die with hunger.

Though many times they would eat that which a hog or a dog would hardly touch, yet by that God strengthened them to be a scourge to His people.

The chief and commonest food was ground-nuts. They eat also nuts and acorns, artichokes, lily roots, ground-beans, and several other weeds and roots that I know not.

They would pick up old bones and cut them to pieces at the joints; and if they were full of worms and maggots, they would scald them over the fire to make the vermin come out, and then boil them, and drink up the liquor, and then beat the great ends of them in a mortar, and so eat them. They would eat horses' guts and ears, and all sorts of wild birds which they would catch, also bear, venison, beaver, tortoise, frogs, squirrels, dogs, skunks, rattlesnakes; yea, the very bark of trees; besides all sorts of creatures and provision which they plundered from the English. I can but stand in admiration to see the wonderful power of God in providing for such a vast number of our enemies in the wilderness, where there is nothing to be seen but from hand to mouth. Many times in a morning the generality of them would eat up all they had, and yet have some further supply against [what] they wanted. It is said, *Psal.* 81: 13, 14: *Oh, that my people had hearkened to me, and Israel had walked in my ways; I should soon have subdued their enemies and turned my hand against their adversaries.* But now our perverse and evil carriages in the sight of the Lord have so offended Him that, instead of turning His hand against them, the Lord feeds and nourishes them up to be a scourge to the whole land.

5.   Another thing that I would observe is the strange providence of God in turning things about when the Indians were at the highest and the English at the lowest. I was with the enemy eleven weeks and five days, and not one week passed without the fury of the enemy and some desolation by fire and sword upon one place or other. They

mourned (with their black faces) for their own losses, yet triumphed and rejoiced in their inhumane and many times devilish cruelty to the English. They would boast much of their victories, saying that in two hours' time they had destroyed such a captain and his company in such a place; and [would] boast how many towns they had destroyed, and then scoff and say [that] they had done them a good turn to send them to heaven so soon. Again, they would say that this summer they would knock all the rogues in the head, or drive them into the sea, or make them flee the country—thinking, surely, Agag-like, *the bitterness of death is past.* Now the heathen begin to think all is their own, and the poor Christians' hopes [begin] to fail (as to man); and now their eyes are more to God, and their hearts sigh heavenward. And [they begin] to say in good earnest, *Help, Lord, or we perish.* When the Lord had brought His people to this, that they saw no help in any thing but Himself, then He takes the quarrel into His own hands. And though they had made a pit, in their own imaginations, as deep as hell for the Christians that summer, yet the Lord hurled themselves into it. And the Lord had not so many ways before to preserve them, but now He hath as many to destroy them.

But to return again to my going home, where we may see a remarkable change of providence: at first they were all against it, except my husband would come for me. But afterwards they assented to it and seemed much to rejoice in it. Some asked me to send them some bread, others some tobacco, others shaking me by the hand, offering me a hood and scarf to ride in—not one moving hand or tongue against it. Thus hath the Lord answered my poor desire and the many earnest requests of others put up unto God for me. In my travels an Indian came to me and told me [that] if I were willing, he and his squaw would run away and go home along with me. I told him, no, I was not willing to run away, but desired to wait God's time, [so] that I might go home quietly and without fear. And now God hath granted me my desire. Oh, the wonderful power of God that I have seen and the experience that I have had. I have been in the midst of those roaring lions and savage bears, that feared neither God nor man nor the devil, by night and day, alone and in company, sleeping all sorts together—and yet not one of them ever offered me the least abuse of unchastity to me, in word or action. Though some are ready to say [that] I speak it for my own credit; but I speak it in the presence of God, and to His glory. God's power is so great now, and as sufficient to save, as when he preserved Daniel in the lions' den, or the three children in the fiery furnace. I may well say, as [in] his *Psal.*, 107: 12, *Oh, give thanks unto the Lord, for He is good, for His mercy endureth forever.* Let the redeemed of the Lord say so, whom He hath redeemed from the hand of the enemy, especially that I should come away in the midst of so many hundreds of enemies quietly and peaceably, and not a dog moving his tongue.

So I took my leave of them, and in coming along my heart melted into tears, more than all the while I was with them; and I was almost swallowed up with the thoughts that ever I should go home again. About the [time of the] sun going down, Mr. Hoar and myself and the two Indians came to Lancaster, and a solemn sight it was to me. There had I lived many comfortable years amongst my relations and neighbors, and now not one Christian [was] to be seen, nor one house left standing. We went on to a farmhouse that was yet standing, where we lay all night; and a comfortable lodging we had, though [with] nothing but straw to lie on. The Lord preserved us in safety that night, and raised us up again in the morning, and carried us along [so] that before noon we came to Concord.

Now was I full of joy, and yet not without sorrow: joy to see such a lovely sight, so many Christians together, and some of them my neighbors. (There I met with my brother and my brother-in-law, who asked me if I knew where his wife was. Poor heart!—He had helped to bury her and knew it not. She, being shot down by the house, was partly burnt, so that those who were at Boston at the desolation of the town, and came back afterward, and buried the dead, did not know her.) Yet I was not without sorrow to think how many were looking and longing, and my own children amongst the rest, to enjoy that deliverance that I had now received; and I did not know whether ever I should see them again. Being recruited with food and raiment, we went to Boston that day, where I met with my dear husband; but the thoughts of our dear children, one being dead, and the other we could not tell where, abated our comfort each to [the] other. I was not [long] before so much hemmed in with the merciless and cruel heathen, but now as much with pitiful, tender-hearted, and compassionate Christians. In that poor and distressed and beggarly condition I was received in, I was kindly entertained in several houses. So much love I received from several (some of whom I knew, and others I knew not) that I am not capable to declare it. But the Lord knows them all by name; the Lord reward them seven-fold into their bosoms of His spirituals, for their temporals. The twenty pounds [which was] the price of my redemption was raised by some Boston gentlemen and Mrs. Usher, whose bounty and religious charity I would not forget to make mention of. Then Mr. Thomas Shepard of Charlestown received us into his house, where we continued eleven weeks; and a father and mother they were to us. And many more tender-hearted friends we met with in that place.

We were now in the midst of love, yet not without much and frequent heaviness of heart for our poor children and other relations who were still in affliction. The week following after my coming in, the Governor and Council sent forth to the Indians again, and that not without success; for they brought in my sister and Goodwife Kettle. Their not knowing where our children were was a sore trial to us still, and yet we were not without secret hopes that we should see them again. That which was dead lay heavier upon my spirit than those which were alive and amongst the heathen—thinking how it suffered with its wounds and I was [in] no way able to relieve it, and how it was buried by the heathen in the wilderness from among all Christians. We were hurried up and down in our thoughts. Sometimes we should hear a report that they were gone this way, and sometimes that, and that they were come in, in this place or that. We kept inquiring and listening to hear concerning them, but [received] no certain news as yet.

About this time the Council had ordered a day of public thanksgiving, though I thought I had still cause of mourning; and being unsettled in our minds we thought we would ride toward the eastward, to see if we could hear anything concerning our children. And as we were riding along (God is the wise disposer of all things) between Ipswich and Rowley, we met with Mr. William Hubbard, who told us that our son Joseph was come in to Major Waldron's, and another with him, which was my sister's son. I asked him how he knew it. He said [that] the Major himself told him so. So along we went till we came to Newbury. And their minister being absent, they desired my husband to preach the Thanksgiving for them. But he was willing to stay there that night, but would go over to Salisbury to hear further, and come again in the morning; which he did, and preached there that day. At night, when he had done, one came and told him that his daughter was come in at Providence. Here was mercy on both hands—now hath God fulfilled that precious scripture which was such a comfort to me in my distressed condition. When my heart was ready to sink into the earth (my children being gone I could not tell whither), and my knees trembled under me, and I was walking through the valley of the shadow of death, then the Lord brought and now has fulfilled that reviving word unto me: *Thus saith the Lord: refrain thy voice from weeping, thine eyes from tears, for thy work shall be rewarded, saith the Lord, and they shall come again from the land of the enemy.* Now we were between them, the one on the east and the other on the west. Our son being nearest, we went to him first, to Portsmouth, where we met with him and with the Major also—who told us he had done what he could, but could not redeem him [for] under seven pounds, which the good people thereabouts were pleased to pay. The Lord reward the Major and all the rest, though unknown to me, for their labor of love. My sister's son was redeemed for four pounds, which the Council gave order for the payment of. Having now received one of our children, we hastened toward the other. Going back through Newbury, my husband preached there on the Sabbath-day, for which they rewarded him many-fold.

On Monday we came to Charlestown, where we heard that the Governor of Rhode Island had sent over for our daughter to take care of her, [she] being now within his jurisdiction; which should not pass without our acknowledgments. But she being nearer Rehoboth than Rhode Island, Mr. Newman went over and took care of her, and brought her to his own house. And the goodness of God was admirable to us in our low estate, in that He raised up passionate friends on every side to us, when we had nothing to recompense any for their love. The Indians were now gone that way, [so] that it was apprehended danger-ous to go to her. But the carts which carried provision to the English army, being guarded, brought her with them to Dorchester, where we received her safe. Blessed be the Lord for it; for great is His power, and He can do whatsoever seemeth [to] Him good. Her coming in was after this manner. She was traveling one day with the Indians, with her basket at her back; [and] the company of Indians were got before her, and gone out of sight, all except one squaw. She followed the squaw till night, and then both of them lay down, having nothing over them but the heavens and under them but the earth. Thus she traveled three days together, not knowing whither she was going, having nothing to eat or drink but water and green hirtle-berries. At last they came into Providence, where she was kindly entertained by several of that town. The Indians often said that I should never have her [for] under twenty pounds; but now the Lord hath brought her in upon free-cost and given her to me the second time. The Lord make us a blessing indeed, each to others. Now have I seen that scripture also fulfilled, *Deut.., 30: 4, 7: If any of thine be driven out to the outmost parts of heaven, from thence will the Lord thy God gather thee, and from thence will He fetch thee. And the Lord thy God will put all these curses upon thine enemies, and on them that hate thee, which persecuted thee.* Thus hath the Lord brought me and mine out of that horrible pit, and hath set us in the midst of tender-hearted and compassionate Christians. It is the desire of my soul that we may walk worthy of the mercies received and which we are receiving.

Our family being now gathered together (those of us that were living), the South Church in Boston hired a house for us. Then we removed from Mr. Shepard's, those cordial friends, and went to Boston, where we continued about three-quarters of a year. Still the Lord went along with us, and provided graciously for us. I thought it somewhat strange to set up housekeeping with bare walls; but, as Solomon says, *Money answers all things*, and that we had through the benevolence of Christian friends, some in this town, and some in that, and others, and some from England—[so] that in a little time we might look and see the house furnished with love. The Lord hath been exceeding good to us in our low estate, in that when we had neither house nor home nor other necessaries, the Lord so moved the hearts of these and those towards us, that we wanted neither food nor raiment for ourselves or ours, *Prov.*, 18:24. *There is a friend which sticketh closer than a brother.* And how many such friends have we found, and [are] now living amongst! And truly such a friend have we found him to be unto us in whose house we lived, *viz*, Mr. James Whitcomb, a friend unto us near [at] hand and afar off.

I can remember the time when I used to sleep quietly, without workings in my thoughts, whole nights together; but now it is otherwise with me. When all are fast [asleep] about me, and no eye open but His who ever waketh, my thoughts are upon things past, upon the awful dispensation of the Lord towards us, upon His wonderful power and might, in carrying of us through so many difficulties, in returning us in safety, and [in] suffering none to hurt us. I remember, in the night season, how the other day I was in the midst of thousands of enemies and nothing but death before me. It is then hard work to persuade myself that ever I should be satisfied with bread again. But now we are fed with the finest of the wheat, and, as I may say, with honey out of the rock; instead of the husk, we have the fatted calf. The thoughts of these things, in the particulars of them, and of the love and goodness of God towards us, make it true of me what David said of himself, *Psal.*, 6:5: *I watered my couch with my tears!* Oh! the wonderful power of God that mine eyes have seen, affording matter enough for my thoughts to run in that when others are sleeping mine eyes are weeping.

I have seen the extreme vanity of this world. One hour I have been in health and wealth, wanting nothing; but the next hour in sickness and wounds and death, having nothing but sorrow and affliction.

Before I knew what affliction meant, I was ready sometimes to wish for it. When I lived in prosperity, having the comforts of the world about me, my relations by me, my heart cheerful, and taking little care for anything—and yet seeing many, whom I preferred before myself, under many trials and afflictions, in sickness, weakness, poverty, losses, crosses, and cares of the world—I should be sometimes jealous lest I should have my portion in this life. And that scripture would come to my mind, *Heb.*, 12: 6: *For whom the Lord loveth He chasteneth, and scourgeth every son whom He receiveth.* But now I see the Lord had His time to scourge and chasten me. The portion of some is to have their afflictions by drops, now one drop and then another; but the dregs of the cup, the wine of astonishment, like a sweeping rain that leaveth no food, did the Lord prepare to be my portion. Affliction I wanted, and affliction I had—full measure (I thought), pressed down and running over. Yet I see [that] when God calls a person to anything, and through never so many difficulties, yet He is fully able to carry them through and make them see, and say they have been gainers thereby. And I hope I can say in some measure, as David did, *It is good for me that I have been afflicted.* The Lord hath showed me the vanity of these outward things: that they are the vanity of vanities, and vexation of spirit; that they are but a shadow, a blast, a bubble, and things of no continuance; that we must rely on God Himself, and our whole dependence must be upon Him. If trouble from smaller matters begins to arise in me, I have something at hand to check myself with; and [I] say, "Why am I troubled? It was but the other day that if I had had the world, I would have given it for my freedom, or to have been a servant to a Christian." I have learned to look beyond the present and smaller troubles, and to be quieted under them, as Moses said, *Exod.*, 14: 13: *Stand still and see the salvation of the Lord.*

FINIS

40

How to Fight Savages

Bitter memories of King Philip's War lingered for many years along the New England frontier. Relations between the settlers and the Indians remained uneasy at best and were marred periodically by individual acts of violence. In 1702 new troubles loomed ahead, as France and England became locked in open warfare on both sides of the Atlantic. The French made common cause with the Abenaki Indians of northern New England and helped to initiate a series of raids against outlying communities in Massachusetts, New Hampshire, and Maine.

The dread—indeed, the general demoralization—that enveloped the inhabitants of such places is vividly revealed in the following letter from the Reverend Solomon Stoddard to Governor Joseph Dudley. Stoddard was for many years the minister of Northampton, Massachusetts, but in this case his concern was for the people of Deerfield, a neighboring town that seemed particularly vulnerable to surprise attack. Events would prove that his fears were not misplaced, for, a few months after the date of his letter to Dudley, a combined force of Frenchmen, Abenakis, and Canadian Indians descended on Deerfield, killed some fifty of its inhabitants, and carried another hundred or so away as captives. This was one of the most notorious of all Indian "massacres."

Letter from the Reverend Solomon Stoddard to Governor Joseph Dudley

(Massachusetts, 1703)

Excellent Sir

The town of Deerfield has suffered much formerly from the Indians, [and] of late two of their young men are carried into captivity. This

Letter from Rev. Solomon Stoddard to Gov. Joseph Dudley, October 22, 1703, in *New England Historical and Genealogical Register*, XXIV (1870), pp. 269–270.

makes a great impression on the spirits of the people, and they are much discouraged. This puts me upon it to make two proposals to Your Excellency.

The first is that they may be put into a way to hunt the Indians with dogs. Other methods that have been taken are found by experience to be chargeable, hazardous, and insufficient. But if dogs were trained up to hunt Indians as they do bears, we should quickly be sensible of a great advantage thereby. The dogs would be an extreme terror to the Indians; they are not much afraid of us, they know they can take us and leave us. If they can but get out of gun-shot, they count themselves in no great danger, how many soever pursue them. They are neither afraid of being discovered or pursued. But these dogs would be such a terror to them that after a little experience it would prevent their coming, and men would live more safely in their houses and work more safely in the fields and woods. In case the Indians should come near the town the dogs would readily take their track and lead us to them. Sometimes we see the track of one or two Indians but can't follow it. The dogs would discover it and lead our men directly to their enemies—for the want of which help we many times take a great deal of pains to little purpose. Besides, if we had dogs fitted for that purpose, our men might follow Indians with more safety, [and] there would be no hazard of their being shot at out of the bushes. They would follow their dogs with an undaunted spirit, not fearing a surprisal; and indeed the presence of the dogs would much facilitate their victory. The dogs would do a great deal of execution upon the enemy and catch many an Indian that would be too light of foot for us.

If it should be thought by any that this way is unpracticable and that the dogs will not learn to do what we do expect from them, these two things may satisfy them: one is that in a time of war with the Indians in Virginia, they did in this way prevail over them, though all attempts before they betook themselves to this method proved in vain. The other is that our hunters give an account that the dogs that are used to hunt bears mind no other track but the track of a bear; from whence we may conclude that if the dogs were used to pursue Indians they would mind nothing else.

If the Indians were as other people are and did manage their war fairly after the manner of other nations, it might be looked upon as inhumane to pursue them in such a manner. But they are to be looked upon as thieves and murderers; they do acts of hostility without proclaiming war.

They don't appear openly in the field to bid us battle, [and] they use those cruelly that fall into their hands. They act like wolves and are to be dealt withal as wolves.

There must be some charge in prosecuting this design; something must be expended for the purchasing [of] suitable dogs and for their maintenance. The men also who spend their time in this service must be paid, but this will not rise in any proportion to the charge of maintaining a suitable number of garrison solders. I have taken advice with several of the principal persons amongst us, and they look upon this way as the most probable expedient in this case.

The other proposal is that the town of Deerfield may be freed from country rates during the time of the war. Their circumstances do call for commiseration: sometimes they are alarmed and called off from their business; sometimes they dare not go into the field (and when they do go, they are fain to wait 'till they have a guard); they can't make improvement of their outlands as other towns do; the houses are so crowded sometimes with soldiers that men and women can do little business within doors; and their spirits are so taken up about their dangers that they have little heart to undertake what is needful for advancing their estates. It seems to me to be a thing acceptable to God that they should be considered and freed from rates.

Your excellency will not take it amiss that I take my accustomed freedom and am so officious as to tender my advice before it be asked. The good Lord guide Your Excellency and the General Assembly to do that which shall be serviceable to this afflicted country, which is the hearty prayer of your humble servant,

Solomon Stoddard.

Northampton
Oct. 22d, 1703

Since I wrote, the father of the two captives belonging to Deerfield has importunately desired me to write to Your Excellency, that you would endeavor the redemption of his children. I request that if you have any opportunity you would not be backward to such work of mercy.

Part Six
Nature

41

Lay of the Land

From the moment of their arrival colonists sought to learn the physical shape of the new continent. At first, their understanding—like their experience—was limited to the coastlines. But gradually, as they pushed inland, they filled the blank spaces.

The maps they drew, and sometimes published, reflected this expanded knowledge. The example reproduced here dates from 1675, a time when its subject (New England) had become quite fully investigated. The outlines of the region, as drawn by the cartographer, are generally correct—though not, to be sure, the details. Coasts are rendered with special care, and rivers stand out like the arteries and veins of a human body. These features represent, of course, actual priorities in the colonists' lives: commerce and communication went overwhelmingly by water.

The Seller map is, however, much more than an assemblage of cartographic lines; at many points it is frankly pictorial. The fauna and flora of New England, the fish of the surrounding sea, ships, soldiers in battle, Indian villages: the whole makes a portrait as much as a map proper,

A Map of New England

(1675)

John Seller

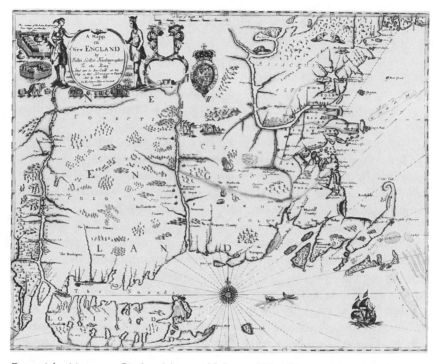

From *Atlas Maritimus*. Sterling Memorial Library, Yale University. Used with permission.

42

Ways and Means of Agriculture

Throughout the colonial period people were bound to, and bound *by*, their natural environment to an extent that is hard to imagine today. They were, of course, exposed all the time to the vagaries of wind and weather. The routine of their lives was tightly shaped by basic diurnal and seasonal rhythms. And their perceptual field—what they saw, and heard, and smelled, and touched—encompassed much that was entirely free of human intervention. But most simply, and most important by far, their livelihood was quite literally wrenched from nature by dint of unending struggle with woods and soil and water. It is necessary to emphasize that some 95 percent of all colonial Americans were farmers. No other historical fact has such profound implications for the difference between their world and our own.

But it is not easy to recapture this vital part of their lives, either in general or in detail. For the most part, it belonged to a realm of assumed, instinctive, unspoken (or at least unwritten) behavior. To record such matters would seem quite superfluous—except, perhaps, from the standpoint of an interested "outsider."

Luckily, the Rev. John Clayton was just such an outsider—an Englishman born and bred, a "parson with a scientific mind" (in the words of his recent biographers), and a tourist in the southern colonies near the end of the seventeenth century. The reports he sent back to his friends at the Royal Society of London have much to say about agriculture, for Clayton fancied himself something of an expert on the subject. They describe a pattern (or perhaps a *non*-pattern) that already displayed a number of distinctively "American" features. The letter of August 17, 1688, is a representative specimen.

Letter from the Reverend John Clayton to the Royal
Society of London

(Virginia, 1688)

Sir:

My last was the journal of Thomas Bats, Thomas Woods, and Robert Fallam. I know Colonel Byrd very well, that's mentioned to have been about that time as far as the Totemas. He's one of the intelligentest gentlemen in all Virginia, and knows more of Indian affairs than any man in the country. I discoursed [with] him about the River on the other side of the mountains, said to ebb and flow, which he assured me was a mistake in them. For [he said] that it must run into a lake now called Lake Petite, which is fresh water. For since that time a colony of the French are come down from Canada and have seated themselves on the back of Virginia, where Fallam and the rest supposed there might be a bay; but [there] is a lake to which they have given the name of Lake Petite, there being several larger lakes between that and Canada. The French, possessing themselves of these lakes, no doubt will in short time be absolute masters of the beaver trade, the greatest number of beavers being caught there. The Colonel told me likewise that the common notion of the lake of Canada he was assured was a mistake; for the river supposed to come out of it had no communication with any of the lakes, nor the lakes one with another, but were distinct. But [it is well] not to ramble after hearsay and other matters.

But with them [?] [it is necessary] to return to the parts of Virginia inhabited by the English, which in general is a very fertile soil, far surpassing England, for there English wheat—as they call it to distinguish it from maize, commonly called Virginia wheat—yields generally between 15 and 30 fold, the ground only once plowed, whereas 'tis a good crop in England that yields above 8 fold, after all their toil and labor. And yet in truth 'tis only the barrenest parts that they have cultivated— tilling and planting only the high lands, leaving the richer vales unstirred because they understand not anything of draining. So that the richest

Letter of Rev. John Clayton to the Royal Society of London, August 17, 1688, in Edmund Berkeley and Dorothy Smith Berkeley, eds., *The Reverend John Clayton, a Parson with a Scientific Mind* (Charlottesville, Va., 1965), pp. 78–90. I am grateful to the Virginia Historical Society, owner of the copyright to this book, for permission to reprint Clayton's letter. I am similarly indebted to the Royal Society of London, owner of the manuscript itself.

meadow lands, which is one third of the country, is boggy marsh and swamp, whereof they make little advantage, but loose in them abundance of their cattle, especially at the first of the spring when the cattle are weak and venture too far after young grass. Whereas vast improvements might be made thereof, for the generality of Virginia is a sandy land with a shallow soil. So that after they have cleared a fresh piece of ground out of the woods, it will not bear tobacco past two or three years, unless cow-penned; for they manure the ground by keeping their cattle, as in the south you do keep your sheep, every night confining them within hurdles, which they remove when they have sufficiently dunged one spot of ground.

But, alas, they cannot improve much thus; besides, it produces a strong sort of tobacco in which the smokers say they can plainly taste the fulsomeness of the dung. Therefore every three or four years they must be [ready] for clearing a new piece of ground out of woods, which requires much labor and toil, it being so thick grown all over with massy timber. Thus their plantations run over vast tracts of ground, each ambitioning to engross as much as they can [in order] that they may be sure [to] have enough to plant, and [enough] for their stocks and herds of cattle to range and feed in; [so] that plantations of 1000, 2000, or 3000 acres are common, whereby the country is thinly inhabited, their living is solitary and unsociable, trading [is] confused and dispersed; besides other inconveniences. Whereas they might improve 200 or 300 acres to more advantage, and would make the country much more healthy; for those that have 3000 acres have scarce cleared 600 acres thereof, which is peculiarly termed the plantation, being surrounded with the 2400 acres of woods. So that there can be no free or even motion of the air; but the air is kept either stagnant, or the lofty sulphurous particles of the air, that are higher than the tops of the trees, which are above as high again as the generality of the woods in England, descending when they pass over the cleared spots of ground, must needs in the violent heat of summer raise a preternatural ferment and produce bad effects. Nor is it any advantage to their stocks or crops; for did they but drain their swamps and low lands they [would] have a very deep soil that would endure planting 20 or 30 years, and some would scarce ever be worn out, but be ever longer better. For they might lay them all winter or when they pleased in water, and the product of their labor would be double or treble, whether [for] corn or tobacco. And [I am certain] that this is no fond projection —though when I [have] discoursed the same to several and [have] in part shown them how their particular grounds might be drained at a very easy rate, they have either been so conceited of their old way, so sottish as not to apprehend, or so negligent as not to apply themselves thereto.

But on the plantation where I lived, I drained a good large swamp, which fully answered expectation. The gentlewoman where I lived was a very acute, ingenious lady, who one day [was] discoursing [with] the overseer of her servants about pitching the ensuing year's crop. The overseer was naming one place where he designed to plant 30000 plants, another place for 15000, another for 10000, and so forth—the whole crop designed to be about 100000 plants. Having observed the year before [that] he had one the like and [had] scattered his crop up and down the plantation at places a mile or a mile and a half asunder, which was very inconvenient and whereby they lost much time, I interposed and asked why they did not plant all their crop together. The fellow smiled, as it were at my ignorance, and said there was very good reason for it. I replied that was it [which] I inquired after. He returned [that] the plantation had been an old, planted plantation, and being but a small plot of ground [it] was almost worn out; so that they had not ground all together that would bring forth tobacco. I told him then [that] they had better ground than ever yet they had planted, and more than their hands could manage. He smiled again, and asked me where. I then named such a swamp. He then said scornfully [that] he thought what a planter I was, [and] that I understood better how to make a sermon than managing tobacco. I replied with some warmness: though I hoped so, that was impertinence, and no answer. He then said that the tobacco there would drown and the roots rot. I replied that the whole country would drown if the rivers were stopped, but it might be laid as dry as any land on the plantation. In short we discoursed [about] it very warmly, till he told me he understood his own business well enough and did not desire to learn of me.

But the gentlewoman attended somewhat better to my reasoning, and got me one day to go and show her how I projected the draining of the swamp, and thought it so feasible that she was resolved to have it done, and therefore desired me I would again discourse [with] her overseer, which I did several times. But he would by no means hearken thereto and was so positive that she was forced to turn him away to have her servants set about the work; and with three men in thirteen days I drained the whole swamp. It, being sandy land, soaks and drains admirably well, and, what I little expected, laid a well dry at a considerable distance. The gentlewoman was in England last year, and I think Dr. Moulin was by when she asked me. Now to teach her how she might make her tobacco that grew in the swamp less—for it produced so very large that it was suspected to be of the Aranoko kind—I told her [that] though the complaint was rare, yet there was an excellent remedy for that. In letting every plant bear eight or nine leaves instead of four or five she would have more tobacco and less leaves. Now you must know [that] they top their tobacco, that is, take away the little top bud when the plant has put forth as many leaves as they think the richness of the ground will bring to a substance, but generally when it has shot forth four or six leaves. And when the top bud is gone, it puts forth no more leaves, but side branches instead which they call suckers [and] which they are careful ever to take away that they may not impoverish the leaves.

I have been more tedious in the particulars, the fuller to evince how resolute they are and conceitedly bent to follow their old practice and custom, rather than to receive directions from others, though plain, easy, and advantageous. There are many other places [that] are as easy to drain as this, though of larger extent and richer soil, for some of which I have given directions and have only had the return perhaps of a flout afterwards. Even in Jamestown Island, which is much [?] of an oval figure, there's a swamp [which] runs diagonal-wise over the island, whereby is lost at least 150 acres of land that would be meadow which would turn to as good account as if it were in England. Besides, it is the great annoyance of the town and no doubt but makes it much more unhealthy. If therefore they but scoured the channel, and made a pretty ordinary trench all along the middle of the swamp, placed a sluice at the mouth where it opens into the Back Creek (for the mouth of the channel there is narrow, has a good hard bottom, and is not past two yards deep when the flood is out, as if nature had designed it beforehand), they might thus drain all the swamp absolutely dry or lay it under water at their pleasure. I have talked several times hereof to Mr. Sherwood, the owner of the swamp, yet nothing is essayed in order thereto.

And now, since we are speaking of Jamestown, give me leave to adjoin some reflections as to the situation and fortifications of the place. The natural situation of the place is such as perhaps the world has not a more commodious place for a town, where all things conspire for [the] advantage thereof. To give you some idea of the place, the river and island lie thus. [Clayton included a map of Jamestown, here omitted.]

Jamestown Island is rather a peninsula, being joined to the continent by a small neck of land, not past 20 or 30 yards over, and which at spring tides is overflowed and is then an absolute island. Now they have built a silly sort of a fort, that is a brick wall in the shape of a half moon, at the beginning of the swamp, because the channel of the river lies very nigh the shore, but it is the same as if a fort were built at Chelsea to secure London from being taken by shipping. Besides, ships passing up the river are secured from the guns of the fort till they come directly over against the fort, by reason [that] the fort stands in a vale; and all the guns directed down the river, that should play on the ships as they are coming up the river, will lodge their shot within ten, twenty, or forty yards in the rising bank, which is much above the level of the fort, so that if a ship gave but a good broadside, just when she comes to bear upon the fort, she might put the fort into that confusion as to have free passage enough. There was indeed an old fort of earth in the town, being a sort of tetragon with something like bastions at the four corners, as I remember; but the channel lying further off to the middle of the river there, they let it be demolished and built that new one [already] spoken of, of brick, which seems little better than a blind wall to shoot wild ducks or geese.

If they would build a fort for the security of the town and country, I conceive it should be on Archer's Hope Point, for that would stop the ships from passing up the river before they came to the town, and would secure the town from being blocked up by sea. The channel at Archer's Hope Point lies close by the shore and makes such an angle there (by reason of Hogg Island) that going up or down the river, let the wind be where it will, they must there bring the contrary tack on board; and generally when they about the ship, as they call it, they are so nigh the shore that a man may almost fling a finger-stone on board. How much this hinders the motion of a ship, and what confusion it must be to them to bring a contrary tack on board whilst they have all the guns of a fort playing so nigh upon them, may readily be conceived. Archer's Hope is a neck of land that runs down three miles long [and] not much past half a mile broad between the main river and Archer's Hope Creek, which has large marshes and swamps; so that a citadel built upon the point would almost be impregnable, being it could be attacked [in] no way but one (which is so narrow a slender neck of land that it would be difficult to take it that way). And it would secure Jamestown from being blocked, being it would not be past a mile by water to the point of Jamestown Island. The island is s surrounded with water and marshy land that the town could never be bombed by land.

But now to return to the reflections of improving and manuring of land in Virginia: hitherto, as I have said, they have used none but that of cow-penning. Yet I suppose they might find very good marl in many places. I have seen both the red and blue marl at some breaks of hills. This would be the properest manure for their sandy land if they spread it not too thick—theirs being, as I have said, a shallow, sandy soil, which was the reason I never advised any to use lime, though they have very good lime of oyster shells, but that's the properest manure for cold clay land and not for a sandy soil. But as most lands have one swamp or another bordering on them, they may certainly get admirable slitch, wherewith to manure all their uplands. But this, say they, will not improve ground, but [rather] clods and grows hard. 'Tis true [that] it will do so for some time, a year or two at the first; but did they cast it in heaps and let it lie for two or three years after a frost or two had seized it and it has been well pierced therewith, I doubt not [that] it would turn to good account. And for this too I have something more then bare conjecture; for discoursing [about] it once with a good, notable planter, we went to view a heap thereof that casually he had cast up between three and four years before, and we found it not very binding but rather a fine natural mold, whereupon he did confess [that] he then remembered that out of a ridge of the like mold he had had very large plants, which must have been of the like slime or slitch cast up before. But [he] said that himself and others despaired of this manure, because they had taken some of this slitch fresh and moist out of the swamp, and filled tobacco hills with it, and in the midst of it planted their plants, which so bound the roots of their plants that they never came to anything. But he said he then saw his error, yet I have not heard [that] he has remembered to correct it.

But 'tis strange in how many things besides they are remiss, which one would think Englishmen should not be guilty of. They neither house nor milk any of their cows in winter, having a notion that it would kill them; yet I persuaded the aforementioned lady where I lived to milk four cows the last winter that I stayed in the country (whereof she found so good effect that she assured me she would keep to my advice for the future), and also, as I had further urged, house them too—for which they have mighty conveniences, their tobacco houses being empty ever at that time of the year and may easily be [re-]fitted in two or three days' time without any prejudice, whereby their cattle would be much sheltered from those pinching, sharp frosts that some nights on a sudden become very severe. I had another project for the preservation of their cattle [which] proved very successful. I urged the lady to sow her wheat as early as possibly she could, so that before winter it might be well rooted, to be early and flourishing at the first of the spring—so that she might turn thereon her weak cattle and such as should at any time be swamped, whereby they might be recruited and saved and it would do the wheat good also. I advised her likewise to save and carefully gather her Indian corntops and blades and all her straw and whatever could be made [into] fodder for her cattle, for they got no hay (though I was urging her to [grow] that, too), and to sow sainfoin, for being a sandy soil I'm confident [that] it would turn to very good account. They have little or no grasses in winter, so that their cattle are pined and starved; and many that are brought low and weak, when the spring begins, venture too far into the swamps after the fresh grass, where they perish, so that several persons lose 10, 20, or 30 head of cattle in a year.

I observed [that] this was much owing to their inadvertancy and error in their way of managing and feeding them, for they get little fodder; but as they think [of] corn [as] being more nourishing, [they] feed them with their Indian corn, which they give them morning and evening. They spend thus a great quantity of corn; and when all's done, what signifies two or three heads of corn to a beast in a morning? It makes them only linger about the houses for more, and after that sweet food they are not so prompt to browse on the trees and the coarse grass which the country affords. So that thus their guts shrink up; they become belly-shot, as they call it. I advised therefore never to give them anything in a morning, whereby as soon as they were set forth of the cow pens they would fall a-feeding; and though they filled their bellies only with such coarse stuff as had little nourishment in it, yet it would keep out their bellies and they would have a better digestion. And then when they were come home at nights [I said] to fodder them, beginning with straw and their coarsest fodder, which they would learn to eat by degrees before they tasted that that was more delicate, and whilst their digestion was strong would yield them nourishment to keep them still so. Afterwards when the winter pinched, their fine fodder then would stand them instead; and hereby they might preserve their weakest cattle by these methods and [with] the help of the wheat patch. She, the gentlewoman where I lived, saved all her cattle and lost not one in two winters after that I stayed there. Besides, she saved about 20 barrels of corn, as I remember, that she told me she used to spend upon her stock. And a barrel of corn is commonly worth 10 shillings. Nay, further, the last spring she fed two beasts, a bullock and a cow, fat upon her wheat with the addition only of a little boiled corn; and yet the wheat was scarce eaten down enough.

But to return again to the nature of the earth, which may be pretty well gathered from what I have already said: I have observed that at five or six yards deep, at the breaks of some banks, I have found veins of clay, admirably good to make pots, pipes, or the like of—and whereof I suppose the Indians make their pipes and pots to boil their meat in, which they make very handsomely, and [which] will endure the fire better than most crucibles. I took [some] of this clay, dried, powdered, and sifted it; powdered and sifted potsherds and glass; [and mixed the whole in a ratio of] 3 parts, 2 parts, and 1 part, as I remember, and therewith made a large crucible which was the best I yet tried in my life. I took it, once [it had become] red-hot, out of the fire and clapped it immediately into water, and it started not at all. The country abounds mightily with iron ore that, as I have been assured by some upon trial, has been found very good. There are rocks thereof [which] appear at the precipice of hills, at the foot whereof there runs a river fit for a forge; and there's wood enough to supply it with charcoal. As I have heard, there was formerly some persons [who] undertook the work, and when they had made but a small quantity of iron (which proved very good) the Indian Massacre happened. And they, being higher-seated than the then-inhabited part of the country, were all cut off, and the work demolished; so that it has frightened others, I think, from the like attempt. Besides, such a work requires a greater fund and bank of money to carry it on than any there are able to lay out; and for persons in England to meddle therewith is certainly to be cheated at such a distance. Some Indians brought Colonel Byrd some black lead, whereof he has told me there was great store. There's very curious talc towards the falls of [the] Rappahannock River, which they burn and make a delicate white wash of it. The Secretary of State, Colonel Spencer, has assured me there were vitriolic or alluminous earths on the banks of [the] Potomac.

And thus far, of what my memory supplies me, referring to the earth. In the next I shall give a short account of the Byrds. My humble respects and service to the honorable society, more peculiarly to my acquaintance and friend. I am,

Sir,

yours to serve,

J. Clayton

Wakefield, August the 17th/88

43

Problems of Travel and Transport

The agricultural orientation of the colonists is clear and incontrovertible, but they did reach out at many points to a wider world of trade. Even those who were most tightly bound to subsistence farming hoped, in the long run, to be able to grow surpluses that would be suitable for sale. Thus, as the commercial nexus grew to intercolonial and even to international dimensions, problems of transport and communication assumed a special importance.

In fact, the means of transport available in that era are reducible to two—the sailboat and the horse-drawn cart—and there were in either case a multitude of hazards and petty harassments to overcome. Some of these can be glimpsed in the following short "log," kept by an anonymous sailor on a journey from Red Bank, New Jersey, to New York City in the autumn of 1734. The distance covered was barely thirty miles, and the time elapsed on the outward leg was fully six days. It is a striking measure of the altered relationship between humankind and nature that today the same trip is made in about two hours.

Log of a Journey from Red Bank, New Jersey, to New York City

(1734)

A journal of our intended voyage, by God's permission, from Red Bank to New York, distant 12 leagues, in the sloop *Portland*, and back again.

On Saturday, the 9th [of] November, 1734, we went on board in order for to come to sail; but in weighing the best bower it got fast under the stern, and it not being got light we could not clear it until the tide was so much fallen that we could not get away. So we was obliged to

From John E. Stilwell, ed., *Historical and Genealogical Miscellany*, I (New York, 1903), pp. 222–224.

go on shore again, the wind [being] west-southwest, and went home; and likewise the passengers went home.

On Sunday, the 10th, we went on board without the passengers early in the evening and got down the river as far as Mr. Pintard's, it being one mile; but it was with much labor, for there was no wind and we were obliged to row and set all the way. When we came there seven passengers came on board, but went on shore again for the wind sprung up at [the] east and south; and that being contrary, we went home again on foot [in] wet weather.

On Monday, the 11th, at 12 o'clock we went on board again with five passengers and sailed down the river as far as Rocky Point, the wind [being] at [the] south, and there got aground and lay until high water, that being at 9 o'clock, when we weighed again. And with abundance of difficulty and hard labor we got to Black Point then, it being late in the night. Though it being but one mile, yet the wind being at [the] south [and] contrary, we were obliged to row and set all the way, and got aground several times. Then, being come to an anchor, we went on shore, and some of our passengers lodged on shore, the weather being all day lowering—the distance from Mr. Pintard's to Black Point being two leagues.

On Tuesday we went on board again with all our passengers in the morning, and set sail, and sailed towards the inlet about one mile, and there got aground. And though we carried out an anchor and strove very hard for it, yet we could not get off [on] that tide. Then there came a canoe and fetched one of our passengers, and some of us went on shore and barbecued a pig and ate him. Then towards evening [we] went on board again, and at high water we strove to get off again, but could not though we carried out an anchor and took much trouble. In the evening [there] came in a sloop from Rhode Island (Captain John Watson, commander) and [it] ran aground in call of us. At dark [there] came a canoe on board and took one of our passengers on shore. So we finding our labor in striving to get off to be in vain, we went to sleep—the wind [being] at [the] west and north [and] clear weather.

On Wednesday, by [the] break of day, we began [to] beat and thump and at high water we got off, and got over the shoal [that] we lay upon, and came to an anchor. Likewise the other sloop got off, and slipped her cable, and left her boat with it, and got some of our passengers to carry it to Black Point. In the afternoon they came back with that passenger that left us the night before. Then we went on shore, four of us, and got some wood. While we were on shore one of the passengers that came on shore with us had a fit of fever and ague. When we came on board again we weighed anchor, and in casting the anchor the cat-rope broke and the anchor fell down again; and before we could get it up again we got aground and were obliged to carry out an anchor again. And in about half an hour's time we got off and sailed down to the bar; but it being low water, we struck upon the bar and lay thumping [for] about one hour. By this time the sun was down, and when we got out the wind was at west [by] north. We sailed along Sandy Hook [for] about two miles, and then the wind began scant upon us and at last came to north-west. Then we were obliged to turn it, and in three trips we got within the hook. We had a very rough time and several of our passengers were sick. We ran against shoal harbor and came to anchor there at 11 o'clock at night and went to sleep. Some of our passengers were yet sick; the weather [was] indifferent and clear. She rode all the night. [The] wind [was] still at [the] north-west and blew fresh.

On Thursday, towards day, we awoke and boiled a pot of potatoes and ate [some] of them by daylight. We weighed anchor and came to sail. The wind [being] still at [the] north-west that morning, we got into Permy City Cove where lay two vessels, one of them from Egg Harbor which was full of water. The people came on board of us to get some meat. We, having a small shoat, let them have half of it; and [we] took part of the other and carried it on shore with some potatoes, which we exchanged with the other people for musty Indian meal and made doughboys of it at an Indian wigwam. So having ate our doughboys, potatoes, and pork and got some wood, toward evening we went on board again—all but two passengers, who left us and went home on foot. So then we had lost three of our passengers. The wind [was] still at [the] north-west, [and] clear weather. The man that had a fit of the fever and ague yesterday had another this day. Also I cut my right hand with a shell very badly.

On Friday we boiled more potatoes and pork and ate that, for our bread was all spent. Towards evening there came a man and hailed us. Four of us went on shore to him, and he told us he wanted a passage to [New] York. We told him the wind was contrary and we could not tell when we should go, for it was at [the] north-west still; so he left us. Then, having got some wood, we went on board again. By this time we found the wind was shifted [and was] fair for us. We quickly came to sail, and with much difficulty we got out of the cove. The wind [was] at the south-west by this time. It was dark; however, we steered our course. Then we boiled more potatoes and ate them without anything. Then, being obliged to steer by the compass, we had no candle but were obliged to put some tallow in a rag and [make] do with that. Then, having made the narrows at 10 o'clock at night, we had one small bottle [of] rum which [we] finished by the time we got into the narrows. Then the wind died away and we hoisted our square sail; but presently the wind sprang up, and broke the oar we turned it out with, and had like to have carried the square sail away. But having a brisk gale and fair, we got to [New] York by 11 o'clock that night; but in coming to run into the dock, we ran with our bolt sprit upon the Long Bridge.

I had like to have broke it and tore the jib; but having cleared her again, we with much difficulty haled her along the dock, where, having fastened her and landed part of our passengers and secured all things, the rest of us went to sleep. The wind [was] at [the] south-west, and clear weather.

On Saturday we haled close to the wharf (for we could not get close last night, the tide being too low), and landed our wood which was a cord and three quarters. Then, having some barrels upon deck, we went to lower them into the hold; and they laying upon the side next to the dock, when we took them off, she listed off, and broke the down haul of the jib (which was made fast) off, and stove a barrel of flour and a barrel of meat, and broke a cheese. But having lighted her again and put things in order, by this time it was night. The wind [was] west by north, and clear weather.

On Sunday, the 17th [of] November, at night [there] came to town two of the passengers we left behind. This day [there was] all good weather.

On Monday we landed some leather and cheese—we then being got onto Conches' Dock. The weather [was] clear.

On Wednesday we took on board four pipes of cider. In taking them on we split one of the tackle blocks and were put to much trouble to get them in.

Also we took on board eight barrels and two crates and other goods. At night, by candle light, we spliced the down haul of the jib, intending to sail at 4 o'clock the next morning—for then the tide did serve, and the down wind [was] at [the] south, [and] fair and good weather. On Thursday by 2 o'clock in the morning we got all things in order for to sail and got water on board. But there being four vessels of us, all desiring to sail together, and [since we] had appointed to call upon one another, and we trusting to that, [we] went to sleep. They all went away without calling upon us; so when we awoke our vessel was aground and we could not go [on] that tide though the wind was fair. When we floated again we came to sail, the wind [being] at east by north, and rain. By the time that we got down to the narrows the wind was got to [the] north-east and the tide of ebb was made for us. Then we had a debate among us [as to] whether we should come to an anchor there and stay until better weather or stand along. But at length we concluded to stand along and see it out, but the fog was so thick that we were obliged to steer by the compass; and in crossing the bay the cask shifted in the hold, the seas being so rough—likewise our main sail gave way out of the bolt rope, the wind being so hard. However, after some time we made Sandy Hook. We then being within, we made for Permy City Cove; but in going in we ground upon the point of the cove. But having a fresh breeze we rubbed over. But being desirous to get as far in as we could, we went to put her in stays, but she misstayed several times. Then we wore her; but with misstaying so often, we were got so near the shoal that in wearing she struck, but rubbed over. Then we found the wind so hard that it was impossible to bring her to stays [and] we came to an anchor in the mouth of the cove. So, having put things in order, we went and kindled a fire and warmed ourselves. There being but two passengers, we went to sleep. The wind [was] still at [the] north-east, and [there was] rain and cold, uncomfortable weather. On Friday morning [we] went to mending the main-sail, but for want of a needle we were obliged to make one [out] of an old fork, [with] which we made holes through the sail, and put the twine through, and so around the bolt rope. So, having mended some parts and hooped the others by taking a reef, we came to sail [with] the wind at [the] north-west. And in three trips we got around the point of the rock. The wind then being fair, we in a little time got on the river; but just as we came to Black Point —the wind being contrary there—we got around and were obliged to carry out an anchor before we could get her off. But having got her afloat . . . [The remainder of this document has been lost.]

44

The Forms and Uses of Wildlife

The wildlife of the New World was, understandably, of great interest both to the settlers themselves and to many people who followed the process of colonization from overseas. Nearly all reports from those on the scene contained some account of flora and fauna, and as time passed the whole subject evoked an increasingly scientific curiosity. For the most part the colonists seem to have maintained a fairly balanced posture toward the "beasts" around them: there is little fear, and not much fantasy, in any of their comments on wildlife. Indeed, most such comments display a spirit of calculating utilitarianism. Usually the central question was: what useful purposes can these animals, or their carcasses, be made to serve? From the standpoint of results, this was an attitude fully as exploitative and wasteful as the corresponding attitude of many settlers toward the land.

John Lawson's book, *A New Voyage to Carolina*, is the source of the following document. Lawson was born and educated in England, and came to America as a young man in the year 1700. Soon after his arrival (in North Carolina) he was assigned important work as a surveyor and boundary commissioner. He also acquired land of his own in several different locations and helped to found the towns of Bath and New Bern. His book was, therefore, based on extensive personal experience. First published in London in 1709 and reprinted many times thereafter, it remains today one of the best descriptive accounts of the southern colonies in the early eighteenth century.

The Beasts of Carolina

(1709)

John Lawson

The Beasts of Carolina are the:

Buffalo, or wild Beef	Water Rat
Bear	Rabbit, two sorts
Panther	Elks
Cat-a-mount	Stags
Wild Cat	Fallow Deer
Wolf	Squirrel, four sorts
Tiger	Fox
Polecat	Lion, and Jackel on the lake
Otter	Rats, two sorts
Beaver	Mice, two sorts
Muskrat	Moles
Possum	Weasel, Dormouse
Raccoon	Bearmouse
Minx	

The buffalo is a wild beast of America, which has a bunch on his back, as the cattle of St. Lawrence are said to have. He seldom appears amongst the English inhabitants, his chief haunt being in the land of Mississippi, which is, for the most part, a plain country; yet I have known some killed on the hilly part of Cape Fair River, they passing the ledges of vast mountains from the said Mississippi before they can come near us. I have eaten of their meat, but do not think it so good as our beef; yet the younger calves are cried up for excellent food, as very likely they may be. It is conjectured that these buffalos, mixed in breed with our tame cattle, would much better the breed for largeness and milk which seems very probable. Of the wild bull's skin, buff is made. The Indians cut the skins into quarters for the ease of their transportation, and make beds to lie on. They spin the hair into garters, girdles, sashes, and the like, it being long and curled and often of a chestnut or red color. These monsters are found to weigh (as I am informed by a traveler of credit) from 1600 to 2400 weight.

John Lawson, *A History of Carolina* (London, 1714), pp. 118–130.

The bears here are very common, though not so large as in Greenland and the more northern countries of Russia. The flesh of this beast is very good and nourishing and not inferior to the best pork in taste. It stands betwixt beef and pork, and the young cubs are a dish for the greatest epicure living. I prefer their flesh before any beef, veal, pork or mutton; and they look as well as they eat, their fat being as white as snow and the sweetest of any creature's in the world. If a man drink a quart thereof melted, it will never rise in his stomach. We prefer it above all things to fry fish and other things in. Those that are strangers to it may judge otherwise; but I who have eaten a great deal of bear's flesh in my lifetime (since my being an inhabitant in America) do think it equalizes, if not excels, any meat I ever ate in Europe. The bacon made thereof is extraordinary meat; but it must be well saved, otherwise it will rust. This creature feeds upon all sorts of wild fruits. When herrings run, which is in March, the flesh of such of those bears as eat thereof is nought all that season and eats filthily. Neither is it good, when he feeds on gumberries, as I intimated before. They are great devourers of acorns, and oftentimes meet the swine in the woods, which they kill and eat, especially when they are hungry and can find no other food. Now and then they get into the fields of Indian corn or maize, where they make a sad havoc, spoiling ten times as much as they eat. The potatoes of this country are so agreeable to them that they never fail to sweep 'em all clean, if they chance to come in their way. They are seemingly a very clumsy creature, yet are very nimble in running up trees and traversing every limb thereof. When they come down they run tail foremost. At catching of herrings they are most expert fishers. They sit by the creeksides (which are very narrow) where the fish run in; and there they take them up, as fast as it's possible they can dip their paws into the water. There is one thing more to be considered of this creature, which is that no man, either Christian or Indian, has ever killed a she-bear with young.

It is supposed that the she-bears, after conception, hide themselves in some secret and undiscoverable place till they bring forth their young, which in all probability cannot be long; otherwise the Indians, who hunt the woods like dogs, would at some time or other have found them out. Bear hunting is a great sport in America, both with the English and Indians. Some years ago there were killed five hundred bears in two counties of Virginia in one winter, and but two she-bears amongst them all, which were not with young, as I told you of the rest. The English have a breed of dogs fit for this sport, about the size of farmers' curs, and [which] by practice come to know the scent of a bear—which, as soon as they have found, they run him by the nose till they come up with him, and then bark and snap at him till he trees, when the huntsman shoots him out of the trees, there being for the most part two or three with guns, lest the first should miss or not quite kill him. Though they are not naturally voracious, yet they are very fierce when wounded. The dogs often bring him to a bay, when wounded, and then the huntsmen make other shots, perhaps with the pistols that are stuck in their girdles. If a dog is apt to fasten and run into a bear, he is not good, for the best dog in Europe is nothing in their paws; but if ever they get him in their clutches, they blow his skin from his flesh like a bladder and often kill him; or if he recovers [from] it, he is never good for anything after that. As the paws of this creature are held for the best bit about him, so is the head esteemed the worst and always thrown away, for what reason I know not. I believe none ever made trial thereof, to know how it eats. The oil of the bear is very sovereign for strains, aches, and old pains. The fine fur at the bottom of the belly is used for making hats, in some places. The fur itself is fit for several uses, as for making muffs, facing caps, and etc.; but the black cubskin is preferable to all sorts of that kind for muffs. Its grain is like hogskin.

The panther is of the cat's kind—about the height of a very large greyhound of a reddish color, the same as a lion. He climbs trees with the greatest agility imaginable, is very strong-limbed, catching a piece of meat from any creature he strikes at. His tail is exceeding long; his eyes look very fierce and lively, are large, and of a grayish color; his prey is swine's flesh, deer, or anything he can take; no creature is so nice and clean as this in his food. When he has got his prey, he fills his belly with the slaughter and carefully lays up the remainder, covering it very neatly with leaves, which, if anything touches, he never eats any more of it. He purrs as cats do; if taken when young, [he] is never to be reclaimed from his wild nature. He hallos like a man in the woods, when killed, which is by making him take [to] a tree, as the least cur will presently do; the huntsmen shoot him. If they do not kill him outright, he is a dangerous enemy when wounded, especially to the dogs that approach him. This beast is the greatest enemy to the planter of any vermin in Carolina. His flesh looks as well as any shambles-meat whatsoever; a great many people eat him as choice food; but I have never tasted panther, so [I] cannot commend the meat by my own experience. His skin is a warm covering for the Indians in winter, though not esteemed amongst the choice furs. This skin [when] dressed makes fine women's shoes or men's gloves.

The mountain cat, so called because he lives in the mountainous parts of America is a beast of prey, as the panther is, and nearest to him in bigness and nature.

This cat [wildcat] is quite different from those in Europe, being more nimble and fierce and larger; his tail does not exceed four inches. He makes a very odd sort of cry in the woods in the night. He is spotted as the leopard is, though some of them are not (which may happen when their furs are out of season). He climbs a tree very dexterously, and preys as the panther does. He is a great destroyer of young swine. I knew an island which was possessed by these vermin, unknown to the planter —who put thereon a considerable stock of swine, but never took one back, for the wild cats destroyed them all. He takes most of his prey by surprise, getting up the trees which they pass by or under, and thence leaping directly upon them. Thus he takes deer (which he cannot catch by running) and fastens his teeth into their shoulders and sucks them. They run with him till they fall down for want of strength and become a prey to the enemy. Hares, birds, and all he meets that he can conquer, he destroys. The fur is approved to wear as a stomacher, for weak and cold stomachs. They are likewise used to line muffs and coats withal in cold climates.

The wolf of Carolina is the dog of the woods. The Indians had no other curs, before the Christians came amongst them. They are made domestic. When wild they are neither so large nor fierce as the European wolf. They are not manslayers; neither is any creature in Carolina unless wounded. They go in great droves in the night to hunt deer, which they do as well as the best pack of hounds. Nay, one of these will hunt down a deer. They are often so poor that they can hardly run. When they catch no prey, they go to a swamp and fill their belly full of mud; if afterwards they chance to get anything of flesh, they will disgorge the mud and eat the other. When they hunt in the night [in such a way] that there is a great many together, they make the most hideous and frightful noise that ever was heard. The fur makes good muffs. The skin [when] dressed to a parchment makes the best drum heads, and if tanned makes the best sort of shoes for the summer countries.

Tigers are never met withal in the settlement, but are more to the westward, and are not numerous on this side [of] the chain of mountains. I once saw one that was larger than a panther and seemed to be a very bold creature. The Indians that hunt in those quarters say they are seldom met withal. It seems to differ from the tiger of Asia or Africa.

Polecats or skunks in America are different from those in Europe. They are thicker and of a great many colors—not all alike, but each differing from another in the particular color. They smell like a fox, but ten times stronger. When a dog encounters them they piss upon them, and he will not be sweet again in a fortnight or more. The Indians love to eat their flesh, which has no manner of ill smell when the bladder is out. I know no use their furs are put to. They are easily brought up tame.

There have been seen some otters from the westward of Carolina, which were of a white color, a little inclining to yellow. They live on the same prey here as in Europe and are the same in all other respects; so I shall insist no further on that creature. Their furs, if black, are valuable.

Beavers are very numerous in Carolina, there being abundance of their dams in all parts of the country where I have traveled. They are the most industrious and greatest artificers (in building their dams and houses) of any four-footed creatures in the world. Their food is chiefly the barks of trees and shrubs, viz. sassafras, ash, sweet-gum, and several others. If you take them young they become very tame and domestic, but are very mischievous in spoiling orchards by breaking the trees and blocking up your doors in the night with the sticks and wood they bring thither. If they eat anything that is salt it kills them. Their flesh is a sweet food —especially their tail, which is held very dainty. Their forefeet are open like a dog's, their hindfeet webbed like a water fowl's. The skins are good furs for several uses, which every one knows. The leather is very thick; I have known shoes made thereof in Carolina which lasted well. It makes the best hedger's mittens that can be used.

Muskrats frequent fresh streams and no other, as the beaver does. He has a cod of musk, which is valuable, as is likewise his fur.

The possum is found nowhere but in America. He is the wonder of all the land animals, being the size of a badger and near that color. The male's pizzle is placed retrograde; and in time of coition they differ from other animals, turning tail to tail, as dog and bitch when tied. The female doubtless breeds her young at her teats; for I have seen them stick fast thereto when they have been no bigger than a small raspberry and seemingly inanimate. She has a paunch, or false belly, wherein she carries her young after they are [removed] from those teats till they can shift for themselves. Their food is roots, poultry, or wild fruits. They have no hair on their tails, but a sort of a scale or hard crust, as the beavers have. If a cat has nine lives, this creature surely has nineteen; for if you break every bone in their skin and mash their skull, leaving them for dead, you may come an hour after and they will be gone quite away, or perhaps you meet them creeping away. They are a very stupid creature, utterly neglecting their safety. They are most like rats of anything. I have for necessity in the wilderness eaten of them. Their flesh is very white and well tasted; but their ugly tails put me out of conceit with that fare. They climb trees as raccoons do. Their fur is not esteemed or used, save that the Indians spin it into girdles and garters.

The raccoon is of a dark gray color. If taken young [he] is easily made tame, but is the drunkenest creature living if he can get any liquor that is sweet and strong. They are rather more unlucky than a monkey. When wild they are very subtle in catching their prey. Those that live in the salt water feed much on oysters which they love. They watch the oyster when it opens and nimbly put in their paw and pluck out the fish. Sometimes the oyster shuts and holds fast their paw till the tide comes in, [so] that they are drowned, though they swim very well. The way that this animal catches crabs, which he greatly admires and which are plenty in Carolina, is worthy of remark. When he intends to make a prey of these fish he goes to a marsh, where, standing on the land, he lets his tail hang in the water. This the crab takes for a bait and fastens his claws therein—which, as soon as the raccoon perceives, he of a sudden springs forward a considerable way on the land and brings the crab along with him. As soon as the fish finds himself out of his element he presently lets go his hold; and then the raccoon encounters him, by getting him crosswise in his mouth, and devours him. There is a sort of small land crab, which we call a fiddler, that runs into a hole when anything pursues him. This crab the raccoon takes by putting his forefoot in the hole and pulling him out. With a tame raccoon this sport is very diverting. The chief of his other food is all sorts of wild fruits, green corn, and such as the bear delights in. This and the possum are much of a bigness. The fur makes good hats and linings. The skin [when] dressed makes fine women's shoes.

The minx is an animal much like the English fillimart or polecat. He is long, slender, and [in] every way shaped like him. His haunts are chiefly in the marshes, by the seaside and salt water, where he lives on fish, fowl, mice, and insects. They are bold thieves and will steal anything from you in the night, when asleep, as I can tell by experience; for one winter by misfortune I ran my vessel aground and went often to the banks to kill wild fowl (which we did a great many). One night we had a mind to sleep on the banks (the weather being fair) and wrapped up the geese which we had killed and not eaten very carefully in the sail of a canoe, and folded it [in] several doubles, and for their better security laid 'em all night under my head. In the morning when I waked a minx had eaten through every fold of the canoe's sail and through one of the geese, most part of which was gone. These are likewise found high up in the rivers, in whose sides they live—which is known by the abundance of fresh water mussel shells (such as you have in England) that lie at the mouth of their holes. This [creature] is an enemy to the tortoise, whose holes in the sand, where they hide their eggs, the minx finds out and scratches up and eats. The raccoons and crows do the same. The minx may be made domestic; and were it not for his paying a visit now and then to the poultry, they are the greatest destroyers of rats and mice that are in the world. Their skins, if good of that kind, are valuable, provided they are killed in season.

The water rat is found here the same as in England. The water snakes are often found to have [some] of these rats in their bellies.

That which the people of Carolina call a hare is nothing but a hedgeconey. They never burrow in the ground but much frequent marshes and meadowland. They hide their young in some place secure from the discovery of the buck, as the European rabbits do, and are of the same color; but if you start one of them and pursue her, she takes into a hollow tree and there runs up as far as she can, in which case the hunter makes a fire and smokes the tree, which brings her down and smothers her. At one time of the year great bots or maggots breed betwixt the skin and the flesh of these creatures. They eat just as the English ones do;

but I never saw one of them fat. We fire the marshes and then kill abundance [of them].

The English or European coneys are here found, though but in one place that I ever knew of—which was in Trent River where they burrowed among the rocks. I cannot believe [that] these are natives of the country, any otherwise than that they might come from aboard some wreck— the sea not being far off. I was told of several that were upon Bodies Island by Roanoke, which came from that ship of Bodies; but I never saw any. However, the banks are no proper abode of safety because of the many minxes in those quarters. I carried over some of the tame sort from England to South Carolina, which bred three times going over, we having a long passage. I turned them loose in a plantation, and the young ones and some of the old ones bred great maggots in their testicles. At last the great gust in September, 1700, brought a great deal of rain and drowned them all in their holes. I intend to make a second trial of them in North Carolina, and doubt not but to secure them.

The elk is a monster of the venison sort. His skin is used almost in the same nature as the buffalo's. Some take him for the red deer of America; but he is not. For, if brought and kept in company with one of that sort of the contrary sex, he will never couple. His flesh is not so sweet as the lesser deers. His horns exceed (in weight) all creatures which the New World affords. They will often resort and feed with the buffalo, delighting in the same range as they do.

The stags of Carolina are lodged in the mountains. They are not so large as in Europe, but [are] much larger than any fallow deer. They are always fat, I believe, with some delicate herbage that grows on the hills; for we find all creatures that graze much fatter and better meat on the hills than those in the valleys—I mean towards and near the sea. Some deer on these mountains afford the Occidental Bezoar, not coming from a goat as some report. What sort of beast affords the Oriental Bezoar I know not. The tallow of the harts make incomparable candles. Their horns and hides are of the same value as others of their kind.

Fallow deer in Carolina are taller and longer-legged than in Europe, but neither run so fast nor are so well-haunched. Their singles are much longer, and their horns stand forward, as the others incline backward;

neither do they beam, or bear their antlers, as the English deer do. Towards the salts they are not generally so fat and good meat as on the
hills. I have known some killed on the salts in January that have had
abundance of bots in their throat, which keep them very poor. As the
summer approaches these bots come out and turn into the finest butterfly
imaginable, being very large and having black, white, and yellow stripes.
Deerskins are one of the best commodities Carolina affords to ship off
for England, provided they be large.

Of squirrels we have four sorts. The first is the fox-squirrel, so called
because of his large size, which is the bigness of a rabbit of two or
three months old. His color is commonly gray; yet I have seen several
pied ones, and some reddish and black. His chiefest haunts are in the
piney land, where the almond pine grows. There he provides his winter
store—they being a nut that never fails of bearing. He may be made
tame, and is very good meat when killed.

The next sort of squirrel [the small gray squirrel] is much of the nature
of the English, only differing in color. Their food is nuts (of all sorts
[that] the country affords) and acorns. They eat well; and like the bear
[they] are never found with young.

This squirrel [the flying squirrel] is gray, as well as the others. He is
the least of the three. His food is much the same with the small gray
squirrels. He has not wings, as birds or bats have, there being a fine
thin skin covered with hair, as the rest of the parts are. This is from
the forefeet to the hinderfeet, which is extended and holds so much air
as buoys him up from one tree to another, that are greater distances
asunder than other squirrels can reach by jumping or springing. He is
made very tame, is an enemy to a cornfield (as all squirrels are), and
eats only the germinating eye of that grain which is very sweet.

Ground squirrels are so called because they never delight in running up
trees and leaping from tree to tree. They are the smallest of all squirrels.
Their tail is neither so long nor bushy, but [is] flattish. They are of a
reddish color and [are] striped down each side with black rows, which
make them very beautiful. They may be kept tame in a little box with
cotton. They and the flying squirrels seldom stir out in cold weather,
being tender animals.

The fox of Carolina is gray, but smells not as the foxes in Great Britain and elsewhere. They have reddish hair about their ears and are generally very fat; yet I never saw anyone eat them. When hunted they make a sorry chase, because they run up trees when pursued. They are never to be made familiar and tame, as the raccoon is. Their furs, if in season, are used for muffs and other ornaments. They live chiefly on birds and fowls and such small prey.

Supposed lion and jackal: I have been informed by the Indians that on a lake of water towards the head of Neus River there haunts a creature, which frightens them all from hunting thereabouts. They say he is the color of a panther, but cannot run up trees; and that there abides with him a creature like an Englishman's dog, which runs faster than he can and gets his prey for him. They add that there is no other of that kind that ever they met withal, and that they have no other way to avoid him but by running up a tree. The certainty of this I cannot affirm by my own knowledge, yet they all agree in this story. As for lions, I never saw any in America; neither can I imagine how they should come there.

Of rats we have two sorts: the house rat, as in Europe; and the marsh rat, which differs very much from the other [in] being more hairy and has several other distinctions too long here to name.

Mice are the same here as those in England that belong to the house. There is the sort that poisons a cat as soon as she eats of them, which has sometimes happened. These mice resort not to houses.

The dormouse is the same as in England; and so is the weasel, which is very scarce.

The bat or rearmouse [is] the same as in England. The Indian children are much addicted to eat dirt, and so are some of the Christians. But roast a bat on a skewer, then pull the skin off and make the child that eats dirt eat the roasted rearmouse—and he will never eat dirt again. This is held as an infallible remedy. I have put this amongst the beasts, as partaking of both natures—of the bird and mouse kind.

45

Land Law:
Some New World Variants

The economy of colonial America seemed to some observers visibly distorted, at least when measured against traditional patterns in the Old World. Especially notable in this regard was the changed relationship between land and the labor of the people who worked it. The abundance of the one and the scarcity of the other exerted a profound influence on many aspects of the evolving culture.

Consider, for example, the matter of inheritance. In England a modified system of primogeniture had obtained for generations—both in custom and, for certain situations, in legal process as well. But in the colonies "partible inheritance" became increasingly prevalent. This meant equal bequests to each of a man's (male) children (though usually with an extra share reserved for the first-born). The New England colonies led the way here, and some of them made partible divisions the law in dealing with estates for which there was no will. In time, however, their system was challenged on the grounds of conflict with long-established statutory precedents in the mother country. The defense prepared by the Connecticut House of Representatives in 1727 details some of the historical and practical points at issue. It was sent, in the form of "instructions" to the colony's London agent, for eventual submission to Whitehall.

Tenure—the forms and conditions of land ownership—was another area of significant change. The "quitrent," a regular (though modest) yearly charge on land, was still familiar enough in seventeenth-century England, and some of the big investors in early America counted on it as a source of revenue. These expectations, however, were repeatedly frustrated. Many small farmers and frontiersmen simply would not pay the specified sums, or would avoid "quitrent land" in the first place. After all, the wilderness offered a range of alternative properties that would come entirely free of such "encumbrances." Some aspects of this situation are evident in a statement presented in about 1736 by one William Leeds in reference to land at Swimming River, New Jersey. It is all very personal, even petty, but for exactly this reason it conveys with particular vividness the truth of the New World experience.

Instructions to the Agent Jonathan Belcher, Esq., from the House of Representatives of Connecticut

(1727)

Sir: After you have presented an address to their Majesties and acquainted yourself with the state of our affairs by Mr. Drummer, and [after you] shall have obtained a reconsideration of that which affects us in the determination of His Majesty in Council, namely, the vacating [of] our law concerning intestate estates, the arguments which we have prepared for you are as follows:

1. Although it be said that no time occurs to the King, yet many corporations and courts are allowed to prescribe for their authorities. And it has been the uninterrupted practice of the people settled within the limits of Connecticut to make laws to govern themselves by, which now runs well nigh to an hundred years, as appears by all our ancient monuments and records. . . .

2. That this is a reasonable custom will appear if it be considered that in the first settlement of the country lands were the least valuable part of men's estates, and so should be much rather subject to a division than his chattels. Land was plenty and chattels scarce; so that without a division of the lands as well as chattels, very little could be assigned to any except the eldest son. And the land itself must have remained unoccupied, if it had not been divided. It was esteemed much in favor of creditors when they were not obliged to take lands in satisfaction of their debts (quote the law) and it remains so to this time. It was inhabitants and not land that was wanting; yea, it was common in dividing lands among the inhabitants to oblige them to hold the land they had once accepted, that they might bear the burden of the taxes and fencing. And much of our lands remain yet unsubdued, and must continue so without the assistance of the younger sons, which in reason can't be expected

Instructions to Jonathan Belcher, from the House of Representatives of Connecticut, December 19, 1727, in *Collections of the Connecticut Historical Society*, IV (Hartford, Conn., 1892), pp. 143–147.

if they have no part of the inheritance. For in this poor country, if the landlord lives, the tenant starves: few estates here will let for little more than for maintaining fences and paying taxes. By this custom of dividing inheritances, all were supplied with land to work upon, the land as well occupied as the number of hands would admit of, the people universally employed in husbandry. Thereby considerable quantities of provisions are raised; and from our stores the trading part of the Massachusetts and Rhode Island [colonies] are supplied, the fishermen are subsisted, and the most of the sugars in the West Indies are put in casks made of our staves. By this means our predecessors were enabled to furnish themselves with almost all their clothing, nails, and most other necessaries from their neighbors at Boston (who transport them from Great Britain), and so we do [to] this day. By means of this custom His Majesty's subjects are here increased, the younger brethren do not depart from us, but others are rather encouraged to settle among us; and it's manifest that New England does populate faster than the colonies where the land descends according to the rules of the common law. And such measures as will furnish with the best infantry does most prepare for the defense of a people settled in their enemy's country. If this custom be so ancient and so useful, *non est abolenda, sed privare debet communem legem.*

3. That this law should be favored and allowed of, appears from the inconveniences that will follow upon its being vacated.

In that, all the settlements of lands left intestate and all the alienations under such settlements will be overthrown thereby, by which means almost every man in the colony will be turned out of his house and land or some of his improvements. We are now arrived to the third, fourth, and fifth generation, and many families who proceeded from one stock are branched into twenty, forty, and it may be some sixty or more descendants; and by their sweat and toil and the labors of their fathers and grandfathers, the lands they now possess were reduced from a mere chaos, and a thing of little or no value, to be sufficient to subsist a numerous offspring. And now to be turned out of all by the eldest descendants from our great-grandfathers, who had nothing but a thing of nought in it, will be so far from the rules of equity and justice that we presume the common law will never put it upon us. Quarrels and lawsuits will abound when matters of fact shall be judged of by rules unknown to the transactors of them. Most of our lands will lie unoccupied. Multitudes will be undone and beggared when their lands are taken from them, not being brought up in manufactures but husbandry only. Creditors who have by their estates subsisted others whilst they have been making a spot of the earth habitable, which they could not have done without their assistance, and have died and not left wherewith to repay them, without the sale of some part of the debtors' lands, will be defrauded —if their lands descend by the common law and are not chargeable with the debts of the deceased.

The just designs and dependence of the deceased, to have their children provided for after their decease, by this law will be frustrated. And by plentiful evidence it might be made to appear that many, and not of the least estate, have declared they would not make any will because the law of the country was agreeable to their minds, and so died without making any other, but resigning what they had to the disposal of the said law.

And the further inconveniences on others, which the vacating [of] this law will have a tendency to, are too manifest. The abatement of our husbandry will abate the trade of the neighboring provinces, the fishery, etc., who have a considerable dependence on our husbandry, and the abatement of the fishery will affect the British trade.

The increase of His Majesty's subjects in this colony will be diminished. And as to the younger generation, necessity will require their being brought up to trades, or leave their country, and the promoting [of] manufactories here will not be favored in Great Britain.

And since there are innumerable instances in the laws of Great Britain, wherein things are allowed for the quiet of the commonwealth when the strict rules of justice would tend to the subversion and destruction of many men's estates, which from time to time they have enjoyed without contradiction, as in entailing, copyhold, cutting off entails, *et similia*: we pray that might apologize for us in this, if it appear within the same reason. . . .

Letter from William Leeds to ——— Cox

(New Jersey, circa 1736–1737)

I am informed by Captain Throckmorton as you threaten to sue me for some land I detain from you (as you say). Friend Cox, if you had in your possession any land, or a pig, or a lamb as I thought to be mine,

Letter from William Leeds to ——— Cox, Monmouth County, N.J., ca. 1736–1737, in John E. Stilwell, ed., *Historical and Genealogical Miscellany* (New York, 1914), III, pp. 448–449.

I should think it a Christian duty in me to come to you or to talk with you. When I did meet you and ask you your reasons of your detainer and give you my reasons, I had to demand. And I should think I was very unneighborly if I should keep a noise at 30 miles distance against you and never say nothing to you. It runs in my mind [that] your mother and I had some words, but she gave me but little room to make a reply. But, however, the good respect I have had for the Coxes dost something oblige me to give you some account of what I have heard, and know of the case; and that is as follows.

Richard Stout married a girl in Shrewsbury and settled there, and his father lived in Middletown; and passing and repassing from one to the other he took a liking to some land at Swimming River. The general surveyor then being measuring land thereabouts to the people, Stout got him to measure him a piece [on] the first [of] June, 1676, in order to settle it; but Stout's wife would not go so far unless he would get a neighbor to go with her. Stout goes down [to] the town of Shrewsbury to Thomas Wright and proposes to let him have half of it if he liked it. Wright viewed it and liked it and agreed to give Stout a cow and calf for the half, and went to Samuel Leonard at the Falls to draw a writing, and it was signed [on] the twenty-second of the same June. The thirtieth of the same June Governor Cartwright and his council made Stout a title by patent under the broad seal of the province. In the fall the patent was sent to Stout from Elizabethtown. Then they went to Leonard to read it to them (for neither of them could read); and when Wright heard the words of the patent—that is, yielding and paying one-half penny yearly for every [one] of the said acres—Wright got in a passion. Stout then demanded the cow and offered him a deed, and Wright swore— godzooks, he would have nothing to do with land as payed quitrents, for they paid none in New England. This was done and acted above 60 years ago when I was a little child and could not know it, but I heard my father and the Leonards and Stout talk and laugh about it several times. About four or five years after the date of the patent Stout comes down [to] Shrewsbury to my father, and offered to sell him his land at Swimming River, and [they] agreed conditionally: if Wright would accept of one half, he was to give such a price, and if Wright would not, then such a price for the whole. My father looked on it and liked it, and he and Stout invited Wright to the Falls along with them in order to get deeds drawn for each half. And Stout then and there offered Wright a deed [for] the second time, upon the delivery of the cow and calf; and Wright refused to be further concerned because he would not pay quitrents. And so my father and Stout agreed for the whole and ordered the deed to be written. A little time after we came to Swimming River Thomas Wright and his wife died, and my father planted the land then as Wright had cleared. And Jaratt Wall was in a pucker—he would arrest my father for a trespass, ay, that he would. But Samuel Leonard met with him and showed him [that] it was [done] out of Stout's power to make a lawful title for any land at Swimming River [acquired] the twenty-second of June, 1676. Then he said he would [press charges] at Stout. "No," said Leonard, "you can't have him; for to my certain knowledge and several evidences more, Stout offered Wright a lawful deed for one half of that land, and Wright refused to accept because he would not be obliged to pay quitrents." And so Jaratt had done [with the matter], and we heard no more for several years. But at last it came in his head, as he said, that he would get the articles of agreement of writing acknowledged and recorded and so let it lie.

So, had you said [this] any time in thirty years before the Leonards were dead, we would have proved that Wright refused to accept of a deed and the delivery of a cow and calf, and that he was present in company when Stout sold the land to my father and [when] the deed [was] ordered to be writ for same, and [he] opposed not. After Richard Gardiner and the Leonards were dead, I got Richard Stout and Job Throckmorton before Justice Allen (about 20 years ago). Stout upon oath says that he did agree with Wright for the half of the land at Swimming River for a cow and calf, and [that] when the patent came he offered Wright a deed and demanded the cow and calf, and Wright refused both and said he would not be concerned with quitrent land. Throckmorton upon oath says his brother-in-law Samuel Leonard told him that Stout offered Wright a deed and urged him to take it, but Wright refused to take it and said he would not be concerned with it because it was quitrent land. These affidavits I think I have by me, and if you were at my house I would let you see them. Friend Cox, by these affidavits, and by all that I heard the Leonards say and Stout and my father say, the truth of the matter is [that] Wright got mad with the quitrents, and would not let Stout have the cow nor accept a lawful deed, and said he would not be concerned with it. So that I cannot see any wrong done, for Stout upon oath says Wright would not deliver the cow nor accept of a deed, and I have heard the Leonards and my father say the same several times. Stout made some pretence to buy the Indian right, but he did not [buy it] of the right owner; for my father was obliged to buy it of Ireeseek, Waquehela's father, and Stout allowed him for so doing. This [is] from one who desires to be your friend,

William Leeds

Part Seven
The Supernatural

46

Images of Another World

As every schoolchild knows, the colonists were extremely attentive to a variety of supernatural phenomena. Even as they went about the practical business of clearing land, raising crops, tending animals, and managing local and provincial governments, their thoughts turned repeatedly to an unseen realm—where, they felt, the ultimate questions of their lives would be decided. But to say that they were a religious people scarcely does justice to the importance of these matters. It was not simply that they worshiped God with an unquestioning devotion, or that they measured all their behavior against Christian ethical standards. It was, more particularly, their sense of the realness and immediacy of the whole "other world." Heaven and hell, angels and devils: such things were as real to them as the fields and the forest and the house next door.

Some of this comes through in the "commonplace book" kept by a young New Englander named Joseph Green. Green was born in Cambridge, Massachusetts, in 1675, was educated at Harvard, taught at the Roxbury Latin School, and became in time the minister at Salem Village. It was while working as a schoolmaster that he wrote out the following passages—part diary, part "instructions" for his students.

Extracts from the Commonplace Book of Joseph Green

(Massachusetts, 1696)

April 18, 1696. I have heretofore laid down some motives before you to engage you to be religious now in your younger days; and I have endeavored to instruct you in the principles of the Christian religion contained in the catechism—as far as what offices does Jesus Christ execute, etc.

From the Commonplace Book of Joseph Green, as published in *Publications of the Colonial Society of Massachusetts*, XXXIV (Boston, 1943), pp. 203–212. I am grateful to the Colonial Society of Massachusetts for permission to reprint from this document.

—and I intend to proceed. But because, as I have before told you, that all lies in the practicing of what we know, therefore I shall lay down a few more motives and directions to move you to do that which is well pleasing to God, and then I shall (*Deo volente*) *proceed*, etc.

1. Pray to God in secret; whatever you do, let not this be neglected. Remember your creator in the days of your youth; pray to God that He would pardon your sins for His Son Jesus Christ's sake. Pray to Jesus Christ to pardon you—He is as able now as He was when on the earth. And pray that He would save you from hellfire and from eternal misery. I am sure there is none of you that is willing to have your portion with Devils and [be] damned forever—oh, then be persuaded to pray in secret.

2. Read the Scriptures; labor to take delight in reading the Gospel of Jesus Christ.

3. Keep holy the sabbath day. Do not speak your own words, nor think your own thoughts on the sabbath; but spend the whole day in reading and praying and other holy duties.

4. Give good attention to the word preached, not only to remember something to tell me but [to] remember something for your souls and for eternity. Remember it is God that speaks to you by His servants.

5. Remember death; think much of death; think how it will be on a death bed—whether then you will not wish that you had prayed and done that [which] you know to be our duty.

6. Think much of the Day of Judgement, when every secret thing shall be discovered before the whole world. All secret sins shall [then] be discovered and shall be punished with eternal burnings; and then also all secret good duties shall be discovered and shall be rewarded with life eternal.

7. Think of eternity: the greatest thing that I would ask of you for all my pains is that every day you would think seriously of eternity. Think of those that are in hell that must abide under all the pain imaginable to eternity, and those that are in heaven [that] shall live in the greatest happiness with God forever.

Oh, then, be persuaded to be religious betimes: these are no trifling things, these are for eternity. Think, then, every day when you rise, and say to yourselves, "I may die before night," and then ask seriously, "if it should be so, where will my soul lodge throughout eternal ages?" And say every night when you go to bed, "If I should die before morning, where shall I live forever? Should I go down to eternal misery where there is nothing but weeping and wailing and blaspheming God's name forever? Or should I go to heaven to live with and to love and serve [God] unto all eternity?"

Be awakened then to set about your duty and secure your own souls by getting an interest in Jesus Christ. And once more I charge you in the fear of God to think of these things seriously, for know assuredly that God will call you to a strict account, not only for every sermon but also for every such opportunity as this. And [if] you be found despisers of Jesus Christ, He will give that sentence: "Depart, ye cursed, into everlasting fire prepared for the Devil and his angels." But if ye be found [among] those that fear Him and serve Him, He will at that day own you openly before the whole world, and will say to you: "Come, ye blessed of My Father, inherit a kingdom prepared for you before the foundation of the world."

April 25, 1696. I was sick of the toothache.

May 2, 1696. I come now to show you that Jesus Christ, the early redeemer of God's elect, did while on earth in His state of humiliation, and does also now in heaven, perform the offices of a prophet, of a priest, and of a king, in order to [bring about] our conversion, justification, sanctification, and eternal glorification.

As a prophet, Christ reveals to us what God would have us believe in order to [gain] our salvation. And it is Christ alone that teaches us this, the way to everlasting salvation; and this He does by sending His ministers, by His word, and by His spirit. Hereby, He effectually calls home all His elect, and builds them unto salvation. As a priest, Christ continually appears in the presence of God and presents before Him the infinite satisfaction of His perfect obedience in fulfilling the law and in dying for sinners, and He continually pleads that the benefits of His death may be applied to believers. And indeed if it were not for this intercession of Jesus Christ, the best performances of the best men would be rejected by God.

And as a king, Jesus Christ rules in the hearts of His elect; His kingly power is exercised in their conversion, and in defending them from all their enemies and temptations that they meet with. And although there are very few that did believe in Christ while He was on the earth, or do now believe Christ to be such a prophet, priest, and king as He is (I mean so as to obey Him), yet all the world shall know and be forced to own that He is God over all blessed forever, in that day when they shall call upon the rocks and unto the mountains to fall on them, when Jesus Christ shall be revealed from heaven in flames of fire, taking vengeance on them that know not God and that obey not His Gospel. But of this Day of Judgement I desire to discourse at large.

May 9, 1696. Among all the truths that are revealed in the scriptures there is none that is more plainly and clearly asserted than this, viz: that there will be a general Day of Judgement. There will certainly be a day when the Lord Jesus Christ Himself will appear with all His holy angels in the clouds of heaven to judge the whole world. And all the dead shall rise out of their graves and appear before Him; and then before the whole world every one shall give an account for all things done here in the flesh, and Christ Himself will give sentence to everyone according to what they have done in this life. Indeed when Jesus Christ humbled Himself in His first appearance, He showed His power in working miracles, and His knowledge in looking into men's hearts; and He showed his great wisdom in His doctrine, and His holiness in His exact walk and perfect obedience; and He wonderfully showed His goodness and mercy in all the infinite love and kindness He showed to the children of men and in all that He did for them. These excellencies shined at His first appearance, though it was but darkly, as being veiled; and indeed these are abundantly shining in Him now, especially His goodness and mercy, for He stands now and entreats sinners to be reconciled to God by Him; and He is really willing to save and accept of all that will forsake their sins and come to Him for forgiveness and salvation.

But at His second appearance, there [will] be no mercy to be obtained for them who in this life have neglected to get an interest in Him. He will then appear as a merciful saviour to them that love Him and fear Him; but to them that do not keep all His commandments He will appear as an angry judge and His eyes will look as flames of fire, and then poor sinners will call to the rocks and to the mountains to fall on them and to hide them from the wrath of the lamb, but all will be in vain.

Indeed to set forth the power and glory and splendor of Christ's second coming is beyond the skill of men or angels; but yet we have something revealed to us in the scriptures of the manner of it.

1. He shall [have] power in heaven and earth given to Him; there will then be no hiding from Him. All things will then obey Him, the grave shall give up her dead, and He shall then have power over men and devils. All good men that have served Him faithfully He will receive to eternal glory; but wicked men and devils shall be bound in chains under darkness for ever. He will then send wicked men and angels into that lake of fire and brimstone, which shall burn throughout eternal ages.

2. Christ Jesus will come in great glory; He will then be clothed with honor and glory, and there shall be ten thousand times ten thousand holy angels waiting on Him to do His will.

Now the angels are some in heaven and some on earth ministering to God's servants, but then they will be all gathered together into one innumerable company, there to attend on our blessed Lord Jesus.

Then the sun shall be darkened and the moon shall vanish, and the heaven and earth shall flee away before Him, and his brightness shall exceed the brightness of the sun, moon, and stars; and Christ shall come with a glorious and dreadful noise which will make wicked men and devils to quake and tremble, but it will make the hearts of good men to leap for joy.

Then the heavens shall roar, and there will be terrible thunderings and lightnings, and the earth shall be in flames of fire, and there shall be such a shout as shall awake the dead out of their graves. And all the men shall hear that voice [saying], "Arise, ye dead, and come to judgement;" and then the whole world shall ring and tremble. Surely this will startle all such and fill them with amazement.

3. The end of Christ's coming. And that will be to judge the whole world. Then He will raise the dead out of their graves, and the sea shall give up her dead, and the saints shall find their own bodies, and He will cause those that are in hell to come out; and they shall all be joined, soul and body, and so be prepared for the last judgement.

Then all nations shall be gathered together, and there will be an innumerable number of saints—but 1000 times as many wicked. The righteous shall stand at Christ's right hand, and the wicked at His left hand. There will then be no mistake: those that are God's children and servants shall every one be secured forever. And then, all nations being there gathered together, and the righteous being filled with unspeakable joy and the wicked with irrepressible horror, grief, and amazement, then the books shall be opened and the judgement shall be set. Then it shall be openly declared what every one's name was, and in what age and place they lived, and especially all men's actions shall openly be declared to the whole world. It will then be told what their carriage was to God and towards one another. It will then be known who prayed in secret and read the Scriptures, and who were obedient to their parents, and who were diligent to perform what they found to do. It will then be known who loved to pray and read and keep holy the Sabbath Day, and who made conscience to keep a strict watch over their thoughts, words, and actions, etc.

And then all the sinful actions of men will be made known. It will then be said [that] such a one did never pray, or if he did it was but seldom, and he did not take delight in praying and in reading the Scriptures, but it was a burden to them; [and] such were disobedient to parents; and such played on the Sabbath Day. And it shall be said [that] such a one did not give serious attention to the word preached, or were careless in family prayer, or in public worship.

And then it will be known to the world who were dishonest, intemperate, unclean; then all secret sins will be manifested, for God's eyes are as a flame of fire and He perfectly sees all the secret abominations which are unknown to men.

And these things will not only be declared by God Himself, but then conscience shall be as a thousand witnesses; and although men forget many sins which now they commit, yet at that day they shall all be remembered, and then a good conscience will be worth ten thousand worlds. For then wicked men shall be judged by the law and shall be condemned because they did not perform perfect obedience to the law, neither did they fly to Christ for salvation. But then the righteous shall be accepted through the intercession of Jesus Christ and shall be judged by the Gospel, and Christ Jesus who will then be judge will acquit them before the whole world, and then none shall be able to object anything against them.

Oh, then, be persuaded before it be too late—even now while the day of grace lasts—to set about it with all diligence and get your sins pardoned, and while Christ Jesus Himself is entreating you to come to God by Him. I say now give all diligence to get an interest in Him and in His righteousness, and then it shall go well with you in that day and forever.

May 16, 1696. I desire now to proceed in discoursing more particularly of the judgement of the righteous and of the wicked, that so you may be awakened to improve all the advantages you are entrusted withal to get into Christ Jesus and not be found among devils and damned spirits at the left hand of Christ at that day—but at His right hand with holy saints and angels.

The righteous shall be raised up in glory; those that now are (perhaps) despised in the world and want many good things, as Lazarus did, shall then in a moment be raised out of their graves with inexpressible pleasure. And then the holy angels shall meet them and bid them welcome, and then saints shall meet one with another and shall every one know one another. And then they shall all be caught up to meet the Lord in the air; then all the disciples and servants of Christ which never saw Him in the flesh shall meet Him with inexpressible delight and rejoicing; and

He will rejoice to see them and will place them at His right hand.

And Christ will take an account of them. Although I cannot say whether Christ will then mention the sins and infirmities of His servants, yet this I know: that if He does it will only be as so many sins that are pardoned, and so it will tend to the exaltation of the glory of Christ's blood and to the rejoicing of His redeemed. But doubtless He will take an account of their graces and virtues, and how they have improved all the endowments and talents and opportunities that He has privileged them withal. He will then take an account [of] what they have done for their fellow creatures in order to [bring about] their eternal salvation; and He will then take an account of all the injuries and affronts that they have met with for His name's sake. And all this shall be open before the whole world, and every one shall see and hear it; and Christ Jesus Himself will then proceed to give sentence to them, and they shall hear that blessed call, "Come, ye blessed of My Father, inherit a kingdom prepared for you before the foundation of the world."

Thus I have told you in short how it will fare with the righteous at that day; and I hope that you will every one of you be of that number at that day. And surely that thought of their blessedness is enough to stir you up to a care to secure to yourselves an interest in Christ, which alone will make you blessed.

For then all that are out of Him shall arise out of their graves, and their miserable souls shall come out of hell and they shall be reunited. But, oh, what an unhappy meeting will this be. Oh, what sighs and groans and cries will then be uttered by poor miserable sinners at that their doleful meeting. Oh, how will they be cast down to think that they are lost forever, and that they must lie in hell, soul and body, in extremity of pain unto all eternity. And then they shall meet with devils, which will torment and spit their malice in their faces, and will laugh them to scorn because they hearkened to them and suffered them to tempt them and lead them to eternal darkness. And then wicked men shall meet with one another, and shall look back upon their former sins with sorrow and shame, but then it will be too late.

And they shall look forward, and shall see nothing but an angry God and an endless eternity of misery and their company [with] devils and damned spirits forever. And then the wicked that shall be alive at the second appearance of Christ shall see all this, and it will be a surprise to them, for there shall not be more warning than now there is, but the world will be careless and unconcerned about it. It may be I shall be teaching and you be learning.

And suppose that now you should hear terrible thunderings and see heaven and earth in a flame, and should hear the words, "Come to judgement"—would your heart leap with joy within you, and could you with great comfort look back upon your past lives, or could you claim an interest in Christ? Or would your hearts sink within you for sorrow? Would you not then cry out for mercy and beg of God's children to take you up with them? But, alas, then it will be too late. Now you are called to repent and believe and love God, and to make conscience of praying and keeping holy the Sabbath Day, and to keep a strict watch over your thoughts, words, and actions, and to make it your business to be religious; and now Christ Jesus is abundantly willing to save you. But then all cares and tears will be too late, if now we neglect to get an interest in Him; then He will look with an angry countenance on them that have despised Him, and they shall be filled with confusion and shame, and in the meanwhile they [will] see the righteous on the right hand of Christ, and then they will be past all hopes of obtaining one smile from Christ or one jot of mercy unto eternity. But there poor sinners must stand trembling in expectation of their last judgement (the particular description whereof I shall leave until next time). Thus I have shown you what a blessed estate the righteous will be in, and what a miserable condition the wicked will be in at that day. And we shall every one of us stand naked before Christ's judgement seat, and therefore it highly concerns us to look to ourselves; for unless we get out of our natural estate and get an interest in Jesus Christ we shall be miserable forever. These are no trifling things, but they are of eternal concernment to every one of us; and if we that have the Gospel and the way to heaven made known to us should miscarry, it would have been better for us that we had never been born. Oh, then, think much of this day, and live every moment as if it were to be the last, and do not allow yourselves in any sin; for all, even the most secret sins, shall be laid open before the whole world, and the least sin deserves eternal wrath. And therefore break off all sin by a speedy and thorough repentance, lest God cut you off now in your younger days and never give you an opportunity to repent, or lest God give over striving with you—and so you be found at the left hand of Christ at the great day.

47

A Case of Diabolical Possession

The men and women of seventeenth-century America saw themselves as participants in a cosmic struggle between God and Satan (and their respective legions) for control of the universe. History was, from this perspective, a theater of unceasing warfare—grand in scale, terrifying in character, and fraught with the gravest consequences for all concerned. Much of this combat was unseen, of course, but from time to time it intruded unmistakably into the everyday course of human events. In most such cases the Devil would take the initiative, by conspiring to entrap certain vulnerable individuals into joining his cause.

"Diabolical possession" was the name given to some of these episodes. The basic format was fairly well standardized. A girl in her teens (or perhaps several such girls) would begin to experience "fits." Her friends and relatives would rally to her side. The local minister would arrange prayer meetings as a means to her cure and would question her repeatedly in order to discover the cause of her particular afflictions. A neighbor (usually an older woman) would be suspected of using witchcraft against the girl, presumably on orders from the Devil. The case might or might not go to the courts, and the accused might or might not be convicted. Indeed, the final outcome would be determined by a variety of different circumstances and pressures: no two episodes were identical in detail. Sometimes (as in the following narrative) human witches were eliminated from consideration, and the Devil himself was left as the sole culprit. But in every instance the *context* was as vast as the conflict between good and evil, and as particular as a specific village or neighborhood.

The "possession" of Elizabeth Knapp in the winter of 1671–1672 exemplified many aspects of the familiar pattern. Elizabeth was at the time sixteen years old, the daughter of an average yeoman of Groton, Massachusetts, and living temporarily as a servant in the home of the town pastor, Samuel Willard. It was Willard who wrote the extremely careful account of her condition reprinted below.

A Brief Account of a Strange and Unusual Providence of God Befallen to Elizabeth Knapp of Groton

(1672)

Samuel Willard

This poor and miserable object, about a fortnight before she was taken, we observed to carry herself in a strange and unwonted manner. Sometimes she would give sudden shrieks, and if we inquired a reason would always put it off with some excuse; and then [she] would burst forth into immoderate and extravagant laughter, in such ways as sometimes she fell onto the ground with it. I myself observed oftentimes a strange change in her countenance, but conceived she might be ill, and therefore diverse times inquired how she did, and she always answered well—which made me wonder.

But the tragedy began to unfold itself upon Monday, October 30, 1671, after this manner (as I received by credible information, being that day myself gone from home). In the evening a little before she went to bed, [while] sitting by the fire she cried out, "Oh, my legs!" and clapped her hand on them. Immediately [she cried], "Oh, my breast!" and removed her hands thither. And forthwith, "Oh, I am strangled," and put her hands on her throat. Those that observed her could not see what to make of it, whether she was in earnest or dissembled; and in this manner they left her (excepting the person that lay with her), complaining of her breath being stopped.

The next day she was in a strange frame (as was observed by diverse), sometimes weeping, sometimes laughing, and [making] many foolish and apish gestures. In the evening, going into the cellar, she shrieked suddenly; and being inquired of the cause, she answered that she saw two persons in the cellar; whereupon some went down with her to search, but found none—she also looking with them. At last she turned her head and, looking one way steadfastly, used the expression, "What cheer, old man?" (which they that were with her took for a fancy), and so ceased. Afterwards (the same evening), the rest of the family being in bed, she was (as one lying in the room saw, and she herself also afterwards related) suddenly thrown down into the midst of the floor with violence, and

Samuel Willard, "A brief account of a strange and unusual providence of God befallen to Elizabeth Knapp of Groton," in Samuel A. Green, *Groton in the Witchcraft Times* (Groton, Mass., 1883), pp. 7–21.

taken with a violent fit, whereupon the whole family was raised; and with much ado was she kept out of the fire from destroying herself. After which time she was followed with fits, from thence till the Sabbath Day, in which she was violent in bodily motions, leapings, strainings, and strange agitations, scarce to be held in bounds by the strength of three or four—violent also in roarings and screamings, representing a dark resemblance of hellish torments, and frequently using in these fits diverse words, sometimes crying out "money, money," sometimes "sin and misery," with other words.

On Wednesday [November 1], being in the time of intermission questioned about the case she was in with reference to the cause or occasion of it, she seemed to impeach one of the neighbors—a person (I doubt not) of sincere uprightness before God—as though either she, or the Devil in her likeness and habit, particularly her riding hood, had come down the chimney [and] stricken her that night [when] she was first taken violently, which was the occasion of her being cast into the floor. Whereupon those about her sent to request the person to come to her, who, coming unwittingly, was at the first assaulted by her strangely. For though her eyes were (as it were) sealed up (as they were always, or for the most part, in those fits, and so continue in them all to this day), she yet knew her very touch from any other, though no voice were uttered, and discovered it evidently by her gestures, so powerful were Satan's suggestions in her. Yet afterward God was pleased to vindicate the case and justify the innocent—even to remove jealousies from the spirits of the party concerned, and [to the] satisfaction of the bystanders. For after she had gone to prayer with her she confessed that she believed Satan had deluded her, and [she] hath never since complained of any such apparition or disturbance from the person.

These fits continuing (though with intermission), diverse [people], when they had opportunity, pressed upon her to declare what might be the true and real occasion of these amazing fits. She used many tergiversations and excuses, pretending she would [declare it] to this and that young person—who coming, she put it off to another—till at the last, on Thursday night [November 2], she broke forth into a large confession in the presence of many, the substance whereof amounted to thus much: that the Devil had oftentimes appeared to her, presenting the treaty of a covenant and proffering largely to her—viz. such things as suited her youthful fancy, [like] money, silks, fine clothes, ease from labor, to show her the whole world, etc.; that it had been then three years since his first appearance, occasioned by her discontent; that at first his apparitions had been more rare, but lately more frequent (yea, [during] those few weeks that she had dwelt with us almost constantly, [so] that she seldom went out of one room into another but he appeared to her, urging of her); and that he had presented her a book, written with blood, of covenants made by others with him, and told her such and such (of some whereof we hope better things) had a name there; that he urged upon her constant temptations to murder her parents, her neighbors, our children, especially the youngest—tempting her to throw it into the fire, on the hearth, into the oven; and that once he put a bill-hook into her hand to murder myself, persuading her I was asleep—but coming about it she met me on the stairs, at which she was affrighted. (The time I remember well, and observed a strange frame in her countenance and saw she endeavored to hide something, but I knew not what; neither did I at all suspect any such matter.) And [she also declared] that often he persuaded her to make away with herself, and once she was going to drown herself in the well, for, looking into it, she saw such sights as allured her, and was gotten within the curb, and was by God's providence prevented.

Many other like things she related, too tedious to recollect. But being pressed to declare whether she had not consented to a covenant with the Devil, she with solemn assertions denied it—yea, asserted that she had never so much as consented to discourse with him, nor had ever but once before that night used the expression, "what cheer, old man?" And this argument she used, that the providence of God had ordered it so that all his apparitions had been frightful to her. Yet this she acknowledged (which seemed contradictory), that when she came to our house to school, before such time as she dwelt with us, she delayed her going home in the evening till it was dark (which we observed), upon his persuasion to have his company home; and [she said] that she could not, when he appeared, but go to him.

One evident testimony whereof we can say something to [is the following], viz.: The night before the Thanksgiving, Oct. 19, she was with another maid that boarded in the house, where both of them saw the appearance of a man's head and shoulders, with a great white neckcloth, looking in at the window, at which they came up affrighted both into the chamber where the rest of us were. They declaring the case, one of us went down to see who it might be; but she ran immediately out of the door before him, which she hath since confessed was the Devil coming to her. She also acknowledged [that] the reason of her former sudden shriekings was from a sudden apparition, and that the Devil put these excuses into her mouth, and bit her, so to say, and hurried her into those violent (but she said feigned and forced) laughters. She then also complained against herself of many sins, disobedience to parents, neglect of attendance upon ordinances, attempts to murder herself and others; but this particular of a covenant she utterly disclaimed—which relation seemed fair, especially in that it was attended with bitter tears, self-condemnations, and good counsels given to all about her (especially the youth then present), and an earnest desire of prayers. She sent to Lancaster for Mr. Rowlandson, who came and prayed with her, and gave her serious counsels; but she was still followed, all this notwithstanding, with these fits.

And in this state (coming home on Friday) I found her, but could get nothing from her. Whenever I came in [her] presence she fell into those fits—concerning which fits I find this noteworthy, [that] she knew and understood what was spoken to her, but could not answer, nor use any other words but the aforementioned, "money," etc., as long as the fit continued. For when she came out of it, she could give a relation of all that had been spoken to her. She was demanded a reason why she used those words in her fits, and [she] signified that the Devil presented her with such things to tempt her, and with sin and misery to terrify her; she also declared that she had seen the devils in their hellish shapes, and more devils than anyone there ever saw men in the world. Many of these things I heard her declare on Saturday at night. On the Sabbath [November 5] the physician came, who judged a main part of her distemper to be natural, arising from the foulness of her stomach and corruptness of her blood, occasioning fumes in her brain and strange fantasies; whereupon (in order to [make] further trial and administration) she was removed home, and the succeeding week she took physic and was not in such violence handled in her fits as before, but enjoyed an intermission and gave some hopes of recovery; in which intermission she was altogether senseless (as to our discovery) of her state, held under security and hardness of heart, [and] professing [that] she had no trouble upon her spirits she cried [that] Satan had left her. A solemn day was kept with her, yet it had then (as I apprehend) little efficacy upon her. She that day again expressed hopes that the Devil had left her, but there was little ground to think so, because she remained under such extreme senselessness of her own estate.

And thus she continued—being exercised with some moderate fits, in which she used none of the former expressions, but sometimes fainted away, sometimes used some strugglings, yet not with extremity—till the Wednesday following [November 15], which day was spent in prayer with her, when her fits something more increased and her tongue was for many hours together drawn into a semicircle up to the roof of her mouth, and not to be removed (for some tried with the fingers to do it). From thence to the Sabbath seven nights following she continued alike. Only she added to former confessions [an account] of her twice consenting to travel with the Devil in her company between Groton and Lancaster, who accompanied her in [the] form of a black dog with eyes in his back, sometimes stopping her horse, sometimes leaping up behind, and keeping her (when she came home with company) 40 rods at least behind, leading her out of the way into a swamp, etc. But still no conference would she own, but urged that the Devil's quarrel with her was because she would not seal a covenant with him, and that this was the ground of her first being taken. Besides this nothing observable came from her; only one morning she said "God is a father," the next morning "God is my father"—which words (it is to be feared) were words of presumption put into her mouth by the adversary. I, suspecting the truth of her former story, pressed whether she never verbally promised to covenant with him, which she stoutly denied; [she] only acknowledged that she had had some thoughts so to do.

But on the forenamed Nov. 26 she was again with violence and extremity seized by her fits in such ways that six persons could hardly hold her; but she leaped and skipped about the house perforce, roaring and yelling extremely and fetching deadly sighs as if her heartstrings would have broken and looking with a frightful aspect, to the amazement and astonishment of all the beholders, of which I was an eye witness. The physician, being then again with her, consented that the distemper was diabolical, refused further to administer, [and] advised to extraordinary fasting; whereupon some of God's ministers were sent for. She meanwhile continued extremely tormented, night and day, till Tuesday about noon —having this added on Monday and Tuesday morning, that she barked like a dog and bleated like a calf, in which her organs were visibly made use of. Yea (as was carefully observed) on Monday night and Tuesday morning, whenever any [person] came near the house, though they within heard nothing at all, yet would she bark till they were come into the house.

On Tuesday [November 28], about 12 of the clock, she came out of the fit which had held her from Sabbath day about the same time [for] at least 48 hours with little or no intermission. And then her speech was restored to her, and she expressed a great seeming sense of her state. Many bitter tears, sighings, sobbings, complainings she uttered, bewailing of many sins aforementioned, begging prayers, and in the hour of prayer expressing much affection. I then pressed if there were anything behind in reference to the dealings between her and Satan, when she again professed that she had related all. And [she] declared that in those fits the Devil had assaulted her [in] many ways: that he came down the chimney and she essayed to escape him but was seized upon by him; that he sat upon her breast, and used many arguments with her; and that he urged her at one time with persuasions and promises of ease and great matters, told her that she had done enough in what she had already confessed, [that] she might henceforth serve him more securely—[and] anon told her [that] her time was past and there was no hope unless she would serve him. And it was observed in the time of her extremity, once when a little moment's respite was granted her of speech, [that] she advised us to make our peace with God and use our time better than she had done. The party advised her also to bethink herself of making her peace, [and] she replied, "It is too late for me."

The next day was solemnized, when we had the presence of Mr. Bulkley, Mr. Rowlandson, and Mr. Estabrook—whither coming, we found her returned to a sottish and stupid kind of frame. Much was pressed upon her, but no affection at all [was] discovered, though she was little or nothing exercised with any fits. And her speech also continued, though a day or two after she was melancholy—and being inquired of a reason, she complained that she was grieved that so much pains were taken with her, and did no good; but this held her not long. And thus she remained till Monday [December 4], when to some neighbors there present she related something more of her converse with the Devil, viz., that it had been five years or thereabouts since she first saw him. And [she] declared methodically the sundry apparitions from time to time till she was thus dreadfully assaulted, in which the principal [matter] was that after many assaults she had resolved to seal a covenant with Satan, thinking she had better do it than be thus followed by him. [She also declared] that once, when she lived at Lancaster, he presented himself and desired of her blood, and she would have done it but wanted a knife. In the parley she was prevented—by the providence of God interposing my father— a second time. In the house he met her and presented her with a knife; and as she was going about it my father stepped in again and prevented [it], [so] that when she sought and inquired for the knife it was not to be found. (And [she said] that afterward she saw it sticking in the top of the old barn, and some other like passages.) She again owned an observable passage which she also had confessed in her first declaration but is not there inserted, viz. that the Devil had often proffered her his service but she accepted not. And once in particular [he offered] to bring her in chips for the fire, [and] she refused; but when she came in she saw them lie by the fireside, and was afraid. And this I remark: I, sitting by the fire, spoke to her to lay them on, and she turned away in an unwonted manner. She then also declared against herself her unprofitable life she had led, and how justly God had thus permitted Satan to handle her, telling them [that] they little knew what a sad case she was in. I after[ward] asked her concerning these passages, and she owned the truth of them and declared that now she hoped the Devil had left her. But being pressed whether there were not a covenant, she earnestly professed that by God's goodness she had been prevented from doing that which she of herself had been ready enough to assent to; and she thanked God there was no such thing.

The same day she was again taken with a new kind of unwonted fit, in which, after she had been awhile exercised with violence, she got her a stick and went up and down, thrusting and pushing here and there, and anon looking out at a window, and cried out of a witch appearing in a strange manner in [the] form of a dog downward, with a woman's head. And [she] declared the person, other whiles that she appeared in her whole likeness, and described her shape and habit, [and] signified that she went up the chimney and went her way. What impression we read in the clay of the chimney, in [the] similitude of a dog's paw by the operation of Satan, and in the form of a dog's going in the same place she told of, I shall not conclude; though something there was, as I myself saw, in the chimney in the same place where she declared the foot was set to go up. In this manner was she handled that night and the two next days, using strange gestures, complaining by signs when she could not speak, explaining that she was sometimes in the chamber, sometimes in the chimney; and anon [she] assaults her, sometimes scratching her breast, beating her sides, strangling her throat, and she did oftentimes seem to our apprehension as if she would forthwith be strangled. She declared that if the party were apprehended she should forthwith be well, but never till then; whereupon her father went and procured the coming of the woman impeached by her, who came down to her on Thursday night [December 7], where (being desired to be present) I observed that she was violently handled and lamentably tormented by the adversary, and [that she] uttered unusual shrieks at the instant of the person's coming in, though her eyes were fast closed. But having experience of such former actings, we made nothing of it but waited the issue.

God therefore was sought to, to signify something where the innocent might be acquitted or the guilty discovered; and He answered our prayers, for by two evident and clear mistakes she was cleared, and then all prejudices ceased, and she never more to this day hath impeached her of any apparition. On the aforementioned allegation of the person she also signified that sometimes the Devil also, in the likeness of a little boy, appeared together with the person.

Friday was a sad day with her; for she was sorely handled with fits, which some perceiving pressed that there was something yet behind not discovered by her. And she (after a violent fit, holding her between two and three hours) did first to one, and afterwards to many, acknowledge that she had given of her blood to the Devil and made a covenant with him—whereupon I was sent for to [visit] her. And understanding how things had passed, I found that there was no room for privacy. In another, already made by her so public, I therefore examined her concerning the matter; and [I] found her not so forward to confess, as she had been to others, yet thus much I gathered from her confession: that after she came to dwell with us, one day as she was alone in a lower room, all the rest of us being in the chamber, she looked out at the window and saw the Devil in the habit of an old man coming over a great meadow lying near the house. And suspecting his design she had thoughts to have gone away, yet at length resolved to tarry it out and hear what he had to say to her. When he came he demanded of her some of her blood, which she forthwith consented to, and with a knife cut her finger. He caught the blood in his hand and then told her she must write her name in his book. She answered [that] she could not write; but he told her he would direct her hand and then took a little sharpened stick and dipped it in the blood and put it into her hand and guided it, and she wrote her name with his help.

What was the matter she set her hand to I could not learn from her; but thus much she confessed, that the term of time agreed upon with him was for seven years—one year she was to be faithful in his service, and then the other six he would serve her and make her a witch. She also related that the ground of contest between her and the Devil, which was the occasion of this sad providence, was this, that after her covenant [was] made the Devil showed her hell and the damned, and told her if she were not faithful to him she should go thither and be tormented there. She desired of him to show her heaven, but he told her that heaven was an ugly place, and that none went thither but a company of base rogues whom he hated; but if she would obey him, it should be well with her. But afterward she considered with herself that the term of her covenant was but short and would soon be at an end; and she doubted [not] (for all the Devil's promises) [that] she must at last come to the place he had shown her, and withal feared [that] if she were a witch she should be discovered and brought to a shameful end, which was many times a trouble on her spirits. This the Devil perceiving [he] urged upon her to give him more of her blood and set her hand again to his book, which she refused to do. But partly through promises, partly by threatenings, he brought her at last to a promise that she would sometime do it; after which he left not incessantly to urge her to the performance of it. Once he met her on the stairs, and often elsewhere, pressing her with vehemence; but she still put it off, till the first night she was taken, when the Devil came to her and told her he would not tarry any longer. She told him she would not do it; he answered she had done it already, and what further damage would it be to do it again, for she was his sure enough. She rejoined she had done it already, and if she were his sure enough, what need [had] he to desire any more of her; whereupon he struck her the first night, [and] again more violently the second, as is above expressed.

This is the sum of the relation I then had from her, which at that time seemed to be methodical. These things she uttered with great affection, overflowing of tears, and seeming bitterness. She complained of her sins, and some in particular (profanation of the Sabbath, etc.); but [she said] nothing of this sin of renouncing the government of God and giving herself up to the Devil. I therefore (as God helped) applied it to her and asked her whether she desired not prayers with and for her. She assented with earnestness and in prayer seemed to bewail the sin, as God helped, then in the aggravation of it; and [she] afterward declared a desire to rely on the power and mercy of God in Christ. She then also declared that the Devil had deceived her concerning those persons impeached by her, that he had in their likeness or resemblance tormented her, persuading her that it was they—that they bore her a spleen, but he loved her and would free her from them—and pressed on her to endeavor to bring them forth to the censure of the law. In this case I left her; but (not being satisfied in some things) I promised to visit her again the next day, which accordingly I did. But coming to her, I found her (though her speech still remained) in a case sad enough, her tears dried up and senses stupefied. And (as was observed) when I could get nothing from her and therefore applied myself in council to her, she regarded it not but fixed her eye steadfastly upon a place, as she was wont when the Devil presented himself to her, which was a grief to her parents and brought me to a stand. In this condition I left her.

The next day [December 10], being the Sabbath, whether upon any hint given her or any advantage Satan took by it upon her, she sent for me in haste at noon. Coming to her, she immediately with tears told me that she had belied the Devil in saying she had given him of her blood, etc., professed that the most of the apparitions she had spoken of were but fancies, as images represented in a dream, [and] earnestly entreated me to believe her. [She] called God to witness to her assertion. I told her I would willingly hope the best and believe what I had any good grounds to apprehend. If therefore she would tell a more methodical relation than the former, it would be well; but if otherwise, she must be content that everyone should censure according to their apprehension. She promised so to do and expressed a desire that all that would might hear her. [She declared] that as they had heard so many lies and untruths, they might now hear the truth, and engaged that in the evening she would do it. I then repaired to her, and diverse more then went. She then declared thus much: that the Devil had sometimes appeared to her; that the occasion of it was her discontent; that her condition displeased her, her labor was burdensome to her, [and] she was neither content to be at home nor abroad; and [that she] had oftentimes strong persuasions to practice in witchcraft, had often wished the Devil would come to her at such and such times, and [had] resolved that if he would she would give herself up to him soul and body. But though he had oft times appeared to her, yet at such times he had not discovered himself, and therefore she had been preserved from such a thing. I declared a suspicion of the truth of the relation and gave her some reasons; but by reason of the company [I] did not say much, neither could anything further be gotten from her.

But the next day I went to her and opened my mind to her alone and left it with her. [I] declared (among other things) that she had used preposterous courses, and therefore it was no marvel that she had been led into such contradictions; and [I] tendered her all the help I could, if she would make use of me and more privately relate any weighty and serious case of conscience to me. She promised me she would, if she knew anything; but [she] said that then she knew nothing at all, but stood to the story she had told the foregoing evening. And indeed what to make of these things I at present know not, but am waiting till God (if He sees meet) wind up the story and make a more clear discovery. It was not many days before she was hurried again into violent fits after a different manner, being taken again speechless, and using all endeavors to make away with herself and do mischief unto others—striking those that held her, [and] spitting in their faces. And if at any time she had done any harm or frightened them, she would laugh immediately; which fits held her sometimes longer, sometimes shorter. Few occasions she had of speech; but when she could speak she complained of a hard heart, counselled some to beware of sin for that had brought her to this, bewailed that so many prayers had been put up for her and [that] she [was] still so hard-hearted and no more good wrought upon her. But being asked whether she were willing to repent, [she] shaked her head and said nothing.

Thus she continued till the next Sabbath [December 17] in the afternoon; on which day, in the morning, being something better than at other times, she had but little company [who] tarried with her in the afternoon—when the Devil began to make more full discovery of himself. It had been a question before whether she might properly be called a demoniac, or person possessed of the Devil, but it was then put out of question. He began (as the persons with her testify) by drawing her tongue out of her mouth most frightfully to an extraordinary length and greatness, and [making] many amazing postures of her body. And then [he continued] by speaking vocally in her, whereupon her father and another neighbor were called from the meeting—on whom (as soon as they came in) he railed, calling them rogues, charging them for folly in going to hear a black rogue who told them nothing but a parcel of lies and deceived them, and many like expressions.

After exercise I was called, but understood not the occasion till I came and heard the same voice. A grum, low, yet audible voice it was. The first salutation I had was, "Oh! you are a great rogue." I was at first something daunted and amazed, and many reluctances I had upon my spirits, which brought me to a silence and amazement in my spirits, till at last God heard my groans and gave me both refreshment in Christ and courage. I then called for a light to see whether it might not appear a counterfeit, and [I] observed not any of her organs to move. The voice was hollow, as if it issued out of her throat. He then again called me a great black rogue. I challenged him to make it appear [so]; but all the answer was, "You tell the people a company of lies." I reflected on myself, and could not but magnify the goodness of God not to suffer Satan to bespatter the names of His people with those sins which He Himself hath pardoned in the blood of Christ. I answered, "Satan, thou art a liar and a deceiver, and God will vindicate His own truth one day." He answered nothing directly, but said, "I am not Satan; I am a pretty black boy [and] this is my pretty girl. I have been here a great while." I sat still and answered nothing to these expressions. But when he directed himself to me again —[saying] "Oh! you black rogue, I do not love you"—I replied, "Through God's grace I hate thee." He rejoined, "But you had better love me." These manner of expressions filled some of the company there present with great consternation. Others put on boldness to speak to him, at which I was displeased and advised them to see their call clear, fearing lest by his policy and [the] many apish expressions he used he might insinuate himself and raise in them a fearlessness of spirit of him. I no sooner turned my back to go to the fire but he called out again, "Where is that black rogue gone?"

I seeing little good to be done by discourse, and questioning many things in my mind concerning it, I desired the company to join in prayer unto God. When we went about that duty and were kneeled down, with a voice louder than before he cried out, "Hold your tongue, hold your tongue; get you gone, you black rogue; what are you going to do; you have nothing to do with me," etc. But through God's goodness he was silenced, and she lay quiet during the time of prayer; but as soon as it was ended [he] began afresh, using the former expressions—at which some ventured to speak to him, though I think imprudently. One told him [that] God had him in chains; he replied, "For all my chains, I can knock thee on the head when I please." He said he would carry her away that night, [and] another answered, "But God is stronger than thou." He presently rejoined, "That's a lie, I am stronger than God"—at which blasphemy I again advised them to be wary of speaking, counselled them to get serious persons to watch with her, and left her, commending her to God.

On Tuesday [December 19] following she confessed that the Devil entered into her the second night after her first taking, that when she was going to bed he entered in (as she conceived) at her mouth, and had been in her ever since, and professed that if there were ever a devil in the world there was one in her, but in what manner he spoke in her she could not tell. On Wednesday night [she said] she must forthwith be carried down to the Bay in all haste; she should never be well till an assembly of ministers was met together to pray with and for her, and in particular Mr. Cobbet. Her friends advised with me about it; I signified to them that I apprehended [that] Satan never made any good motion but it was out of season, and that it was not a thing now feasible, the season being then extremely cold, and the snow deep—that if she had been taken in the woods with her fits she must needs perish. On Friday [December 22] in the evening she was taken again violently, and then the former voice (for the sound) was heard in her again, not speaking but imitating the crowing of a cock, accompanied with many other gestures, some violent, some ridiculous, which occasioned my going to her, where by signs she signified that the Devil threatened to carry her away that night. God was again then sought for her. And when, in prayer, that expression was used that God had proved Satan a liar, in preserving her once when he had threatened to carry her away that night, and was entreated so to do again, the same voice which had ceased two days before was again heard by the bystanders five times distinctly to cry out, "Oh, you are a rogue," and then ceased. But the whole time of prayer, sometimes by violence of fits, sometimes by noises she made, she drowned her own hearing from receiving our petition, as she afterwards confessed.

Since that time she hath continued for the most part speechless, her fits coming upon her sometimes often, sometimes with greater intermission, and with great varieties in the manner of them, sometimes by violence, sometimes by making her sick, but (through God's goodness) so abated in violence that now one person can as well rule her as formerly four or five. She is observed always to fall into fits when any strangers go to visit her—and the more go, the more violent are her fits. As to the frame of her spirits, she hath been more averse lately to good counsel than heretofore; yet sometimes she signifies a desire of the company of ministers. On Thursday last [January 11, 1671–72], in the evening, she came [in] a season to her speech, and (as I received from them with her) again disowned a covenant with the Devil, disowned that relation about the knife aforementioned, declared the occasion of her fits to be discontent, owned the temptations to murder, [and] declared that though the Devil had power of her body she hoped he should not of her soul. [She also declared] that she had rather continue so speechless than have her speech and make no better use of it than formerly she had, expressed that she was sometimes disposed to do mischief (and [it] was as if some had laid hold of her to enforce her to it, and had double strength to her own), [and said] that she knew not whether the Devil were in her or no [and] if he were she knew not when or how he entered. [She declared further] that when she was taken speechless, she feared as if a string was tied about the roots of her tongue and reached down into her vitals and pulled her tongue down—and then most when she strove to speak. On Friday, in the evening, she was taken with a passion of weeping and sighing, which held her till late in the night. At length she sent for me, but the unreasonableness of the weather and my own bodily indisposition prevented [my going]. I went the next morning, when she strove to speak something but could not, but was taken with her fits—which held her as long as I tarried, which was more than an hour, and I left her in them.

And thus she continues speechless to this instant, Jan. 15, and followed with fits—concerning which state of hers I shall suspend my own judgement and willingly leave it to the censure of those that are more learned, aged, and judicious. Only I shall leave my thoughts in respect of two or three questions which have risen about her: viz.

(1.) Whether her distemper be real or counterfeit? I shall say no more to that but this: the great strength appearing in them, and great weakness after them, will disclaim the contrary opinion; for though a person may counterfeit much, yet such a strength is beyond the force of dissimulation.

(2.) Whether her distemper be natural or diabolical? I suppose the premises will strongly enough conclude the latter. Yet I will add these two further arguments: First, the actings of convulsion, which these [fits] come nearest to, are (as persons acquainted with them observe) in many —yea, the most essential—parts of them quite contrary to these actings. Second, she hath [in] no ways wasted in body or strength by all these fits, though [they are] so dreadful; but [she hath] gathered flesh exceedingly, and hath her natural strength when her fits are off, for the most part.

(3.) Whether the devil did really speak in her? To that point, which some have much doubted of, thus much I will say to countermand this apprehension. First, the manner of expression I diligently observed, and [I] could not perceive any organ, any instrument of speech (which the philosopher makes mention of) to have any motion at all. Yea, her mouth was sometimes shut without opening, sometimes open without shutting or moving; and then both I and others saw her tongue (as it used to be when she was in some fits, when speechless) turned up circularly to the roof of her mouth. Second, the labial letters, diverse of which were used by her, viz. B, M, P—which cannot be naturally expressed without motion of the lips [and] which must needs come within our ken if observed —were uttered without any such motion. If she had used only linguals, gutturals, etc., the matter might have been more suspicious. Third, the reviling terms then used were such as she never used before nor since in all this time of her being thus taken. Yea, [she] hath been always observed to speak respectfully concerning me. Fourth, they were expressions [with] which the Devil (by her confession) aspersed me and others withal, in the hour of temptation. Particularly, she had freely acknowledged that the Devil was wont to appear to her in the house of God, and divert her mind, and charge her [that] she should not give ear to what that black-coated rogue spoke. Fifth, we observed [that] when the voice spoke her throat was swelled formidably, as big at least as one's fist. These arguments I shall leave to the censure of the judicious.

(4.) Whether she have covenanted with the Devil or no? I think this is a case unanswerable. Her declarations have been so contradictory, one to another, that we know not what to make of them; and her condition is such as administers many doubts. Charity would hope the best, love would fear the worst, but thus much is clear: she is an object of pity, and I desire that all that hear of her would compassionate her forlorn state. She is (I question not) a subject of hope, and therefore all means ought to be used for her recovery. She is a monument of divine severity; and the Lord grant that all that see or hear may fear and tremble. Amen.

S.W.

48

Defense Against Evil

The colonists were not defenseless against witchcraft and other forms of malign power. A variety of magical objects and procedures served them—so they believed—as protection. Obscure chants and rhymes, amulets worn close to the body, horseshoes set over a doorway, bay leaves buried under a threshold: these would all, in their way, ward off evil.

And two more. The stone boundary marker pictured here still sits on the Massachusetts farmland where it was first set up in the mid-seventeenth century. Its startling, scarecrow-like figure conveyed a "keep-out" message to the spirit as well as the human world. Bearded-man jugs (so called) performed a similar combination of practical and magical function. Manufactured in Germany and shipped all over the Euro-American world, they were in frequent use as storage vessels. But they were also known as "witch bottles"; in that connection they could prevent—or, possibly, promote—supernatural evil. Examples unearthed in recent years have been found to contain human hair, urine, fingernails, and even a cloth heart pierced with pins.

Boundary Marker and "Bearded-Man Jug"

Boundary marker, Witchstone Farm, Byfield Parish, Newbury, Mass. Photograph by Dan Farber.

Bearded-man jug, made in Raeren, Germany, 1617, Museum of Fine Arts, Boston, bequest of George W. Wales. Used with permission.

49

An Astrological Almanac

Americans of the colonial era, like most of their contemporaries in Europe, watched the heavens for clues to their present and future experience. Astrology was for them a resource of much practical importance.

Celestial events of several kinds demanded notice. Some were singular in their timing and appearance: eclipses, comets, meteors. Others were entirely regular and recurrent: the phases of the moon, the positioning of the planets. *All* kinds were thought to hold significance for human, earthbound activity.

An ancient lore, rising in some respects to the level of science, spelled out particular meanings behind the recurrences and regularities. The roots of this lay far back in medieval, even classical, times. Passed down through the generations by both word of mouth and writing, it was carried to America as part of the larger cultural "baggage." There it coexisted, sometimes uneasily, with other forms of supernatural belief, including witchcraft, fortune telling, and prevalent Christian dogma.

This coexistence must not be missed: the intellectuals of the time —for example, the clergy—were no less astrology-minded than the "plain people." Indeed, the next document is drawn from the manuscript journal of Seaborn Cotton, a prominent Puritan "divine." Born in 1630 while his parents were en route to the New World—hence his given name—Cotton was raised in Boston, graduated from Harvard, and served a long ministry in the town of Hampton, New Hampshire. Other sections of the journal include sermon notes, parish records, business accounts, and love poems—all, together with astrology, within his everyday orbit of concern.

Actually, the writing on the "disposition" of the moon and planets is not in Cotton's own hand, but that of his wife. Its archaic diction, no less than its sometimes obscure content, betrays its remote and (to us) exotic provenance. No other selection in this volume is as difficult now to read and understand. And none underscores more sharply the distance between their world and our own.

The Nature and Disposition of the Moon,
in the Birth of Children
[Dorothy Cotton?]

In the first day, all things are profitable. And that [which] thou seest in thy sleep shall be well and turned into joy. If thou seemest to be overcome, nevertheless thou shalt overcome. A child that is born shall soon increase and be of long life and rich. He that falleth sick shall long wail and suffer a long sickness. It is good to let [a] little blood.

In the second day of the moon, whatsoever thou shall see in thy sleep, sudden effect shall it [have?], whether it be good or evil. To let blood is good. A child that is born soon shall wax, and he shall be a lecher [?], and if a woman [shall] prove a strumpet.

The third day of the moon, abstain from doing anything, [for] thou would not have it prosper. Theft done shall soon be found. Whatsoever thou seest in thy sleep, it is naught. The man-child shall grow for a time, but [shall] die young. The sick man that falleth in his bed shall travail, and not escape. To let blood is good.

The fourth day of the moon, whatsoever thou doest is good, in each travail. The dream [which] thou seest hath effect, [through?] hope in God and counsel good. A child that is born shall be a good creature [?] and much praised. A man that falleth sick either soon shall be healed, or soon shall die. It is good to let blood.

The fifth day of the moon, do nothing of errands or work. He that flyeth shall be taken or killed. The dream that thou shalt see shall be well. Beware that thou reject not counsel. A child that is born shall die young. He that falleth in his bed soon shall die. To let blood is good.

The sixth day of the moon: to send children to school is good. The dream thou shalt see shall not come to pass. But beware thou [should] say naught to any man, nor discover thy counsel. A child born shall be of long life, and sickly. A sick [illegible word] shall escape. To let blood is good.

In the seventh day of the moon, he that falleth sick shall die. He that is born shall be of long life. It is good to let blood and take drink. A dream that thou seest long after shall be [fulfilled?]. Who that flyeth long after shall be found. A sick man, if he be medicined, he shall be healed.

From Seaborn Cotton's Journal, ms. original in the New England Historic Genealogical Society, Boston. Used with permission.

440

And in the eighth day of the moon, whatsoever thou will do is good, all things that thou will treat of: to go in counsel, to buy manciples and beasts, to lay foundations, to sow seeds. A child that is born shall be sick and die young, but if he live he shall be a purchaser. A dream shall be certain and soon shall be [fulfilled]. If thou seest sorry things, turn them to the east. Though an old man wax sick, he shall live. Theft shall be found.

In the ninth day of the [moon], to do all things is profitable. What [ever] thing thou wilt enterprise shall come to good effect. A dream that thou seest shall come [to pass] in the day following or in the second day, and thou shalt see signs in the east. And that [which] shall appear in thy sleep openly within eleven days shall come to pass. A child born in all things shall be a purchaser and good and of long life. A sick man shall wail much and arise. Who[ever] shall be chased [shall] not be found. And who that is oppressed shall be comforted. Let not blood.

In the tenth day of the moon, whatsoever thou wilt do shall pertain to light. Dreams are in vain, and within four days shall come without [illegible word]. A child that is born shall see many countries and die old. Whatsoever is done shall be hid. Whosoever is bound shall be unbound. Who that flyeth after shall be found. Who that falleth in travail without peril shall be delivered. Who that falleth sick in his bed shall long abide. To let blood is good.

The eleventh day of the moon: it is good to begin works, to journey, to make a wedding. A dream within four days shall be fulfilled without peril. A child that is born shall be of long life and religious; and he shall have a sign [illegible word] in the forehead or in the mouth or in the eye, and in the later age he shall be made better. A wench shall have a sign that she shall be learned with wisdom. He that is sick, be he long sick, shall be healed. Each day to [let?] blood is good.

In the twelfth day of the moon, nothing shall begin, for it is a grievous day. And a dream shall be certain and joy to thee after[ward]. That [which] thou seest within two days shall be fulfilled. To wed and to do errands is profitable. And that [which] is lost shall be found. And a child that is born shall be of long life, angry, and honest. A sick man shall be grieved and arise. Who that is taken shall be let go. Theft done shall be found.

In the thirteenth day of the moon: after that thou wakest thy dream shall be [fulfilled] and within four days come to gladness. But take heed to psalms and orisons. A child born shall come to adversity, and he shall be angry and not long of life. Who that is bound shall be loosed. That which is lost shall be found. Who that waxeth sick long shall travail and seldom still recover, but die. To wed a wife is good, and to let blood each day.

[In the] fourteenth day of the moon, all things whatever [which] thou do shall come to thee to good purpose. A dream within six days shall be [fulfilled]. To make a wedding is good, and to go in the way. Ask of thy friend or thy enemy, and it shall be done to thee. A child that is born shall be a traitor. A sick man shall be changed, and rise, and [be] healed by medicine. To let blood is good.

The fifteenth day of the moon: begin no work, [for] it is a grievous day. A sick man shall long travail, but he shall escape. A dream that thou seest nothing shall annoy, but [it will] come to good event. A child born shall die young. That [which] is lost shall be found. To let blood is good.

The sixteenth day of the moon: to buy and sell is good, [and] to tame oxen and other beasts. A dream is not good; after a long time it shall not come, and it shall be harmful. To take a wife is good. A child born shall be of long life, but he shall be poor, foresworn, and accused. A sick man, if he change his place, he shall live. To let blood is good.

The seventeenth day of the moon: it is evil to do an errand. A dream after a long time shall be [fulfilled], or within 30 days. A child that is born shall be silly. He that is sick shall be grieved, and arise. He that is lost shall be found. To send children to school, to be wedded, to make medicine and to take it, is good, but not to let blood.

The eighteenth day of the moon is good for all things to be done. Dreams are good and shall be done with[in] twenty days. He that hath sickness shall soon arise, or be long sick and then recover. Theft done shall be found. A man-child born shall be valiant and eloquent, proud, unpeaceable, and not long of life. And a maid-child born shall be chaste, laborious, serviceable, and better in her later age. They shall be both marked above the knees. Not so hardy be thou to let blood this day.

The nineteenth day of the moon: it is indifferent to begin anything. Dreams shall come [to pass] within twenty days. Who that hath sickness shall soon rise, if he take medicine. Theft then done shall not be found. A man-child then born shall be true, benign, slight, wise, [and] shall ever wax better and better, in great worship, and [shall] have a mark in the brow. A maid-child then born shall be right sick, yet wedded to one man. That day is good to bleed.

The twentieth day of the moon: whatever thou do is good. A dream that thou seest shall appear, but tell it to no man. To make a wedding is good, [and] to buy a servant. A child that is born shall be a fighter, [and] he shall have many arrivings. That [which] is lost shall be found. A sick man shall long wail, or soon arise.

The twenty-first day of the moon: a dream is true, and [shall] come to pass within four days. A child [that] is born shall come to much evil; he shall be a thief, and witty, or a traitor, and travailous. It behooveth to abstain from gaming. To go in the way is good. A sick man shall arise. Theft shall be found. Let no blood, neither night nor day.

The twenty-second day of the moon: if thou doest any errand, thou shall find it grievous. Dreams shall be certain and come to joy. A child born in all days shall be a purchaser, merry, fair, and religious. A sick man born late is confirmed and healed. And to let blood is good.

The twenty-third [day of the moon]: whatever thou wilt do is good. A dream that thou seest shall turn to joy. Nothing shall trouble thee, and other while [?] it is wont to fall within eight days. A child born shall be an outcast, and many adventures he shall have, and in sins he shall die. A sick man shall arise. To let blood is good.

In the twenty-fourth day of the moon, a dream that thou seest signifieth thy health, and nothing shall annoy. A child born shall be sudden in his actions and do wonderful things. A sick man shall languish and be healed.

The twenty-fifth day of the moon: fear is threatened. The dream signifieth hard things, and within ten days it was wont to come early; then bow thy head into the east. A child born shall be an evil man; many perils he shall suffer. A sick man shall sustain injury, and [illegible word] escape. It is good to let blood.

The twenty-sixth day of the moon, thou shalt begin nothing. The dream that thou seest shall be certain and turned into joy. Pilgrims must beware of spies and enemies. A child born shall be full, lonely, but neither rich nor poor. A sick man shall travail and arise; if he have the dropsy, he shall die. To let blood a little is needful.

The twenty-seventh day of the moon: the dream thou shall [see?] [shall] come either to good or evil. A child born shall be of long life, most loved, and, if a man, neither rich nor poor. A sick man shall rise to life; he shall be holden in much languor, but he shall be healed. To let blood is good.

The twenty-eighth day of the moon: whatsoever thou wilt do is good. A dream that thou seest shall turn to joy. A child born shall be much loved, [but] he shall be holden in sickness. A sick man that fasteth in infirmity soon shall be saved. To let blood is good.

The twenty-ninth day of the moon: begin nothing. Thy dream shall be certain and good, gladness and joy it signifieth. An errand begun is good to fulfill. To take a wife is good, but yet make no dowers nor write testaments. A child born shall be of long life, wise, holy, and meek. To fish [and] hunt is good. A sick man shall not be grievously sick, but escape. It is good to let blood.

The thirtieth day of the moon: whatsoever thou doest is good. A dream that appeareth to the certain [?], and within two days thou shalt see, and thou shalt find a red sign in the east within nine days. A child born shall be of long life, and profitable, and well-measured in each thing. A sick man shall nigh come to death. In no manner let blood.

These and many others pertain to men as the course of the moon followeth.

The Disposition of the Planets

Saturn, Jupiter, Mars, Sol, Venus, Mercury, Luna.

Saturn is the cause of death, dearth, and peace. Jupiter is the cause of long peace, rest, and virtuous living. Mars is the cause of dryness, debate, and war. Sol is the cause of life, health, and waxing. Venus is the cause of lusty love and lechery. Mercury is the cause of much speech, [illegible word], and sleights. Luna [is the cause of] great waters and violent floods.

Saturn's hour is good and strong to do all things that asketh strength, and to nought else but to battle; for it is a wondrous evil. That man or woman that hath this star Saturn to his planet is melancholy, black, and goeth swiftly. He hath a void heart, wicked and bitter as wormwood. He will lightly be wroth. He is quarrelsome, witty, covetous, and ireful. He eateth hastily in dining, with shining eyes as a cat. He hath in the forehead a mark—a wound [as] if [caused] by fire. He is poor. His clothes [are] rent, and thus he hath open signs. And all his riches are by other men's possessions, and not by his own.

Jupiter's hour is good in all things, namely, peace, love, accord. Who that hath this star to his planet, he is sanguine, ruddy, and goeth a large pace, neither too swift nor too soft. His strength is [illegible words] and shining. He hath a fair visage, lovely semblance, red lips, fair hair, broad face, good brows. His clothes are good and strong. He is sweet, peaceable, and soft.

Mars' hour is evil, and better by night than by day. For it is masculine in the night, and feminine in the day. It is good to do anything, but with great strength. By night it is good to enter battle, and also by day. Who that hath this star to his planet, his making is of good defense. And oftentimes his face is red with blood. His face is small and subtle and laughing, and he hath eyes as a cat. And all the days of his life he will accuse many men of evil. He hath a wound of a sword in his face. He is most choleric, and thus he hath open signs.

Sol's hour is the worst of all other hours. No man in this hour may do his will, save kings and lords, and that with great strength. Whoso [ever] in this hour enterest battle shall be dead there. Whoso[ever] hath this star to his planet hath sharp eyes, great speech, and wicked thoughts in his heart. He [is] wicked and avaricious, neither white nor black but betwixt both. He hath a mark in his face or a wound, [and] a wound in his body by fire. And he is right wicked and grudging in his deeds.

Venus's hour is good in all things, and it is better by night than by day, even till mid-day. At mid-day it is not good, for the sun covereth it. On Sunday the ninth hour is Venus's hour. Sue not then to any lord nor potentate, for if thou do thou shalt find him wroth. Who that hath this star to his planet—namely, if he be born by night in Venus's hour —he is white and hath a round face, [and] little forehead [and] round beard. He hath a middle nose and hairy eyes. He is laughing and litigious, and he hath a mark in his face. His making is fair and plain, and oft times his nether lip is greater than his upper. And who that is born under Venus when she is not in full power, he hath a sharp nose and somewhat crooked, fair hair, [and] soft eyes, [as] if running water. He is a singer. He longeth much after games, and loveth them well. His tales [will?] be sweet.

Mercury's hour, from the beginning to the middle, is good in all things, and from the middle to the end is hardy. And it is not much better on night than on day, and each time on the night and on the day [that] he standeth before the sun or behind the sun he hath his power much more by night than by day. From moon till the [illegible word] hour of the day he hath his power, and from then to the ninth he hath no power. Who that hath this star to his planet, he hath a sharp stature and a sharp, long face, long eyes, long nose, great hair on his eyes, thick, narrow forehead, long beard, thin hair, long arms, long fingers, long feet, long head. He is meek and lonely [?]. He will do each thing to [a] certain space. He is more white than black, and oft times right white, and he hath great shoulders. And whoso[ever] is born under Mercury when he is not in full power—that is to say, from the first hour of the day to the ninth—he is black and dry. He hath [illegible word] teeth and sharp. He hath a wound in his body with fire. He is scourged with wounds [?] or [illegible words], and men speak evil of him for lying and manslaughter.

The moon's hour is right good and right evil. From the ninth to the seventeenth [day] it is good, namely, to all those that are born in it. And from this day to the twentieth day, it is somewhat good, but not so good. And from the twentieth day to the twenty-seventh day it is evil, namely, to those that are born in it. Who that [hath] this star to his planet and is there under [it] when it is in its full power, he hath a plain face and pale. [He is] sometimes quarreling, and doth his will to [illegible word]. He hath a seemly semblance, and is rich. He hath mean stature, neither too long nor too short. He hath straight lips and hollow eyes. Who that is born under this star when it is not in full power, he hath a straight face and dry, and is malicious. He hath little teeth, [and] a white streak in the [illegible word].

50

A Range of Remarkables

Heaven, hell, the Day of Judgment, conversion to "sainthood," pacts with the Devil: these were the ultimate terms of human involvement in the moral struggles that governed the universe. But for most of the colonists there were countless lesser experiences that also expressed an unseen purpose. Indeed, anything that departed from the normal, expected course of everyday affairs was liable to be viewed in this way. Life was full of signs and portents which, when properly understood, might yield valuable clues as to God's current and future disposition toward humankind.

A determination to scrutinize events for their inner meaning is evident in each of the following documents. John Eliot, who won for himself a transatlantic reputation as a missionary to the Indians, also served for many years as pastor to the First Church of Roxbury in Massachusetts Bay. Among the records he kept for this church was a kind of diary of "remarkable providences"—from which the first selection is taken. The Reverend John Clayton we have met before. His account of "a strange accident" experienced by a Maryland lady was transmitted as part of a letter to the famous British scientist Sir Robert Boyle. The authors and protagonists of the other two documents included here cannot be further identified.

Extracts from John Eliot's Records of
the First Church of Roxbury, Massachusetts

(1643–1646)

1643, month 8, day 29: Robert Potter was excommunicated. His sins were: First, in the time of Mistress Hutchinson, when diverse of our church were seduced to familism and schism, he was of their side and company,

John Eliot, Records of the First Church of Roxbury, Mass., *New England Historical and Genealogical Register*, XXXIII (1879), pp. 62–65.

and so fled with them as that he departed to the [Rhode] Island rather than forsake them; and being there he refused to hear the church who had lovingly sent after him. Secondly, [he sinned in] that he was now tossed with other winds of new doctrine, forsaking the [Rhode] Island and joining with Gorton—and that not only in his heresies but also in his heretical, blasphemous, and reproachful writings; and [he] publicly owned them in Court, and made himself guilty of all those wicked ways.

There happened (by God's providence) a dreadful example of God's judgement this year upon one William Franklin, who belonged to Boston town and took Mr. Ting's farm above Muddy River belonging to Boston. But he spent his Sabbaths at our town, being nearer; and after a season [he] desired to join to our church, and had approbation so to do, and was received. But Satan presently did enter into him. And having a boy who he had bought for some years' time, and [the boy] proving sick and naughty, after he was joined to the church he grew more passionate, cruel and fierce against him. (Though he had been sharp before, yet [this was] unknown or undisposed to us.) But now he grew outrageous, so that by sundry cruel stripes and other kind of ill usage the boy died under his rigorous hand. And that [happened], by a strange providence of God and his own folly, at Boston, as if God meant to bring him on the stage for an example to all others—for which sin, [on] that day [and] month that he was admitted, he was excommunicated. And though much pains were taken to have brought him to repentance and reconciliation to the church, yet all [was] in vain—he protesting, partly to deny and partly to mince his cruel actions towards the boy, so that in that estate he was executed at Boston as public records will show.

1644. A strange providence of God fell out at Boston, where a piece of iron in a dung-cart was smote into the head and brains of the daughter of Jacob Eliot, deacon of the church, and brought forth some of the brains. And after[ward] more of the brains came forth. And yet the Lord cured the child, the brains lying next [to] the skin in that place.

Soon after that one William Curtis of Roxbury was cast off from a cart of logs onto the ground with such violence that his head and one side of his face were bruised, blood gushed out of his ear, his brain was shaken, [and] he was senseless [for] diverse days; yet by degrees through God's mercy he recovered his senses, yet his cheek [was] drawn awry and [was] paralytic; but in a quarter of a year he was pretty well recovered, to the wonder of all men.

1645. Toward the end of the first month, called March, there happened (by God's providence) a very dreadful fire in Roxbury street. None know-

eth how it was kindled, but [there] being a fierce wind it suddenly prevailed. And in this man's house was a good part of the country's magazine
of powder of 17 or 18 barrels, which made the people [so fearful] that
none durst come to save the house or goods till that was blown up;
and by that time the fire had taken the barns and outhousing (which
were many and great) so that none were saved.

In this fire [there] were strange preservations of God's providence to
the neighbors and town; for the wind at first stood to carry the fire to
other houses but suddenly turned and carried it [away] from all the other
houses, only carrying it to the barns and outhousing nearby. And it was
a fierce wind, and [it] thereby drove the vehement heat from the neighboring houses, which in a calmer time would by the heat have been set
on fire.

But [remarkable] above all [was] the preservation of all people from
hurt and [the] other houses from fire at the blowing up of the powder
—many being in great danger yet none hurt, and sundry houses set on
fire by the blow and yet all quenched—through God's rich mercy in
Christ.

1645. About the 16th of the 5th month was this anagram sent to Mr.
Dudley, then the Governor, by some nameless author.

> Thomas Dudley—
> ah! old, must die.
> A death's head on your hand you need not wear;
> A dying head you on your shoulders bear.
> You need not one to mind you, you must die;
> You in your name may spell mortality.
> Young men may die, but old men these die must;
> (or) it can't be long.
> T'will not be long, before you turn to dust.
> Before you turn to dust! ah! must! old! die!
> What shall young do, when old in dust do lie?
> When old in dust lie, what N. England do?
> When old in dust do lie, it's best die too.

This year we had sundry strange and prodigious signs. [There was]
a storm of hail at Boston where the stones were as big or bigger than
musket bullets, and fell terribly.

The week after the like was at Dedham, where some were in fashion
like cross-bar cannon shot, others like musket bullets. There was also
a fierce hurricane at Braintree soon after. The Narragansetts resolved [on]
a war that year, but through mercy a peace was made.

449

Daulny that year took La Tour's Fort.

Mr. Hawkins and another ship, great vessels both, [were] cast away at Spain. The country suffered many losses at sea, at least lb. 10000 in less than two years, besides many lives; yea, some think [a] twenty or thirty thousand-pound loss.

This winter we had much sickness at Roxbury and greater mortality than ever we had before in so short a time. Five died in eight days and more followed, as appeareth in the record thereof. Yet this mercy the Lord showed New England this year, that the iron works were brought to perfection—[a] trial proving [them] excellent well. This year there was also a great scarcity of wine in the winter, which had not so been [in any] of three years before. It was a gracious awakening [of] the land, to consider of the excess that hath here been [in] that way.

1646. This year [there] arose a great disturbance in the country by such as are called the petitioners—a trouble raised by Jesuited agents to molest the peace of the churches and commonwealth.

Gorton found favor in England, having none to inform against him [as to] what he was; but Mr. Winslow was sent over—whom the Lord direct, protect, and prosper.

A synod was held this year at Cambridge, and [was] adjourned to the summer following after some questions were discussed.

This year, about the end of the fifth month, we had a very strange hand of God upon us, [in] that upon a sudden innumerable armies of caterpillars filled the country all over the English plantations, which devoured some whole meadows of grass and greatly devoured barley (being the most green and tender corn), eating off all the blades and beards. But [they] left the corn, only many ears they quite ate off by biting the green straw asunder below the ear. So that barley was generally half spoiled, [and] likewise they much hurt wheat by eating the blades off; but wheat had the less hurt because it was a little forwarder than barley, and so harder and dryer, and they the less meddled with it. As for rye it was so hard and near ripe that they touched it not, but above all grains they devoured Scylly oats. And in some places they fell upon Indian corn and quite devoured it; in other places they touched it not. They would go across highways by the thousand. Much prayer there was made to God about it, with fasting in diverse places; and the Lord heard, and on a sudden took them all away again in all parts of the country, to the wonderment of all men. It was of the Lord, for it was done suddenly.

This winter was one of the mildest that ever we had—no snow all winter long nor [any] sharp weather. But they had long floods at Connecticut, which was much spoil to their corn in the meadows. We never had a bad day to go preach to the Indians all this winter, praised be the Lord.

Correspondence between the Commissioners of Albany and Captain A. Brockholles, on the Sighting of a Comet

(1680)

1st January, 1681

Honored Sir:

According to former practice in this season of the year, we have sent this post to acquaint you how all affairs are here with us—which is (thanks be to God) all in peace and quietness. The Lord continue the same through the whole government. We doubt not but you have seen the dreadful comet star which appeared in the southwest on the 9th of December last about 2 o'clock in the afternoon, [in] fair sunshine weather, a little above the sun, [and] which takes its course more northerly and was seen the Sunday night after about twilight with a very fiery tail or streamer in the west, to the great astonishment of all spectators, and is now seen every night with clear weather. Undoubtedly God threatens us with dreadful punishments if we do not repent. We would have caused the *Domine* [to] proclaim a day of fasting and humiliation tomorrow, to be kept on Wednesday, the 12th [of] January, in the town of Albany and [it]s dependencies—if we thought our power and authority did extend so far and would [not] have been well resented by yourself. For all persons ought to humble themselves in such a time and pray to God to withdraw His righteous judgements from us, as He did to Ninevah. Therefore, if you would be pleased to grant your approbation, we would willingly cause a day of fasting and humiliation to be kept, if it were monthly; your answer we shall expect with the bearer.

We cannot forbear to acquaint you with the very great scarcity of corn throughout our jurisdiction, which is ten times more than was expected, now when the people thresh; so that it is supposed there will

Correspondence between the Commissioners of Albany, N.Y., and Captain A. Brockholles, January 1681, in E. B. O'Callaghan, ed., *The Documentary History of the State of New York* (Albany, N.Y., 1850), III, pp. 882–883.

scarce be corn to supply the inhabitants here with bread. This is all at present. Wishing you and [the] council a happy New Year, [we] shall break off and remain,

Your humble and obedient servants,
The Commissioners of Albany

The Indian Wattawitt must have a
blanket and shirt at York.

Gentlemen,

Yours of the first instant by the Indian post received, and [I] am glad to hear [that] all things [are] well. We have seen the comet, [but] not at the time you mention, only in the evening—the stream being very large. But [we] know not its predictions or events. And as they certainly threaten God's vengeance and judgements and are premonitors to us, so I doubt not of your and each of your performance of your duty by prayer, etc., as becomes good Christians especially at this time. And [I] hope the next year will make amends for and supply your present scarcity of corn. The Governor went hence [on] the 7th and sailed from Sandy Point the eleventh instant. No news here but all well. I remain,

Your affectionate friend,
A. Brockholles.

The Reverend Stephen Hosmore's Account of the Noises at East Haddam, in a Letter to the Reverend Thomas Prince of Boston

(1729)

As to earthquakes, I have something considerable and awful to tell you: Earthquakes have been here (and nowhere but in this precinct, as [far as] can be discovered, i.e., they seem to have their center, rise, [and] original among us), as has been observed for more than 30 years. I have been informed that in this place (before the English settlement) there were great numbers of Indian inhabitants, and that it was a place of extraordinary Indian powwows—or, in short, that it was a place where the

From a letter by Rev. Stephen Hosmore to Rev. Thomas Prince, August 13, 1729, in *Collections of the Connecticut Historical Society*, III (Hartford, Connecticut, 1890), pp. 280–281.

Indians drove a prodigious trade of worshipping the Devil. Also, I was informed that (many years past) an old Indian was asked what was the reason of the noises in this place, to which he replied that the Indian's God was very angry because [the] Englishman's god was come here. Now whether there be anything diabolical in these things I know not; but this I know, that God Almighty is to be seen and trembled at in what has been often heard among us. Whether it be fire or air distressed in the subterraneous caverns cannot be known, for there is no eruption, no explosion perceptible, but by sounds and tremors, which sometimes are very fearful and dreadful. I have myself heard eight or ten sounds successively and imitating small arms, in the space of five minutes. I have (I suppose) heard several hundreds of them within this [past] twenty years; some more, some less terrible. Sometimes we have heard them almost every day, and great numbers of them in the space of a year. Oftentimes I have observed them to be coming down from the north, imitating slow thunder, until the sound came near or right under; and then there seemed to be a breaking like the noise of a cannon shot or severe thunder which shakes houses and all that is in them. They have in a manner ceased ever since the general earthquake. As I remember, there has been but two heard since that time, and those but moderate.

The Strange Experiences of
Mrs. Susanna Sewall of Maryland

(1684)

Virginia, James-City, June 23, 1684

Honored and worthy Sir,

In England having perused, among the rest of your admirable treatises, that ingenious discourse of the *Noctiluca* wherein, as I remember, you gave an account of several nocturnal irradiations, [and] having therefore met with the relation of [a] strange accident in that nature, from very good hands, I presumed this might not prove unwelcome—for the fuller confirmation of which I have enclosed the very paper Colonel Diggs gave me thereof, under his own hand and name, to attest the truth. The same

Letter from Rev. John Clayton to Sir Robert Boyle (with enclosure), June 23, 1684, in Edmund Berkeley and Dorothy Smith Berkeley, eds., *The Reverend John Clayton, a Parson with a Scientific Mind* (Charlottesville, Va., 1965), pp. 6–9. I am grateful to the Virginia Historical society for permission to reprint this document.

has been likewise asserted to me by Madam Diggs, his lady, sister to the said Susanna Sewall, daughter to the Lord Baltimore, lately gone for England—who I suppose may give you fuller satisfaction of such particulars as you may be desirous to be informed of. I cannot but admire the strangeness of such a complicated spirit of a volatile salt and exalted oil, as I deem it to be from its crepitation and shining flame. How it should transpire through the pores and not be inflamed by the joint motion and heat of the body, and afterwards so suddenly to be actuated into sparks by the shaking or brushing of her coats, raises much my wonder.

Another thing [that] I am confident your honor would be much pleased at the sight of [is] a fly we have here, called the firefly, about the bigness of the cantharides, its body of a dark color, the tail of it a deep yellow by day, which by night shines brighter than the glow-worm; which bright shining ebbs and flows, as if the fly breathed with a shining spirit. I pulled the tail of the fly in several pieces, and every part thereof would shine for several hours after and cast a light around it. Be pleased favorably to interpret this fond impertinency of a stranger. All your works have to the world evidenced your goodness, which has encouraged the presumption; and it is that which bids me hope its pardon. If there be anything in this country I may please you in, be pleased to command. It will be my ambition to serve you, nor shall I scruple to ride two or three hundred miles to satisfy any query you shall propound. If you honor me with your commands, you may direct your letter to Mr. John Clayton, parson of James-City, Virginia.

Your humble servant, and, though unknown, your friend,

John Clayton

[Enclosure]   Maryland, Anno 1683

There happened about the month of November to one Madam Susanna Sewall, wife to Major Nicholas Sewall, of the province abovesaid, a strange flashing of sparks (seemed to be of fire) in all the wearing apparel she put on; and so [it] continued till Candlemas. And in the company of several—viz. Captain Edward Poulson, Captain John Harris, Mr. Edward Braines—the said Susanna did send several of her wearing apparel; and when they were shaken, it would fly out in sparks and make a noise much like unto bay leaves when flung into the fire. And one spark lit on Major Sewall's thumb-nail, and there continued [for] at least a minute before it went out, without any heat, all [of] which happened in the company of William Diggs.

My Lady Baltimore, her mother-in-law, for some time before the death of her son Caecelius Calvert, had the like happen to her, which has made Madam Sewall much troubled at what has happened to her. They carried Mrs. Susanna Sewall one day to put on her sister Diggs' petticoat, which they had tried beforehand, and [it] would not sparkle; but at night, when Madam Sewall put it off, it would sparkle as the rest of her own garments did.